BARRON'S
BUSINESS
REVIEW
SERIES

Finance

Second Edition

Ehsan Nikbakht

Associate Professor of Finance
Banking and Finance Department
Hofstra University

A. A. Groppelli

Professor of Finance
Banking and Finance Department
Hofstra University

BARRON'S

All inquiries should be addressed to:
Barron's Educational Series, Inc.
250 Wireless Boulevard
Hauppauge, New York 11788

Library of Congress Catalog Card No.: 89-18317

International Standard Book No. 0-8120-4373-1

Library of Congress Cataloging-in-Publication Data

Nikbakht, Ehsan.
   Finance / Ehsan Nikbakht, A.A. Groppelli. — 2nd ed.
      p.   cm. — (Barron's business review series)
   ISBN 0-8120-4373-1
   1. Business enterprises—Finance.   2. Corporations—Finance.
I. Groppelli, Angelico A.   II. Title.   III. Series.
HG4026.N54 1990
658.15—dc20   89-18317
                                                              CIP

PRINTED IN THE UNITED STATES OF AMERICA

   23   800   9876543.

CONTENTS

INVESTING, FINANCING, AND DIVIDEND DECISIONS

MANAGING WORKING CAPITAL

SPECIAL TOPICS

PREFACE

The field of finance has undergone dramatic changes in the last 10 years. For persons engaged in the practical conduct of businesses a knowledge of finance is now essential. In turn, academicians have revised their theories to reflect real-world situations. Financial markets have developed a variety of investment instruments and methods to raise capital. Lease contracts, mergers, acquisitions, stock options, and currency options—to name just a few—have revolutionized the subject of finance, which has become complicated and, at the same time, greatly in demand. The growth of enrollment in finance courses has been so phenomenal that business schools across the country have difficulty in finding qualified instructors to satisfy the demand. There is good evidence that finance will remain a most popular academic discipline for many years to come.

Unfortunately, many articles and books in this field are technical in nature and are written in complicated language. There is a tendency for authors to stress mathematics and theory, and this emphasis may frustrate students and practitioners who want to understand finance in simple terms. In response to this need we have written this book to explain finance in an easy way, with the hope that the book will provide a sound understanding of the fundamentals and will make learning an enjoyable experience.

The book is designed primarily for students enrolled in finance courses and for persons in business who need a basic knowledge of finance to run firms efficiently and make profitable investment decisions. We have made extensive use of tables, numerical examples, and graphs to explain theories and practical business applications. Although complicated issues and concepts have been simplified, there is no compromise in regard to accuracy.

The book covers the following major areas of finance:

1. The time value of money and the risk/return analysis of investment decisions such as bonds and stock valuation.

2. Methods of capital budgeting and techniques to discount returns and deduct costs in order to compare the profitability of various projects.

3. The theory of the firm, including dividend policy, cost of capital, and capital structure.

4. Financial planning and control and working capital management, including the monitoring of accounts receivable, accounts payable, inventory, and cash management.

5. Current trends in finance, for example, mergers, convertible bonds, currency options, and leasing.

At the end of each chapter there are questions to test understanding of the basic concepts presented, and mathematical problems for practice in applying what has been learned are provided for all chapters except the first and the last. Explained answers to questions and most problems follow.

An appendix at the end of the book contains helpful tables and a glossary of terms commonly used in finance.

Ehsan Nikbakht
A. A. Groppelli

AN INTRODUCTION

1
WHAT IS FINANCE ALL ABOUT?

Finance is the application of a series of economic principles to **maximize the wealth** or overall value of a business. More specifically, maximizing the wealth of a firm means making the highest possible profits at the least risk. No one really knows when maximum wealth is achieved, though it is assumed to be the ultimate goal of every firm. One way of finding out the wealth of a firm is through the price of its common stock. When the price of a firm's shares increases, it is said that the wealth of the firm's shareholders has increased.

Finance has developed many sophisticated approaches to provide financial managers with tools for solving difficult business problems. Before 1970, the emphasis was on new ways of achieving effective working capital management, improving methods for maintaining financial records and interpreting balance sheets and income statements. Finance has extended its horizons in the last 15 years, and the emphasis is now on ways to budget scarce resources effectively and to invest funds in the assets or projects that yield the best risk/return trade-offs. Attention has been drawn to the study of different alternatives and the effect of each alternative on the value of the firm. More attention has been given to determining the proper proportion between debt and stock financing, as well as the correct dividend policy. The need to develop long-term plans, to take advantage of new financial instruments, and to understand multinational finance principles is becoming increasingly evident.

Knowledge of finance should not be limited to treasurers, controllers, and financial planners. In any firm, if the accountants, statisticians, and marketers have an appreciation and understanding of the principles of finance, they will be able to participate more effectively in the decision-making process. Different departments should participate in the final plans made by the finance division.

ADAPTING TO CHANGES

Finance is part science, part art. **Financial analysis** provides a means of flexible judgment for making the right investment decisions at the right and most advantageous time. When financial managers succeed in doing the right things, they help improve the value of the firm's shares.

A manager gives favorable signals to investors by establishing a record of sound financial statements with returns that are growing rapidly and steadily at a minimum level of risk. Why are the right signals so necessary? Because *stockholders (investors) ultimately determine the market value of the firm as reflected in the prices of the securities it issues.* If the firm has a good record, and these people believe that its record will continue, valuation will be high. Conversely, a poor record, with expectations of unfavorable returns and high risk levels, will produce a low valuation.

To be successful, financial managers have to deal with the changes constantly occurring in the field of finance. They must adopt more sophisticated methods so they can plan better in an increasingly competitive climate. They need to deal effectively with constant change inside and outside the company. In short, financial managers are responsible for recognizing and responding to the changing factors in the private, public, and financial environments.

There is a growing need for timing new product introductions correctly, for delivering products and services that meet current and developing needs, and for ensuring that decisions are backed up by alternative plans. Changes in research efforts and production are sometimes called for to ensure that new products can meet the challenges of an increasingly competitive marketplace.

PLANNING AHEAD

Financial planning, a crucial part of financial management, includes the making of daily decisions to help the firm meet its cash requirements. It requires close attention to intermediate changes in business activity. Analysis of the business cycle helps the financial manager keep financing costs low and avoid excesses in inventories and capacity. Proper timing of business activity leads to better production and inventory decisions to meet changes in economic activity.

Long-range plans must be developed to give proper direction to research and development and to make sound capital expenditure decisions. If properly managed, the lower risk and higher expected returns that result will be recognized by investors, who are likely to raise their assessment of the value of the firm. By adopting these approaches, financial managers have a better-than-even chance of maintaining a healthy firm and maximizing shareholders' wealth.

• *THE MANAGER AS AN AGENT*

At one time or another, most people have had occasion to hire agents to take care of a specific matter. In doing so, responsibility is delegated to another person.

For example, when suing for damages, individuals may represent themselves or may hire a lawyer to plead their case in court. As an agent, the lawyer is given the assignment to get the highest possible award. And so it is with stockholders when they delegate the task of running a firm to a financial manager, who, though not strictly correct, legally may be thought of as an agent of the company. Obviously, the goal is to achieve the highest value of a share of stock for the firm's owners. But there are no standard rules that indicate which course of action should be followed by managers to achieve this. The ultimate guideline is how investors perceive the actions of managers.

POLICY CONFLICTS

In general, managers should seek to use sound investment policies that minimize risk. However, some managers interpret their mission differently. As agents, they envision their role as one of avoiding big mistakes. As a result, these agents may overlook good opportunities with acceptable levels of risk. This conflict between agent and stockholders is unlikely to produce the best results.

There is no guarantee that managers, acting as agents, will make the appropriate decisions and take the best course of action. For example, in assessing the risks of different projects against their expected returns, managers may concentrate on only certain investments, failing to diversify the assets of the firm to achieve a lower risk level.

Agents are often caught in the middle by trying to satisfy two major factions: the creditors and the stockholders. This consideration is especially important when debt becomes an important source of financing. Creditors impose certain constraints on the firm, such as limiting dividend payments when profits are too low, and otherwise force the managers to maintain the liquidity of the firm at a given level to ensure repayment of loans. In trying to satisfy the claims and restrictions imposed by these creditors, financial managers may have to devote too much attention to creditors and not enough attention to stockholders. This conflict can make managers less efficient and prevent them from taking advantage of the best opportunities.

There are no easy answers to ensure compatibility between agents and their stockholders. It is up to the stockholders—acting through the board of directors—to hire the right managers and to make sure they are properly compensated. This means meeting the market price to attract the right talent. Offering stock to these managers also helps ensure that they will seek to maximize the value of the firm's shares.

In any event, capable managers have the right judgment and instincts to know what policies to implement and when to implement them. They know when to raise funds and how to control assets. These correct decisions are translated into favorable signals to investors, usually resulting in a higher valuation of the firm's common stock.

YOU SHOULD REMEMBER

If there is one problem that enters into the decision-making process, it is the uncertainty and the risk aspects of investments. When a firm makes investment decisions, it automatically attempts to put together (invest in) the best asset mix. This means utilizing the best quality assets in the most efficient way so that they will yield the fastest and least risky returns in the future. In addition, the firm must be concerned with the way it generates internal and external funds, since too much outstanding stock can cause earnings-per-share dilution, and too much debt can increase the financial riskiness and fixed loan commitments of the firm. Proper utilization of these factors, however, can produce a higher valuation for the firm. Consequently, it is important for financial managers to adopt a balanced financing policy so that investors can be assured that their invested funds are well managed and safe.

• *RISK VERSUS PROFITS*

Profit maximization is a less important objective than wealth maximization. All firms would like to achieve the highest profits possible, but attempts to maximize profits may prove inconsistent with wealth maximization because of risk considerations.

In finance, higher risks are generally associated with higher possible gains—but there is also a greater chance of loss. The same principle applies to Aunt Jane or John Doe. Both would like to strike it rich, but they know that to do so they must be willing to face the dangers of heavy losses. Aunt Jane and John Doe are aware that it is safer to purchase a U.S. treasury bill than to buy pork belly contracts. The chances of incurring losses from owning a treasury bill are slim indeed, while pork belly contracts could mean high gains or large losses.

Managers are faced with a similar dilemma. Some projects may be more profitable than others, but the risk associated with them could be too high and might jeopardize the solvency of the firm. This situation is analogous to gamblers who insist on betting on long-shot horses. Although the payout is great if the long shot wins, the chances are that these gamblers will be consistent losers. Bettors who play to "show" or put their money on the favorite horse have a better chance of winning, but their gains will be lower. The same applies to the policies adopted by managers. There is a constant conflict between engaging in highly profitable ventures and maintaining a sound financial status. These managerial decisions involve a compromise between taking excessive risks to maximize profits and accepting investments that will probably result in lower risk and lower profitability—but will lead to a sound financial posture for the firm.

THE LONG-RANGE VIEW

Management can, in the short run, gain high profits by buying inferior materials and hiring poorly trained or unskilled workers. This decision may temporarily yield lower costs and lower prices than those charged by competitors. The first results may be higher profits. These short-sighted policies, however, tend to produce long-range problems. Inferior machinery produces more than the usual number of rejects. Machinery breakdowns become more frequent, costs of repairs mount, and fewer products meet quality standards. The outcome is likely to damage the image of the firm, affecting the price of the firm's stock adversely. The better course of action is to incur the added expense of maintaining quality control, thereby reducing the potential risk of unfavorable feedback from investors.

High profits gained at the expense of increased risk generally produce unsatisfactory reactions by stockholders and investors in the long run. Investors generally give more value to earnings generated by a firm with a steady profit record than to the same level of earnings generated by a firm in highly risky investments with a widely fluctuating earnings record.

As a result, the objective of profit maximization may conflict with that of the maximization of wealth. Attempts to increase profits beyond a certain level may mean the taking of greater than necessary risks and may also impair, to some extent, the ability of the firm to maintain solvency. Wealth maximization implies a constant concern with risk. This goal may not be achieved if the firm pursues a policy of profit maximization.

There are many tools for accomplishing the maximization of wealth, among them the understanding and application of the principles of economics, accounting, statistics, and related disciplines.

YOU SHOULD REMEMBER

The primary goal of a financial manager is to maximize the wealth of stockholders. Maximizing profits is a short-term goal which does not address itself to some key factors, one of which is an acceptable risk level. The goal to maximize wealth may conflict with the aim to optimize profits in the short run, but wealth maximization should always be the primary consideration.

ESSENTIAL SKILLS
OF FINANCIAL MANAGEMENT

• *UNDERSTANDING ECONOMIC FACTORS*

Almost everyone applies some economic principles on one occasion or another. Take the case of a flea market. Most of us have either gone to one or have been vendors at these markets. Whether one is buying or selling, it is obvious that the vendors displaying the items most in demand usually wind up with the biggest sales. Price is another important consideration. If it is too high, few customers will buy. Some of these simple economic principles are useful in making the right sell/buy decisions in any market.

Similarly, financial managers can make better decisions if they apply these basic economic principles. For example, economic theory teaches us to seek the best allocation of resources in the economy. To this end, financial managers are given the responsibility to find the best and least expensive sources of funds and to invest these funds into the best and most efficient mix of assets. In doing so, they try to find the mix of available resources that will achieve the highest return at the least risk. Good or bad performances by managers are recognized by investors and are finally reflected in corresponding changes in the value of a stock. Good financial management excludes the taking of excessive risks to maximize profits.

MICROECONOMIC FACTORS

Financial managers do a better job when they understand how to respond effectively to changes in supply, demand, and prices (**micro factors**), as well as to the more general and overall economic factors (**macro factors**). Learning to deal with these factors provides important tools for effective financial planning.

When making investment decisions, financial managers consider the effects of changing supply, demand, and price conditions on the firm's performance. Understanding the nature of these factors helps managers make the most advantageous financing and operating decisions. More specifically, managers can thus determine more accurately when it is best to issue stock, bonds, or other financial instruments.

The sale of products at a profit depends heavily on how well managers are able to analyze and interpret supply and demand conditions. Supply considerations relate specifically to the control of production costs, where the key element is to hold costs down so that prices can be set at competitive levels. The best machinery for the price must be bought; and the most productive workers available must be hired. The goal is to squeeze out the biggest possible profit under given supply conditions. Maintaining a low-cost operation will enable the firm to charge competitive prices for its product and maintain its market share while still obtaining a reasonable return.

Knowledge of economic principles can be useful in generating the highest sales possible. Understanding and appropriately responding to changes in demand allows financial managers to take full advantage of market conditions. To accomplish this, the best managers develop and adopt reliable, workable statistical techniques that forecast demand and pinpoint when directional changes in sales take place.

This task, however, is not an easy one. Economic factors cannot be forecast with any degree of accuracy, and many projections are subject to large errors. Good managers, however, can modify forecasts of supply and demand to make them come reasonably close to the actual results. In other words, good financial managers know when to raise and/or lower prices. If demand estimates are high, they institute actions to avoid overproduction and excessive inventories. Therefore, while all managers are faced with forecasting problems, the good ones can deal effectively with difficult situations.

Assuming that demand and prices can be forecast fairly accurately, the next step is to make a decision on the kind of plant and equipment needed to produce goods at the cheapest cost. Obviously, this decision calls for a great deal of judgment regarding the efficiency of different types of equipment and whether or not—or when—this equipment might become outdated. The choice of one machine over another involves considering the risks associated with each machine. This risk decision must also consider that future shifts in demand can make a particular machine useless. These are some of the important microeconomic questions which financial managers must answer.

MACROECONOMIC FACTORS

Peoples' decisions are influenced by changing economic conditions. By reading the newspapers and listening, people develop a sense about the economic climate. If it seems to be deteriorating, consumers tend to cut spending and become more conservative in their buying habits. Conversely, when conditions improve, people are likely to loosen their purse strings. These reactions to changing external economic forces, such as rising or declining business activity and changes in tax laws, influence the decisions made by a firm.

When business is expanding, a firm increases its investment and production; it pulls in its horns when faced by a business contraction. The important thing is to be able to detect when these changes in activity occur. This is why financial management relies on internal and external models that forecast expected business activity in future months and years. A firm must also develop a flexible strategy to deal with major shifts in demographics, changes in legislation or tax laws, and new technological breakthroughs. It behooves managers to engage in financial planning so that they can be armed with different alternatives under different economic conditions.

Failure—or success—in dealing with macroeconomic problems can have an impact on the price of the firm's shares.

TIMING OF ECONOMIC DECISIONS

Most consumers know that one can get a good buy on a product once the demand for it fades. This kind of timing can pay off handsomely. Christmas greeting cards, for example, sell for half-price right after the holidays.

In the same way, the successful manager instinctively knows how to react in a timely fashion to changes in supply, demand, and price conditions. Buying raw materials at low prices can give a cost advantage to a firm. Conversely, if investments are undertaken and demand does not increase as expected, a firm may expand too early, getting stuck with large inventories and an underutilized capacity. The way financial managers time their decisions with respect to changing microeconomic factors can be reflected in higher or lower prices of the company's stock.

Equally valued is the ability to properly time decisions dealing with changing macroeconomic factors. Knowledgeable managers have the judgment to be able to take full advantage of profitable opportunities at reasonable risks when general business activity is expanding. It is important, therefore, for financial managers not only to forecast levels of business and related activities accurately, but also to make sound judgments with respect to expected changes in the direction of related macro and micro factors.

Financial managers must make sure that their decisions to invest or not to invest, to raise capital or not to raise capital, are justified. To do this they must judge the future direction of interest rates, the behavior of stock prices, the expected changes in overall business activity, the anticipated rate of inflation, the status of financial markets, and even the trend of foreign exchange rates. Wrong timing in regard to any of these factors can mean higher costs of generating funds in financial markets. If corporate managers misjudge the business cycle at the peak, they may get stuck with unwanted and costly inventories. A decision to increase capital expenditures and to produce more at the peak of a business cycle could lead to excess inventory once demand contracts. By correctly timing a rise in the rate of inflation, managers can make better judgments about purchasing raw materials at low prices, building inventories, and buying equipment at the most advantageous terms.

Proper timing of these factors also reduces volatility and the uncertainty of future profits.

• *IMPORTANCE OF ACCOUNTING*

Financial managers cannot do without accountants and related record keepers. The importance of accounting to finance is demonstrated by the common use of financial ratios, pro forma statements, sources and uses of funds, and cash budgeting.

By analyzing income and balance sheet statements, managers can direct new financing to the most cost-effective areas. Other reasons for evaluating these accounting statements are to constantly monitor the efficiency of operations, to achieve the best allocation of available funds among assets, and to avoid financial problems before they get out of hand.

It should be pointed out that the managers of a firm are supplied with more detailed statistical information than appears in published financial statements. These data are especially important in developing cash flow concepts for evaluating the relative merits of different investment projects. This information permits managers to determine incremental cash flows (an approach that looks at the net returns a given project generates in comparison with alternative investments), thus enabling them to make more accurate assessments of the profitabilities of specific investments. It is the responsibility of managers to direct their accountants to prepare internal statements that include this information so that they can make the best investment decisions possible.

• *SIGNIFICANCE OF STATISTICS*

Statistical analysis supplies a basis for forecasting and for comparing a firm's financial health and profitability with that of other companies. In this connection, statistics are most effective when computers are used to make projections of future returns or to calculate risk and to estimate the probable receipts or returns associated with a project. Statistics can be employed to plan long-term investments and capacity decisions. Statistical relationships are also invaluable in simulating the success or failure of research projects. This, in turn, can be useful in developing product cycle analyses and exploring the alternatives available to the managers under different sets of conditions. These so-called simulation models are important for determining the degree of uncertainty involved in different investment decisions.

Firms use statistics to find out when business activity is expected to change and, consequently, when it is best to invest or borrow, refund debt or increase working capital and expand capacity. With statistics, a firm can calculate the seasonal patterns of sales, using the information to effectively budget interim-year cash requirements, time the purchase of raw materials, and build—or reduce—inventories.

For example, everyone knows that retail industry sales increase substantially during the Christmas season. By employing appropriate statistical techniques, a firm can estimate just how much sales will increase in this period. In doing so, it can maintain production at a fairly constant pace while still building inventories ahead of this surge in demand. All in all, statistical models used to forecast the returns and the risks of the firm have become an essential part of the decision-making process.

YOU SHOULD REMEMBER

Managers should learn how to use statistical techniques to time and forecast, as accurately as possible, changes in basic micro- and macroeconomic factors. They should make good use of accountants, who supply the financial statements that enable managers to monitor the performance of the firm. In other words, the best managers know how to use all available tools and how to piece together different sources of information to achieve the most effective investment strategies and objectives for the firm.

PUBLIC RESPONSIBILITY AND FINANCIAL MANAGEMENT

Finance is a very challenging and rewarding field. It is an exciting area because financial managers are given the responsibility to plan the future growth and direction of a firm—which can greatly affect the community in which it is based. Many of the tools and techniques for solving financial problems are discussed in the following chapters of this book. One must bear in mind, however, that these models and methods provide only a starting point. The decisions reached by a financial manager ultimately represent a blend of theoretical, technical and judgmental matters that must reflect the concerns of society.

BENEFITS AND OBLIGATIONS TO SOCIETY

All of us grumble occasionally about government regulations, but as good citizens we abide by the law. Voting on election day may take some of our time, but it is a civic duty and right that citizens exercise for the good of society. We go on jury duty even though it takes us away from more productive business endeavors, because we know this is a necessary function if our legal system is to work.

Business firms are faced by similar obligations to society. Though they search for ways to be profitable and achieve the highest wealth, financial managers must accept certain compromises that may impede them from obtaining the highest wealth possible. For example, a firm may be prevented from selecting certain production methods because the government says they cause too much pollution. In other words, firms have obligations to society that can interfere with their profit motives. Social, moral, environmental and ethical considerations are part of the investment decision process and cannot be ignored by financial planners.

The burdens of these costs fall unevenly on different firms. Some firms, especially large corporations, have more resources to deal with these problems. And it seems logical to assume that the most profitable and financially strong corporations should incur a greater share of these social costs. Pollution abatement, enforcement of safety standards, and improved sanitary conditions can reduce employee absences and raise labor productivity. Therefore, a firm can deal with social and legal constraints satisfactorily without critically impairing its ability to maximize the price of its stock.

BENEFITS AND OBLIGATIONS TO THE FIRM

Within this framework, financial managers have certain obligations to those who entrust them with the running of the firm. They must have a clear sense of ethics and must avoid payoffs or other forms of personal gain. Managers should not engage in practices that can damage the image of the firm, but should participate as much as possible in social activities to demonstrate that they are cognizant of the importance of the community and those who buy their products or services.

Financial managers should also ensure that all environmental and legal standards necessary to ensure the health and safety of the community and of the workers are met.

More specifically, if financial managers work in a vacuum and are concerned only with monetary gains, they may overlook other equally important aspects necessary for maintaining a high public opinion of their firms. By allocating funds for the social betterment of employees and the community, managers will attract customers and a more stable shareholder following. Obviously, the costs of social programs must be tempered by the financial ability of the firm to engage in these less-profitable endeavors. Certain socially desirable policies—hiring minorities, providing for worker safety, and refusing to invest in specific profitable ventures because they fail to meet democratic principles—should be part of the financial decision process. There is no conflict between promoting socially responsible programs and the profit motive. It is only a question of maintaining some concern for social needs when pursuing the goal of maximizing the wealth of the firm.

YOU SHOULD REMEMBER

Financial managers must reconcile social and environmental requirements with profit-making motives. Adherence to social values may not produce the most efficient use of assets or the lowest costs, but it will enhance the image of the firm. Looking after the interests of minorities, setting up training facilities, and caring for the safety and the welfare of workers can produce long-term benefits in the form of higher productivity and more harmonious relationships between labor and management.

GOALS OF FINANCIAL PLANNING

A good manager knows how to use the factors just discussed in arriving at final decisions. Financial managers are charged with the primary responsibility of maximizing the price of the firm's shares while holding risk at the lowest level possible. In order to achieve these goals, a manager must determine which investments will provide the highest profits at least risk. Once this decision is reached, the next step involves the selection of optimal ways to finance these investments.

Planning to achieve the best results should be flexible, allowing for alternative strategies to replace existing plans should financial and economic developments diverge from an expected pattern. Furthermore, financial planning involves proper timing of investments in order to avoid over expansion and inefficient use of resources. Optimal use of available funds means exploring different options and selecting those that provide the greatest overall value. It also means adopting effective ways of determining how much to borrow in order to reduce financing risks. The financing used to raise funds should include safety features that will allow managers to refinance when market conditions become favorable.

After a financial decision has been made, there must be constant vigilance and monitoring of developments. If the original plan falls short of expectations, early recognition and remedial action become necessary. Those who delay in taking appropriate action pay the price for poor management. This price is exacted by the market (and the investment community), which in the aggregate represents a highly efficient judge of performance. Poor or inflexible managers are accountable to competitive forces and to the marketplace, where valuation becomes the ultimate determinant of successful or unsuccessful financial management.

That is why it is important to keep abreast of new advances in modern theory of finance as well as of the developments taking place in the financial markets. Finance has emerged as an important discipline that requires constant updating of old and refining of new concepts. The latest advances in valuation methods can help to make better decisions. The emergence of new financial instruments, such as financial futures, options, and other contingency liability claims, provides managers with more sophisticated and effective methods for evaluating and, when necessary, altering financial decisions.

KNOW THE CONCEPTS

DO YOU KNOW THE BASICS?

1. What do financial managers try to maximize, and what is their second objective?

2. In trying to achieve optimum profits, what may a firm ignore?

3. State the kinds of assurances that investors and creditors seek from a firm.

4. What environmental considerations prevent the firm from achieving the best results in terms of cost control and profitability? Explain what this means.

5. What are some of the micro- and macroeconomic factors that influence the decisions of a firm?

6. What kinds of conflicts confront the financial manager as an agent of the firm? How can a firm attract the best managers?

7. What two accounting statements help the manager monitor a firm's performance? What can the balance sheet tell the firm about its assets and financial structure?

8. In what way can statistics be used to help managers succeed?

9. What are some of the nonfinancial aspects of the manager's role in society, such as responsibility toward workers and minorities?

10. What happens when the firm issues either too much debt or too much common stock?

11. Does knowledge of financial theory and statistical approaches give a manager all the answers in solving financial problems? Explain.

12. Besides maximizing the wealth of the firm, what are some of the other goals of financial management?

TERMS FOR STUDY

finance	maximize the wealth
financial analysis	micro factors
financial planning	macro factors
	risk

ANSWERS

KNOW THE CONCEPTS

1. The primary objective of financial managers is to maximize the wealth of the firm or the price of the firm's stock. A secondary objective is to maximize earnings per share.

2. In striving for optimum profits, a firm may overlook risk. In other words, investment decisions based on high profits can cause profits to disappear or fluctuate excessively; this could lead to insolvency or a great deal of uncertainty.

3. Investors are looking for the highest returns at the lowest risk. Creditors want to be assured that the firm maintains a sound financial structure and that its policies ensure payment of interest and repayment of principal. Creditors don't want the firm to take unnecessary chances which could lead to insolvency.

4. Firms must try to minimize such environmental hazards as air and water pollution. By buying pollution equipment, a firm allocates funds to unproductive and unprofitable equipment. In doing so, it cannot achieve the highest financial returns.

5. Micro factors are mainly supply, demand, and prices. Macro factors are external in nature and include the business cycle, the rate of inflation, trends in the financial field, and changes in foreign exchange rates. Correct timing and forecasting of these macro factors are essential.

6. By acting as agents of stockholders, managers may adopt conservative approaches to avoid making big mistakes. They may also be forced to reconcile the different aims of stockholders and creditors. In trying to meet the constraints imposed on the firm by creditors, agents may not be able to devote enough time and effort to achieve maximization of the firm's wealth. Agents may not be willing to assume the added risks of certain projects even though such investments may more than adequately compensate the firm for the risks incurred.

   The best managers can be attracted to the firm in two ways: First, by offering them attractive compensation, and second, by giving them options to buy stock in the firm as an incentive to make decisions that will raise the market value of shares.

7. The income statement and the balance sheet. The balance sheet tells the firm how it is allocating its funds to various assets and how the firm generates funds from internal and external sources.

8. Statistics provides the tools for comparing the financial status of the firm with that of other companies and of its own industry. Statistical techniques are invaluable for projecting the returns and relative risks of different investments. They can be used to simulate the outcome of investments, given different assumptions. Statistics can help managers to monitor operations and correctly time borrowings, purchases of goods, and capacity expansion.

9. Financial managers must be ethical and seek to interact with the community. They must conform to environmental, legal, health, and safety standards. In this connection, they should avoid investments in ventures that transgress democratic principles and should seek to help minorities get jobs. In other words, a balance should be struck between attempts to maximize wealth and the attainment of social betterment.

10. Risk increases and the firm fails to take full advantage of the various sources of funds. In this case, the cost of capital for debt or stock will eventually increase.

11. Financial theory is a starting point. It merely provides some tools which cannot substitute for experience and judgment. However, despite its limitations, theory helps to explain the financial process and show how to avoid pitfalls in making investment decisions.

12. Besides having the responsibility of maximizing the price of a company's shares at the least risk possible, a manager must adopt flexible financing methods in order to control costs. Furthermore, when implementing a plan, constant monitoring is required, and when the plan fails to achieve the desired goal, a new strategy should be adopted.

2
BUSINESS TYPES AND TAXATION METHODS

KEY TERMS

Accelerated Cost Recovery System (ACRS) a depreciation method in which assets are classified according to their specifications and to the number of years over which they can be depreciated

active income income generated from a trade or business in which an investor actively and materially participates; otherwise, called *passive income*

capital gain profit from the resale of an asset (selling price minus book value)

capital asset a real and tangible asset such as real estate or machinery

cash flow a measure of a company's liquidity, consisting of net income plus noncash expenditures (such as depreciation charges)

financial asset assets that are not real on their own; for example, bonds, stocks, certificates of deposit

marginal tax rate a rate a taxpayer pays on his/her last unit of income

S Corporation small business with a corporate form but in which all profits (and losses) are passed through to the shareholders, as in a partnership

triple tax a situation where taxes are paid three times: income tax on corporate income, tax on stockholders' dividends, and tax on dividend income of the firm from its outside investment

FORMS OF BUSINESS ORGANIZATIONS

There are three main types of business organizations in the United States: proprietorships, partnerships, and corporations. The general characteristics of each type of organization are explained in this section.

PROPRIETORSHIP

A **proprietorship** is the oldest form of organization for a business owned by only one individual. Anyone with money can buy basic working tools and start a proprietorship to produce goods or offer services thought to be marketable.

A main advantage of a proprietorship is its easy formation process. The formation of a proprietorship doesn't require the approval of any regulatory agency. Once the working conditions of the business are present the sole proprietorship is in existence. (The only exception is that certain professions require a license in order to practice.) Another advantage is the straightforward taxation method used for proprietorships: The proprietor's income is simply included on the owner's individual tax return each year.

A main disadvantage of this form of organization is that the owner is responsible for the entire liability of the proprietorship. Since the owner has unlimited liability, personal properties that are not used in the business may be lost to creditors.

Another disadvantage is that a proprietorship can't use organized capital markets—such as stock and bond markets—to raise needed capital. A proprietorship therefore has limited opportunities for growth, because its capital can be expanded only so far. **Capital,** in the form of either debt or equity, is the means to buy assets and expand a company. Since a proprietorship cannot raise equity capital by outside means, it cannot enjoy the benefits of continuous growth.

Although more than 80% of the businesses in the United States are proprietorships, they represent only 10% of the total sales in the marketplace! The reason? *Proprietorships are small businesses with limited means to finance operations and limited resources to compete and survive in the market.*

PARTNERSHIP

A **partnership** is a form of business organization in which two or more individuals are the owners. A partnership can be viewed as a proprietorship with more than one owner.

There are two kinds of partners: general partners and limited partners. General partners have unlimited liability in running a business, but limited partners are liable only up to the amount of their investments or for a specified amount of money. In a **general partnership** all partners have unlimited liability. In a **limited partnership** there is at least one limited partner in the business.

Business publications such as the *Wall Street Journal* often contain advertisements for limited partners in real estate businesses. In such a case, an individual typically invests a certain amount of money in a partnership for the purpose of building a shopping center, buying or leasing a rental property, or purchasing land. The profits of the partnership are divided among the limited and general partners according to predetermined ratios. Since the risk of a limited partner is confined to the loss of the investment, his or her portion of the total profit is usually less than that of a general partner. In order to bring more capital to some undertakings, particularly lucrative real estate ventures, existing general partners may sometimes offer nearly equal shares of profits to new limited partners.

CORPORATION

The third form of organization is the **corporation,** which, in terms of dollars, dominates today's business world. A corporation can be formed by a person or a group of persons. The "personality" of the corporation, under the law, is totally separate from its owners. Precisely speaking, a corporation, is a "legal entity"; therefore, the corporation, rather than the owners, is responsible for paying all debts.

Because of the legal status of a corporation, the owners have limited liability and can't lose more than their invested money. Unlike a proprietor, the owners of a corporation do not have to withdraw from their personal savings or sell their personal belongings to satisfy creditors if the corporation goes bankrupt. An owner of a corporation is called a stockholder or shareholder.

The purpose of a corporation is to increase the wealth of stockholders, who elect a board of directors from among themselves and from people outside the corporation to set general guidelines for the corporation. If the corporation is relatively large, the board hires managers to work as agents of the stockholders.

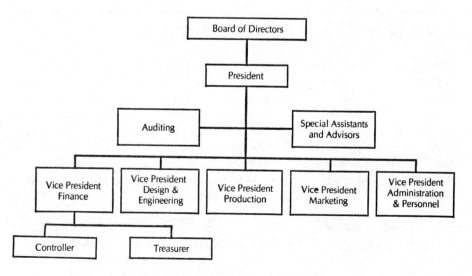

Figure 2–1 A Typical Corporate Organization

Managers have a responsibility to set long-range corporate strategy, which specifies the objectives that the corporation must achieve in the future. Managers have other responsibilities, including hiring employees, purchasing assets, borrowing money, issuing stock, controlling the work of other employees, and reporting the status of the corporation to the board of directors and stockholders on a periodic basis. Figure 2–1 illustrates the basic organization of a corporation.

YOU SHOULD REMEMBER

The three major forms of business organizations are proprietorships, partnerships, and corporations. An owner of a proprietorship or a general partnership has unlimited liability, but the liabilities of shareholders in a limited partnership or a corporation do not exceed the value of their investments. Unlike a proprietorship or a partnership, a business corporation is a "legal entity" separate from its owners.

Proprietorships and partnerships are small firms with very limited ways to raise capital and to expand operations. While more than 80% of U.S. business firms are either proprietorships or partnerships, they have a market share of only 10% of the national economy.

BASICS OF TAXATION

The U.S. tax law was revised several times in the 1980s. The current tax law is the outcome of various revisions made by the Economic Recovery Tax Act of 1981, the Tax Equity and Fiscal Responsibility Act of 1982, the Tax Reform Act of 1984 and, most drastically, the Tax Reform Act of 1986. In the following sections, we will introduce the basic concepts of taxation and illustrate how the existing tax law works in the case of individuals and corporations. Without a good understanding of taxation, a financial analyst may not be able to arrive at correct decisions in capital budgeting, leasing versus buying, dividend policy, alternative sources of financing, and other cases related to finance and investment.

• *FEDERAL INCOME TAX FOR INDIVIDUALS*

Before the Tax Reform Act of 1986, individuals were taxed at fifteen progressive rates from 11% to 50%. The old structure has been reduced to two basic tax brackets, 15% and 28%. However, in the case of high-income taxpayers (over $71,900 for joint taxpayers and over $43,150 for single individuals), the benefit of 15% is gradually removed by taxing income above those limits at a 33% rate. Table 2–1 illustrates the personal income tax brackets that are currently in effect. Note that the marginal tax rate, the rate a taxpayer pays on the last unit of his/her income, increases from 15%, to 28%, to 33%, and then decreases to a flat rate of 28%. Because of the increasing-and-then-decreasing rates, the existing tax law could be called a "progressive-and-regressive" tax system.

MARGINAL VERSUS AVERAGE TAX RATE

The distinction between marginal and average tax rates is simple, yet very important. In the previous case, the Joneses were in a marginal tax rate of 28%, the rate they had to pay on their additional income. For instance, if they had an income of $100,000, their marginal tax rate would be 33%, because a $100,000 income is in the range of $71,951 to $171,090. (See Table 2–1) Mr. and Mrs. Jones should always consider the marginal tax rate as a basis for their investment decisions.

For the sake of argument, suppose that the marginal rate for the Jones family, in a hypothetical tax system, is 75%. The Jones family may decide not to work harder or to take more risk to increase their income if the marginal rate is 75%. Why? Because, of every additional dollar they make, their income after taxes would increase only by 25 cents, and this may not be sufficient to compensate for the extra efforts and risk of making an additional dollar. Therefore, the marginal tax rate is the only tax rate that need be considered before undertaking new income-producing ventures.

What is an average tax rate? It is basically the percentage of total taxes paid on total

Table 2–1   Marginal Tax Rates on Individual Taxable Income

Tax Rate	Single Returns	Joint Returns
15%	Up to $17,850	Up to $29,750
28%	$17,851–43,150	$29,751–71,950
33%	$43,151–89,560	$71,951–171,090
28%	$89,561 and over	$171,091 and over

Example: Computing Taxes for Individuals

PROBLEM   Mr. and Mrs. Jones file a joint taxable income of $185,000. What is their tax liability?

SOLUTION   We refer to Table 2–1 and calculate taxes as follows:

$$
\begin{array}{lcr}
29{,}750 \times .15 & = & \$\ 4{,}462.50 \\
(71{,}950 - 29{,}750) \times .28 & = & 11{,}816.00 \\
(171{,}090 - 71{,}950) \times .33 & = & 32{,}716.20 \\
(185{,}000 - 171{,}090) \times .28 & = & \underline{3{,}894.80} \\
\text{Total Taxes} & & \$52{,}889.50
\end{array}
$$

taxable income. In the case of Mr. and Mrs. Jones, it is 29%. ($52,889/$185,000) This percentage does not have any significant meaning for investment purposes. However, it may satisfy the curiosity of a taxpayer as to what portion of his/her income is spent on taxes.

HOW TO FIGURE TAXABLE INCOME

To arrive at taxable income, we need to go through three steps: First, we determine the total income. Total income includes all kinds of income minus certain exclusions, such as interest from tax-exempt securities and some Social Security benefits. Second, the total income should be reduced by certain adjustments such as IRA deductions (if eligible), contributions to other acceptable retirement plans, alimony payments, and penalty on early withdrawals of savings. The balance is called the adjusted gross income. Third, we subtract the standard deductions or the itemized deductions (whichever is higher) and the total exemptions from the adjusted gross income; the remaining figure is the taxable income on which we must pay taxes.

Example: Determine the Amount of Taxable Income

PROBLEM   Mary and John have a total income of $40,000. They have made $3,000 contributions to an acceptable self-employed retirement plan and have also paid a $400 penalty on an early withdrawal of a certificate of deposit from their bank. Including their child, they are entitled to three personal exemptions ($2,000 each). Their total itemized deductions are $10,500. What is the taxable income of Mary and John?

SOLUTION   Adjusted gross income = Total income − Adjustments
            = 40,000 − 3,000 − 400 = 36,600
            Taxable income = Adjusted gross income −
            Deductions − Exemptions
            = 36,600 − 10,500 − 6,000 = 20,100

Therefore, Mary and John would pay taxes on $20,100.

STANDARD DEDUCTIONS VERSUS ITEMIZED DEDUCTIONS

Once the adjusted gross income is computed, a taxpayer has the choice of taking a fixed amount of deductions as stated by the law or reporting a detailed and itemized list of deductions. As a rational person, the taxpayer should compute and compare both amounts and claim the higher amount. The itemized deductions, subject to limits, include medical and dental expenses, state and local income taxes, real estate taxes, home mortgage interest, some other interest expenses, gifts to charity, casualty and theft losses, job-related expenses, and a broad category of miscellaneous expenses.

Itemized deductions were severely limited by the Tax Act of 1986. For instance, medical expenses that are not reimbursed by insurance companies may be deductible to the extent that they exceed 7.5% of the adjusted gross income. For instance, a taxpayer with an adjusted gross income of $30,000 is not entitled to any medical deduction before he/she pays $2,250 of medical expenses (30,000 × .075). If total expenses are $3,000, deductions would be $750; assuming a marginal tax rate of 28%, the tax benefit of this deduction is only $210 ($750 × .28). Stated differently, under current tax law, a taxpayer in a 28% tax bracket, with an adjusted gross income of $30,000 who pays $3,000 for medical expenses, receives only $210 in the form of a tax benefit.

Another example of a major limitation on itemized deductions is that in 1989 only 20% of interest expenses (except on home mortgages) were deductible. In 1990, the corresponding percentage was 10%, and in 1991 and later, such interest expenses will be nondeductible. An exception to this rule is the interest on one's principal residence or a second residence, though the deduction is limited to the interest on a mortgage no greater than the home's purchase price plus the cost of home improvement. If the extra debt on the principal or second residence is used for educational or medical purposes, interest expenses may also be considered deductible.

CAPITAL GAINS AND LOSSES

By definition, if a capital asset is sold above its book value, a capital gain is realized; if the asset is sold for less than the book value, there is a capital loss. A capital asset could be a "real asset," such as real estate, or a "financial asset," such as stocks and bonds. One of the most controversial provisions of the Tax Reform Act of 1986 was the elimination of the long-term capital gain deduction. Under previous tax law, a capital gain of $1,000 on an asset that an investor had owned for six months or longer was exempt by 60%. Since the maximum tax bracket in the previous system was 50%, the most one had to pay on long-term capital gains was only 20%. (50%) × (1 − 60%) In the new Act, there is no capital gain deduction; therefore, capital gains and ordinary income (wages, salaries, rent, etc.) are taxed at the same rates. Congress and the President are currently looking into the possibility of revising the capital gains provision.

Regarding capital losses, under both the old law and the new law, capital losses may be offset against other ordinary income up to a limit of $3,000 with the balance carried to the following years. There is a major difference in this respect between the two laws. In the previous system, a taxpayer had to have two dollars worth of capital gain to offset one dollar of ordinary income. In the new system, long-term capital losses could be offset against ordinary income on a dollar-to-dollar basis.

Example: Treating Capital Losses Under the New and Old Tax Systems

PROBLEM   Jack has $30,000 of salary and a $3,000 capital loss on the stocks he purchased on January 15 and sold on December 15 of the same year. Determine Jack's taxable income under the new and old tax laws.

SOLUTION   Following are the calculations for taxable income under the new tax law versus the old tax law:

	New Tax Law	Old Tax Law
Ordinary income	$30,000	$30,000
Capital loss on stocks	3,000	1,500
Taxable Income	$27,000	$28,500

PASSIVE INCOME VERSUS ACTIVE INCOME

The current tax law makes a distinction between "passive" income and "active" income. What is the difference between the two? Passive income is generated from a trade or business in which the taxpayer "does not materially participate." With certain exceptions, investments in rental properties and limited partnerships are defined as passive. Investments in which a taxpayer is continuously and rigorously involved are called active. Why does this distinction matter? The answer is that a taxpayer cannot deduct a passive loss from his/her salary, portfolio income, or business income. Passive losses are deductible to the extent that there is a net income from passive activities. A dollar loss from one limited partnership can be deducted from a dollar net income of another passive investment. If there is no income from any other passive investment, passive losses should be carried toward future years.

The effect of the change in the rules for passive losses has adversely affected a number of limited partnerships, especially in the real estate and motion picture industries. Regarding passive losses, legislators made a minor exception for the people who are actively involved in buying and managing rental properties only on a small scale. Up to $25,000 of losses from investment in rental properties may be deducted from ordinary income (including portfolio income), provided that the investor actively and materially participates. The $25,000 deduction is phased out between an adjusted gross income of $100,000 and $150,000. The way this works is that one dollar of deduction is phased out for every two dollars of additional income above the $100,000 threshold. Therefore, a taxpayer who has an adjusted gross income of $125,000 is entitled to $12,500 deduction, and there is no deduction if the income is $150,000 or more. There is an element of unfairness in the case of a couple who are married and file jointly. They are entitled to a $25,000 deduction together. Were they not married, and reporting separately, they would enjoy the benefit of a $25,000 deduction each, a total of $50,000 in deductions!

YOU SHOULD REMEMBER

The Tax Reform Act of 1986 changed the tax law for individuals and corporations. The current tax law has two tax brackets, 15% and 28%, and in the case of high-income taxpayers there is a surcharge of 5%, making the maximum tax rate 33%. Since the tax rate became flat and remained at 28% beyond a certain level, the current tax law is called "progressive-and-regressive." Marginal tax rate is the only relevant factor to consider for calculations of after-tax benefits of a new investment. Taxpayers may elect a standard deduction or itemize their deductible expenses, though itemized deductions are severely limited in the current tax law. The capital gain provision does not exist, and passive losses cannot be deducted from ordinary and portfolio income.

The only exception is for people who, on a small scale, actively engage in owning and managing a real estate property. A maximum deductible loss in this case is $25,000, and it is proportionally phased out for people with incomes between $100,000 to $150,000 annually.

CORPORATE TAXATION

Prior to the 1986 Act, corporations were taxed at five different rates ranging from 15% to 46%. There is now a three-bracket system: the corporate income up to $50,000 is taxed at 15%, between $50,001 to 75,000 at 25%, and over $75,000 at 34%. While corporate tax rates have been reduced, the capital gain tax rate of 28%, which was optional in the previous system, has been repealed. Capital gains are taxed in the same way corporate ordinary income is treated. Capital losses are also applied only against capital losses. The $3,000 capital loss deduction against ordinary income of individual taxpayers is not allowed for corporations. Because capital losses are treated differently—in the sense that they are deducted from capital gains only—their distinction from noncapital losses is important. A noncapital loss, such as merchandise sold below cost or a loss due to fire in the place of business, is treated like a business expense and can be deducted from ordinary business income in the same year. In the case of capital losses, however, if there are no offsetting capital gains, the losses must be carried forward.

TAXES ON DIVIDENDS RECEIVED BY CORPORATIONS

Corporations, like individuals, may invest in the financial securities of other corporations or institutions. Since corporations pay taxes on their income and stockholders also pay taxes on distributed dividends, the law permits an exemption of 80% of the dividends that corporations receive on their investment outside the company. In other words, corporations pay taxes only on 20% of their dividend income. Since the maximum corporate tax rate is 34%, the effective highest tax rate on dividends is 6.8%. (.34 × .20). The exclusion rate has recently been changed to 70% for most cases.

Taxes on a corporation's dividend income, which is in addition to taxes a corporation pays on its earnings and that stockholders pay on their dividends, is usually called a triple tax. The rationale for an 80% tax exemption of the dividend income of corporations is basically to minimize the effects of a triple tax.

INVESTMENT TAX CREDIT

Intended to encourage business firms to expand their assets and produce more goods and services, the previous law allowed a 6% or 10% tax credit against the tax liability of business firms. Assets with a life span of 3 years used to receive a 6% tax credit, and assets with depreciation lives of 5, 10, or 18 years could be qualified for a tax credit of 10%. The concept and provision of the investment tax credit was repealed in the Tax Act of 1986. Except for only a few types of properties, including those constructed or acquired before December 31, 1985, there is no such thing as investment tax credit in the current law.

Example: Computing Total Tax Liability of a Corporation

PROBLEM   The ABC Company has $640,000 in sales revenue, of which 60% is the cost of goods sold. Other costs include selling expenses of $20,000, administrative expenses of $10,000, interest expenses of $8,000 and depreciation charges of $15,000. In addition, the company has capital gains income of $80,000 and capital losses of $60,000 from the resale of equipment. A dividend income is $40,000. Determine the total tax liability of the ABC Company.

SOLUTION   Using an income-statement format, the taxable income of the Company is computed as follows:

Sales	$640,000
Dividend income (20% of $40,000)	8,000
Capital gain income net of	
capital losses ($80,000 − $60,000)	20,000
Cost of goods sold (60% of Sales)	(384,000)
Selling expenses	(20,000)
Administrative expenses	(10,000)
Interest expenses	(8,000)
Depreciation	(15,000)
Taxable income	$231,000

On the taxable income of $231,000, we calculate the tax liability of the firm as follows:

15% on the first $50,000	$ 7,500
25% on the next $25,000	6,250
34% on the remaining $156,000	53,040
Total tax liability	$66,790

• *BASICS OF DEPRECIATION*

Depreciation is the allocation, for accounting and tax purposes, of the purchase costs of fixed assets (such as machinery and equipment) over a number of years. Since depreciation is a major expense, it has a significant effect on the net income of the firm. **Overdepreciation** (depreciating more than the purchase price) of assets decreases the net income of the firm, and **underdepreciation** (depreciating less than the purchase price) increases it. In simple terms, then, when a company depreciates an asset at more than the normal rate, total expenses go up and lower profits are reported. Therefore, profits vary depending on the method of depreciation used in preparing financial statements.

To prevent inconsistent use of depreciation methods by different companies from one year to another, the Internal Revenue Service (IRS) requires all firms to depreciate their assets based on certain procedures approved by Congress. However, firms can use different depreciation methods in various internal or external reports, or for evaluation of their own performance.

A company or individual cannot depreciate an asset more than its original price. In other words, an asset purchased for $100 can be depreciated for no more than $100. This may sound unreasonable, because annual rates of inflation can sometimes raise the price of an asset above its initial price. Unfortunately, the existing depreciation laws ignore inflation and limit the total depreciation charges to the purchase price and installation cost.

• *MAJOR METHODS OF DEPRECIATION*

An asset can be depreciated in several ways. Although IRS regulations require a certain method for tax purposes, management can use different depreciation methods for internal evaluation and other nontax purposes. The major methods of depreciation are the accelerated cost recovery system and the straight-line, sum-of-the-years'-digits, and double-declining balance methods.

ACCELERATED COST RECOVERY SYSTEM (ACRS)

In the **Accelerated Cost Recovery System (ACRS),** all properties, except real estate, are classified into six groups for the purpose of depreciation, as listed in Table 2–2. Depreciation life for residential real estate properties is 27½, and for nonresidential 31½. The precise application of the ACRS is cumbersome and may deviate our attention from finance, the focus of this book. Therefore, throughout the examples, we will use a simplified ACRS table for more common assets of 3, 5, 7, or 10 years. Annual factors of depreciation for these assets are presented in Table 2–3. For example, an asset with a 3-year depreciable life is depreciated at 33% of its cost in the first year, 44% in the second year, and 23% in the third year.

An important point to keep in mind is that depreciation is a "noncash" expenditure, in the sense that the firm does not pay cash for depreciation as it does for wages and salaries. Depreciation reduces taxable income; therefore, it produces additional cash flows for the company. **Cash flow** is the sum of net earnings and depreciation.

Table 2-2   **Property Classes for Depreciation (Tax Act of 1986)**

Example of Property	Normal Recovery Period
Short-lived assets and general tools	3 years
Light trucks, buses, autos, electronics	5 years
Manufacturing equipment, office furniture railroad cars, riding equipment for amusement	7 years
Heavy-duty manufacturing equipment, petroleum refining equipment	10 years
Electric generators, pipelines, communication plants	15 years
Some utility and railroad properties	20 years

Table 2-3   **Annual Depreciation Factors: Simplified ACRS**

3-year asset		5-year asset		7-year asset		10-year asset	
Year	%	Year	%	Year	%	Year	%
1	33	1	20	1	14	1	10
2	44	2	32	2	25	2	18
3	23	3	19	3	17	3	14
		4	15	4	13	4	12
		5	14	5	11	5	9
				6–7	10	6–7	8
						8–10	7

Cash flow = Net earnings + Noncash expenditures (such as depreciation)

As depreciation charges increase, the cash flow of the firm improves, providing more funds for further business activities. Since depreciation has a favorable effect on the cash flow and the activities of the firm, Congress passed the ACRS, under which assets are depreciated at faster rates than they were under the previous system.

Tax relief in the business sector also means decreased government revenue and an increased budget deficit. Supply-side economists, however, argue that tax relief stimulates the economy, generates new business activities, and increases the profits of firms. Once profits in the business sector have increased, they say, the government will have a broader tax base from which to collect taxes. From a supply-side economic view, then, the ACRS not only increases business sector profits, but also improves government tax revenues in the long run. To prove this theory, of course, would require a staggering amount of research.

STRAIGHT-LINE METHOD

In the **straight-line method,** information about the purchase price of the asset, the life of the asset, and its **salvage value** (or scrap value) is required. Annual depreciation charges are calculated by using the following formula:

$$\text{Annual depreciation} = \frac{\text{Purchasing costs} - \text{Salvage value}}{\text{Number of years the asset will be used}}$$

Example: Calculating Straight-Line Depreciation

PROBLEM Determine the annual depreciation of a piece of equipment with a useful life of 5 years, a purchase price of $62,000, and a salvage value of $12,000.

SOLUTION
$$\text{Annual depreciation} = \frac{\$62,000 - \$12,000}{5 \text{ years}} = \$10,000 \text{ per year}$$

In this method, it is assumed that the asset is used at a constant rate over its useful life.

The straight-line method is recommended for performance evaluation of various departments in the same company or for comparison of company performance from one year to another.

SUM-OF-THE-YEARS'-DIGITS METHOD

In the **sum-of-the-years'-digits** method, it is assumed that the asset is used more often either in the earlier part or the later part of its useful life. The procedure to figure out annual depreciation charges contains three steps:

1. Add all the digits of the years of depreciation together.

2. Make annual fractions of the sum so that the first year's numerator is the highest digit, the second year's numerator is the next highest digit, and so on.

3. Multiply the fraction for each year by the value of the asset to get the depreciation charges for that particular year.

Take a look at the following example—this method is really a lot easier than it seems.

Example: Calculating Sum-of-the-Years'-Digits Depreciation

PROBLEM Suppose the purchase cost of an asset, after the salvage value, is $62,000, and the useful life of the asset is 3 years. Find the depreciation amount for each year of its useful life.

SOLUTION In this case, the sum of the years' digits (3 years) is 1 + 2 + 3, or 6. The fractions for years 1 to 3 are 3/6, 2/6, and 1/6, respectively. The annual depreciation charges are computed as follows, using these fractions:

$$\text{Depreciation of first year} = \tfrac{3}{6} \times \$62{,}000 = \$31{,}000$$
$$\text{Depreciation of second year} = \tfrac{2}{6} \times \$62{,}000 = \$20{,}666$$
$$\text{Depreciation of third year} = \tfrac{1}{6} \times \$62{,}000 = \$10{,}333$$

This method of computation (the *accelerating* method) is appropriate when the management of a company believes that the asset is used more in the first half of its life. If the asset is used more in the later part of its useful life, the order of the fractions has merely to be reversed (the *decelerating* method):

$$\text{Depreciation of first year} = \tfrac{1}{6} \times \$62{,}000 = \$10{,}333$$
$$\text{Depreciation of second year} = \tfrac{2}{6} \times \$62{,}000 = \$20{,}666$$
$$\text{Depreciation of third year} = \tfrac{3}{6} \times \$62{,}000 = \$31{,}000$$

DOUBLE-DECLINING BALANCE METHOD

In the **double-declining balance method,** which was popular before the ACRS became mandatory, the firm uses an annual depreciation ratio equal to double the

Table 2–4 Double-Declining Balance Depreciation Method

Year	Depreciation Ratio (%) (*R*)	Book Value (undepreciated balance) (dollars) (*B*)	Annual Depreciation Charges (dollars) (*R*) (*B*)
1	40	80,000	32,000
2	40	48,000	19,200
3	40	28,800	11,520
4	40	17,280	6,912
5	40	10,368	4,147

NOTE: In the double-declining balance method, the salvage value is not subtracted from the purchase cost. In this example, the total depreciation charges are $73,779, which can be computed from Table 2–4 ($32,000 + $19,000 + $11,520 + $6,912 + $4,147 = $73,779). When $73,779 is subtracted from the purchase cost of $80,000, the undepreciated amount remaining—which can be considered the salvage value of the asset—is $6,221.

straight-line ratio. This ratio is multiplied by the book value (undepreciated balance) of the asset to get depreciation charges for that particular year.

Example: Calculating Double-Declining Balance Depreciation

PROBLEM Suppose the purchase cost of an asset is $80,000 and its useful life is 5 years. Find the depreciation amount for each year of useful life.

SOLUTION The annual straight-line ratio is ⅕, or 20%. Twice this is 40%. Annual depreciation charges are calculated in Table 2–4, using the ratio of 40%.

• S CORPORATIONS AND ADVANTAGES

Certain businesses that adopt the organization of a corporation are not subject to corporate income tax regulations. This type of organization is called an S corporation. A basic reason to apply for S corporation status is to enjoy the corporate benefit of limited liability and meantime pay taxes at individual rates like a proprietorship. Thus, the tax advantage of an S corporation is that dividends are taxed only once. A regular corporation pays taxes before dividends are paid, and then shareholders pay income taxes on the same dividends. This can be avoided if an S corporation is formed. Owners of an S corporation combine their business and personal income, subtract business losses, and pay taxes only once. Note that like an individual taxpayer, an S corporation is also entitled to a $3,000 capital loss deduction against its business or personal income. Of course, before applying for S corporation status, taxes should be estimated for a regular corporation and compared to taxes on an S corporation, in order to determine which status is more advantageous.

Among main requirements for the formation of an S corporation are: the firm must be domestic, have only one class of stock, and be owned by no more than 35 shareholders. Financial institutions and most insurance companies, no matter how small, cannot apply to become an S corporation.

• SMALL BUSINESS ADMINISTRATION (SBA)

The **Small Business Administration** (SBA) is a federal agency established in 1935 whose purpose is to help small businesses. The SBA offers three types of loans: direct loans, participation loans, and economic opportunity loans. *Direct loans* are available to small businesses that have no source of financing. *Participation loans* are offered by a local bank or financial institution but are guaranteed by the SBA. *Economic opportunity loans* are generally given to minority individuals who own and run small businesses.

Interest rates on SBA loans are usually lower than those on regular commercial loans.

YOU SHOULD REMEMBER

There are three tax brackets in corporate taxation: 15%, 25%, and 34%. Capital gains and ordinary income are taxed the same way. Dividends received on investments outside the company are exempt by 80%; therefore, the maximum tax rate on such dividends is 6.8%. [.34 × (1 − .80)] The reason behind this exemption is to reduce the effect of a triple tax. Investment tax credit does not any longer exist in corporate taxation. Some firms may adopt the organization of a corporation but pay taxes like individuals. These firms, called S corporations, enjoy the limited liability of a corporation but are not subject to corporate tax law.

KNOW THE CONCEPTS

DO YOU KNOW THE BASICS?

1. What are the three types of business organizations? Define them.
2. Name the major tax acts that changed tax laws in 1980s.
3. What are current individual tax rates?
4. What are current corporate tax rates?
5. How are capital gains and ordinary income taxed in the current tax system?
6. What major tax changes may we expect in future?
7. What is the ACRS depreciation procedure for an asset with a useful life of 5 years?
8. Is a firm allowed to use the straight-line depreciation method?
9. How are capital losses treated in the new tax law?
10. What percentage of dividend income received by a corporation is subject to tax?
11. Is investment in real estate considered active or passive?
12. At what level of income is a person *not* entitled to any passive loss from investment in real estate, no matter how actively he/she is involved in managing his/her rental property?
13. Are corporations entitled to investment tax credit?
14. A corporation has 40 owners. They like to pay taxes as individuals, but they do not want to give up their limited liability status. What is your advice?

TERMS FOR STUDY

Accelerated Cost Recovery System
   (ACRS)
capital

capital gains
cash flow
corporation

depreciation
dividend income
double-declining balance method
general partnership
investment tax credit
limited partnership
ordinary income
overdepreciation
partnership

proprietorship
salvage value
S corporation (Subchapter S
    corporation)
Small Business Administration (SBA)
straight-line method
sum-of-the-years'-digits method
underdepreciation

PRACTICAL APPLICATION

COMPUTATIONAL PROBLEMS

1. XYZ Inc. has $700,000 in sales revenue, of which 70% is the cost of goods sold. Other costs are selling expenses of $60,000, administrative expenses of $18,000, interest expenses of $12,000, and depreciation charges of $17,000. The company also has capital gains income of $70,000 from the resale of an old machine, and has received a dividend income of $60,000. Calculate the total tax liability of XYZ Inc.

2. The future net earnings of the XYZ Co. are estimated as follows:

Year:	1	2	3	4	5
Net earnings:	$100,000	$150,000	$200,000	$250,000	$300,000

Assets worth $400,000 will be depreciated using the ACRS method for the next 5 years. Determine the annual cash flows for those years.

3. Calculate the annual depreciation charges, assuming no salvage value and a depreciation life of 3 years, for an asset bought for $200,000 using the following four methods:

   (a) Straight-line
   (b) Sum-of-the-years'-digits (accelerating)
   (c) Double-declining
   (d) ACRS

4. XYZ Corporation sells personal computers. During the past year, the company's sales were $2,400,000. The combined cost of goods sold and operating expenses were 62.5% of sales. In addition, the company paid $20,000 in interest on a bank loan and $30,000 in preferred stock dividends. The firm also received $25,000 in dividend income and sold land for $70,000. The land was purchased 2 years ago at a cost of $55,000. Calculate XYZ's tax liability. Find the average tax rate and marginal tax rate.

ANSWERS

KNOW THE CONCEPTS

1. The three types of business organizations are proprietorships, partnerships, and corporations. A proprietorship is owned by one individual. A partnership is owned by more than one person. A corporation can be formed by a person or a group of persons; the identity or "persona" of the corporation is totally separate from those of the owners.

2. The Economic Recovery Tax Act of 1981, the Tax Equity and Fiscal Responsibility Act of 1982, the Tax Reform Act of 1984, and the Tax Reform Act of 1986.

3. 15%, 28%, and 33%.

4. 15%, 25%, and 34%.

5. The same, like ordinary income.

6. The capital gain tax provision may come back again.

7. .20, .32, .19, .15, and .14 (Total 100%)

8. Yes, only for internal purposes.

9. In the case of individuals, capital losses may be offset against other ordinary income up to a limit of $3,000, with the balance carried forward. The $3,000 limit is not allowed for corporations.

10. 20%

11. Passive

12. $150,000

13. Not in the current tax system. Investment tax credit, like capital gains deductions, could be the subject of a future debate among legislators.

14. Number of shareholders should be reduced to 35, if possible.

PRACTICAL APPLICATION

1.
Sales	$700,000
Cost of goods sold (70% of Sales)	(490,000)
Selling expenses	(60,000)
Administrative expenses	(18,000)
Interest expenses	(12,000)
Depreciation	(17,000)
Ordinary income	$103,000
Plus capital gain	70,000
Taxable income	$173,000

Taxes = 50,000 (.15) + 25,000 (.25) + (173,000 − 75,000) (.34)
     = 7,500 + 6,250 + 33,320 = $47,070

Taxes on Dividends $= (60,000)\ (.20)\ (.34)$
$$= 4080$$
Total Taxes $= 47,070 + 4080 = 51,150$

2.

Year	Net Earnings	Depreciation	Cash Flow = Net Earnings + Depreciation
1	100,000	80,000	180,000
2	150,000	128,000	278,000
3	200,000	76,000	276,000
4	250,000	60,000	310,000
5	300,000	56,000	356,000

3.

Depreciation methods	Year 1	Year 2	Year 3
Straight line	$ 66,666	$ 66,666	$ 66,666
Sum-of-the-years'-digits	100,000	66,666	33,333
Double-declining	133,333	44,444	14,815
ACRS	66,000	88,000	46,000

4.

Sales	$2,400,000
Cost of goods and operating expenses (62.5% of sales)	(1,500,000)
Interest expenses	(20,000)
Ordinary income	880,000
Capital gain (70,000−55,000)	15,000
Taxable dividend income after 80% exemption	5,000
Total taxable income	$900,000

Taxes $= 50,000 \times .15 + 25,000 \times .25 + (900,000-75,000) \times .34$
$$= 7,500 + 6,250 + 280,500 = \$294,250$$

In this case, the marginal tax rate is 34% and the average tax rate is 33% ($294,500/900,000). Do you know why the average tax rate is close to the marginal tax rate in this problem? The reason is that most of the total income is taxed at 34%.

VALUATION
(TIME AND RISK)

3
THE VALUE OF MONEY OVER TIME

KEY TERMS

future value the value of an initial investment after a specified period of time at a stated rate of interest

inflation a general price increase in the economy

liquidity a measure of how easily assets can be converted into cash

present value the cash value, today, of future returns on income after adjustments are made for risk

risk uncertainty about the future

securities company assets guaranteed to lenders to ensure repayment of a loan

WHY THE VALUE OF MONEY CHANGES OVER TIME

The old saying "A bird in the hand is worth two in the bush" makes a great deal of sense when applied to finance. In monetary terms, it means that cash today is worth more than cash in the future. In other words, the value of money changes over time. Investors have a natural preference for cash now rather than later, so they can *increase* its value. This, of course, is a major goal of a financial manager. Aside from this basic reason why cash now is worth more than cash later, you should also be aware of factors that *decrease* the value of money over time. Three important reasons why the value of money decreases progressively over time are as follows:

1. Inflation
2. Risk
3. Preference for Liquidity

INFLATION

Inflation refers to a general price increase in the economy. When prices increase, the value of a dollar decreases, and since prices are expected to rise in the future, the value of a dollar in future years will be less than it is today. In other words, the purchasing power of a dollar today is higher than it will be tomorrow, because rising prices will diminish the value of that dollar. Therefore, it is possible to buy more goods with one dollar a year from now than two years from now, and so on.

Example: Inflation

If general prices increased by 5% annually, the purchasing power of one dollar today would be 5% less one year from now. In other words, $1.00 today would depreciate in value to $0.95 one year from now. If consumers could buy 100 pins with a dollar today, they would be able to buy only 95 pins a year from now. Simply stated, the higher the rate of inflation, and the longer the period of time involved, the less a given amount of money will be worth in the future.

RISK

Risk, or uncertainty about the future, also causes a decline in the value of money. Because the future is uncertain, risk increases with time. Most people wish to avoid risk, so they value cash today more than the promise of cash in the future. Most people are willing to give up cash for promised cash only if properly compensated for the risk they are asked to take.

No one can predict with certainty either the future of the U.S. economy or economic and financial trends in other parts of the world. It is impossible to predict accurately whether money invested today will be available tomorrow. There is no assurance that a financially sound firm will remain so in the years ahead. Investors cannot be guaranteed dividends or price appreciation in stocks they purchase, nor can they be completely certain that the interest and principal on fixed-income securities will be paid as agreed by the issuer. Financial analysts or sophisticated investors, no matter how competent they are, cannot be assured that the returns they project from a given investment will turn out as originally visualized.

Since uncertainty increases the further one looks into the future, risk also increases—and the value of money promised in the future diminishes accordingly.

PREFERENCE FOR LIQUIDITY

Liquidity is important to an investor or a firm. Liquidity refers to how easily assets can be converted into cash. Cash, government bonds, and other marketable **securities** (company assets guaranteed to lenders to ensure repayment of a loan) increase the liquidity of a firm. By the same token, fixed assets such as plant and equipment are not considered very liquid. Investors have a **preference for liquidity;** that is, they prefer to hold ready cash for unexpected emergencies and financial claims rather than commit funds into future-yielding assets. If they do give up current liquidity by buying assets that promise future returns, they are trading an assured cash asset for a riskier future asset. The trade will take place only if the promised rewards of the future assets are sufficiently high to warrant taking the risk.

When lenders or investors give up cash for very risky future returns, they require high premiums, or returns, on their invested cash to compensate for less liquidity. Conversely, when they invest in low-risk assets, the premiums they expect in return are relatively low.

Example: Liquidity versus Future Returns

If a person deposits cash in a bank that is FDIC insured, she will be willing to accept 5% interest, whereas if she buys the long-term bond of an unknown company, a higher rate of interest, say 15%, would be required. In both cases, cash, or 100% liquidity, is given up, and the return must compensate for the risk.

It is clearly essential for lenders or investors to know how much their cash investments will grow so they can determine whether their investments are worthwhile. Borrowers also want to know how much, and over what period of time, they will have to repay the lenders, and whether the returns from these borrowed funds will be greater than the costs of borrowing. This all boils down to the concept of future value, as determined by the compound rate of interest, and the present value of future returns once they are adjusted for risk.

YOU SHOULD REMEMBER

Aside from the fact that money invested wisely today will yield a return in the future (a fact that creates a natural investor desire for cash today), money loses value over time because of inflation, risk, and preference for cash. The concept that the value of a dollar today is more than the value of a dollar tomorrow is central to financial theory.

FUTURE VALUE AND COMPOUND INTEREST

Any reasonable investment or commitment of cash must provide for an increase in value over time. Given the amount of cash that you want to commit, you can find out how much that cash value will increase in the future once the expected rate of return is known. This calculation is called finding the **future value** of an investment.

Example: Future Value after One Year

Suppose an investor saves $100. This cash is deposited in the bank at a 10% annual interest rate. After one year the investor will have the original $100 plus $10 in interest:

$$\text{Original deposit} + \text{Interest on deposit} = \text{FV}$$
$$\$100 \quad + \quad (10\%)(\$100) \quad = \$110$$

At the time of deposit the $100 was worth 100%, or $100. Since the bank promised to pay an additional 10%, the future value of the $100 one year from now is equal to $110 ($100 plus 10).

Calculating future value for 1 year is perfectly straightforward, but what happens when someone wants to know how much money will be in an account after 20 years? Luckily, there is an easy formula to calculate future values:

$$FV = P(1 + R)^N$$

where FV = future value
$\quad\quad\;\; P$ = initial deposit (principal)
$\quad\quad\;\; R$ = annual rate of interest
$\quad\quad\;\; N$ = number of years

Example: Future Value after Any Number of Years

The equation just introduced can be used for any number of years. Here are two instances involving a $100 deposit at a 10% interest rate:

1 Year on Deposit	2 Years on Deposit
$FV = P(1 + R)^1$	$FV = P(1 + R)^2$
$FV = \$100(1 + .10)$	$FV = \$100(1 + .10)^2$
$FV = \$100(1.10)$	$FV = \$100(1.10)(1.10)$
$FV = \$110$	$FV = \$121$

If the preceding example had involved 10 years, you would have had to calculate $(1.10)^{10}$, which is equal to 2.594. So the future value of $100 in 10 years would be $100(2.594), or $259.40. Note that each year the cash value increases, not by 10% of the original $100, but by 10% of each subsequently higher amount. In other words, you earn interest not only on your initial deposit, but also on your interest:

Original $100 × 1.10 = $110 future value (*FV*) after 1 year
$110 × 1.10 = $121 *FV* after 2 years
$121 × 1.10 = $133 *FV* after 3 years

This method of computing future value is cumbersome. Fortunately, future value tables are available to speed the computations. These tables calculate all of the factors $(1 + R)^N$ for a given number of years. If the rate of interest is known, you can easily find the factor by which to multiply the original cash investment to obtain the future value.

Table 3–1 shows what is known as a Future Value Interest Factor (*FVIF*). It is a highly useful tool for obtaining different values related to future values

USING FUTURE VALUE TABLES

Reading the future value table is fairly simple. Suppose you wish to find the *FV* of an original investment of $100 over a 3-year period at 10% interest. Look up the factor (1.33), and multiply it by the original investment: $100(1.33) = $133. If the intent is to find out how fast an investment will grow over 3 years, just deduct 1.00 from the factor and you get the total percentage increase (1.33 − 1.00 = .33, or 33%). In other words, a $100 investment that grows to $133 in 3 years represents an increase in value of 33%.

If your goal is to find out the annual rate of compound interest that applies to an investment of $100 which is expected to grow 33% in 3 years, all that is required is to locate the factor (133%, or 1.000 + .33 = 1.33) by going to the third year and finding 1.33. By looking up the column, you find that the rate of interest for a $100 investment expected to grow 33% in 3 years is 10%. Conversely, if you want to find out how many years it will take for an investment growing at 10% annually to increase 33%, merely look up 10% and the factor 1.33, and then move your eyes horizontally along the row to obtain the corresponding time of 3 years.

ANNUITY

An **annuity** is a series of equal payments (or receipts) made at any regular interval of time. An annuity can be a payment or an investment each year, each half-year (semiannually), each quarter, or each month. Examples are the monthly mortgage payments on a house, quarterly investments in a trust account for a child's future education, and periodic loan payments.

FV factors can be used to find the total future value of an annuity. Even long-term annuities can be handled easily in this manner.

Example: Using FV *Factors to Calculate Annuities*

PROBLEM   Find the total future value of payments for a $100 annuity paid once a year over a period of 4 years. Assume 10% compound interest.

Table 3–1 Future Value of $1 After *n* Periods

| | Interest Rate | | | | | | | | | | | |
Periods	1%	2%	3%	4%	5%	6%	7%	8%	9%	10%	11%	12%
1	1.0100	1.0200	1.0300	1.0400	1.0500	1.0600	1.0700	1.0800	1.0900	1.1000	1.1100	1.1200
2	1.0201	1.0404	1.0609	1.0816	1.1025	1.1236	1.1449	1.1664	1.1881	1.2100	1.2321	1.2544
3	1.0303	1.0612	1.0927	1.1249	1.1576	1.1910	1.2250	1.2597	1.2950	1.3310	1.3676	1.4049
4	1.0406	1.0824	1.1255	1.1699	1.2155	1.2625	1.3108	1.3605	1.4116	1.4641	1.5181	1.5735
5	1.0510	1.1041	1.1593	1.2167	1.2763	1.3382	1.4026	1.4693	1.5386	1.6105	1.6851	1.7623
6	1.0615	1.1261	1.1941	1.2653	1.3401	1.4185	1.5007	1.5869	1.6771	1.7716	1.8704	1.9738
7	1.0721	1.1487	1.2299	1.3159	1.4071	1.5036	1.6058	1.7138	1.8280	1.9487	2.0762	2.2107
8	1.0829	1.1717	1.2668	1.3686	1.4775	1.5939	1.7182	1.8509	1.9926	2.1436	2.3045	2.4760
9	1.0937	1.1951	1.3048	1.4233	1.5513	1.6895	1.8385	1.9990	2.1719	2.3580	2.5580	2.7731
10	1.1046	1.2190	1.3439	1.4802	1.6289	1.7909	1.9672	2.1589	2.3674	2.5937	2.8394	3.1059
11	1.1157	1.2434	1.3842	1.5395	1.7103	1.8983	2.1049	2.3316	2.5804	2.8531	3.1518	3.4786
12	1.1268	1.2682	1.4258	1.6010	1.7959	2.0122	2.2522	2.5182	2.8127	3.1384	3.4985	3.8960
13	1.1381	1.2936	1.4685	1.6651	1.8857	2.1329	2.4098	2.7196	3.0658	3.4523	3.8833	4.3635
14	1.1495	1.3195	1.5126	1.7317	1.9799	2.2609	2.5785	2.9372	3.3417	3.7975	4.3104	4.8871
15	1.1610	1.3459	1.5580	1.8009	2.0789	2.3966	2.7590	3.1722	3.6425	4.1773	4.7846	5.4736
16	1.1726	1.3728	1.6047	1.8730	2.1829	2.5404	2.9522	3.4259	3.9703	4.5950	5.3109	6.1304
17	1.1843	1.4002	1.6529	1.9479	2.2920	2.6928	3.1588	3.7000	4.3276	5.0545	5.8951	6.8660
18	1.1962	1.4283	1.7024	2.0258	2.4066	2.8543	3.3799	3.9960	4.7171	5.5599	6.5436	7.6900
19	1.2081	1.4568	1.7535	2.1069	2.5270	3.0256	3.6165	4.3157	5.1417	6.1159	7.2633	8.6128
20	1.2202	1.4860	1.8061	2.1911	2.6533	3.2071	3.8697	4.6610	5.6044	6.7275	8.0623	9.6463
21	1.2324	1.5157	1.8603	2.2788	2.7860	3.3996	4.1406	5.0338	6.1088	7.4003	8.9492	10.804
22	1.2447	1.5460	1.9161	2.3699	2.9253	3.6035	4.4304	5.4365	6.6586	8.1403	9.9336	12.100
23	1.2572	1.5769	1.9736	2.4647	3.0715	3.8198	4.7405	5.8714	7.2579	8.9543	11.026	13.552
24	1.2697	1.6084	2.0328	2.5633	3.2251	4.0489	5.0724	6.3412	7.9111	9.8497	12.239	15.179

SOLUTION   Finding the total future value of this series of payments is a relatively easy task. All you have to do is sum up the future value factors for the number of years that cover the annuity. From the *FV* table, then, the factor for a 4-year annuity at a 10% compound interest rate would be 1.000 + 1.100 + 1.210 + 1.331, or 4.641. In 4 years, annuity payments of $100 would be worth $100(4.641), or $464.10.

USING FUTURE VALUE ANNUITY TABLES

The simple mathematical formula for computing the *FV* of an annuity is

$$Sn = a(FVI_{R,N}FA)$$

where *Sn* = total future value of the annuity at the end of a given period
      a = annuity payments
$FVI_{R,N}FA$ = annuity factor, or future value interest annuity factor

Future value annuity tables merely simplify your computations by adding up interim compound interest rate factors and providing you with a single factor. Table 3–2 is a sample future value annuity table. Using the figures from the preceding example, you can find the 4-year annuity factor, or 4.641, directly.

YOU SHOULD REMEMBER

There are two ways to determine the future value of a deposit: using a formula and using a future value table. The formula for the future value is

$$FV_N = P(1 + R)^N$$

where FV_N = future value in period N.
      P = initial deposit (principal)
      R = annual rate of interest
      N = number of periods

If you want to use the table, multiply your initial deposit by the value of *FVIF*. In the case of annuities, you should multiply the amount of annuity by the value of *FVIFA* available in the table.

Table 3–2 Future Value Interest Factor Annuity

Period	1%	2%	3%	4%	5%	6%	7%	8%	9%	10%
1	1.000	1.000	1.000	1.000	1.000	1.000	1.000	1.000	1.000	1.000
2	2.010	2.020	2.030	2.040	2.050	2.060	2.070	2.080	2.090	2.100
3	3.030	3.060	3.091	3.122	3.152	3.184	3.215	3.246	3.278	3.310
4	4.060	4.122	4.184	4.246	4.310	4.375	4.440	4.506	4.573	4.641
5	5.101	5.204	5.309	5.416	5.526	5.637	5.751	5.867	5.985	6.105
6	6.152	6.308	6.468	6.633	6.802	6.975	7.153	7.336	7.523	7.716
7	7.214	7.434	7.662	7.898	8.142	8.394	8.654	8.923	9.200	9.487
8	8.286	8.583	8.892	9.214	9.549	9.897	10.260	10.637	11.028	11.436
9	9.368	9.755	10.159	10.583	11.027	11.491	11.978	12.488	13.021	13.579
10	10.462	10.950	11.464	12.006	12.578	13.181	13.816	14.487	15.193	15.937
11	11.567	12.169	12.808	13.486	14.207	14.972	15.784	16.645	17.560	18.531
12	12.682	13.412	14.192	15.026	15.917	16.870	17.888	18.977	20.141	21.384
13	13.809	14.680	15.618	16.627	17.713	18.882	20.141	21.495	22.953	24.523
14	14.947	15.974	17.086	18.292	19.598	21.015	22.550	24.215	26.019	27.975
15	16.097	17.293	18.599	20.023	21.578	23.276	25.129	27.152	29.361	31.772
16	17.258	18.639	20.157	21.824	23.657	25.672	27.888	30.324	33.003	35.949
17	18.430	20.012	21.761	23.697	25.840	28.213	30.840	33.750	36.973	40.544
18	19.614	21.412	23.414	25.645	28.132	30.905	33.999	37.450	41.301	45.599
19	20.811	22.840	25.117	27.671	30.539	33.760	37.379	41.446	46.018	51.158
20	22.019	24.297	26.870	29.778	33.066	36.785	40.995	45.762	51.159	57.274
21	23.239	25.783	28.676	31.969	35.719	39.992	44.865	50.422	56.764	64.002
22	24.471	27.299	30.536	34.248	38.505	43.392	49.005	55.456	62.872	71.402
23	25.716	28.845	32.452	36.618	41.430	46.995	53.435	60.893	69.531	79.542
24	26.973	30.421	34.426	39.082	44.501	50.815	58.176	66.764	76.789	88.496
25	28.243	32.030	36.459	41.645	47.726	54.864	63.248	73.105	84.699	98.346
30	34.784	40.567	47.575	56.084	66.438	79.057	94.459	113.282	136.305	164.491
40	48.885	60.401	75.400	95.024	120.797	154.758	199.630	259.052	337.872	442.580
50	64.461	84.577	112.794	152.664	209.341	290.325	406.516	573.756	815.051	1163.865

PRESENT VALUE AND DISCOUNT RATES

Why is present value of crucial interest to financial people? The answer is that it provides them with a basis for comparing the profitability of different projects or investments over a period of years. **Present value,** therefore, is the cash value of future returns or income once a discount (capitalization) rate has been applied to it. The **discount, or capitalization, rate** is an interest rate applied to a series of future payments to adjust for risk and the uncertainty of the time factor.

ADJUSTING FOR RISK

To calculate present value, a discount rate must be determined that takes into consideration how much risk is associated with each project or investment. Risk levels follow a simple rule:

> High risk means a high discount (capitalization) rate, and low risk means a low discount rate.

For example, if an investor decides that the discount rate assigned to a stock should be 5%, another stock having double this risk will have a discount rate of 10%.

Once the risk level is determined, the next step is to adjust returns or future income for the uncertainty of time. Generally speaking, the following principles apply to evaluating discount rates.

Evaluating Discount Rates

1. Between two future incomes, the one that will take longer to reach maturity should have a higher discount rate.

2. The lower the perceived risk, the lower the discount rate should be.

3. If general interest rates in the market rise, the discount rate should increase also.

Risk can decline because of a more favorable business outlook, the prospect of declining inflation and interest rates, or less uncertain economic conditions. As risk declines, the present value of future income will increase, as illustrated in Table 3–3.

Table 3–3   **Inverse Relationship between Present Value and Risk**

Future Income (3 years from now) (dollars)	Discount Rate (%)	PV of $1 in 3 Years	PV of Future Income (dollars)
1,000	15 (high risk)	.658	658
1,000	10 (average risk)	.751	751
1,000	5 (low risk)	.864	864

ADJUSTING FOR TIME

The present value of any future returns declines the further out into the future you look. Obviously, this procedure employs a mathematical adjustment for the time value of money. As it turns out, the principle involved is not a difficult one to grasp—*the present value of future returns is merely the reverse of future value compounding.*

An arithmetic illustration will provide a better understanding of this principie. Assume you wish to find out the present value of $1,000 3 years from now, and you expect the level of risk associated with the project to be 10% annually. Thus, if

$$FV = P(1 + R)^N$$

then

$$PV = \frac{FV}{(1 + R)^N}$$

It is evident from Table 3–1 that the factors increase as time passes and as the compound interest rate rises. You can observe that, if these factors are plugged into the denominator in the last equation, the present value of $1,000 3 years hence is

$$\frac{\$1,000}{(1 + .10)^3} = \$751$$

How was this value found? Simply by multiplying 1.10 three times (1.10 × 1.10 × 1.10 = 1.33), and using this factor to discount:

$$\frac{\$1,000}{1.33} = \$751$$

The present value table saves all the work required to compute the different *PV* factors. This table indicates, for example, that the values decrease the longer the time period considered, and that these values also decline as the discount rate increases. The table merely indicates the factor which, when multiplied by a future value, will yield the present value. A sample present value table is available in Table 3–4.

It is evident that, if you had two projects with the same costs and same economic lives but different risk factors, it would be possible to find out their present values and then determine which is more favorable. Capital budgeting evaluation, which is designed to determine the relative merits of projects or investments, employs the present value concept as a guideline. The whole idea is to discount the future returns by a level of risk plus the uncertainty of time. The present value method accomplishes this objective.

USING PRESENT VALUE TABLES

In the last illustration, in which you had to find the present value of $1,000 3 years hence, all you had to do was look up the length of time and its corresponding present value factor at a given discount rate in Table 3–4. This factor is shown to be .751. To obtain the present value of $1,000 3 years from now at a discount rate of 10%, calculate the product of the present value times the factor ($1,000 × .751 = $751), which is the same amount you obtained using the long method.

The present value table obviously saves investors and financial managers a great deal of time. Note that when the discount rate declines the present value increases, and that when it increases the present value decreases. It should be clear by now that the present value concept is an important tool in making investment and other financial decisions.

• *PRESENT VALUE OF AN ANNUITY*

When financial managers are faced by a steady and constant stream of future payments or receipts, and they want to evaluate the present value of these figures, they can do two things:

1. Calculate the present value of each future year by discounting each payment or receipt with its appropriate present value factor. This is a long and redundant method.

2. Calculate the *PV* annuity of future cash flows by employing a present value annuity factor. This is the short and easy method.

An example will help show you which method is easier. Assume you expect a cash flow of $100 in the next 3 years and wish to find out the *PV* of these cash flows given a discount rate, or risk level, of 10%.

Table 3–4   Present Value of $1

Periods	1%	2%	3%	4%	5%	6%	7%	8%	9%	10%	11%	12%
1	.99010	.98039	.97087	.96154	.95238	.94340	.93458	.92593	.91743	.90909	.90090	.89286
2	.98030	.96117	.94260	.92456	.90703	.89000	.87344	.85734	.84168	.82645	.81162	.79719
3	.97059	.94232	.91514	.88900	.86384	.83962	.81630	.79383	.77218	.75131	.73119	.71178
4	.96098	.92385	.88849	.85480	.82270	.79209	.76290	.73503	.70843	.68301	.65873	.63552
5	.95147	.90573	.86261	.82193	.78353	.74726	.71299	.68058	.64993	.62092	.59345	.56743
6	.94204	.88797	.83748	.79031	.74622	.70496	.66634	.63017	.59627	.56447	.53464	.50663
7	.93272	.87056	.81309	.75992	.71068	.66506	.62275	.58349	.54703	.51316	.48166	.45235
8	.92348	.85349	.78941	.73069	.67684	.62741	.58201	.54027	.50187	.46651	.43393	.40388
9	.91434	.83675	.76642	.70259	.64461	.59190	.54393	.50025	.46043	.42410	.39092	.36061
10	.90529	.82035	.74409	.67556	.61391	.55839	.50835	.46319	.42241	.38554	.35218	.32197
11	.89632	.80426	.72242	.64958	.58468	.52679	.47509	.42888	.38753	.35049	.31728	.28748
12	.88745	.78849	.70138	.62460	.55684	.49697	.44401	.39711	.35553	.31683	.28584	.25667
13	.87866	.77303	.68095	.60057	.53032	.46884	.41496	.36770	.32618	.28966	.25751	.22917
14	.86996	.75787	.66112	.57747	.50507	.44230	.38782	.34046	.29925	.26333	.23199	.20462
15	.86135	.74301	.64186	.55526	.48102	.41726	.36245	.31524	.27454	.23939	.20900	.18270
16	.85282	.72845	.62317	.53391	.45811	.39365	.33873	.29189	.25187	.21763	.18829	.16312
17	.84438	.71416	.60502	.51337	.43630	.37136	.31657	.27027	.23107	.19784	.16963	.14564
18	.83602	.70016	.58739	.49363	.41552	.35034	.29586	.25025	.21199	.17986	.15282	.13004
19	.82774	.68643	.57029	.47464	.39573	.33051	.27651	.23171	.19449	.16351	.13768	.11611
20	.81954	.67297	.55367	.45639	.37689	.31180	.25842	.21455	.17843	.14864	.12403	.10367
21	.81143	.65978	.53755	.43883	.35894	.29415	.24151	.19866	.16370	.13513	.11174	.09256
22	.80340	.64684	.52189	.42195	.34185	.27750	.22571	.18394	.15018	.12285	.10067	.08264
23	.79544	.63414	.50669	.40573	.32557	.26180	.21095	.17031	.13778	.11168	.09069	.07379
24	.78757	.62172	.49193	.39012	.31007	.24698	.19715	.15770	.12640	.10153	.08170	.06588
48												

Discount Rate

In long method of calculation you would look up the factors in the *PV* table, derive the *PV* for each $100 in the next 3 years, and sum the products:

Year	Cash Flow	PVIF (10%)	Present Value
1	$100	.909	$ 90.90
2	100	.826	82.60
3	100	.751	75.10
	Total	2.486	$248.60

Recall that when *FV* annuities were discussed it was pointed out that annuity factors represent the summation of the future value factors. The same principle applies in calculating the present value annuity for an equal series of future cash flows. All that you have to do is add up the *PV* factors for the period under analysis and apply this total annuity factor to the cash flow for any year. Mathematically, the equation for *PV* annuity is

$$PV_a = \frac{A}{(1 + R)^N}$$

where PV_a = present value of an annuity
A = amount of annuity
R = discount rate
N = number of years or periods

Example: Calculating Present Values of Annuities—The Long Way

PROBLEM   Calculate the present value of a $100 annuity for a 3-year period. Assume a discount rate of 10%.

SOLUTION

$$\text{Present value of 1st payment} = \frac{\$100}{(1 + .10)^1} = \$90.90$$

$$\text{Present value of 2nd payment} = \frac{\$100}{(1 + .10)^2} = \$82.60$$

$$\text{Present value of 3rd payment} = \frac{\$100}{(1 + .10)^3} = \$75.10$$

$$\text{Present value of all three payments} = \$90.90 + \$82.60 + \$75.10$$
$$= \$248.60$$

The above calculations show that the three payments of $100 each are currently worth only $248.60 if the discount rate is 10%. This is exactly what discounting is all about. The difference between $300 and $248.60 is called the time value of money, or the total discount.

USING PRESENT VALUE ANNUITY TABLES

Instead of having to go through laborious calculations, a table has been set up that sums the *PV* factors. Table 3–5 is a present value annuity interest factor table, and it is relatively easy to read. Assume that you contemplate buying stock A, which will return $1,000 annually over 5 years, and stock B, which will return $1,025 yearly during the same period. You wish to find out which annuity is the better investment. A security analyst tells you that stock A is discounted at 10% and stock B at 12%. To compare the *PV* annuities of these two stocks all you have to do is go to the annuity table and look up the present value interest factor annuity (*PVIFA*) for these two streams of returns. At 10% in 5 years the factor is 3.7908 and at 12% it is 3.6048. Given these factors you can calculate the *PV* of the two stocks:

$$PV_{\text{stock A}} = \$1,000(3.791) = \$3,791$$
$$PV_{\text{stock B}} = \$1,025(3.605) = \$3,695$$

After adjusting, or discounting, these cash flow annuities it is evident that stock B, which will return less than stock A, is less attractive on a risk/reward basis.

• *PRESENT VALUE OF VARIABLE CASH FLOWS*

Suppose a firm expects to receive the following varying amounts of money over the next 4 years:

Year	Cash Flow
1	$1,000
2	1,200
3	1,500
4	900

The present value of this mixed cash flow is simply the sum of the present values of the four individual cash flows. If the discount rate is 10%, then the present value of such a mixed cash flow will be $3,642.43:

Year	Cash Flow	PVIF (see Table 3–4)	Present Value
1	$1,000	.9091	$ 909.10
2	1,200	.8264	991.68
3	1,500	.7513	1,126.95
4	900	.6830	614.70
		Present value of 4-year cash flow =	$ 3,642.43

Table 3–5 Present Value Interest Factor Annuities

Discount Rate

Periods	1%	2%	3%	4%	5%	6%	7%	8%	9%	10%	11%	12%
1	.9901	.9804	.9709	.9615	.9524	.9434	.9346	.9259	.9174	.9091	.9009	.8929
2	1.9704	1.9416	1.9135	1.8861	1.8594	1.8334	1.8080	1.7833	1.7591	1.7355	1.7125	1.6901
3	2.9410	2.8839	2.8286	2.7751	2.7233	2.6730	2.6243	2.5771	2.5313	2.4868	2.4437	2.4018
4	3.9020	3.8077	3.7171	3.6299	3.5459	3.4651	3.3872	3.3121	3.2397	3.1699	3.1024	3.0374
5	4.8535	4.7134	4.5797	4.4518	4.3295	4.2123	4.1002	3.9927	3.8896	3.7908	3.6959	3.6048
6	5.7955	5.6014	5.4172	5.2421	5.0757	4.9173	4.7665	4.6229	4.4859	4.3553	4.2305	4.1114
7	6.7282	6.4720	6.2302	6.0020	5.7863	5.5824	5.3893	5.2064	5.0329	4.8684	4.7122	4.5638
8	7.6517	7.3254	7.0196	6.7327	6.4632	6.2098	5.9713	5.7466	5.5348	5.3349	5.1461	4.9676
9	8.5661	8.1622	7.7861	7.4353	7.1078	6.8017	6.5152	6.2469	5.9852	5.7590	5.5370	5.3282
10	9.4714	8.9825	8.7302	8.1109	7.7217	7.3601	7.0236	6.7101	6.4176	6.1446	5.8892	5.6502
11	10.3677	9.7868	9.2526	8.7604	8.3064	7.8868	7.4987	7.1389	6.8052	6.4951	6.2065	5.9377
12	11.2552	10.5753	9.9539	9.3850	8.8632	8.3838	7.9427	7.5361	7.1607	6.8137	6.4924	6.1944
13	12.1338	11.3483	10.6349	9.9856	9.3935	8.8527	8.3576	7.9038	7.4869	7.1034	6.7499	6.4235
14	13.0038	12.1062	11.2960	10.5631	9.8986	9.2950	8.7454	8.2442	7.7861	7.3667	6.9819	6.6282
15	13.8651	12.8492	11.9379	11.1183	10.3796	9.7122	9.1079	8.5595	8.0607	7.6061	7.1909	6.8109
16	14.7180	13.5777	12.5610	11.6522	10.8377	10.1059	9.4466	8.8514	8.3125	7.8237	7.3792	6.9740
17	15.5624	14.2918	13.1660	12.1656	11.2740	10.4772	9.7632	9.1216	8.5436	8.0215	7.5488	7.1196
18	16.3984	14.9920	13.7534	12.6592	11.6895	10.8276	10.0591	9.3719	8.7556	8.2014	7.7016	7.2497
19	17.2261	15.2684	14.3237	13.1339	12.0853	11.1581	10.3356	9.6036	8.9501	8.3649	7.8393	7.3650
20	18.0457	16.3514	14.8774	13.5903	12.4622	11.4699	10.5940	9.8181	9.1285	8.5136	7.9633	7.4694
21	18.8571	17.0111	15.4149	14.0291	12.8211	11.7640	10.8355	10.0168	9.2922	8.6487	8.0751	7.5620
22	19.6605	17.6581	15.9368	14.4511	13.1630	12.0416	11.0612	10.2007	9.4424	8.7715	8.1757	7.6446
23	20.4559	18.2921	16.4435	14.8568	13.4885	12.3033	11.2722	10.3710	9.5802	8.8832	8.2664	7.7184
24	21.2435	18.9139	16.9355	15.2469	13.7986	12.5503	11.4693	10.5287	9.7066	8.9847	8.3481	7.7843
48												

• *PRESENT VALUE OF PERPETUITIES*

A perpetuity is an annuity forever! Stated otherwise, a **perpetuity** is a certain amount of money that will be paid at regular periods of time permanently. Dividends on a preferred stock or benefits from an education endowment fund may be viewed as examples of perpetuities.

The present value of a perpetuity is the sum of the present value of infinite payments.

$$PV_p = \frac{D_1}{(1 + R)^1} + \frac{D_2}{(1 + R)^2} + \frac{D_3}{(1 + R)^3} + \cdots + \frac{D_\infty}{(1 + R)^\infty}$$

where PV_p = present value of a perpetuity
D = amount of regular payment
R = discount factor
∞ = infinity

Do you have to solve this unpleasant-looking equation to determine PV_p in the case of perpetuities? No! Mathematicians have proved that the answer to this equation is much simpler than you might think. The compact but precise equation for the present value of a perpetuity is

$$PV_p = \frac{D}{R}$$

For instance, the present value of a $2 perpetuity discounted at 8% is

$$PV_p = \frac{2}{.08} = \$25$$

YOU SHOULD REMEMBER

There are two ways to determine the present value of a future income: using a simple formula and using a present value table. The formula for the present value is

$$PV = \frac{FV_N}{(1 + R)^N}$$

where PV = present value of a future income
FV_N = future income in period N
R = interest or discount rate
N = number of years or periods

If you want to use the table, multiply your future income by the value of *PVIF*. In the case of annuities, multiply the amount of annuity by the value of *PVIFA* as available in the table.

INTERIM-YEAR COMPOUNDING

So far, it has been assumed for the sake of simplicity that interest is compounded only once a year. But this sort of simplicity rarely occurs in actual practice. Happily, the general tables and equations with which you have become familiar are unaffected by changes in the frequency of compounding. And the factors that *are* affected—interest rate (R) and period (N)—are easily adjusted.

If an interest rate is 10% annually, it is clear that the semiannual rate is 5%, and the quarterly rate 2.5%. Therefore, if you want to determine the annual interest on an investment that pays 10% annual interest compounded semiannually, you would look in the proper table for a 5% interest rate, *but for two periods of time*. Accordingly, interest compounded quarterly can be calculated using a 2.5% interest rate for four periods of time.

If *m* is the number of times interest is compounded in a year, future values can be calculated by

$$FV_N = P\left(1 + \frac{R}{M}\right)^{mN}$$

For instance, the future value of $100, compounded monthly at an annual rate of 12%, after 2 years is determined as follows:

$$FV_2 = \$100\left(1 + \frac{.12}{12}\right)^{(12)(2)} = \$100(1.01)^{24} = \$112.70$$

Example 1: Interim-Year Compounding

PROBLEM   Assume you deposit $100 in a bank that pays 8% interest compounded quarterly. This means that at the end of each quarter your deposit gets bigger and interest is paid on the original deposit plus any accrued interest. How much will your bankbook show at the end of 1 year?

SOLUTION   Using 2% as the interest rate $\left(\frac{8\%}{4} = 2\%\right)$, compound as follows:

$$
\begin{array}{l}
\text{1st quarter: } \$100.00 \times 1.02 = \$102.00 \\
\text{2nd quarter: } \$102.00 \times 1.02 = \$104.04 \\
\text{3rd quarter: } \$104.04 \times 1.02 = \$106.12 \\
\text{4th quarter: } \$106.12 \times 1.02 = \$108.24
\end{array}
$$

At the beginning of the following year the bankbook will record a total of $108.24 on deposit.

It is easier, however, to use the future value table to compute the final value of the deposit. Since the time involves 4 periods, look up 4 periods (years) in the table at 2% and find that the FV factor is

1.0824. As a result, the figure on deposit in the bank at the beginning of the following year equals $108.24 (or 100 × 1.0824). One point requires clarification. *It is important to remember when using the tables that the figure in the first column is not necessarily the number of years. It is the number of time periods—and the other columns give the interest rate for each time period.*

Example 2: Interim-Year Compounding

PROBLEM   Determine the future value after 2 years of $100 deposited today if the annual interest rate is 12% and interest is compounded monthly.

SOLUTION   There are 12 months in a year; therefore, *N*, the number of periods, is 24 (2 years × 12 months). Since interest is compounded monthly, *R*, the monthly compounding rate, is 1% (12% ÷ 12 months). Looking through Table 3–1, you can find that the future value of $1 after 24 periods at the rate of 1% is $1.27. The future value of $100 is, therefore, $127 (1.27 × $100).

CALCULATING GROWTH RATES

Knowing growth rates can be very valuable. They can give you the rates of annual returns that can be obtained from any given shares of stock. These rates can then be compared to the annual return rates of other assets to find out if they are faster or slower.

You can use present value or future value tables to find out the annual growth rates of revenues, earnings, dividends, and so on. Suppose the dividend per share has been $2, $2.10, $2.40, and $3.04 from year 1 to year 4, respectively. What is the annual rate of growth of this stream of dividends?

The first step is to find out the total percentage growth in the above series of dividends. This can be done in the following manner: $\frac{FV}{PV} = \frac{3.04}{2.00} = 1.520$. The value 1.520 is the factor to look up in the *FV* table corresponding to 4 years; the annual rate of growth obtained is approximately 11%. The procedure for computing rates of growth, then, is:

1. Divide the terminal value by the first figure in the series.

2. For the given number of years (or periods), find the rate in the future value table that corresponds with the value you calculated in step 1.

YOU SHOULD REMEMBER

In actual practice, interest rates are usually compounded more often than once a year. If *m* is the number of times that interest is compounded in a year, the future value (*FV*) of an initial deposit (*P*) at an interest rate of *R* after *N* years is calculated as follows:

$$FV = P\left(1 + \frac{R}{m}\right)^{mN}$$

To determine the rate of growth, divide the terminal value by the first value in the series to get a figure. Then, for the given number of years (or periods), find the growth rate in the future value table that corresponds with that particular figure.

KNOW THE CONCEPTS

DO YOU KNOW THE BASICS?

1. Is a dollar today worth more than a dollar next year if the annual rate of inflation is zero?

2. Does preference for liquidity increase or decrease the cash value of a future income? Explain in your own words.

3. Which offer would you rather accept: an investment paying 10% compounded annually, or an investment paying 10% compounded quarterly?

4. Give two examples of common annuities.

5. What happens to present values when the interest is compounded more frequently?

TERMS FOR STUDY

annuity	perpetuity
capitalization rate	preference for liquidity
discount rate	present value
future value	risk
inflation	securities
liquidity	

PRACTICAL APPLICATION

COMPUTATIONAL PROBLEMS

1. Using the basic formula for future value, determine how much an investor will collect after 5 years if $1 is deposited and is compounded annually at the rate of 8%.

2. Using the future value table, determine the future value of $500 invested for 8 years if the rate of interest is 12% compounded annually.

3. What is the future value of a $250 annuity at the end of the next 5 years if the annual compounding rate is 10%?

4. The future value of an annuity after 4 years is $4,000. If the annual compounding interest rate is 8%, what is the value of each annuity payment?

5. A government bond can be converted to $25,000 at maturity 10 years from now. What is the value of this bond if the discount rate in the bond market is 9%? (Ignore interest payments on the bond.)

6. Which alternative do you prefer: $4,500 cash or $1,200 each year for a period of 4 years? Assume a discount rate of 10% annually.

7. You have borrowed $6,000 from the ABC Bank for a period of 4 years. The annual interest rate is 12%. Can you determine your annual repayment of the loan? (Hint: $6,000 is the present value of your annual loan repayment.)

8. Determine the future value of $1,200 after 4 years under the following assumptions:

   (a) Interest is compounded annually at 12%.
   (b) Interest is compounded semiannually at 12%.
   (c) Interest is compounded quarterly at 16%.
   (d) Interest is compounded monthly at 24%.

9. A share of preferred stock is usually viewed as a perpetuity. If the annual dividend of a preferred stock is $5 and the discount rate is 10%, what is the value of that preferred stock? (Hint: Calculate the present value of a $5 perpetuity.)

10. Suppose a bond will give you $100 annual interest forever. Can you determine the present value of such a perpetuity? (Assume an annual discount rate of 12%.)

ANSWERS

KNOW THE CONCEPTS

1. No. If the inflation rate is zero, a dollar today and a dollar next year have the same purchasing power.

2. As preference for liquidity goes up, the cash value of future income declines, because future income becomes less certain and less desirable.

3. The investment paying 10% compounded quarterly is preferable because the interest paid will be greater.

4. Mortgage or home loans; pension funds.

5. The value declines.

PRACTICAL APPLICATION

1. $\$1(1.08)^5 = \$1.469$

2. $500 (*FVIF* of 12%, 8 yrs) = $500(2.476) = $1,238

3. $250 (*FVIFA* of 10%, 5 yrs) = $250(6.1051) = $1,526

4. $4,000/*PVIFA* of 8%, 4 yrs = $4,000/4.506 = $888

5. $25,000 (*PVIF* of 9%, 10 yrs) = $25,000(.4224) = $10,560

6. $1,200 (*PVIFA* of 10%, 4 yrs) = $1,200(3.1699) = $3,803
   Therefore, $4,500 cash is preferred.

7. $6,000/*PVIFA* of 12%, 4 yrs $= \dfrac{\$6,000}{3.0373} = \$1,975$

8. a. $1,200 (*FVIF* of 12%, 4 yrs) = $1,200(1.5735) = $1,888
   b. $1,200 (*FVIF* of 6%, 8 periods) = $1,200(1.5938) = $1,912
   c. $1,200 (*FVIF* of 4%, 16 periods) = $1,200(1.873) = $2,247
   d. $1,200 (*FVIF* of 2%, 48 periods) = $1,200(2.587) = $3,104

9. $\dfrac{\$5}{.10} = \$50$

10. $\dfrac{\$100}{.12} = \$833$

4
RISK AND RETURN

RELATIONSHIP BETWEEN RISK AND RETURN

Risk and return are the foundations upon which rational and intelligent investment decisions are made. Broadly speaking, **risk** is a measure of the volatility, or uncertainty of returns, and **returns** are the expected receipts or cash flows anticipated from any investment.

The following example may help explain the meaning of risk. Everyone knows that deposits at a savings bank are safer than money bet on a horse race. Bank deposits yield a steady but low rate of interest year by year and are insured by the Federal Deposit Insurance Corporation (FDIC). There is a high degree of confidence that these returns and the original deposit will be paid back. The returns from bank deposits don't fluctuate very much, and for this reason they are considered to be safe and to have a low degree of risk. On the other hand, when people gamble they don't know the outcome. They may win big, but they can also lose everything. Returns from horse betting are highly uncertain, very volatile, and subject to a high degree of risk. When two investments yield the same returns, the final choice will be based on the evaluation of the riskiness of each project. The project having the lower risk will be selected.

WHY DIFFERENT INVESTMENTS PAY DIFFERENT RETURNS

Some investments pay a high return, and others a low return. Certainly, you can't expect a high return from a "sure thing." But it is reasonable to demand a high return when asked to invest money in an uncertain or risky venture. In other words, investors must be properly compensated for the risks they take.

RELATIONSHIP BETWEEN RISK AND RETURN

The return on your money should be proportional to the risk involved.

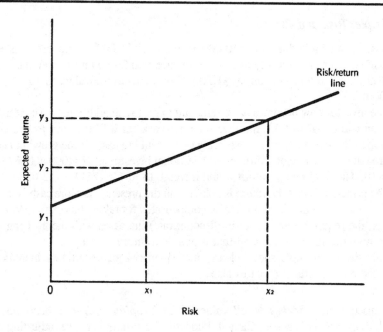

Figure 4–1 Relationship between Risk and Return

Risk is the degree of uncertainty associated with an investment. The more volatile the returns from an investment, the greater its risk. When two projects have the same expected returns, choose the one with the least risk.

Low risk is associated with low returns and high risk with high returns. The relationship between risk and expected returns is illustrated in Figure 4–1. At zero risk investors will get Y_1 returns, at X_1 risk they will get Y_2 returns, and at X_2 risk they will get Y_3 returns. Figure 4–1 presents the trade-off between risk and expected returns. Under normal circumstances, low risk will bring low returns and high risk is associated with high returns.

In finance, risk is measured by the degree of volatility associated with expected returns. **Volatility** is the amount of fluctuation that occurs in a series of figures as they deviate from a representative average. For example, the average of the series 1, 2, 3 is 2, and the average of the series 1, 3, 5 is 3. The second series is considered more volatile than the first series of figures. The higher the volatility, then, the higher the level of risk.

Another factor that adds to risk is time. Present cash is worth more to investors than future cash. When an investor lends money, there is always the risk or uncertainty that the loan may not be repaid. To get lenders to take the risk of parting with their cash, lenders have to be properly compensated. An example should help explain this principle.

Example: Risk and Return

Assume an individual has $10,000 in cash. If $1,000 is lent or invested, the individual gives up the safety of cash for an uncertain future return, and might ask for a $100 return to lend this initial $1,000. The return is equivalent to 10% ($100 ÷ $1,000).

The investor now becomes more reluctant to part with additional cash. If asked to lend an additional $1,000, the investor might ask for a $110 return to overcome a growing reluctance to give up the safety of cash and to assume the growing risk of a future return. The rate of return on the additional investment of $1000 is 11% ($110 ÷ $1,000). The total rate of return would increase to 10.5% ($210 ÷ $2,000).

The principle is that the future is riskier than the present. As more cash is invested, risk increases and investors want to be compensated for taking this extra risk. In other words, the required rate of return (discount rate) increases with the growing risk of tying up more funds in an asset that promises a future return.

This simple example shows clearly that when risk or uncertainty increases, the required rate of return increases also.

Consequently, *the key to all valuation and capital budgeting decisions is the analysis of risk and return.* Capital budgeting decisions involve adjusting future expected returns for risk and comparing these returns with the cost of a project. In this way, it is possible to determine whether or not a project is acceptable, and whether it is more or less profitable than some other project.

YOU SHOULD REMEMBER

There is a trade-off between risk and return. Generally, the more risk, the higher the expected return, and the lower the risk, the lower the expected return.

• *MEASURING RETURN*

Investments are made because investors expect to gain a return. This return is the future expected receipts or returns obtained from a given investment. From the lender's, or bondholder's, point of view, expected returns are the periodic interest payments on the loan plus the repayment of principal at maturity.

$$\begin{matrix} \text{Bondholder's} \\ \text{expected} \\ \text{return} \end{matrix} = \frac{\begin{matrix}\text{Annual coupon}\\\text{or interest}\\\text{payment}\end{matrix} + \begin{matrix}\text{Change in}\\\text{the value}\\\text{of the bond}\end{matrix}}{\text{Value of bond in period } (t-1)} = \frac{C_{P_t} + (P_t - P_{(t-1)})}{P_{t-1}}$$

where t = time periods

C_{P_t} = coupon paid by issuer of bond

P_t = price of bond in the current year

P_{t-1} = price of bond in prior year

Stockholders look for dividends plus the capital gains which accrue from the appreciation of their stock.

$$\begin{matrix} \text{Stockholder's} \\ \text{expected} \\ \text{return} \end{matrix} = \frac{\text{Dividend + Capital appreciation}}{\text{Value of stock in period } (t-1)} = \frac{D_t + (P_t - P_{(t-1)})}{P_{t-1}}$$

where D_t = dividend in current year

P_t = price of stock in current year

P_{t-1} = price of stock in previous year

t = period of time

The above formulas measure expected returns in terms of the series of future annual returns and the change in the value of an asset. The total return for stocks consists of *dividend yield* plus *capital appreciation* (or loss). Bond returns consist of interest yield plus changes in the value of the bond. Therefore, if a stock or bond yields 5% annually and the annual average rate of price appreciation is equal to 10%, the total expected rate of return of these securities equals 15%.

When a corporation makes an investment decision regarding a project, the returns a manager looks at are the *cash flow* generated by the investment. In corporate finance, returns are defined as cash flows after taxes, Earnings before interest and taxes $(i - t)$ + depreciation (T).

Obviously, these returns differ from accounting profits, which deal only with the netting out of costs, interest, and taxes from sales. The goal of managers is to find out how much cash flow an investment will yield or return in the future. This can then be compared to the original cost to find out whether the investment is profitable.

ESTIMATING CASH FLOWS

The usual procedure for determining future cash flows that a firm will generate from a given investment is to prepare a pro forma income statement that projects the earnings before taxes and the depreciation originating in the investment. An example should help to explain how this is done.

Example: Estimating Cash Flows

PROBLEM   A firm invests $120,000 for 3 years. On the basis of acceptable statistical methods, the firm anticipates this investment to generate sales of $100,000, $150,000, and $200,000 during the next 3 years. Calculate the cash flows for each year.

SOLUTION

	Forecasted Years		
	1990	1991	1992
Sales	$100,000	$150,000	$200,000
Costs	(50,000)	(70,000)	(100,000)
Earnings before interest and taxes (EBIT)	50,000	80,000	100,000
Interest	10,000	10,000	10,000
Earnings before taxes	40,000	70,000	90,000
Taxes (@ .40 rate)	20,000	32,000	40,000
Earnings after taxes	30,000	48,000	60,000
Depreciation (T)	16,000	16,000	16,000
Cash flow after taxes (CFAT)*	$ 46,000	$ 64,000	$ 76,000

*Note: CFAT = EBIT$(i - t)$ + Depreciation (T)

The table contains the factors for obtaining cash flows after taxes. Depreciation is shown separately at the bottom of the income statement. Given the $120,000 investment and assuming the firm uses the straight-line depreciation method, the yearly depreciation is $40,000 ($120,000 ÷ 3). The tax saved from this depreciation

(T) $16,000 = ($40,000 × .40) plus the operating earnings of the firm EBIT *(i − T)* add up to total cash flow after takes over the next 3 years. These cash flows represent the inflows of returns anticipated from an investment in a given project.

The determination of expected returns for investments are subject to certain forecasting errors. No one can say with certainty that the projections will be accurate. However, the less risky and more stable past relationships have been, the more confidence you can place on the outcome. Therefore, it is important not only to forecast as accurately as possible, but also to measure the riskiness (volatility) of cash flows or the degree of instability associated with the expected returns. To do this, it is necessary to calculate risk.

• *MEASURING RISK*

Risk is defined as the deviation of expected outcomes from a mean or anticipated value. It can also be regarded as the chance of incurring a loss or gain by investing in an asset or project. The chances of making a profit or incurring a loss can be high or low depending on the degree of risk (variability of expected returns) associated with a given investment.

The simplest way to look at risk is to break it down into two components: the level of risk and the risk of time.

THE LEVEL OF RISK

The level of risk can be determined by comparing the risk of one asset to that of another. For example, the risk associated with IBM is much less than that for a very small computer firm. In other words, some firms have a low degree of risk while others have a high degree of risk. This is important because low-risk firms can borrow funds more cheaply than high-risk firms. Their discount rate or required rate of return is lower, which means that a return for the low-risk firm gets a better valuation in the marketplace than the same return generated by a high-risk firm.

The chances of getting back an investment in IBM are much better than they are for an unknown company. Usually, it is easier to forecast the returns of a low-risk company than to forecast the returns of a high-risk company. Why? Because the volatility of the low-risk company returns is usually small (the returns vary only slightly), whereas the returns of high-risk companies are subject to high volatility.

THE RISK OF TIME

In financial jargon, risk is an increasing function of time. In other words, the longer an amount is invested, the greater is the risk involved. If the investment has no chance of loss and is made for a very short period, it is called risk-free. If a longer time period is considered, though, a premium must be paid to lenders for assuming this time risk. Therefore, the usual procedure is to divide risk into a risk-free rate and a risk premium when dealing with the element of time.

The risk-free rate is the interest rate paid on assets that provide a sure return, like U.S. Treasury bills, which come due in 90 days and are backed by the federal government's guarantee to pay on maturity. This risk-free rate provides the benchmark for measuring how risky other assets are. A **risk premium** is the required rate of return of an asset over and above the risk-free rate. Because long-term government securities mature years from now, they have a higher risk premium than 1-year government notes. You can see that this kind of risk rating helps investors to measure the relative risks of different assets.

The way to measure the risk of a project is to calculate the volatility of the expected returns of that project. If the expected returns are highly volatile, the chances of knowing the outcome will be less than when returns fluctuate in a narrow range. For example, in Figure 4–2 the returns of Company A are more volatile than those of Company B. Investors would feel more confident in judging the outcome of Company B's returns than those of A.

Since the risk-free rate provides a benchmark, the risk premiums of more risky assets can be measured as the difference between the total risk of different assets and the risk-free rate. This measurement is shown in Table 4–1 for government securities differing in the time to maturity.

This ranking of risk levels helps to evaluate the relative merits of assets. A study of the returns of these assets would indicates that the prices of short-term securities are less volatile than those of long-term securities. The chances of default are smaller for short-term securities than for long-term securities. Consequently, the risk level assigned to them is less than for longer term and less certain securities.

The same principle applies in measuring the riskiness of other assets. The volatility of the returns of any asset measures the level of risk. The wider dispersion of Company A's returns in Figure 4–2 indicates that there is a greater chance that an estimate will fall either below or above the straight line. This range is unwieldy to work with and makes the merits of investments more difficult to evaluate. Some

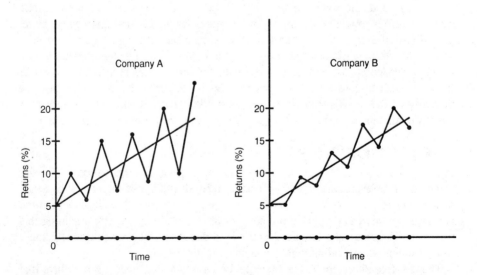

Figure 4–2 Volatility of Returns for Company A and Company B.
Note: Company A and Company B have same percentage scale of returns

Table 4-1   How Risk Changes Over Time

	Time to Maturity	Risk Free Rate (%)	Risk Premium (%)	Total Risk (%)
Treasury bills	90 days	5	0	5
Government notes	1 year	5	2	7
Government bonds	20 years	5	4	9
Corporate bonds	20 years	5	5	10

judgment must be applied that will help bring the range down to a more manageable single figure. To do this, it is necessary to assign probabilities to the different estimated values in the range. These probabilities, of course, must add up to 1.00.

YOU SHOULD REMEMBER

In the securities market, returns consist of capital gains plus dividend or interest yield. The returns of a firm consist of cash flows. These returns provide a basis for calculating the present values of securities or projects and their ultimate profitabilities.

The valuation of securities and the determination of the merits of investments involve the use of risk and return concepts. Investors will part with their money as long as discounted future returns exceed the cost of the original investment.

CALCULATING EXPECTED RETURNS IN UNCERTAIN CONDITIONS

ASSIGNING PROBABILITIES

Probabilities help us to determine the likelihood or chance of an event occurring. Some probabilities can be obtained from actual observations. For example, the risk of getting heads or tails from a coin can be readily measured by flipping it many times and finding out the actual outcomes. On the other hand, there are instances—such as the introduction of a new product—when the outcome is highly uncertain. In these cases, there usually is no past experience to draw on. The manager must make a judgment as to the probable outcome. Because the future returns from the new product are highly uncertain, a manager will work with the assumption that projected returns will probably fall within a particular range. The more uncertain the outcome, the bigger the range. Since it is difficult to interpret returns from a range, managers assign weights or probabilities to the values in the range in order to bring the figures in the range down to a single and more manageable figure. One way this can be done is shown in Table 4–2.

This table compares the returns of Project A with the returns of Project B. Note that Project A's returns fluctuate within a narrower range than Project B's. Based on subjective judgments, it is assumed that the most likely outcome should get a weight of 50% while the extreme values in the range should get a value of 25% each. When the returns are multiplied by these weights (probabilities) and the resulting products are added, the result is known as an expected value $(\bar{E}_R)$.

Notice that the expected returns in Project A and Project B are the same, or 320. The dispersions (or range over which the returns vary) from this expected value, however, are different for each project. Project A's returns range from 100 to 500, whereas Project B has a dispersion ranging from 80 to 600. What does this mean? It indicates that, because the volatility around the expected return is smaller for Project A than for Project B, its risk is lower. This is precisely the way the individual risk of each project is measured—namely, by how much or how little the returns deviate from the expected values. The measure of this dispersion is called standard deviation.

STANDARD DEVIATION AS A MEASURE OF RISK

One common way to measure the risk of an asset is to calculate its deviation from a mean or an expected return. Since the expected returns of both projects in Table 4–2 are the same (320), it is evident that the higher dispersion of Project B (100–500 for

Table 4–2   Assigning Probabilities to Projected Returns

Probable Outcome	Projected Return	Weight or Probability (%)	Probable Return
Project A			
Pessimistic	100	.20	20
Most likely	333	.60	200
Optimistic	500	.20	100
		1.00	320 $(\bar{E}_R)$
Project B			
Pessimistic	80	.25	20
Most likely	300	.50	150
Optimistic	600	.25	150
		1.00	320 $(\bar{E}_R)$

$\bar{E}_R$ = Expected returns.

A vs. 80–600 for B) implies greater risk. By assuming that all values are distributed normally—that the returns are distributed equally between the higher and lower sides of expected returns—it is possible to measure the volatility of returns for each project and, in turn, to measure their comparative risk. This can be done, for Project A, by subtracting the actual returns (100, 333, and 500) in the range from the expected return ($\bar{K}$) of 320: $(K-\bar{K})$. The values derived from these calculations are then squared to eliminate the problem of minus signs. In a world of uncertainty, probabilities are assigned to each deviation to obtain a single representative value, which is called **variance.** The square root of variance is none other than the **standard deviation.**

$$\text{Standard deviation } (\sigma) = \sqrt{\sum_{t=1}^{N} (K - \bar{K})^2 \, P_i}$$

where N = number of observations
  t = time periods
  $\bar{K}$ = expected returns
  P_i = probabilities of returns
  K = actual returns

Table 4–3 presents a simple example that shows how the standard deviation of Project A is computed.

What does all this mean? First, you must assume that the probability distribution is normal. This implies that half the values in the distribution are likely to fall below the expected value and half to fall above the expected value. The closer a distribution is to the expected value, the more likely it is that the actual outcomes will be closer to the mean or expected value. Chances will be higher that the outcomes will be close to the expected value in a narrow distribution than in a wide distribution.

As Figure 4–3 shows, probability distributions for both A and B are normal,

Table 4–3 Calculating the Standard Deviation of Project A

i	k	$\bar{k}$	$(k-\bar{k})$	$(k-\bar{k})^2$	P_i (probabilities)	$(k-\bar{k})^2 \, P_i$
1	100	320	−220	48,400	.20	9,680
2	333	320	+ 13	169	.60	101
3	500	320	+180	32,400	.20	6,480
						Variance = 16,261

Standard deviation of Project A = $\sqrt{\text{variance}}$ or $\sqrt{16,261}$ = 128. Using the same approach, the standard deviation of Project B (see Table 4–2 for figures) is 185.

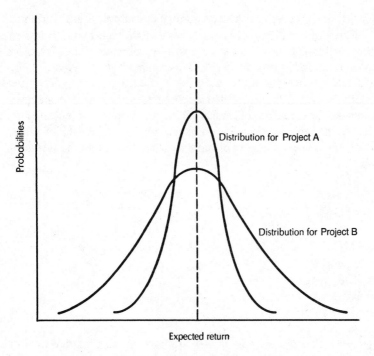

Figure 4–3 Normal Probability Distributions of Two Projects, A and B

but B has a wider dispersion away from the expected value. Consequently, the distribution for B is considered riskier than the distribution for A. Note: Both probability distributions have the same expected value, but A has a narrower distribution, indicating less volatility relative to the expected value and hence less risk.

In finance, it is statistically acceptable to assume that probability distributions are normal, because this assumption facilitates the calculation of expected outcomes. For example, statisticians have discovered that in cases involving normal distributions one can expect 68% of the outcomes or returns to fall within plus or minus one standard deviation of the expected value. In the preceding example, when you subtract and add one standard deviation (128) from the expected return of 320, the result will be a range of 192 to 448. This range indicates that, in 68 out of 100 times, you can expect returns to fall within the range of 192 to 448. When two standard deviations (256) are used, practically all of the values in the distribution (or 95%) should fall within a range of 64 to 576. The accepted procedure is to work with one standard deviation.

Table 4–3 indicates that the standard deviation of Project B is 185. In the case of Project B, a deviation of plus or minus one standard deviation produces a range of 135 to 505. Given these parameters, the risk of Project A to that of Project B can be compared. They have the same expected return, but because Project A has a smaller dispersion around the expected value—its standard deviation is lower—its risk is lower than that of Project B.

YOU SHOULD REMEMBER

Risk is measured by taking into account the variability of expected returns. The more the returns fluctuate, the higher the risk. This variability can be measured by using standard deviation. When returns are uncertain, the accepted procedure for calculating expected values and probable standard deviations is to assign weights or probabilities to the figures in a projected range.

COEFFICIENT OF VARIATION: THE RISK/RETURN TRADE-OFF

What if the expected returns of one project differ from those of another project? In this case, it is difficult to compare absolute measures of dispersion as provided by standard deviation. The way to deal with this problem is to determine the risk of a project relative to its expected returns. This measure is called the **coefficient of variation,** or **risk/return trade-off ratio.** It is calculated as follows:

$$\text{Coefficient of variation } (CV) = \frac{\text{Standard deviation of returns}}{\text{Expected returns}} = \frac{\sigma}{\overline{K}}$$

Example: Calculating the Risk/Return Trade-off

PROBLEM   Interpret the risk/return trade-off by using the figures calculated in the preceding example, where the standard deviations are 128 and 185 for Projects A and B, respectively.

SOLUTION   Expected returns in both cases are 320. The coefficients of variation (*CV*) for the two projects are:

$$CV \text{ of Project A: } \frac{128}{320} = .40$$

$$CV \text{ of Project B: } \frac{185}{320} = .58$$

Even though Project A's expected return is the same as Project B's, the risk or standard deviation of Project A is lower, and it has a better risk/return trade-off ratio.

When the coefficients of variation of different projects are compared, the lower the *CV*, the better the project from a risk/return trade-off point of view. Project A is a better investment because, despite having the same expected return, it has a lower risk than Project B. Therefore, Project A is better than Project B.

YOU SHOULD REMEMBER

In order to compare the risk/return trade-offs of different investments, it is necessary to state these values on a relative basis. The coefficient of variation, which represents the standard deviation divided by the expected return, accomplishes this feat. The lower the value of the coefficient of variation, the better the merits of an investment from a risk/return standpoint.

• PORTFOLIO RISK

So far, risk and return have been analyzed for individual projects. Firms, however, have a number of assets and liabilities in their balance-sheet, and investors usually have a number of securities in their portfolios. Presumably, these investments are made with the goal in mind to maximize returns and minimize risk. It is important, therefore, to consider the risk/return characteristics of individual assets as well as their specific contributions to the risk and returns of a given **portfolio** (the sum total of a firm's or investor's assets).

The approach to measuring the risk and returns of a portfolio starts with the calculations of the standard deviations and expected returns of each security in the portfolio. This procedure was discussed previously in this chapter. The objective is to spread the risk among several assets or securities, thereby reducing overall risk.

There are two ways this can be done. One way is to diversify by adding more securities to the portfolio, and the other way is to search for securities whose returns move differently from the returns of the securities (assets) already in the portfolio. Up to a certain point, adding more assets and securities to a portfolio can reduce risk. However, if investors add securities that have the same patterns of dispersion and movement as the securities already in the portfolio, risk will remain unchanged. The idea is to find securities that move differently.

COVARIANCE PRINCIPLE

The search for securities that move differently is made easier by the use of a measure called **covariance.** Covariance is a statistical method used to compare the movements of two variables—or, in this case, the returns of assets in a portfolio.

A proxy for covariance, which limits the values within a range of $+1.0$ and -1.0, is called coefficient of correlation (R). It tells us how closely asset returns correlate or move relative to one another. If they move exactly the same way, the (R) has a value of $+1.0$. If they move exactly in opposite directions, (R) has a value of -1.0. When asset returns do not correlate with one another, the (R) equals zero. The mathematical formula for the correlation coefficient involving two assets is

$$R = \frac{\sum_{T=1}^{N} (K_a - \overline{K}_a)(K_b - \overline{K}_b)/N}{\sigma_a \sigma_b} = \frac{\text{Covariance } (a, b)}{\sigma_a \sigma_b}$$

This formula measures the volatility $(K - \overline{K})$ of asset A relative to asset B (in the numerator), and this covariance is standardized by the product of the two assets' standard deviations (in the denominator).

Figure 4–4 explains the principle visually. The graph to the left shows that security A's expected returns move the same way as the returns of the portfolio. That is why it has an $R = +1.0$. Adding security A to the portfolio does not change its volatility, hence the risk of this portfolio remains unchanged. The graph to the right indicates that security B's returns fluctuate inversely with the portfolio returns. That is why it has an R value of -1.0. Adding securities like B to the portfolio reduces the volatility of the portfolio, hence lowers its risk.

It is important to understand how risk changes in a portfolio context. Corporate managers should be aware that by diversifying the mix of their assets or of their marketable securities, they can reduce the risk to the firm, thus helping to reduce costs of borrowing and to increase the profits and value of the firm.

These portfolio considerations play a key role in the decision-making process. For example, some investors who wish to lower their risk exposure may consider adding stocks and bonds to their portfolios because the prices of these two types of securities usually move in opposite directions over a complete business cycle.

Understanding portfolio theory can help a corporate manager improve performance. However, it is easier to explain this concept using securities rather than corporate assets. Modern portfolio theory demonstrates how investors can employ sophisticated mathematical models to determine an efficient frontier (curve) that provides optimal returns at different risk levels. The principle in portfolio theory is

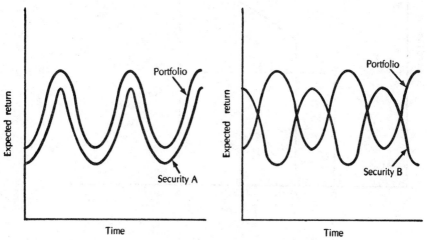

Figure 4–4 Covariance and Volatility

the same as in any asset: the greater the risk, the higher the return. And so, Figure 4–5 reveals the results of mathematical calculations that determine the efficient frontier.

Risk A has a corresponding optimal return X . The level of risk B should yield a return equal to Y. Notice that since B risk > A risk, then X return < Y return. Provided with these risk/return alternatives, an investor should decide how much risk to assume and then proceed to construct a portfolio that will yield an optimal expected return.

Assume the investor wants to take risk B and constructs a portfolio that yields returns equal to C. The performance of this portfolio is subnormal. The investor can improve the performance of the portfolio in two ways. First, there are other securities available that yield higher returns at risk level B. So, all the investor has to do is find these securities, change the mix of the portfolio, and increase the return to Y. The investor's other option is to diversify the portfolio and change its mix by adding new securities with returns that fluctuate differently than the securities in the existing portfolio. In this way it will be possible for the investor to achieve the same returns as C (see Point E, which is equal to C) but at a much lower risk level (see point D).

In the field of corporate finance, it is more difficult to change the mix or diversify the asset composition of a firm. Still, the principles of portfolio theory provide a benchmark for making intelligent investment decisions that will improve perfor-mance, help raise returns at the least risk, and promote the maximization of the stockholders' wealth.

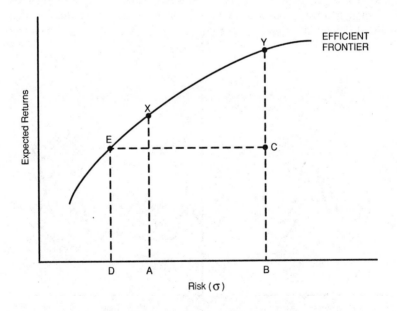

Figure 4–5 Portfolio Theory and the Efficient Frontier

YOU SHOULD REMEMBER

The risk of a single asset is greater than the risk of a portfolio of assets. The more assets you have, the more you spread the risk. This is known as diversification. The addition of new assets to a portfolio will reduce its variability or risk. When the movements of the returns of new assets are different from the movements of assets in an existing portfolio, the total risk of the portfolio is reduced. The relationship between the movements of various assets is studied by a statistical measure called covariance. A standardized covariance is the correlation coefficient which varies from -1.0 to $+1.0$. New assets with a correlation coefficient of $+^{1}1.0$ move similarly to the portfolio, and will not help reduce risk. As the correlation coefficient declines from $+1.0$ to -1.0, portfolio risk also declines. Managers can improve the firm's performance by understanding and applying the principles that underlie portfolio theory.

MEASURING RISK AND RETURN WITH THE CAPITAL ASSET PRICING MODEL (CAPM)

Measuring risk is not an easy task, partly because of the many factors to be considered. The mathematics of risk include knowledge of probability theory and understanding of how portfolio risks and returns are brought together into a meaningful model. Attempts have been made to simplify the measurement of risk, and one of the more successful efforts has been the development of the **Capital Asset Pricing Model (CAPM),** a model that relates predicted undiversifiable risks to the expected returns of a project. Although the CAPM is more readily applicable to security analysis, it can be employed to evaluate the risk/return merits of investments and assets at the corporate level.

The CAPM starts by dividing risk into two major components: diversifiable risk and nondiversifiable risk. The premise is that there is a close relationship between the returns of individual securities and the returns of the market. These returns, whether for a given stock or for the market, consist of capital gains plus dividend yields. It has been established by academicians that the stock market is a highly efficient vehicle because it quickly incorporates all available information. If so, the volatility of the market provides a common denominator for evaluating the degrees of risk of individual assets and securities. This degree of risk is determined by finding out how sensitive the returns of a stock are to the returns of the market. In this way, you employ a common index that measures the sensitivity of the individual stocks against a common index—namely, the market. If a stock's returns move up and down more than the market returns, the stock is said to be more risky than the market. When a stock's returns move up and down less than market returns, the stock is said to be less risky than the market. It is possible, therefore, to classify the risks of different securities simply by relating them to the common market index.

Example: Finding the Sensitivity of a Stock to the Market

PROBLEM   An investor calculates that the volatility of market returns averaged 5% annually over the past 10 years. When the volatility of the returns of these stocks are computed, the investor finds that stock A averaged 10%, stock B averaged 5%, and stock C averaged 3%. Using the market as a common denominator, compare these returns to the market and determine the risk characteristics of each stock.

SOLUTION   The sensitivity of these stocks to the market can be computed using the formula

$$\frac{\text{Volatility of Stock returns}}{\text{Volatility of Market returns}} = \text{Sensitivity}$$

$$\text{Stock A} = \frac{.10}{.05} = 2.00$$

$$\text{Stock B} = \frac{.05}{.05} = 1.00$$

$$\text{Stock C} = \frac{.03}{.05} = .60$$

According to this formula, stock A is more sensitive (hence, more risky) than the market, stock B has the same sensitivity (hence, as risky) as the market, and stock C is less sensitive (hence, less risky) than the market.

The CAPM uses a more sophisticated approach than the simple arithmetic example outlined above, but the concept is very similar.

THE BETA COEFFICIENT

The three characteristic lines in Figure 4-6 can be calculated mathematically, but they simply represent the relationship between stock returns and market returns. The slope, or slant, of each line is called **beta** (β), and it is precisely this beta that measures the sensitivity or risk of a stock (R_s) compared to the market return (K_m). Statistically, the equation, known as the characteristic line, which describes this relationship is

$$R_s = a + BK_m + e$$

where

$$\beta = \text{beta coefficient (slope)}$$
$$K_m = \text{market return}$$
$$R_s = \text{return of stock}$$
$$a = \text{constant}$$
$$e = \text{error term}$$

Let us assume that the monthly returns of stock A were correlated with the monthly returns of a market indicator like the Standard & Poor's 500 Composite Index. If one uses the Standard equation $y = a + b \, (K_m) + e$, the characteristic lines of three securities A, B and C are as follows:

$$R_a = 0 + 2.0 \, (K_m) + e$$
$$R_b = 0 + 1.0 \, (K_m) + e$$
$$R_c = 0 + 0.6 \, (K_m) + e$$

The B values (2.0, 1.0, 0.6) in each equation are the crucial factors. These values are called betas and are relative measures of undiversifiable risk associated with the returns of a stock relative to the returns of the market index. Instead of using a characteristic line to calculate beta, this risk value can be calculated as follows:

$$\text{Beta} = \frac{\sigma_a}{\sigma_m} R_{a,m}$$

Therefore, given the standard deviations of the A stock (σ_a) and the market (σ_m) plus the coefficient of correlation $(R_{a,m})$, beta can be determined in this alternate way:

$$\sigma_b = 10$$
$$\sigma_m = 10$$
$$R_{bm} = +1.0$$

The beta of stock B equals

$$\text{Beta of stock B} = \frac{10}{10} \times 1.0 = 1.0$$

This beta should equal 1.0 because stock B's returns are the same as the market's and they correlate perfectly (positively) with the market index.

The characteristic or representative lines presented above are graphically depicted in Figure 4–6.

In the CAPM, the a and e terms are assumed to be equal to zero. Given these conditions, the returns of a stock (R) and its beta are determined solely by its relationship with the market (K_m).

When stock returns, correlated against market returns, produce a line with a 45° angle, this implies a 1-to-1 relationship. Stated another way, a 1% change in market

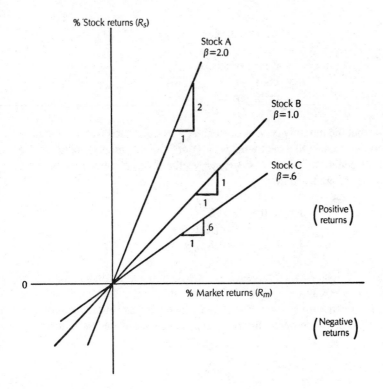

Figure 4-6 Using the CAPM to Compute Betas (βs) of Individual Stocks

returns produces a 1% change in stock returns. The co-movement between the returns of a stock (R_s) and market (K_m) is perfect when the beta has a value of 1.0. When using beta analysis, then, the obvious starting point for comparing risk among securities or assets is a beta of 1.0. Security B, with a 1.0 beta, will move up and down at the same rate as the market, and it has the same nondiversifiable risk as the market. Security C, with a .6 beta, moves up and down less than the market, and has a lower risk than the market. And Security A, with a 2.0 beta, moves up and down more than the market, and is said to have a higher risk than the market.

It is evident that the CAPM provides an easy way to compare the various risk levels of individual stocks. An important precondition, though, is that the dispersion around the representative line is not large. If the dispersion is large, there are additional sources of risk to be considered and the market alone may not be a good measure of the risk of an individual security.

Furthermore, theoreticians have engaged in a lively controversy centering around the nature of the market index. Some academicians claim that no one knows what the true market indicator is, and, therefore, a good measure of nondiversifiable risk cannot be obtained. In practice, however, it is acceptable to employ well-known market indexes, such as the Standard & Poor's 500 Composite Stock Index, as a proxies for the true market index.

CAPM furnishes an alternative measure of risk in contrast to standard deviation. The next step is to employ beta to obtain a corresponding required rate of return. This can be done by using the security market line (SML) principle.

YOU SHOULD REMEMBER

The capital asset pricing model (CAPM) compares or correlates individual stock returns with market returns. The market is a standard or common denominator for deriving what is known as nondiversifiable risk, sometimes also called systematic risk. The measure of the sensitivity of a stock to the market is called beta (β). If the beta of the market equals 1.0, all securities having betas greater than 1.0 are riskier than the market, and securities with assigned betas of less than 1.0 are less risky than the market. In constructing a portfolio, investors who select low-beta stocks are likely to achieve a lower overall return than those who select stocks with higher and therefore riskier betas.

THE SECURITY MARKET LINE (SML)

In the earlier part of this chapter it was shown that the required rate of return for an asset consists of the sum of the riskless rate plus a risk premium. In beta analysis, the risk premium consists of the market return minus the risk-free rate $(K_m - R_F)$ multiplied by the security's index of nondiversifiable risk, or beta. You now have the tools to undertake the risk/return analysis of a security when the market is the standard for measuring risk. In other words, given the risk level of market returns, you can find out the required rate of return of an individual stock. All you have to do is calculate a risk-free rate, get the rate of return of the market, and adjust this return for the riskiness of the individual stock.

Suppose the normal riskless rate is computed to be 5% and the average return of the market is 10%, while a stock's beta is 1.2. Given these inputs, you can establish the required rate of return of a particular stock. The formal equation to obtain this required rate of return (RRR_s) is

$$RRR_s = R_F + (K_m - R_F)\, \beta_s$$

where RRR_s = required rate of return of a stock

$\quad\quad R_F$ = risk-free rate

$\quad\quad K_m$ = average return of the market

$\quad\quad \beta_s$ = beta or nondiversifiable risk

With the data given above, the required rate of return is easily found:

$$RRR_s = .05 + (.10 - .05)1.2 = 11\%$$

This 11% figure means that any stock with a risk, or beta, of 1.2 should return 11%. A return lower than 11% makes the stock unattractive, and it should be sold. A return greater than 11% means the stock is undervalued and should be bought. This relationship is presented in Figure 4-7 in the form of a **security market line (SML)** which is a graphical presentation of the CAPM.

Note that various required rates of return can be found if the SML line and the betas of the different securities are known. A stock with a beta of .8 would have a RRR_s of 9%, and a stock with a beta of 1.2 would have a required rate of return of 11%.

The security market line provides a basis for evaluating the relative merits of securities. For example, assume that stock B offers returns of 13% when the SML line calls for 11%. This stock is undervalued and will be bought. The opposite occurs in the case of stock A. At a beta of 1.2, stock A should return 11%, but if the actual returns of this stock were 8%, stock A should be sold because it is not a bargain.

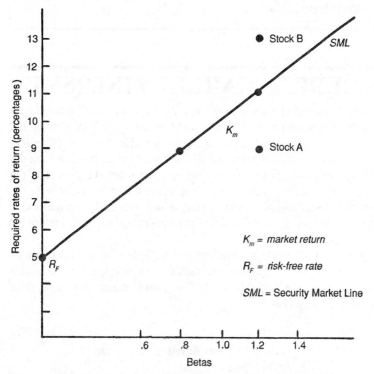

Figure 4-7 The Security Market Line (SML) as a Benchmark for Evaluating Stock Values

If the goal is to keep risk at a low level, then stocks having low betas should be included in the portfolio. Conversely, if the goal is to achieve a higher return, investors should add stocks that have high betas. Clearly, the advantage of employing the CAPM in conjunction with the security market line is simplicity.

The CAPM is a highly useful tool for evaluating securities because it supplies a required rate of return (discount rate) which can be employed to determine the present value of securities.

Instead of saying

$$PV_s = \frac{FV_n}{(1 + R)^n}$$

the same results can be obtained by saying

$$PV_s = \frac{FV_n}{(1 + RRR_s)^n}$$

where PV_s = present value of expected returns
FV_n = future value of expected returns
R = discount rate or required rate of return
$RRR_s = R_F + (K_m - R_F)\beta_s$
n = number of periods or years
R_F = risk-free rate
K_m = average returns of the market
β_s = beta for an individual asset or stock

By providing a risk-adjusted discount rate, the CAPM and the SML equation can be used to adjust the cash flows of projects over time to determine their present values. This model is useful also for calculating the value of a stock by employing the well-known dividend model (see Chapter 5).

YOU SHOULD REMEMBER

The SML model starts with a risk-free rate, then adds a premium consisting of the market returns plus an adjustment called beta, or nondiversifiable risk. The SML approach calculates the rate of return an investor should be getting for a security having a given beta. When the actual return offered by a security is lower than this rate, it means investors are getting less than they are supposed to; hence, the security is overvalued. When actual returns are higher than the required rate of return, investors are getting a bonus over what they should get, which means the security is a bargain. Furthermore, by providing a discount rate, the SML method helps investors to determine the present value and the profitability of investments.

KEEPING THE CAPM
AND SML IN PERSPECTIVE

In the final analysis, whether you calculate risk by using standard deviation or by using beta, both systems provide a basis for determining the valuations of securities and other assets.

The CAPM and SML approaches, however, are not free of problems. There may be other, more important factors besides the market that influence the returns of a security. In this case, beta would not be a good measure of risk. Also, using historical data may not be an appropriate way to calculate expected returns. Some academicians have pointed out that the CAPM and SML approaches are weak because the stock market indexes, like the Standard and Poor's 500 Composite Index, are merely proxies and do not represent the true market index. Others say that the calculation of CAPM values is based on past historical data, while the model is based on expected values. Consequently, historical betas cannot serve as a basis for establishing the true required rate of return for a security. The response to these criticisms is that, although the CAPM and SML approaches provide only a rough approximation, they represent an important tool for determining the risk/return trade-off and the ultimate value of assets.

KNOW THE CONCEPTS

DO YOU KNOW THE BASICS?

1. Under conditions of uncertainty, what kind of weights are used to determine the risk of an investment?

2. If the dispersion of the returns of Project A is large and that for Project B is narrow, which is the riskier project and why?

3. Define standard deviation, and calculate the range within which you can estimate that 68% of the returns will fall within plus or minus one standard deviation. Assume standard deviation equals 10 and the mean or expected return equals 100.

4. Why would you want to use the coefficient of variation to evaluate the merits of two different projects?

5. How does diversification reduce risk? Is it better for the co-movement of the assets in a portfolio to be positive or negative? Why?

6. Why is the market a standard measure of nondiversifiable risk?

7. Given three securities, what do betas of 1.0, .8, and 1.4 tell us about the nondiversifiable risk of each security?

8. Explain how the SML approach can be a useful tool in calculating the net present value of a project.

9. A security's returns, when related to the returns of the market, produce a nondiversifiable line that has a 45° angle. What does this imply?

10. What are some of the weaknesses connected with the beta and SML methods for determining the required rate of return of a security?

11. Define the efficient frontier and explain what can be done to improve a portfolio's expected return that has fallen below the efficient frontier.

TERMS FOR STUDY

beta	probabilities
Capital Asset Pricing Model (CAPM)	return
capital appreciation	risk
cash flow	risk-free rate
coefficient of variation	risk premium
correlation coefficient	risk/return trade-off
covariance	security market line
dividend yield	standard deviation
efficient frontier	variance
portfolio	volatility

PRACTICAL APPLICATION

COMPUTATIONAL PROBLEMS

1. Calculate the standard deviation of returns based on the following information:

Returns:	1, 2, 3
Probabilities:	.25, .50, .25
Expected return:	2

Give the range which covers a 95% confidence level of the returns or outcomes.

2. Calculate the required rate of return of a security, using the SML approach, if the risk-free rate is 8%, the market returns 12%, and the beta of the stock is 1.5. Is this security under- or overvalued if its actual return is 9%?

3. Given the information below on assets A and B, calculate:
   (a) Their expected returns
   (b) Their standard deviations
   (c) Their coefficients of variation

Which asset provides a better risk/return trade-off?

Project A		Project B	
Probability	Return	Probability	Return
.10	10	.15	9
.20	12	.35	13
.40	17	.35	16
.20	22	.15	20
.10	24		

4. If the risk-free rate is 6% and the market return is 10%, calculate the required rates of return for the following investments:

Security	Beta
A	.53
B	1.35
C	.85
D	1.05

5. Stock A, which has a beta of 1.2, is currently selling for $50 per share and will pay a dividend of $2.50 per share this year. On the basis of the company's strong growth, you expect the stock price to be $54 per share at the end of 1 year. The current risk-free rate is 7%, and the market return is 13%. Calculate the stock's required rate of return. Should you purchase the stock?

ANSWERS

KNOW THE CONCEPTS

1. The weights used to determine risk are called probabilities.

2. Project B is less risky than Project A because its volatility, as measured by standard deviation, is lower than Project A's. The more returns fluctuate, the greater the uncertainty of a project and the greater its risk.

3. Standard deviation measures the deviation of actual values from an expected value or the mean of historical observations. It is a measure of risk. When the standard deviation is 10 and the expected returns are 100, the range of the distribution is

(assume $1 \pm \sigma$) 90 to 110

4. It is not possible to compare risk with absolute numbers. A relative measure, such as the coefficient of variation σ/k, provides the basis for comparing the risk/return trade-off between different projects.

5. Diversification reduces risk because the risk is spread among a greater number of assets. A negative covariation is better than a positive one, because different movements of assets in a portfolio tend to dampen its overall fluctuations.

6. The market is a highly efficient vehicle that contains all available information. Therefore, its risk establishes a common indicator against which the nondiversifiable risks of all other securities can be compared.

7. A beta of 1.0 means that a security has the same risk as the market. A beta of .8 indicates that a security is less risky than the market. Conversely, securities with betas of 1.4 are more risky and volatile than the market indicator.

8. The SML equation provides the Required Rate of Returns (*RRRs*) of an asset. This is equivalent to the discount rate. By knowing the initial cost of a project and its discounted future returns, one can determine the *NPV* of the project (*PV* of returns − Initial cost).

9. When the returns of a security are correlated to the returns of the market, a characteristic line emerges implying a one-to-one relationship. In other words, security returns move the same way as market returns. The beta of this relationship is equal to 1.0. A 45° angle implies that the security has the same risk characteristics as the market index.

10. Weaknesses of the beta and SML approaches include:
    (a) There is no true market index that can be used as a benchmark for comparison purposes.
    (b) Past historical patterns are not representative of future required rates of return.
    (c) If the dispersion around the characteristic line is too wide, the line is not representative of the relationship. Consequently, beta is also a poor measure of the nondiversifiable risk of a security.

11. The efficient frontier is a curve that determines the maximum or optimal expected returns of portfolios at different levels of risk. If a portfolio's expected returns fall below the efficient frontier, a manager can diversify the portfolio mix in two ways. First, the manager can find securities with higher returns to increase the expected returns at a given risk level. Second, it is possible to diversify the portfolio by adding securities that have covariance values of zero or −1.0. This will reduce the risk of the portfolio while maintaining the same expected return.

PRACTICAL APPLICATION

1. $\sqrt{.50} = 0.71$

    A mean of 2 and $\pm 2\sigma$ will mean a range of −.58 to 3.42.

2. $RRR_s = .08 + (0.12 - .08)1.5$

    $\qquad .08 + .06 = .14$, or 14%

    If the actual return of this security is 9%, it is overvalued.

3. (a) Expected returns

Project A	Project B
$.10 \times 10 = 1.00$	$.15 \times 9 = 1.35$
$.20 \times 12 = 2.40$	$.35 \times 13 = 4.55$
$.40 \times 17 = 6.80$	$.35 \times 16 = 5.60$
$.20 \times 22 = 4.40$	$.15 \times 20 = \underline{3.00}$
$.10 \times 24 = \underline{2.40}$	$\overline{E}(R)_B = 14.50\%$
$\overline{E}(R)_A = 17.00\%$	

(b) Standard deviations

Project A	Project B
$(10 - 17)^2 \times .10 = 4.90$	$(9 - 14.5)^2 \times .15 = 4.5375$
$(12 - 17)^2 \times .20 = 5.00$	$(13 - 14.5)^2 \times .35 = .7875$
$(17 - 17)^2 \times .40 = 0$	$(16 - 14.5)^2 \times .35 = .7875$
$(22 - 17)^2 \times .20 = 5.00$	$(20 - 14.5)^2 \times .15 = \underline{4.5375}$
$(24 - 17)^2 \times .10 = \underline{4.90}$	$\sigma_B^2 = 10.65$
$\sigma_A^2 = 19.8$	$\sigma_B = 3.26$
$\sigma_A = 4.45$	

(c) Coefficients of variation

$$CV_A = \frac{4.45}{17.00} = .26 \qquad CV_B = \frac{3.26}{14.50} = .22$$

Stock B has a lower risk per unit of return.

4.
Security	Required Rate of Return
A	$.06 + .53(.10 - .06) = 8.12\%$
B	$.06 + 1.35(.10 - .06) = 11.4\%$
C	$.06 + .85(.10 - .06) = 9.4\%$
D	$.06 + 1.05(.10 - .06) = 10.2\%$

5. Expected rate of return $= \dfrac{2.50 + (54 - 50)}{50} = 13\%$

Required rate of return $= .07 + 1.2(.13 - .07) = 14.2\%$

Since the required rate of return exceeds the expected rate of return, stock A is overvalued and you should not purchase it.

5
VALUATION
METHODS

KEY TERMS

bond a long-term debt security issued by a borrower, either a public or private institution

coupon rate the rate of interest received by a bondholder on an annual, semiannual, or quarterly basis

face value the value of a bond at maturity, also called the nominal, or par value

---

THE CONCEPT OF VALUE

The value of an asset, such as a share of common stock or a bond, is influenced by three major factors: cash flow of the asset, growth rate of the cash flow, and risk or uncertainty of the cash flow.

An increase in the amount of cash flow tends to raise the price of an asset. Conversely, the price declines if cash flow becomes more uncertain. These relationships are fundamental to the valuation of an asset. Accordingly, the responsibility of a financial officer is to increase cash flows as much as possible while controlling risk.

The **cash flow** of a share of common stock or preferred stock is measured by its annual dividend and the change in its stock price. The cash flow of a **bond,** which is a long-term debt security issued by a borrower, is the amount of interest received by a bondholder in a year plus the change in its price. Since profits raise the price of an asset and risk reduces the price, all of the following three conditions are required for a continuous increase in the value of any asset:

1. The asset must continuously produce cash flow.

2. Cash flow must have a positive rate of growth (i.e., cash flow must increase over time).

3. Risk must be controlled.

Of the three factors, estimation of risk is the most difficult task. As a result, the subject of risk in the valuation of an asset should receive more attention when the outlook for the economy becomes more uncertain. In Chapters 3 and 4, it was discussed that the discount rate reflects risk, or uncertainty of the future income. To find the current price of an asset, then, future cash flows must be discounted back to present value at an appropriate rate to reflect each aspect of risk. Therefore, the price of an asset is the same as the present value of its future cash flows.

Price of an Asset = Present value of its future cash flows

In order to obtain the present value of future cash flows (returns), you must sum an estimated series of net incomes and depreciations for a number of years in the future. These cash flows are then adjusted for risk to determine their present value.

In Chapter 5, it will be shown that the value of common stocks, preferred stocks, and bonds can be estimated by discounting or by calculating the present value of the future returns that these securities are expected to generate.

YOU SHOULD REMEMBER

The value of an asset is defined as the present value of all future cash flows associated with that particular asset.

• VALUATION OF BONDS

As previously stated, the value of an asset is equal to the present value of its future cash flows. This rule can be applied to any financial asset, including a bond. The U.S. government regularly borrows from the public by issuing government bonds to cover its budget deficit. Corporations issue bonds to raise the capital required to expand their operations. In this manner, the U.S. government and borrowing corporations commit themselves to pay a certain amount of money in interest to bondholders on an annual, semiannual, or quarterly basis. The amount of interest to be received is the **coupon rate** stated on each bond certificate. Other information found on a bond certificate include the maturity date, the face value, and the number of times interest is paid each year. The **maturity date** is the date when the issuer must pay the investor the full price of the bond, thus retiring the debt. The **face value** of a bond is the price of the bond at maturity. When these figures are available, the value of the bond can easily be determined.

How to Determine the Value of a Bond

1. Calculate the present value of interest payments.

2. Calculate the present value of the face value.

3. Add the two present values.

Note that both the interest and the face value must be discounted at the market rate (the rate at which similar bonds are discounted).

Example: Determining the Value of a Bond

PROBLEM   The ABC Co. has issued a 5-year bond with a face value of $1,000 at a coupon rate of 10%. Interest is paid annually, and the discount rate for similar bonds in the market is 12%. Determine the value of the bond.

SOLUTION   To determine the value of this bond, you first discount the annual interest of $100 (10% × $1,000 = $100) at a discount rate of 12% for 5 years. Next, discount the face value of $1,000 at 12% for 5 years and add the two present values;

$$
\begin{aligned}
\text{Bond Value} &= \left[\frac{100}{(1 + 12\%)^1} + \frac{100}{(1 + 12\%)^2} + \frac{100}{(1 + 12\%)^3} \right. \\
(V_b) & \left. \quad + \frac{100}{(1 + 12\%)^4} + \frac{100}{(1 + 12\%)^5} \right] \\
&+ \left[\frac{1,000}{(1 + 12\%)^5} \right] = \textit{Stop!} \text{ Don't work this out by hand.}
\end{aligned}
$$

The answer to this equation can easily be determined by the use of the present value tables in Chapter 3:

$100(PVIFA) + $1,000(PVIF) = $100(3.604) + $1,000(.567)
12%, 5 yr   12%, 5 yr

$$= \$360 + \$567 = \$927$$

where *PVIFA* = present value interest factor annuity
PVIF = present value interest factor

The value of this bond is $927. In other words, an investor would pay $927 for the bond.

A general formula to calculate the value of bonds can be written as

$$V_b = I(PVIFA_{k,n}) + F(PVIF_{k,n})$$

where V_b = value of the bond
   I = interest in each time period
   F = face value of the bond
   k = discount rate
   n = number of periods

The values for the *PVIFA* (present value interest factor annuity) are available in their corresponding tables in Chapter 3. Note that in the preceding example, the value of the bond is only $927—which is below the face value of $1,000. Since the 12% discount rate in the market is higher than the 10% coupon rate, the bond sells at a discount. The bond would sell at a premium if the discount rate were below the coupon rate. For instance, at a discount rate of 8%, the price of this bond would be $1,079:

$$V_b = 100(PVIFA) + 1000(PVIF) = 100(3.99) + 1000(.68) = 1079$$
$$\quad\quad 8\%,\ 5\ \text{yr} \quad\quad 8\%,\ 5\ \text{yr}$$

When the interest rate in the market falls, interest received on old bonds is more than interest on new bonds because of the lower coupon rates. Therefore, old bonds sell at a higher price (premium). The price of a bond moves inversely with the interest rate in the market. If the interest rate rises, the price of a bond with a lower coupon rate declines. This inverse relationship between interest rate and price holds also in the cases of preferred and common stock.

• *VALUATION OF PREFERRED STOCK*

Holders of preferred stock receive a fixed dividend from the issuing companies on a regular basis. There is no maturity date on preferred stock; therefore, a share of preferred stock can be considered a perpetuity, as discussed in Chapter 3. The value of a preferred stock can also be determined by discounting the present value of its dividends over an infinite period of time:

$$V_p = \frac{D}{(1 + K)^1} + \frac{D}{(1 + K)^2} + \frac{D}{(1 + K)^3} + \cdots + \frac{D}{(1 + K)^\infty}$$

where V_p = market value of preferred stock
   D = constant dividend
   K = discount rate

This equation can be rewritten as a simple perpetuity formula:

$$V_p = \frac{D}{K}$$

With this simple equation, the value of a preferred stock can be determined once information about dividends and the discount rate is available. What a straightforward solution to a very important problem!

Example: Determining the Value of Preferred Stock

PROBLEM   The XYZ Co. issues preferred stock, each share paying an annual dividend of $2. The discount rate of similar preferred stock in the market is 10%. Determine the value of a share of preferred stock issued by this company.

SOLUTION   The price of the preferred stock is calculated simply:

$$V_p = \frac{D}{K} = \frac{\$2}{.10} = \$20$$

Although the annual dividends of preferred stock are constant, the price of the stock can change over time. The price of a preferred stock will increase if the market discount rate goes down. By the same token, an increase in the discount rate will lower the price of a preferred stock. For instance, if the discount rate in the preceding example rises to 15%, the preferred stock of the XYZ Co. is worth only $13.33:

$$V_p = \frac{D}{K} = \frac{\$2}{.15} = 13.33$$

• VALUATION OF COMMON STOCK

Buyers of common stock invest in the ownership of the issuing company, that is, they become owners of the company. Dividends on common stock are not guaranteed. Each company's dividend policy depends on the firm's profitability and the availability of funds. Dividends paid in one year may be more or less than dividends paid in a previous year. In some years, no dividend may be paid at all.

Over time, the annual dividend per share may remain fixed, may grow at a constant rate, or may rise at a relatively high rate for a few years and then grow at a constant rate. Because of all these possibilities, calculation of the price of common stock calls for careful projection of future dividends. Since a company is considered to operate forever, the price of common stock is not influenced by the number of years an investor wants to maintain ownership.

The price of common stock is largely determined by three factors: the annual dividends, growth of dividends, and discount rate. The rate at which future dividends are to be discounted is called the required rate of return. If a company has a high level of risk, a high required rate of return is expected by investors. To encourage investors to invest their money in a risky venture, a higher payoff must be offered. The following are the procedures to determine the value of common stock in three possible cases:

VALUING STOCK WITH NO DIVIDEND GROWTH

With D as a constant annual dividend and K_s as a required rate of return, the price of common stock, denoted as P_0, can be determined by discounting future dividends at K_s:

$$P_0 = \frac{D_1}{(1 + K_s)^1} + \frac{D_2}{(1 + K_s)^2} + \frac{D_3}{(1 + K_s)^3} + \cdots + \frac{D_\infty}{(1 + K_s)^\infty}$$

Note that this is the same familiar equation you used earlier for preferred stock. The only difference is the required rate of return (K_s) of common stock, which depends on the risk of that particular common stock. The equation can be simplified further as

$$P_0 = \frac{D}{K_s}$$

Example: Common Stock with No Dividend Growth

PROBLEM   A company pays an annual dividend of $3 per share, expects no growth in future dividends, and has a required rate of return of 12%. What should the price of its common stock be?

SOLUTION

$$P_0 = \frac{\$3}{.12} = \$25$$

VALUING STOCK WITH CONSTANT DIVIDEND GROWTH

Dividends of a firm may increase at a fixed rate on an annual basis. For example, if the latest dividend was $2 and dividends grow at an annual rate of 5%, the dividend in the next year will be $2.10:

$$\$2(1 + .05) = \$2(1.05)^1 = \$2.10$$

The dividend in the second year will be $2.21:

$$\$2(1 + .05)(1 + .05) = \$2(1.05)^2 = \$2.21$$

The pattern, of course, continues with future years.

The price of common stock with a constant rate of growth can also be determined if future dividends are discounted at the required rate of return:

$$P_0 = \frac{D_0(1 + g)^1}{(1 + K_s)} + \frac{D_0(1 + g)^2}{(1 + K_s)^2} + \frac{D_0(1 + g)^3}{(1 + K_s)^3} + \cdots + \frac{D_0(1 + g)^\infty}{(1 + K_s)^\infty}$$

In this equation, $D_0(1 + g)^1$ is the dividend in year 1, $D_0(1 + g)^2$ is the dividend in year 2, and so on. Don't be scared of too many calculations. Professor Myron J. Gordon, a pioneer in the field of finance, made the above equation simple and workable:

$$P_0 = \frac{D_0(1 + g)}{K_s - g} \quad \text{or} \quad \frac{D_1}{K_s - g}$$

where D_0 = latest dividend paid per share
$\quad D_1$ = expected dividend per share in year 1
$\quad K_s$ = required rate of return
$\quad g$ = growth rate of dividends

This equation is often referred to in financial literature as the Gordon model.

Example: Common Stock with Constant Dividend Growth

PROBLEM   The latest dividend per share paid by a company was $1.80. The company is expected to raise its annual dividends at a rate of 6%. Assuming that the required rate of return is 11%, estimate the stock price.

SOLUTION   Using the Gordon model, calculate the price of the common stock as follows:

$$P_0 = \frac{D_0(1 + g)}{K_s - g} = \frac{\$1.80(1 + .06)}{.11 - .06} = \frac{\$1.91}{.05} = \$38.16$$

As in the cases of bonds and preferred stock, the price of common stock will decline if the discount rate, K_s, goes up. For instance, the price of a share of common stock in the preceding example would have been only $21.22 if K_s had increased to 15%.

$$P_0 = \frac{D_0(1 + g)}{K_s - g} = \frac{\$1.80(1 + .06)}{.15 - .06} = \frac{\$1.91}{0.09} = \$21.22$$

Also, note that the price of the stock will increase as the growth rate (g) increases and that the price will decrease as g decreases.

VALUING STOCK WITH UNUSUAL DIVIDEND GROWTH

A firm may have an unusual growth rate of dividends in the first few years and then maintain a normal and constant rate of growth. In this case, the question is how to estimate the stock price when dividends grow at different rates during two periods of time. This problem can easily be solved if we apply the same principle of valuation used for the preceding cases: The price of a financial asset is the present value of its future income.

When a common stock has two or more different growth rates of dividend, future dividends must be projected separately. These projected dividends must be discounted back to present, and finally all of the present values are added together. A numerical approach will clarify the procedure:

Example: Common Stock with Unusual Dividend Growth

PROBLEM   The Profitable Co. paid an annual dividend per share of $4 last year. It is expected that dividends will grow at an annual rate of 20% for the next 3 years and then drop to a normal growth rate of 6%. Assuming a required rate of return of 12%, estimate the price of the common stock today. To help solve this problem, use the future incomes shown in the table.

Year	Income	PVIF at 12%	Present Value of Income
1	$D_1 = \$4.80$	.8929	$ 4.29
2	$D_2 = 5.76$	.7972	4.59
3	$D_3 = 6.91$	.7118	4.92
	$P_3 = 122.08$	.7118	86.90
			Total PV = $100.70

SOLUTION In the table D_1, D_2, and D_3 or dividends in years 1, 2, and 3, respectively—are expected to grow at an annual rate of 20%. The stock price in year 3 (P_3) is calculated as follows:

$$P_3 = \frac{D_3(1 + g)}{K_s - g} = \frac{\$6.91(1.06)}{.12 - .06} = \$122.08$$

Note that, when determining the stock price in a particular year with the Gordon model, the dividend in the following year must be used. Since the growth rate of dividends is constant (6%) after the third year, the Gordon model is used to estimate P_3. The next step is to discount all future income (D_1, D_2, D_3, and P_3) at a given rate of 12%. When the discounted values are summed, the price of the stock is estimated (see the table) to be $100.70.

YOU SHOULD REMEMBER

To determine the price of a bond, its future interest income and principal value must be discounted separately and then added together. The price of preferred stock can be estimated by calculating the present value of annual dividends, as in the case of perpetuities. The valuation of common stock can be estimated using three conditions: no growth rate of dividends, constant growth rate of dividends, and unusual growth rates of dividends.

USING THE CAPM IN VALUATION METHODS

In the preceding sections, the value of an asset was defined as the present value of its future income. It was also assumed that the discount rate was given in all cases. This is not a realistic assumption in practice. Therefore, the CAPM discussed in Chapter 4 can be used to estimate a required rate of return for valuation of a common stock.

The formula for the CAPM is

$$K_s = R_f + \beta(\overline{K}_m - R_f)$$

where K_s = required rate of return
R_f = risk-free rate (such as the return on U.S. treasury bills)
β = beta coefficient of the company
$\overline{K}_m$ = return on a market portfolio

Once K_s (required rate of returns) is computed, the future income is discounted at that rate.

Example: Using the CAPM for Valuation

PROBLEM   The beta of a company is 1.50, the return on the Dow Jones portfolio is 12%, U.S. treasury bills currently yield 9%, the company has historically maintained a growth rate of 6% in dividends, and investors expect to receive a $3 dividend per share in the next year. Using the available data, determine the current price per share.

SOLUTION   In solving this problem, the Gordon model can be used directly if the required rate of return (K_s) is given:

$$P_0 = \frac{D_1}{K_s - g} = \frac{3}{K_s - 6\%}$$

K_s, which is a missing value in the above equation, can be derived by the use of the CAPM, for which all necessary data are available:

$$K_s = R_f + \beta(\overline{K}_m - R_f) = .09 + 1.50(.12 - .09) = 13.5\%$$

Inserting 13.5% as the value of K_s in the Gordon model, the current price per share in this example would be $40:

$$P_0 = \frac{\$3}{.135 - .06} = \$40$$

The use of the CAPM is recommended, of course, in valuation of common stocks for which reliable betas are available. If the beta is not available, the estimated price could be considerably biased.

Prices estimated by using the CAPM may also be different from actual market prices. If the difference is significant, the undervalued stock should be purchased and the overvalued stock should be sold. Undervalued stocks have actual prices lower than the CAPM estimates; overvalued stocks are sold at prices above the CAPM estimates.

YOU SHOULD REMEMBER

The Capital Asset Pricing Model can be used to determine the required rate of return in the valuation of common stock. In the Gordon model, the value of K_s (required rate of return) may be unknown. In this case, a financial analyst may determine K_s by the use of the Capital Asset Pricing Model and then use it in the valuation equation:

$$P_0 = \frac{D_1}{K_s - g}$$

where P_0 = stock price to be estimated
D_1 = dividend in year 1
K_s = required rate of return
g = annual growth rate of dividends

KNOW THE CONCEPTS

DO YOU KNOW THE BASICS?

1. What information do you need to determine the value of the following assets?
   (a) Bonds
   (b) Preferred stock
   (c) Common stock
2. Is it possible that the prices you calculate for bonds and stock are different from actual market prices? Why?
3. What is the general definition of the value of an asset?
4. What happens to the value of a bond if its coupon rate is less than the discount rate required for bonds of similar risk?
5. How can the Capital Asset Pricing Model be used in valuation methods?

TERMS FOR STUDY

bond   face value
cash flow   maturity
coupon rate

PRACTICAL APPLICATION

COMPUTATIONAL PROBLEMS

1. How much will you pay for a 5-year, $1,000-denomination bond if the coupon rate is 10% and interest is paid semiannually? Assume that similar bonds are currently discounted at 12%.

2. How much will you pay for a share of a preferred stock with an annual dividend of $5? Similar preferred stocks are discounted at 13%.

3. Does the value of the preferred stock in Problem 2 change if you know that you will sell your shares next year? Why?

4. The earnings and common stock dividends of Steady Co. have been growing at an annual rate of 7%. The rate of growth is expected to remain unchanged for the foreseeable future. The latest annual dividend per share was $2.50. Determine the value of a share of Steady's common stock with each of the following required rates of return:

   (a) 10%
   (b) 12%
   (c) 20%
   (d) 5%

5. Using the CAPM and the following data, determine the value of a share of Public Utility Co.:

   • The latest annual dividend paid by Public Utility Co. is $1.50.

   • Growth is constant at an annual rate of 4%.

   • The beta of Public Utility Co. is 1.20.

   • The rate of return on a market portfolio is 14%.

   • The rate of return on U.S. treasury bills is 9%.

6. The chairman of World Food Corporation announced that the firm's dividends will grow at a rate of 18% for the next 3 years, and that thereafter the annual rate of growth is expected to be only 6%. The annual dividend per share is estimated to be $4 in the next year. If a required rate of return of 15% is assumed, what is the highest price you are willing to pay for a share of World Food Corporation's common stock?

ANSWERS

KNOW THE CONCEPTS

1. The information required to evaluate bonds, preferred stock, and common stock is as follows:

   (a) *Bonds*: coupon rate, face value, maturity, discount rate, and time between interest payments.

   (b) *Preferred stock*: dividends paid in each period, discount rate

   (c) *Common stock*: expected dividend next year, required rate of return, rate of growth of dividends

2. Yes. The actual market prices may be more or less because of other factors not considered in the formulas.

3. The value of any asset is defined as the present value of the asset's expected future cash flows.

4. Since the price of a bond moves inversely with the market interest rate, the bond price declines and the bond sells at a discount.

5. The CAPM formula calculates the required rate of return for a common stock, which is the discount rate used to find the present value of the stock's dividend stream.

PRACTICAL APPLICATION

1. $50 (*PVIFA*) + $1,000 (*PVIF*) = $50(7.3601) + $1000(.5584) = $926

   6%, 10 periods   12%, 10 periods

2. $\dfrac{\$5}{.13} = \$38.46$

3. No. The assumption is that dividends are paid in perpetuity (forever). Once you have sold the stock, somebody else will own it. Therefore, price has nothing to do with the time period an investor holds the stock.

4. $P_0 = D_1/(K_s - g)$; Note: $D_1 = D_0 (1+g)$

   (a) $\dfrac{\$2.50(1.07)}{.10 - .07} = \$89.17$

   (b) $\dfrac{\$2.50(1.07)}{.12 - .07} = \$53.50$

   (c) $\dfrac{\$2.50(1.07)}{.20 - .07} = \$20.58$

   (d) $\dfrac{\$2.50(1.07)}{.05 - .07} = -\$133.75$

   Answer (d) is not acceptable because the price is negative—which does not make sense!

5. $K_s = R_f + \beta(K_m - R_f) = .09 + 1.20(.14 - .09) = .15$

$P_0 = \dfrac{D_1}{(K_s - g)} = \$1.50(1.04) \div (.15 - .04) = \$14.18$

6.
$$D_1 = \$4$$
$$D_2 = \$4(1.18) = \$4.72$$
$$D_3 = \$4.72(1.18) = \$5.57$$
$$D_4 = \$5.57(1.06) = \$5.90$$
$$P_3 = \dfrac{D_3(1 + g)}{(K_s - g)} = \dfrac{\$5.90}{(.15 - .06)} = \$65.56$$

Value of stock $= (PV \text{ of } D_1) + (PV \text{ of } D_2)$
$+ (PV \text{ of } D_3) + (PV \text{ of } P_3)$
$= \$4(.8696) + \$4.72(.7561)$
$+ \$5.57\,(.6575) + \$65.56\,(.6575)$
$= \$53.82$

INTRODUCTION TO INVESTMENT POLICY: CAPITAL BUDGETING

6

CAPITAL BUDGETING: PRELIMINARY STEPS

KEY TERMS

amortization the gradual, planned reduction in value of capital expenditures

capital budgeting a method for evaluating, comparing, and selecting projects to achieve the best long-term financial return

capital expenditures long-term expenditures that are amortized over a period of time as determined by IRS regulations

current expenditures short-term expenditures that are completely written off in the year when the expenses occur

EBIT earnings before interest and taxes

WHAT IS CAPITAL BUDGETING?

Capital budgeting is a required managerial tool. One duty of a financial manager is to choose investments with satisfactory cash flows and rates of return. Therefore, a financial manager must be able to decide whether or not an investment is worth undertaking and be able to choose intelligently between two or more alternatives. To do this, a sound procedure to evaluate, compare, and select projects is needed. This procedure is called **capital budgeting**.

EFFICIENT USE OF A LIMITED RESOURCE

In the form of either debt or equity, capital is a very limited resource. There is a limit to the volume of credit that the banking system can create in the economy. Commercial banks and other lending institutions have limited deposits from which they can lend money to individuals, corporations, and governments. In addition, the Federal Reserve System requires each bank to maintain part of its deposits as reserves. Having limited resources to lend, lending institutions are selective in extending loans to their customers. But even if a bank were to extend unlimited loans to a company, the management of that company would need to consider the impact that increasing loans would have on the overall cost of financing.

In reality, any firm has limited borrowing resources that should be allocated among the best investment alternatives. One might argue that a company can issue an almost unlimited amount of common stock to raise capital. Increasing the number of shares of company stock, however, will serve only to distribute the same amount of equity among a greater number of shareholders. In other words, as the number of shares of a company increases, the company ownership of the individual stockholder may proportionally decrease.

The argument that capital is a limited resource is true of any form of capital, whether debt or equity (short-term or long-term, common stock) or retained earnings, accounts payable or notes payable, and so on. Even the best-known firm in an industry or a community can increase its borrowing up to a certain limit. Once this point has been reached, the firm will either be denied more credit or be charged a higher interest rate, making borrowing a less desirable way to raise capital.

Faced with limited sources of capital, management should carefully decide whether or not a particular project is economically acceptable. In the case of more than one project, management must identify the projects that will contribute most to profits and, consequently, to the value (or wealth) of the firm. This, in essence, is the basis of capital budgeting.

CURRENT EXPENDITURES AND CAPITAL EXPENDITURES

A firm makes two types of expenditures: current and capital. **Current expenditures** are short-term and completely written off in the same year that the expenses occur. Examples of current expenditures are wages, salaries, cost of raw materials, and various administrative expenses. **Capital expenditures** are long-term, and are **amortized** (their value is gradually reduced) over a period of years according to IRS regulations (discussed previously in Chapter 2). Examples of capital expenditures include an outlay of $100,000 for a new building or machinery, the purchase of a personal computer for business purposes, the purchase of patent rights from an inventor, expenditures for research and development, and so on. For the purposes of this chapter, only capital expenditures will be discussed.

Types of Capital Expenditures

1. New machines and equipment bought for new purposes. In order to expand business operations, firms often buy new equipment. According to IRS regulations, light-duty trucks, different models of automobiles, research and development equipment, and relatively inexpensive equipment are depreciated over a period of 3 years. Other machinery tools are depreciated over

5 years. Public utility capital expenditures generally have a recovery period of 10 or 15 years.

2. Replacement of existing machines. To increase efficiency, management may decide to sell existing still-functioning equipment and replace it with current models. Capital budgeting for replacement projects is concerned not only with the cost of new machines but also with the revenue from the sale of old machines and the tax effects from this sale. Examples later in the chapter will clarify this point.

3. Mandatory projects. With the rise of consumerism, **mandatory projects** are becoming a major component of capital expenditures. These investments are required by law to maintain the safety of consumers and workers as well as a healthy environment.

4. Other capital expenditures. This category encompasses various other long-term investments, such as purchasing land, expanding office buildings, and buying patent rights.

YOU SHOULD REMEMBER

Capital budgeting is investment decision-making as to whether or not a project is worth undertaking. Capital budgeting is basically concerned with the justification of capital expenditures.

Current expenditures are short-term and are completely written off in the same year that expenses occur. Capital expenditures are long-term and are amortized over a period of years are required by the IRS.

DETERMINING INITIAL COSTS

The first important step in deciding whether a project should be accepted is the calculation of its initial cost. The **initial cost**, or cost of initial investment, is simply the actual cost of starting an investment. Once managers know how much it costs to run a project, they can compare the initial investment with future benefits and make a judgment as to whether or not the project is worth undertaking. To determine the cost of the initial investment, financial analysts answer the following questions:

- What is the invoice price of new items (machinery, equipment, services, etc.)?

- What are the additional expenses, such as costs of packing, delivery, installation, and inspection?

- What is the revenue from the sale of existing machinery, if it needs to be replaced?

- How much tax should be paid on the sale of the existing machinery?

Table 6–1 should be used as a checklist to determine the initial cost of a project.

Table 6–1   Calculating the Initial Cost of a Project

Initial Expense	Amount	Initial Revenue	Amount
Price of new items	xx	Revenue from sale of existing machinery	xx
Additional expenses		Tax credit on sale of	
packing and delivery	xx	existing machinery at	
installation	xx	loss	xx
inspection	xx		
other	xx		
Taxes on sale of existing machinery	xx		
Change in net working capital	xx	Total initial revenue	xx
Total initial expense	xx	Initial cost of project*	xx

*Initial cost of project = Total initial expense − Total initial revenue

Example 1: Determining Initial Costs

PROBLEM   XYZ Co. is planning to buy new machinery for $200,000. The machinery has a depreciation life of 5 years. As a result of buying the new machinery, XYZ Co. will sell the existing machinery at $50,000. The existing machinery was purchased 3 years ago for $100,000. The company must pay $4,000 for delivery and $9,000 for installation of the new machinery. As a financial analyst, determine the initial cost of the project. Assume tax rates of 34%. Net working capital does not change.

SOLUTION

**Table 6–2   XYZ Co.—Calculation of the Initial Cost
of Buying New Machinery**

Initial Expense	Amount	Initial Revenue	Amount
Price of new item	$200,000	Revenue from sale of existing machinery	$50,000
Additional expenses		Tax credit on sale of	
packing and delivery	4,000	existing machinery	
installation	9,000	at loss	0
inspection	0		
other	0		
Taxes on sale of existing machinery	$7140		
Change in net working capital			
Total expenses	$220,140	Total revenue	50,000
		Total expenses	220,140
		Net cost	$170,140

As shown in Table 6–2, the total initial expenses are $220,140: including $200,000 for new machinery, $4,000 for packing and delivery, $9,000 for installation, and $7,140 for taxes on the sale of the existing machinery.

Taxes of $7,140 are determined as follows: Since the existing machinery was sold below the original price of $100,000, there is capital gains. The company should pay 34% ordinary tax on any sale price over the book value. Since the existing machinery was purchased 3 years ago, it has been depreciated as follows:

Depreciation in year 1: (.20)($100,000) = $20,000
Depreciation in year 2: (.32)($100,000) = 32,000
Depreciation in year 3: (.19)($100,000) = 19,000
Total depreciation = 71,000

Therefore, the book value of the machinery is $29,000 ($100,000 − $71,000).

Since the machinery has been sold at $50,000, the company has a recaptured depreciation of $21,000. (Remember that **recaptured depreciation** is the difference between the selling price—excluding capital gain—and the book value.) Paying 34% tax on the recaptured depreciation, XYZ Co. should pay 34% of $21,000, which equals $7,140 as reported. (See Table 6–2.)

The total initial revenue is $50,000. Subtracting the total initial revenue of $50,000 from the total initial expenses of $220,140, XYZ Co. will invest $170,140 as the initial cost of this project.

Example 2: Determining Initial Costs

PROBLEM   What would be the initial cost of the project in the preceding example if the existing machinery was sold at $20,000? Assume that all other information remains unchanged.

SOLUTION

Table 6–3 XYZ Co.—Calculation of the Initial Cost of Buying New Machinery

Initial Expense	Amount	Initial Revenue	Amount
Price of new item	$200,000	Revenue from sale of existing machinery	$ 20,000
Additional expenses		Tax credit on sale of	
packing and delivery	4,000	existing machinery at	
installation	9,000	loss	3,060
inspection	0		
other	0		
Taxes on sale of existing			
machinery	0	Total revenue	23,060
Total expenses	213,000	Total expenses	213,000
		Net Cost	$189,940

Since the old machinery is sold below the book value, there is a loss of $9,000 ($29,000 book value minus $20,000 resale price). Therefore, XYZ Co. should receive a tax credit of $3,060 on the loss (34% of $9,000). Table 6–3 shows that, in this case, taxes on the sale of the existing machinery are zero, and the tax credit on the sale is $3,060.

When calculating the initial cost of a project, keep in mind that there is neither a tax to be paid nor a tax to be refunded if existing machinery is sold at its book value. For instance, if the existing machinery in the case of XYZ Co. is sold at the book value of $29,000, taxes on the sale of the machinery—as well as tax credits on the sale of the machine—would be zero.

DETERMINING INCREMENTAL CASH FLOW

The preceding section showed how to calculate the initial cost of a project. In order to decide whether the initial cost will pay off, however, it is also necessary to estimate future cash flows. Management should be concerned only with the incremental cash flow. The **incremental cash flow** is the additional cash flow that the firm will receive over the existing cash flow after the project is accepted. Suppose that the existing cash flow of a firm is $100. If cash flow increases to $150 after starting a new project, the incremental cash flow is $50. Therefore, only $50 is considered as the relevant cash flow, or the benefit of the project. There is a simple method to determine the incremental cash flow of a new project for each year.

Determining Incremental Cash Flow

1. Calculate additional net earnings.

$$\text{Additional net earnings} = \text{Estimated net earnings (including the new project)} - \text{Estimated net earnings (without the new project)}$$

2. Calculate tax benefits of depreciation.

$$\text{Additional tax benefit of depreciation} = \text{Tax rate} \times \text{Additional depreciation}$$

3. Add additional net earnings and tax benefits of depreciation together.

$$\text{Incremental cash flow} = \text{Additional net earnings} + \text{Additional tax benefits of depreciation}$$

Example 1: Calculating Incremental Cash Flow

PROBLEM   The estimated net earnings for the XYZ Co. in the next 3 years are $100,000, $150,000, and $200,000. The annual depreciation amounts for those years are estimated as $30,000, $40,000, and $45,000. As a result of starting a new project, the estimated net earnings will be $120,000, $165,000, and $230,000; and the annual depreciation will increase to $45,000, $62,000, and $66,000. To make it simple, assume that the tax rate is 40%; calculate the incremental cash flow of the new project.

SOLUTION 1. Subtract the estimated net earnings without the new project from the estimated net earnings with the new project for each year. The results are additional net earnings as follows:

Additional net earnings:	Year 1	Year 2	Year 3
	$20,000	$15,000	$30,000

2. Since the annual depreciation increases, so does the tax benefit of depreciation in each year. Subtract to find these benefits:

Additional tax benefit of depreciation (.40 × depreciation increases)	Year 1	Year 2	Year 3
	$6,000	$8,800	$8,400

3. Adding additional net earnings to additional tax benefits of depreciation, determine the incremental cash flow for each year:

Incremental cash flow:	Year 1	Year 2	Year 3
	$26,000	$23,800	$38,400

In other words, the actual benefits of accepting the new project are $26,000 in the first year, $23,800 in the second year, and $38,400 in the third year. In the next chapter, these annual benefits will be compared against the the initial cost of the project (initial investment), and a decision whether to accept or reject the project will then be made.

Example 2: Calculating Incremental Cash Flows

PROBLEM The estimated earnings before interest and taxes (**EBIT**) under two conditions are given in Table 6-4:

Table 6-4   EBIT Under Two Conditions

Year	With the Existing Machine	With the New Machine
1	$100,000	$150,000
2	140,000	250,000
3	280,000	350,000
4	400,000	450,000
5	510,000	550,000

The existing machine was purchased 3 years ago at $400,000. A new machine is under consideration for replacement at a cost of $600,000. Depreciation life is 5 years in both cases, and the tax rate is 34%.

Determine the incremental cash flow for replacing the existing machine.

SOLUTION   In solving this problem, notice that, if the existing machine is kept, only 2 years are left for depreciation. However, if the new machine is purchased, there are 5 years of depreciation. Therefore, the incremental cash flow should include not only the difference between the EBITs, but also the tax benefits from additional years of depreciation if the company buys the new machine. Tables 6–5, 6–6 and 6–7 show a step-by-step solution to the problem.

In calculating depreciation, you multiply the cost of each machine by 20% for the first year, 32% for the second year, and 19%, 15%, and 14% for the years after, as explained in Chapter 2. In Table 6–5 additional values of EBIT were determined, and in Table 6–6 additional tax benefits of depreciation were calculated. If the additional EBIT and the additional tax benefits are added together, the result is the additional, or incremental, cash flow as reported in Table 6–7.

Table 6–5   Step One: Additional EBIT

Year	New EBIT (a)	Existing EBIT (b)	Additional EBIT (a − b)
1	$150,000	$100,000	$ 50,000
2	250,000	140,000	110,000
3	350,000	280,000	70,000
4	450,000	400,000	50,000
5	550,000	510,000	40,000

Table 6–6   Step Two: Additional Tax Benefits

Year	New Depreciation (a)	Existing Depreciation (b)	Additional Depreciation (a − b)	Additional Tax Benefit 34% (a − b)
1	$120,000	$60,000	$ 60,000	$20,400
2	192,000	56,000	136,000	46,240
3	114,000	0	114,000	38,760
4	90,000	0	90,000	30,600
5	84,000	0	84,000	28,560

**Table 6-7 Incremental Cash Flow
in 5 Years**

Year	Incremental Cash Flow = Additional EBIT & Additional Tax Benefit
1	$70,400
2	156,240
3	108,760
4	80,600
5	68,560

From the above example, it can be concluded that

    Incremental cash flow
       = Incremental EBIT + Incremental tax benefit of depreciation

Incremental cash flow is the *only relevant cash flow* for the capital budgeting decisions that will be made in the next two chapters.

YOU SHOULD REMEMBER

Before deciding about a project, management should determine two important values: initial investment and incremental cash flow. Initial investment is the actual cost of a project after adjusting both for the sale of the existing equipment and for taxes. Incremental cash flows are additional benefits that a project will contribute to the existing cash flows. Incremental cash flow should be considered as the only relevant cash flow in the analysis and comparison of projects.

KNOW THE CONCEPTS

DO YOU KNOW THE BASICS?

1. What is capital budgeting?
2. For tax purposes, which type of expenditure is more favorable to the cash flows of a firm: current expenditures or capital expenditures?
3. What major information (data) do you need for capital budgeting?
4. What is the only relevant cash flow when comparing two projects?

5. Explain the tax consequences of selling an old asset at a price above the depreciated value and also above the original purchase price.

TERMS FOR STUDY

amortization	incremental cash flow
capital budgeting	initial cost
capital expenditures	mandatory project
current expenditures	recaptured depreciation
EBIT	

PRACTICAL APPLICATION

COMPUTATIONAL PROBLEMS

1. XYZ Associates are considering the purchase of a new machine for $300,000.
Meanwhile, they are planning to sell their old machine for $60,000. The old
machine was purchased 3 years ago and its book value is $46,200. Both machines
have a depreciation life of 5 years. Delivery expenses are $6,000, and installation
expenses are $10,000. Using tax rates of 34% for ordinary income, calculate the
initial cost of buying the new equipment.

2. Sara & Associates have estimated the EBIT of their firm under two conditions as
follows

Year	EBIT with Old Equipment	EBIT with New Equipment
1	$150,000	$210,000
2	190,000	290,000
3	340,000	380,000
4	450,000	490,000
5	550,000	710,000

The old equipment was purchased 2 years ago for $500,000. New equipment
can be purchased for $710,000. Both pieces of equipment have a depreciation life
of 5 years. Using a tax rate of 34%, calculate the incremental cash flow of
replacing the old equipment. Explain your findings in your own words.

3. ABC, Inc., is considering replacing a machine that originally cost $40,000 with a
new machine that can be purchased for $70,000. The book value of the old
machine is $16,800, and it can be sold for $10,000. Installation costs and
shipping fees associated with the new machine are $3,500. Using a tax rate of
34%, calculate the cost of purchasing the new machine.

4. XYZ Corporation is considering replacing one of its old machines with a new, more efficient machine. The old machine has a book value of $25,000 and can be sold for $100,000. The new machine has a cost of $500,000. Shipping fees are an additional $5,000. Using a tax rate of 34% for ordinary income, calculate the cost of purchasing the new equipment.

5. Calculate the incremental cash flow for replacing old equipment, given the following information:

Year	EBIT with Old Equipment	EBIT with New Equipment
1	$200,000	$225,000
2	215,000	305,000
3	300,000	315,000

The company's tax rate is 34%, the old machine was purchased 2 years ago for $600,000, the new machine costs $920,000, and both machines have a depreciation life of 3 years.

ANSWERS

KNOW THE CONCEPTS

1. Capital budgeting is the procedure used to evaluate, compare, and select projects with satisfactory cash flows.

2. Current expenditures are more favorable for tax purposes, because all expenditures can be written off in 1 year.

3. For capital budgeting, you need to know the initial investment and incremental cash flows.

4. Incremental cash flows are all you need to compare projects.

5. The amount by which the selling price exceeds the original purchase price is considered a capital gain and is taxed as ordinary income. The amount by which the purchase price exceeds the book value is considered a recapture of depreciation and is taxed at the marginal tax rate.

PRACTICAL APPLICATION

1. Cost of equipment	$300,000
Delivery expenses	6,000
Installation	10,000
Sale of old machine	(60,000)
*Tax on the sale of old machine	4,692
	$260,692

*Tax = 34% of recaptured depreciation

Recaptured depreciation = Selling price − Book value
$$= \$60,000 \quad - \$46,200 = \$13,800$$
Therefore, the tax, on the sale of the old machine is 34% × 13,800 = $4,692.

2. Year	New EBIT	Old EBIT	Additional EBIT
1	$210,000	$150,000	$ 60,000
2	290,000	190,000	100,000
3	380,000	340,000	40,000
4	490,000	450,000	40,000
5	710,000	550,000	160,000

Year	New Depreciation	Old Depreciation	Additional Depreciation	Additional Tax Benefit at 34%
1	$142,000	$95,000	$ 47,000	$15,980
2	227,200	75,000	152,200	51,748
3	134,900	70,000	64,900	22,066
4	106,500	0	106,500	36,210
5	99,400	0	99,400	33,796

Incremental cash flow = Additional EBIT + Additional tax benefit

Year	Incremental Cash Flow
1	$ 75,980
2	151,748
3	62,066
4	76,210
5	193,796

3.
Cost of new machine	$70,000
Installation and shipping fees	3,500
Sale of old machine	(10,000)
*Tax credit on sale of old machine	(2,312)
	$61,188

*Loss on sale of old machine = Selling price − Book value
$$= \$10,000 - \$16,800$$
$$= \$6,800$$
Tax credit on sale of old machine = .34 × $6,800
$$= \$2312$$

4. Cost of new machine $500,000
   Shipping fees   5,000
   Sale of old machine   (100,000)
   *Taxes on sale of old machine   25,500
                                                                                                 $430,500

$$\text{Recaptured depreciation} = \text{Purchase price} - \text{Book value}$$
$$\$100,000 - \$25,000$$
$$= \$75,000$$
$$\text{Tax on recaptured depreciation} = \$75,000 \times .34 = \$25,500$$

5. Year	Additional EBIT
1	$225,000 − $200,000 = $25,000
2	$305,000 − $215,000 = $90,000
3	$315,000 − $300,000 = $15,000

Year	New Depreciation	Old Depreciation	Additional Depreciation	Additional Tax Benefit at 34%
1	$303,600	$138,000	$165,600	$ 56,304
2	404,800	0	404,800	137,632
3	211,600	0	211,600	71,944

Year	Incremental Cash Flow
1	$ 81,304
2	227,632
3	86,944

7

CAPITAL BUDGETING METHODS: WITH NO RISK

KEY TERMS

average rate of return (ARR) the ratio of average net earnings to average investment

internal rate of return (IRR) the discount rate that makes the net present value of a project equal to zero

net present value (NPV) the present value of a project's future cash flow less the initial investment in the project

payback period the amount of time required to recover the initial investment in a project

profitability index (PI) the ratio of the present value of future cash flows from a project to the initial investment in the project

---

Capital budgeting refers to the methods for evaluating, comparing, and selecting projects to achieve maximum return or maximum wealth for stockholders. **Maximum return** is measured by profit, and **maximum wealth** is reflected in stock price.

This chapter covers a number of major capital-budgeting techniques. Some techniques focus on return (profit), while others emphasize wealth (stock price). The basic assumption of all capital-budgeting techniques discussed in this chapter is that risk, or uncertainty, is not a major problem for decision makers.

AVERAGE RATE OF RETURN (*ARR*)

Finding the **average rate of return** involves a simple accounting technique that determines the profitability of a project. This method of capital budgeting is perhaps the oldest technique used in business. The basic idea is to compare net earnings against initial costs of a project by adding all future net earnings together and dividing the sum by the average investment.

Example: Finding the Average Rate of Return

PROBLEM   Suppose that net earnings for the next 4 years are estimated to be $10,000, $15,000, $20,000, and $30,000, respectively. If the initial investment is $100,000, find the average rate of return.

SOLUTION   The average rate of return can be calculated as follows:

$$\textbf{1. Average net earnings} = \frac{\$10,000 + \$15,000 + \$20,000 + \$30,000}{4 \text{ years}}$$

$$= \frac{\$75,000}{4} = \$18,750$$

$$\textbf{2. Average investment} = \frac{\$100,000}{2} = \$50,000$$

3. Divide the average net earnings of $18,750 by the average investment of $50,000; you get approximately 38%. For example, the initial investment is assumed to be depreciated on a straight-line basis; therefore, we can use the short method of dividing the initial investment by 2 to arrive at the average investment.

The following formula is used to calculate the average rate of return:

$$\text{Average rate of return (ARR)} = \frac{\text{Average annual future net earnings}}{\text{One-half of initial investment}}$$

Keep in mind that, although the *ARR* concept is easy to understand and work with, this method is not recommended for financial analysis.

Why the *ARR* is Not Recommended for Financial Analysis

1. The *ARR* totally ignores the time value of money.

2. The *ARR* uses book earnings rather than cash flow; it ignores depreciation as a source of cash inflow.

3. The present value of salvaged equipment is not calculated in the average rate of return. Notice that salvage value can reduce the initial investment or increase cash inflow in the future. Therefore, the actual rate of return is underestimated when the salvage value is ignored in calculation.

4. *ARR* ignores the time sequence of net earnings.

Despite these four disadvantages, many financial analysts and managers still use the *ARR* because it is simple to calculate and easy to understand.

YOU SHOULD REMEMBER

The average rate of return is a very simple method that measures the profitability of a project, but it ignores cash flows and the time value of money.

PAYBACK PERIOD

The number of years needed to recover the initial investment is called the **payback period.** If the payback period is of an acceptable length of time to the firm, the project will be selected.

Suppose the maximum acceptable payback period for a firm is 4 years. Assume that a project brings an annual cash inflow of $20,000 for the next 6 years and that the initial investment is $70,000. A simple calculation shows that, after 4 years, the project will contribute an $80,000 cash inflow (4 years × $20,000 = $80,000). Therefore, it should be accepted, because its initial investment is covered in less than 4 years.

When comparing two or more projects, the projects with shorter payback periods are preferred. However, accepted projects should meet the target payback period, which should be set in advance. Keep in mind that cash inflow (net earnings + depreciation), rather than net earnings, should be used to calculate the payback period. In other words, a major difference between this method and the average rate of return is that net earnings are used for the average rate of return, whereas cash inflow should be used in calculating the payback period.

Example: Using the Payback Period to Evaluate a Project

PROBLEM   The ABC Co. plans to invest in a project that has a $3,700 initial outlay. It is estimated that the project will provide regular cash inflows of $1,000 in year 1, $2,000 in year 2, $1,500 in year 3, and $1,000 in year 4. If the company has a target payback period of 3 years, do you recommend that this project be accepted?

SOLUTION The above information should be rewritten in the following format:

Year	Cash Inflow
1	$1,000
2	2,000
3	1,500
4	1,000

You can see from the above information that after 2 years the firm will have recovered $3,000 of its $3,700 investment. Then, compute the portion of the third year the company willl need to recover the remaining $700 of its initial investment ($3,700 − $3,000 = $700). To do this, simply divide $700 by the cash inflow of the third year:

$$\frac{700}{1,500} = .47$$

In round terms, .47 of a year is approximately 24 weeks (.47 × 52 weeks = 24 weeks), making a total of 2 years and 24 weeks before the initial investment is recovered.

Next, compare this payback period with the target period to see if the company should proceed with the investment. In this case, the actual payback period (2 years and 24 weeks) is less than the target period of 3 years. Therefore, the project is acceptable.

ADVANTAGES AND DISADVANTAGES

The payback period method has several advantages and disadvantages. The main advantage is that this method is easy to use. It is not necessary to do a great deal of calculation to find out how many years it takes to get the initial outlay back. The payback period is also easy to understand. Therefore, when analysts need a quick measure of risk, they may use the payback period to see if the invested capital will be paid back in a reasonable period of time.

The payback period method, despite its simplicity, can be of value to even the largest multinational corporations. For such firms, political events—such as the nationalization of industry in a foreign country—are major sources of risk. In terms of possible political events, then, the shorter the payback period, the less risky the project. The payback period method, therefore, can help firms measure the risk of losing capital in foreign countries.

The main disadvantage of this method is that it completely ignores the value of money over time. In the payback period method, there is no difference between the value of a $100 cash inflow in the first year and the same amount of cash inflow in a later year. Additionally, the payback period method does not count the cash inflows produced after the initial investment has been recovered. Because of these severe drawbacks, the payback period method should not be considered as a very good approach to capital budgeting.

YOU SHOULD REMEMBER

The payback period method is widely used to find out how long it takes before the original capital, or initial investment, is recovered. This method is not recommended for two reasons: Like the average rate of return, it does not account for the value of time, nor does it serve as a measure of profitability (since cash flows after the payback period are ignored).

NET PRESENT VALUE (*NPV*)

If the present value of a project's future cash flow is greater than the initial cost, the project is worth undertaking. On the other hand, if the present value is less than the initial cost, a project should be rejected because the investor would lose money if the project were accepted. By definition, the **net present value** of an accepted project is zero or positive, and the net present value of a rejected project is negative. The net present value (*NPV*) of a project can be calculated as follows:

$$NPV = PV - I$$

where PV = present value
I = initial outlay

The critical point of this method is in deciding which discount rate to use in the calculation of the *NPV*. Between two projects, generally speaking, the one with a higher risk should be discounted at a higher rate. Moreover discount rates tend to increase along with interest and inflation rates. When the interest rate goes up, financing projects becomes more expensive; therefore, the cash flows of the projects should be discounted at a higher rate than when the interest rate is declining.

The discount rates used in the *NPV* are also influenced by the lengths of the given projects. Between two projects, the one with a longer life is usually associated with more risk. The further an investment is extended into the future, the more uncertainty is involved in the completion and operation of the project. Therefore, long-term projects should generally be discounted at a higher rate than short-term projects, all other things being equal.

Example: Using the NPV *to Evaluate a Project*

PROBLEM   The ABC Co. is considering an investment that will provide annual after-tax cash flows of $6,000, $4,000, $3,000, and $2,000, respectively, for 4 years. If the discount rate of the project is 10% and the initial investment is $9,000, do you recommend this project?

SOLUTION   **1.** Multiply the annual cash flows of the project by the present value interest factors—at 10%, for 4 individual years—as shown in the table.

Year	Cash Flow		PVIF at 10%		PV for Each Year
1	$6,000	×	.909	=	$ 5,454
2	4,000	×	.826	=	3,304
3	3,000	×	.751	=	2,253
4	2,000	×	.683	=	1,366
			PV of total cash flow of the project =		$12,377

2. Subtract the initial outlay of $9,000 from $12,377, to obtain the net present value of $3,377.

3. Since the net present value is positive, this project is recommended to the ABC Co.

ADVANTAGES AND DISADVANTAGES

The net present value method has three main advantages. First, it uses cash flows rather than net earnings. Cash flows (net earnings + depreciation) include depreciation as a source of funds. This works because depreciation is not a cash expenditure in the year the asset is depreciated. In contrast with accounting, the field of finance considers cash flows rather than net earnings. Therefore, the *NPV* approach, unlike the average rate of return method, is consistent with modern financial theory.

Second, the *NPV* method, unlike the average rate of return and the payback period methods, recognizes the time value of money. The longer the time, the higher the discount. Simply speaking, if the cash flows of a project with an average risk are discounted at 10%, another project with a higher degree of risk should be discounted at more than 10%. Therefore, the time value of money for a project is reflected in the discount rate, which should be selected carefully by the financial analyst. Generally, the discount rate tends to rise if the money supply is tight and the interest rate is expected to go up.

Third, by accepting only projects with positive *NPV*s, the company will also increase its value. An increase in the value of the company is, in fact, an increase in the stock price or in the wealth of stockholders. The *NPV* method of capital budgeting, therefore, should ultimately lead to more wealth for the owners of the company. Since the objective of modern finance is to continuously increase the wealth of stockholders, the *NPV* method should be viewed as the most modern technique of capital budgeting.

There are also some limitations, however, to the *NPV* approach. The method assumes that management is able to make detailed predictions of cash flows for future years. In reality, however, the more distant the date, the more difficult it is to estimate future cash flows. Future cash flows are influenced by future sales, costs of labor, materials and overhead, interest rates, consumer tastes, government policies, demographic changes, and so on. Overestimation or underestimation of future cash flows may lead to the acceptance of a project that should be rejected, or the rejection of a project that should be accepted. Additionally, the *NPV* approach usually assumes that the discount rate is the same over the life of the project. In the preceding example you discounted cash flows of all 4 years at 10%, but a discount rate of 10% for all 4 years may not be realistic. The discount rate of a project, like the interest rate, actually changes from one year to another. Opportunities to reinvest future cash flows, future interest rates, and the costs of raising new capital can all affect the discount rate. It may be suggested that the problem can be resolved by predicting future interest rates, and then discounting the cash flow of each future year at the predicted discount rate. While this is an intelligent suggestion, you may agree that the prediction of the interest rate for the next 5 or 10 years is as uncertain as the outcome of flipping a coin 5 or 10 times! Despite its limitations, however, the *NPV* method is still the best method of capital budgeting.

PROFITABILITY INDEX (*PI*)

The **profitability index,** or *PI,* method compares the present value of future cash inflows with the initial investment on a relative basis. Therefore, the *PI* is the ratio of the present value of cash flows *(PVCF)* to the initial investment of a project:

$$PI = \frac{PVCF}{\text{Initial investment}}$$

In this method, a project with a *PI* greater than 1 is accepted, but a project is rejected when its *PI* is less than 1. Note that the *PI* method is closely related to the *NPV* approach. In fact, if the net present value of a project is positive, the *PI* will be greater than 1. On the other hand, if the net present value is negative, the project will have a *PI* of less than 1. The same conclusion is reached, therefore, whether the net present value or the *PI* is used. In other words, if the present value of cash flows exceeds the initial investment, there is a positive net present value and a *PI* greater than 1, indicating that the project is acceptable.

Example: Using the PI *to Evaluate a Project*

PROBLEM   The ABC Co. is considering a project with annual predicted cash flows of $5,000, $3,000, and $4,000, respectively, for 3 years. The initial investment is $10,000. Using the *PI* method and a discount rate of 12%, determine if the project is acceptable.

SOLUTION   To determine the *PI*, the present value of cash flows should be divided by the initial cost:

Year	Cash Flow (a)	PVIF @12% (b)	PV of Cash Flow (a)(b)
1	$5,000	.893	$4,465
2	3,000	.797	2,391
3	4,000	.712	2,848
		PV of the project =	$9,704

The present value of the project is $9,704. Dividing this figure by the initial investment of $10,000 gives a *PI* of .9704. Since the *PI* value is less than 1, the project is rejected.

The *NPV* of the project can also be determined if the initial investment of $10,000 is subtracted from the present value of $9,704. In this case, the *NPV* is −$296. Since the *NPV* is negative, it is concluded, as with the *PI* method, that the project is not worth undertaking.

An important comment about the *PI* and the *NPV* methods is that, although the two techniques generally lead to the same major decision—whether to accept or reject a project—they often rank alternative projects in different orders.

YOU SHOULD REMEMBER

The net present value and the profitability index are reliable methods for evaluating a project or comparing two or more projects. The *NPV* method compares the present value of a project's future cash flows to its initial cost by means of a simple criterion: Which is the larger figure? The *PI* method compares the same figures, but in the form of a ratio. If *PI* is equal to 1.0 or is greater than 1.0, then accept the project. If *PI* is less than 1.0, reject the project. Financial analysts should be very careful in choosing the discount rate that is most suitable for evaluating the projects.

INTERNAL RATE OF RETURN (*IRR*)

The **internal rate of return,** or *IRR,* is a popular measure used in capital budgeting. The *IRR* is a measure of the rate of profitability. By definition, *IRR* is a discount rate that makes the present value of cash flows equal to the initial investment. In simple terms, the *IRR* is a discount rate that makes the *NPV* equal to zero. The rate below which projects are rejected is called the **cutoff rate,** the target rate, the hurdle rate, or the required rate of return. Firms determine their cutoff rates by the cost of financing and the riskiness of the project. Next, they predict future cash flows and calculate the *IRR.* If the calculated *IRR* exceeds the cutoff rate, the project is added to the list of recommended investments.

Example: Using the IRR *to Evaluate a Project*

PROBLEM   A company has annual cash flows of $5,000 for 6 years. The initial investment is $20,555. Determine the *IRR* of this project.

SOLUTION   First, find a discount rate that makes the present value of the 6-year cash flow equal to an initial investment of $20,555. The unknown discount rate is the value of the *IRR.* First, divide $20,555 by $5,000; 4.111 is the answer.

Next, look at a present value annuity table and read the present value factors for 6 periods. You can easily see that 4.111 is the present value factor at the rate of 12% for 6 periods. This 12% rate is the *IRR* value for the project. If the cutoff rate is 10%, the project will be accepted. By the same token, if the cutoff rate is more than 12%, the project will be rejected.

In the above example, the cash flows were constant. In the case of constant cash flows, the procedure requires only two simple steps.

Calculating *IRR*s with Constant Cash Flows

1. Divide the initial investment by the annual cash flow to obtain a figure (such as 4.111 in the preceding example).

2. Refer to a present value annuity table and look for a discount rate at the specified number of years that matches the figure obtained in step 1. The matching discount rate you find in the table is the *IRR* of the project.

For projects with changing annual cash flows, the procedure becomes one of trial and error. In other words, the cash flows must be discounted at various rates until a rate is found that makes the present value equal to the initial investment. In practice, the *IRR*s of changing cash flows can easily be determined by the use of computers. A numerical example will help make the manual procedure easy and understandable.

Example: Calculating IRRs *with Variable Cash Flows*

PROBLEM   A company is considering an investment with predicted annual cash flows for the next 3 years of $1,000, $4,000, and $5,000, respectively. The initial investment is $7,650. If the cutoff rate is 11%, is the project acceptable?

SOLUTION   At this point, you should realize that the cash flows of the project are not an annuity. Therefore, the present value annuity table cannot be used. Instead, each cash flow should be discounted separately. Starting with an arbitrary number—10%—find the present value cash flows of the 3 years individually and then add them:

Year	Cash Flow (a)	PVIF at 10% (b)	PV of Cash Flow (a)(b)
1	$1,000	.909	$ 909
2	4,000	.826	3,304
3	5,000	.751	3,755
			Total PV = $7,968

The above calculations show that the present values of cash flows for all 3 years add up to $7,968, which is higher than the initial investment of $7,650. Therefore, the discount rate should be raised to get a present value closer to the initial investment. (Remember from Chapter 3 that present value decreases when the discount rate increases.) Try a discount rate of 12%:

Year	Cash Flow	PVIF at 12%	PV of Cash Flow
1	$1,000	.893	$ 893
2	4,000	.797	3,188
3	5,000	.712	3,560
			Total PV = $7,641

You can see that a 12% discount rate makes the present value of future cash flows almost equal to the initial investment of $7,650. This tell us that the *IRR* of the project is very close to 12%. Since the cutoff rate for accepting a project is 11%, and the *IRR* is 12%, you can accept the project.

ADVANTAGES AND DISADVANTAGES

A number of surveys have shown that, in practice, the *IRR* method is more popular than the *NPV* approach. The reason may be that the *IRR* is straightforward, like the *ARR*, but it uses cash flows and recognizes the time value of money, like the *NPV*. In other words, while the *IRR* is easy and understandable, it does not have the drawbacks of the *ARR* and the payback period, both of which ignore the time value of money.

The main problem with the *IRR* method is that it often gives unrealistic rates of return. Suppose the cutoff rate is 11% and the *IRR* is calculated as 40%. Does this mean that management should immediately accept the project because its *IRR* is 40%? The answer is *no*! An *IRR* of 40% assumes that a firm has the opportunity to reinvest future cash flows at 40%. If past experience and the economy indicate that 40% is an unrealistic rate for future reinvestments, an *IRR* of 40% is suspect. Simply speaking, an *IRR* of 40% is too good to be true! So unless the calculated *IRR* is a reasonable rate for reinvestment of future cash flows, it should not be used as a yardstick to accept or reject a project.

Another problem with the *IRR* method is that it may give different rates of return. Suppose there are two discount rates (two *IRR*s) that make the present value equal to the initial investment. In this case, which rate should be used for comparison with the cutoff rate? The purpose of this question is not to resolve the cases where there are different *IRR*s. The purpose is to let you know that the *IRR* method, despite its popularity in the business world, entails more problems than a practitioner may think.

WHY THE *NPV* AND *IRR* SOMETIMES SELECT DIFFERENT PROJECTS

When comparing two projects, the use of the *NPV* and the *IRR* methods may give different results. A project selected according to the *NPV* may be rejected if the *IRR* method is used.

Suppose there are two alternative projects, X and Y. The initial investment in each project is $2,500. Project X will provide annual cash flows of $500 for the next 10 years. Project Y has annual cash flows of $100, $200, $300, $400, $500, $600, $700, $800, $900, and $1,000 in the same period. Using the trial and error method explained before, you find that the *IRR* of Project X is 17% and the *IRR* of Project Y is around 13%. If you use the *IRR*, Project X should be preferred because its *IRR* is 4% more than the *IRR* of Project Y. But what happens to your decision if the *NPV* method is used? The answer is that the decision will change depending on the discount rate you use. For instance, at a 5% discount rate, Project Y has a higher *NPV* than X does. But at a discount rate of 8%, Project X is preferred because of a higher *NPV*.

The purpose of this numerical example is to illustrate an important distinction: The use of the *IRR* always leads to the selection of the same project, whereas project selection using the *NPV* method depends on the discount rate chosen.

PROJECT SIZE AND LIFE

There are reasons why the *NPV* and the *IRR* are sometimes in conflict: the size and life of the project being studied are the most common ones. A 10-year project with an initial investment of $100,000 can hardly be compared with a small 3-year project costing $10,000. Actually, the large project could be thought of as ten small projects. So if you insist on using the *IRR* and the *NPV* methods to compare a big, long-term project with a small, short-term project, don't be surprised if you get different selection results.

DIFFERENT CASH FLOWS

Furthermore, even two projects of the same length may have different patterns of cash flow. The cash flow of one project may continuously increase over time, while the cash flows of the other project may increase, decrease, stop, or become negative. These two projects have completely different forms of cash flow, and if the discount rate is changed when using the *NPV* approach, the result will probably be different orders of ranking. For example, at 10% the *NPV* of Project A may be higher than that of Project B. As soon as you change the discount rate to 15%, Project B may be more attractive.

• *WHEN ARE THE* NPV *AND* IRR *RELIABLE?*

Generally speaking, you can use and rely on both the *NPV* and the *IRR* if two conditions are met. First, if projects are compared using the *NPV*, a discount rate that fairly reflects the risk of each project should be chosen. There is no problem if two projects are discounted at two different rates because one project is riskier than the other. Remember that the result of the *NPV* is as reliable as the discount rate that is chosen. If the discount rate is unrealistic, the decision to accept or reject the project is baseless and unreliable. Second, if the *IRR* method is used, the project must not be accepted only because its *IRR* is very high. Management must ask if such an impressive *IRR* is possible to maintain. In other words, management should look into past records, and existing and future business, to see if an opportunity to reinvest cash flows at such a high *IRR* really exists. If the firm is convinced that such an *IRR* is realistic, the project is acceptable. Otherwise, the project must be reevaluated by the *NPV* method, using a more realistic discount rate.

YOU SHOULD REMEMBER

The internal rate of return (*IRR*) is a popular method in capital budgeting. The *IRR* is a discount rate that makes the present value of estimated cash flows equal to the initial investment. However, when using the *IRR*, you should make sure that the calculated *IRR* is not very different from a realistic reinvestment rate.

KNOW THE CONCEPTS

DO YOU KNOW THE BASICS?

1. Explain in your own words why a positive net present value means that a project is worth undertaking.

2. The *NPV* and *IRR* methods may give different answers in terms of accepting or rejecting projects. Explain the reasons for the conflict, and discuss how the conflict can be resolved.

3. Do the *NPV* and *PI* methods give the same answers in terms of accepting or rejecting projects? Discuss.

4. Which method is superior: *NPV* or payback period? Why?

5. Which method is superior: *NPV* or *IRR*?

TERMS FOR STUDY

average rate of return (*ARR*)	maximum wealth
cutoff rate	net present value (*NPV*)
internal rate of return (*IRR*)	payback period
maximum return	profitability index (*PI*)

PRACTICAL APPLICATION

COMPUTATIONAL PROBLEMS

1. The net earnings of a company for the next 3 years are estimated to be $12,000, $13,000, and $18,000, respectively. Determine the average rate of return if the initial outlay is $80,000.

2. The cash flows of a project are estimated to be as follows:

Year	Cash Flow
1	$2,000
2	4,000
3	6,000
4	5,000
5	1,000

The initial outlay of the project is $14,000. Assuming that the company has a target payback period of 3 years, determine if the project is acceptable.

3. The initial investment of a project is $110,000. Following are the estimated cash flows:

Year	Cash Flow
1	$30,000
2	40,000
3	20,000
4	40,000
5	50,000

Using the *NPV* method and a discount rate of 12%, determine if the project is acceptable.

4. Using the information in Problem 3, determine the profitability index of the project. Explain your findings.

5. A project has annual cash flows of $7,000 for 7 years. The initial investment is $28,500. What is the project's *IRR*?

6. The ABC Co. has to select either Project 1 or Project 2. The projects have the following cash flows:

	Cash Flow	
Year	Project 1	Project 2
0	−$24,000	−$24,000
1	+ 11,000	0
2	+ 11,000	0
3	+ 11,000	0
4	+ 11,000	0
5	+ 11,000	+ 68,000

Using the *NPV* and *IRR* methods, determine which project is preferred. Assume a discount rate of 10%.

7. Using trial and error, determine approximately the *IRR* of the following cash flows:

Year	Cash Flow
0	$1,200
1	780
2	190
3	390

Is this project acceptable if the cutoff rate is 14%?

8. Using the profitability index, rank the following possible investments and discuss their profitabilities:

Investment	Initial Investment	Present Value
A	$100,000	$120,000
B	150,000	180,000
C	200,000	220,000
D	400,000	320,000
E	10,000	30,000
F	280,000	305,000

9. Using the information in Problem 8, rank the listed projects according to their net present values.

ANSWERS

KNOW THE CONCEPTS

1. A positive *NPV* means an excess of return over cost. Therefore, projects with positive *NPVs* should be accepted.

2. Possible reasons for a conflict between the *IRR* and *NPV* are as follows: different sizes and/or lives of the projects to be compared, different patterns of cash flows, and faulty assumptions about reinvestment rates. To help resolve the conflict, the reinvestment rate or the selected discount rate must be realistic.

3. *NPV* and *PI* give the same answers in terms of accepting or rejecting a project, yet they can give different orders of ranking.

4. *NPV*, because it considers the time value of money.

5. *NPV*, because it does not have the problem of multiple rates and the assumption of a reinvestment rate.

PRACTICAL APPLICATION

1. Average net earnings $= \dfrac{(\$12,000 + \$13,000 + \$18,000)}{3} = \$14,333$

   Average investment $= \dfrac{\$80,000}{2} = \$40,000$

   Average rate of return $= \dfrac{\$14,333}{\$40,000} = 36\%$

2. After 3 years, only $12,000 of the $14,000 initial outlay is recovered. Therefore, the project is not acceptable.

3. Net present value = Present value − Initial investment
   Present value = $30,000(.8929) + $40,000(.7972) + $20,000(.7118)
   $$+ \$40,000(.6355) + \$50,000(.5674) = \$126,701$$
   Net present value = $126,701 − $110,000 = $16,701
   Since the *NPV* is positive, the project is acceptable.

4. $PI = \dfrac{PV}{\text{Initial investment}} = \dfrac{\$126,701}{\$110,000} = 1.15$
   The project is acceptable because *PI* > 1.

5. $\dfrac{\$28,500}{\$7000} = 4.07$. The *PVIFA* table for 7 years shows that the *IRR* is about 16%.

6. *NPV* of Project 1 = $11,000(*PVIFA*) − $24,000
   $$\underset{10\%,\ 5}{}$$
   $$= \$11,000(3.791) - \$24,000 = \$17,701$$
   NPV of Project 2 = $68,000(*PVIF*) − $24,000
   $$\underset{10\%,\ 5}{}$$
   $$= \$68,000(.621) - \$24,000 = \$18,228$$
   Thus, Project 2 is preferred.

7. *PV* at 10% = $780(.9091) + $190(.8264) + $390(.7513) = $1,159
   The *IRR* is close to 10%. Therefore, the project is not acceptable.

8.

Rank	Project	PI
1	E	3
2	A, B	1.2
3	C	1.1
4	F	1.09
5	D	.80

Project D is unacceptable because its *PI* is less than 1. The other projects are acceptable as their *PI*s are greater than 1.

9.

Rank	Project	NPV
1	B	$30,000
2	F	25,000
3	A, C, E	20,000
4	D	−80,000

8
CAPITAL BUDGETING METHODS: WITH RISK

RISK IN CAPITAL BUDGETING

Risk is another word for uncertainty and instability. An investment is called **risk-free** if its return is stable and reliable. Investors usually think of the treasury bill, which is a U.S. government security, as a risk-free investment, mainly because its return is certain and guaranteed.

In capital budgeting, there is no such thing as a risk-free project. The future cash flows of a project may unexpectedly decrease or increase. The rate at which future cash flows are invested may not remain the same, as was assumed in earlier chapters. There are many other factors that may reduce expected cash flows: loss of market share, an increase in the cost of goods sold, new environmental regulations, a rising cost of financing. Since there is always risk in capital budgeting, a major job of investment analysts is to select projects under conditions of uncertainty.

CERTAINTY EQUIVALENT APPROACH (CEA)

The idea behind the certainty equivalent approach is to separate the timing of cash flows from their riskiness. Cash flows are converted into riskless (certain) cash flows, which are then discounted at a **risk-free rate.** The rate on a U.S. treasury bill is accepted as risk-free and is the rate generally used.

Calculating Certain Equivalents

1. Estimate the expected cash flows of the project.

2. Determine the **certainty equivalent factors,** or the percentages of the expected cash flows that are certain.

3. Calculate the certain cash flows by multiplying the expected cash flows by the certainty equivalent factors.

4. Calculate the present value of the project by discounting the certain cash flows at a risk-free discount rate—the return on U.S. treasury bills, for example.

5. Determine the net present value of the project by subtracting the initial investment from the present value of the certain cash flows.

6. If the *NPV* is either zero or positive, the project is acceptable. Conversely, the project should be rejected if the *NPV* is negative.

Example: Calculating Certain Equivalents

PROBLEM   The XYZ Co. has estimated that annual cash flows in the next 5 years will be $7,000, $6,000, $5,000, $4,000, and $3,000, respectively. The certainty equivalent factors for the same periods are estimated at 95%, 80%, 70%, 60%, and 40%. The initial investment of the project is $11,000. The risk-free rate (return on the U.S. treasury bill) is 10%. Using the certainty equivalent approach, decide if the project is acceptable.

SOLUTION   First, you should convert expected cash flows into certain cash flows. This can be done by multiplying the expected cash flows by the certainty equivalent factors, as given:

Year	Expected Cash Flow	Certainty Equivalent Factors	Certain Cash Flow
1	$7,000	.95	$6,650
2	6,000	.80	4,800
3	5,000	.70	3,500
4	4,000	.60	2,400
5	3,000	.40	1,200

Once you have the certain cash flows, discount them at the risk-free rate of 10%. (Note: Certain cash flows should be discounted *only* at the risk-free rate. Remember that these cash flows are supposed to be certain.) Using a present value table, you then calculate the present values of the certain cash flows:

Year	Certain Cash Flow	PVIF at 10%	PV of Certain Cash Flow
1	$6,650	.909	$ 6,044.85
2	4,800	.826	3,964.80
3	3,500	.751	2,628.50
4	2,400	.683	1,639.20
5	1,200	.621	745.20
		PV of total certain cash flows =	$15,022.55

The present value of certain cash flows from this project is $15,022.55. Subtracting the initial investment of $11,000 from $15,022.55, you determine the *NPV* of the project to be $4,022.55. By now, of course, you know that a positive *NPV* means that the project is worth undertaking. Therefore, the XYZ Co. should accept this investment.

YOU SHOULD REMEMBER

The certainty equivalent approach (CEA) converts expected cash flows into certain cash flows and discounts them at a risk-free rate.

SENSITIVITY ANALYSIS

Sensitivity analysis is a popular way to find out how the *NPV* of a project changes if sales, labor or material costs, the discount rate, or other factors vary from one case to another. In simple terms, **sensitivity analysis** is a "what if" study. For example, you might be interested in knowing what happens to the *NPV* of a project if cash flow increases by 10%, 20%, or 30% each year. Will the *NPV* still be positive if there is no cash flow in the second year? Which project's *NPV* will fall more sharply if the discount rate goes up from 8% to 11%? These are the kinds of questions financial analysts raise when they want to measure the risk of a project through sensitivity analysis. Remember from the preceding chapters that risk is measured by variation. The more variation or change there is in the *NPV* of a project, the more risky that investment would be.

Example: Using Sensitivity Analysis

PROBLEM   Suppose the cash flows of Project A are $1,000 in year 1 and $1,500 in year 2. Project B has expected cash flows of $1,800 in year 1 and $700 in year 2. The initial investment for each project is $1,600. Which project is more risky if the discount rate changes from 10% to 12%.

SOLUTION   To answer this question, first find out the *NPV* of each project at 10%. Using the *NPV* method that you learned in Chapter 7, you determine that the *NPV* of Project A at 10% is $548, and the *NPV* of Project B at the same rate is $614. (Review: Multiply the cash flows by the present value factors at 10%, add up the answers, and then subtract the initial investment of $1,600.) To see the changes in the *NPVs* of these two projects, you should now calculate the *NPVs* of the cash flows at a new rate. Using the same method, you find that the *NPV* of Project A at 12% is $489, and the *NPV* of Project B at the same rate is $565. Summarize the results:

Project	NPV at 10%	NPV at 12%	Percentage Change in NPV
A	$548	$489	−10.77
B	$614	$565	−7.98

By looking at the above figures, you can see that the *NPVs* of both projects decline when the discount rate rises from 10% to 12%. The sensitivity analysis method, however, poses an additional important question that helps to compare the degrees of risk of these two projects: Which project's *NPV* has a higher percentage of change if the discount rate increases from 10% to 12%? Comparing the above figures, you see that the percentage change in the *NPV* of Project A is -12%, while that of Project B is -9%. Therefore, Project A is more sensitive to a change in the discount rate. In other words, Project A is riskier than project B if the discount rate changes in the future.

YOU SHOULD REMEMBER

Sensitivity analysis measures *NPV, IRR,* and other indicators of profit or risk as sales, costs, the discount rate, or other variables change. The purpose is to find out how sensitive the *NPV* or the *IRR* is to a change in one variable. Of two projects, the one more sensitive to a change is the project considered to have more risk.

THE CAPM IN CAPITAL BUDGETING

The capital asset pricing model (CAPM) was introduced in Chapter 4, where it was used to find the required rate of return on a stock or portfolio. The calculation is very simple if the return on a risk-free asset, beta (β) of the stock or portfolio, and return on the market portfolio are known. The simple equation given in Chapter 4 was

$$K_e = R_f + \beta(K_m - R_f)$$

where K_e = required rate of return
β = beta of the stock
R_f = risk-free rate
K_m = return on a market portfolio

In this chapter the same equation, with only slightly different notation, is used:

$$K_p = R_f + \beta_p(K_m - R_f)$$

where K_p = required rate of return on the project being evaluated
β_p = beta of the project

Other notations are the same as before. This method considers a project as it would a share of stock, arguing that the return from a project is linked to the return on the total assets of the company, or to the return in an industry. If you believe that the project being studied has the same basic risk level as a typical project of the company, you can use the beta of the company as the beta of the project.

Example: Using the CAPM in Capital Budgeting

PROBLEM   Suppose you want to find the *NPV* of a project, but you have no idea what discount rate to use. You do know, however, that the beta of the company is 1.50, the risk-free rate is 8%, and the return on a market portfolio, such as Dow-Jones, is 16%. You also believe that the risk of the project is not much different from the risk of other company projects.

SOLUTION   Since you believe the risks to be similar, you can say that the beta, or the relevant risk, of the project should be close to the beta of the company, which is 1.50.

    Using $K_p = R_f + \beta_p(K_m - R_f)$ and plugging in the given information, you find that the required rate of return on the project will be

$$K_p = .08 + 1.50(.16 - .08) = .20 \text{ or } 20\%$$

    Once you have determined the project's required rate of return—20%—the *NPV* calculation is exactly the same as in preceding chapters. To obtain the *NPV* of the project, discount expected cash flows at 20% and subtract the total present value of cash flows from the initial investment. If the *NPV* is zero or positive, you can accept the project simply because the 20% required rate of return will be maintained.

What happens if a project is not a typical investment of the company? In other words, how can you use the CAPM for a project whose risk and other characteristics are different from average or routine projects that the company undertakes? In this case, you should look into similar projects outside the firm. For instance, if a firm is considering investing in the aluminum industry, the beta for the new project should be the average beta for a group of firms in the aluminum industry. Five other firms in the aluminum industry might have betas of .80, 1.25, 1.10, 1.20, and 1.90. Taking the average of these sample betas, you can say that your project has a beta of 1.25 (.80 + 1.10 + 1.20 + 1.25 + 1.90)/5.

YOU SHOULD REMEMBER

The CAPM calculates the required rate of return for a project. Required rates of return are calculated by the use of the regular equation for the CAPM; of two projects, the one with a higher beta is considered more risky. If a project is similar to other investments in the company, the beta of the company's stock can be used as the beta of the project. Otherwise, the average beta of a group of companies with similar projects should represent the beta of the project.

SIMULATION TECHNIQUES

The word **simulation** comes from the Latin word *similis*, which means "like." Accordingly, the idea behind simulation is basically to make hypothetical situations like real ones. Since the actual cash flows or discount rate that will exist in the future are not known, various cash flows and discount rates are assumed, and the results are studied. These cases based on assumptions are called simulated events. Simulated events in capital budgeting are used to study the *NPVs* or the *IRRs* of a project for different cash flows at different reinvestment rates. After different *NPVs* are computed, the average *NPV* and standard deviation of the project are studied to see if the project is worth undertaking.

If you have more than one project, you can simulate the *NPV* or the *IRR* of each project a number of times and compute the average *NPVs* or *IRRs* and standard deviations. Then rank the projects, starting with the one that has the highest *NPV* or *IRR* and the lowest standard deviation. Ranking projects is much easier if you first divide the average standard deviation by the average *NPV* of each simulated project. The result, as you may remember from Chapter 4, is the coefficient of variation. Finally, rank the projects according to their coefficients of variation, giving the highest rank to the project with the lowest coefficient.

Example: Using Simulation Methods in Capital Budgeting

PROBLEM   Suppose the simulated *NPVs* for Project A are $100, $300, $800, $700, and $600, with corresponding standard deviations of 10, 18, 78, 68, and 50. The simulated *NPVs* for Project B are $300, $150, $700, $640, and $800, with corresponding standard deviations of 62, 29, 98, 102, and 130. Based on the simulated figures, which project is more attractive?

SOLUTION   A simple approach is to calculate the average *NPV* and the average standard deviation of each project:

Project	Average Simulated NPV (x)	Average Simulated Standard Deviation (y)	Simulated Coefficient of Variation (y/x)
A	$500	$45	9%
B	$518	$84	16%

The results of the preceding tabulation indicate that the simulated coefficient of variation (*CV*) for Project A is smaller than for Project B (9% vs. 16%). Since the smaller the *CV* the better the project from a risk-return trade-off basis, then Project A is more attractive than Project B.

Given the fact that both projects have the same average *NPV*, it is evident that Project A's dispersion away from the average simulated value of *NPV* is smaller than Project B's dispersion. (See Figure 8–1.)

The area under curve A is smaller than the one under curve B. This suggests that NPV_B is less certain than NPV_A. By looking at these simulated probability curves, you can see that Project A's *NPV* is less volatile and, therefore, less risky than Project B.

There is a variety of **simulation software** for various personal computers. These programs use variables at random and calculate many more scenarios than anyone would do by hand. The results can also be used to draw curves to show the distribution of the *NPV*s or the *IRR*s. The shapes of distribution curves help financial analysts get a good idea about the riskiness of a project. Figure 8–1 shows the distribution curve of simulated *NPV*s for Projects A and B.

Project A has a steeper curve, which indicates less risk and a higher average *NPV* than Project B. The area under curve A is narrow; the probable *NPV*s do not

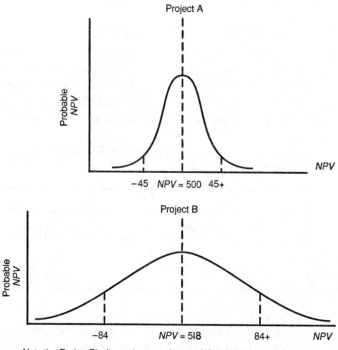

Note that Project B's dispersion away from its *NPV* of 500 is almost twice as large as the dispersion for Project A

Figure 8–1 NPV Simulation Curves

vary very much. Project B has a broader curve, which suggests that its *NPV* is very uncertain. Therefore, by looking at the simulated curves, you can get a clearer idea that Project A is a better choice.

YOU SHOULD REMEMBER

Simulation measures the risk and return of a project. A number of computer packages are currently available to run simulations for project selection. Some of these computer packages will compute results and draw graphs for different assumptions.

ADJUSTING FOR INFLATION

Inflation is a general price increase in the economy. When inflation increases, the real value of expected cash flows decreases. If the analyst does not adjust for risk of inflation, the *NPV* or the *IRR* may be artificially high. In other words, you might accept a project with an unadjusted *IRR* or *NPV*, while the real *IRR* or *NPV*, adjusted for inflation, could be unacceptable. Therefore, capital budgeting techniques that ignore inflation are often misleading. Since inflation has probably become a permanent problem in the economy, you should plan to deal with it anytime you make a major decision.

How can you deal with inflation in capital budgeting? The answer is that you should adjust both the cash flows and the discount rate for the annual rate of inflation.

Example: Adjusting the NPV *for Inflation*

PROBLEM   In 1985, the annual cash flows of a project for the following 3 years are estimated to be $1,000, $2,000, and $3,000. These estimated cash flows are in 1985 dollars. The discount rate is 13%, and the annual rate of inflation is 6%. The initial outlay, or initial investment, of the project is $4,000. What is the *NPV* of this project after adjusting for inflation?

SOLUTION

1   Since the estimated cash flows are in 1985 dollars, you should adjust these amounts for inflation. However, the discount rate of 13% includes a 6% inflation rate. Using a short method, subtract the 6% inflation rate from the discount rate of 13%, getting 7%, which is the real discount rate. Discount the cash flows—which are in 1985 dollars—at 7%, and subtract the initial outlay:

Year	Cash Flow	PVIF at 7%	PV of Cash Flow
1	$1,000	.935	$ 935
2	2,000	.873	1,746
3	3,000	.816	2,448
		Total *PV* at a real discount rate of 7% =	$5,129
		Subtract the initial investment:	−4,000
		NPV adjusted for inflation =	$1,129

SOLUTION

2 Another way of adjusting for inflation is to increase expected cash flows at a 6% annual rate of inflation, and then discount the inflated cash flows at 13%:

Year	Cash Flow Inflated at 6%	PVIF at 13%	PV of Cash Flows
1	$1,060	.885	$ 938
2	2,247	.783	1,759
3	3,573	.693	2,476
		Total *PV* at a discount rate of 13% =	$5,173
		Subtract the initial investment:	−4,000
		NPV adjusted for inflation =	$1,173

As you can see from the preceding example, the *NPV*s of the project are not necessarily the same using the two methods. The project in this example was found acceptable in both calculations, because the *NPV* is positive. However, it is a good idea to use the two methods and compare the *NPV* results. When the *NPV*s are different in these two methods, conservative financial analysts usually use the lower *NPV* as a more reliable figure upon which to base decisions.

YOU SHOULD REMEMBER

There are two methods of adjustment for inflation in capital budgeting. One method is to discount deflated cash flows at a deflated discount rate. The second method is to discount inflated cash flows at an inflated discount rate. Both methods should be tried to examine the effect of inflation on the *NPV* of the project.

KNOW THE CONCEPTS

DO YOU KNOW THE BASICS?

1. Define risk. How can risk be measured?
2. What is a major difference between the CEA and the *NPV* techniques? Do they lead to the same accept/reject decision in capital budgeting?
3. What is sensitivity analysis?
4. How can the CAPM be used in capital budgeting under risk?
5. What is the purpose of simulation in capital budgeting?
6. In practice, how do you find the beta of a project?
7. How can you resolve the problem of inflation in capital budgeting decisions?

TERMS OF STUDY

certainty equivalent factor
inflation
risk
risk-free

risk-free rate
sensitivity analysis
simulation
simulation software

PRACTICAL APPLICATION

COMPUTATIONAL PROBLEMS

1. Using the certainty equivalent approach, determine whether the following project is acceptable:

Year	Cash Flow of Project	Certainty Equivalent Factors
1	$2,000	.93
2	3,000	.91
3	4,000	.80
4	8,000	.75

The intial investment is $15,000. The rate of return on a U.S. treasury bill is 8%.

2. Project M has cash flows of $2,000 in year 1 and $2,500 in year 2. Project N has cash flows of $3,000 in year 1 and $1,500 in year 2. The initial outlay for each project is $2,200. Using sensitivity analysis, determine which project is more risky if the discount rate increases from 12% to 14%.

3. Determine the *NPV* of the following project using the CAPM model:

Year	Cash Flows of Project
0	−$10,000
1	+ 4,000
2	+ 8,000
3	+ 2,000

The rate of return on a market portfolio is 14%, the beta of the project is 1.70, and the risk-free rate is 7%.

4. Company ABC has run five simulations for Projects X, Y, and Z. The results are as follows:

Project X		Project Y		Project Z	
NPV	Standard Dev.	NPV	Standard Dev.	NPV	Standard Dev.
$150	12	$100	34	$100	11
250	17	300	41	200	35
450	21	500	27	300	51
650	20	700	31	700	68
850	33	900	18	900	63

Based on these simulations, which project should the company accept?

5. It is estimated that a project will generate cash flows over the next 5 years of $4,000, $8,000, $12,000, $15,000, and $18,000. The discount rate is 12%, annual inflation is 7%, and the initial investment is $10,000. Using both (a) the deflation and (b) the inflation methods to adjust for inflation, find the adjusted *NPV* on which to base your decisions about the project.

ANSWERS

KNOW THE CONCEPTS

1. Risk means uncertainty and instability. The future cash flows of a project may unexpectedly decrease or increase. The discount rate in the market may rise or decline, leading to a lower or higher price of stock and other financial securities. Risk can be measured by standard deviation, beta analysis in CAPM, and simulation techniques.

2. In the *NPV* method, uncertain cash flows are discounted at a rate appropriate to the level of risk in the project. In the certainty equivalent approach, certain cash

flows are discounted at a risk-free rate. Theoretically, both methods should give the same results.

3. Sensitivity analysis is a technique used to measure risk. The purpose is to estimate net earnings, cash flows, the *NPV*, the stock price, and so on when one or more variables change.

4. When the discount rate is not given, the CAPM can be used to determine a required rate of return: $K_s = R_f + \beta(\overline{K}_m - R_f)$. This rate ($K_s$) can be used as a discount rate in the *NPV* analysis.

5. The purpose of simulation in capital budgeting is to determine which project has a more stable *NPV*, *IRR*, or *PI* when the values of cash flow, discount rate, and other factors change.

6. The beta of a project is approximately equal to the beta of the company's stock. If the project is not a regular one, then the average beta of several companies engaged in similar projects could be used.

7. The problem of inflation in capital budgeting can be partially resolved by taking one of the following approaches:

   (a) Discount deflated cash flows at a deflated discount rate.
   (b) Discount inflated cash flows at an inflated discount rate.

PRACTICAL APPLICATION

1.

Year	Cash Flows	Certainty Equivalent Factor	Certain Cash Flows	PVIF at 8%	PV of Certain Cash Flows
1	$2,000	.93	$1,860	.9259	$ 1,722
2	3,000	.91	2,730	.8573	2,340
3	4,000	.80	3,200	.7938	2,540
4	8,000	.75	6,000	.7350	4,410
				PV at 8% =	$11,012

$NPV = \$11,012 - \$15,000 = -\$3,988$
The project has a negative *NPV*. Thus, it is rejected.

2. *NPV* of Project M at 12% = $1,578
   NPV of Project M at 14% = $1,478

   $$\% \text{ Change in } NPV \text{ of Project M} = \frac{(\$1,478 - \$1,578)}{\$1,578} = -6.3\%$$

   NPV of Project N at 12% = $1,674
   NPV of Project N at 14% = $1,586

   $$\% \text{ Change in } NPV \text{ of Project N} = \frac{(\$1,586 - \$1,674)}{\$1,674} = -5.3\%$$

   Project M is more risky because it has a higher percentage change in *NPV*.

3. $K_s = R_f + \beta(K_m - R_f) = .07 + 1.70(.14 - .07) = 18.9\%$, or 19%
Therefore, cash flows must be discounted at 19% and subtracted from the initial investment of $10,000.
$4,000(.840) + \$8,000(.706) + \$2000(.593) - \$10,000 = \$3,360 + \$5,648 + \$1,186 - \$10,000 = \$194$. Since the *NPV* is positive, the project is acceptable.

4.

Project	Average Simulated NPV	Average Simulated Standard Dev.	Simulated Coefficient of Variation
X	$470	21	4.5%
Y	500	30	6.0%
Z	440	46	10.5%

The lowest simulated coefficient of variation is that for Project X, so that project should be accepted.

5. (a) Deflation Method
   $12\% - 7\% = 5\%$

Year	Cash Flow	PVIF at 5%	PV of Cash Flows
1	$ 4,000	.952	$ 3,808
2	8,000	.907	7,256
3	12,000	.864	10,368
4	15,000	.823	12,345
5	18,000	.784	14,112

Total PV at a real discount rate of 5% = $47,889
Subtract initial investment: −10,000
Adjusted NPV = $37,889

(b) Inflation Method

Year	Cash Flow Inflated at 7%	PVIF at 12%	PV of Cash Flows
1	$ 4,280	.893	$ 3,822
2	9,159	.797	7,300
3	14,701	.712	10,467
4	19,662	.636	12,505
5	25,246	.567	14,314

Total PV at discount rate of 12% = $48,408
Subtract initial investment: −10,000
Adjusted NPV = $38,408

You would use the lower *NPV*, $37,889.

INVESTING, FINANCING, AND DIVIDEND DECISIONS

9
COST OF CAPITAL

KEY TERMS

cost of capital (CC) the rate a firm must pay to investors in order to induce them to purchase the firm's stock and/or bonds

expected return the future receipts that investors anticipate from their investments

opportunity cost the rate of return on the best alternative investment that is not selected

required rate of return (RRR) the minimum future receipts an investor will accept in choosing an investment

marginal cost of capital (MCC) the incremental cost of issuing more securities

risk-adjusted discount rate (RADR) reflects the riskiness of each project

---

BASIC CONCEPTS

Individuals have to decide where to invest the income they have saved. The goal, obviously, is to gain the highest return possible. To determine which assets are profitable and which are not, investors need a point of reference. This point of reference is known as the **required rate of return.**

Given individual preferences and market conditions, investors establish an expected rate of return for each asset they may purchase. **Expected returns** are the future receipts investors anticipate receiving for taking the risk of making investments. If the expected return from an asset falls below the required rate of return, the investment will not be made. If certain assets are expected to return more than the required rate of return, they will be bought. For example, suppose an investor calculates that the required rate of return on an investment is 10%. Given the opportunity to buy an asset with an expected return of 9%, the investor will refuse to purchase this asset. Conversely, assets will be purchased if they return 11%, 12% or more.

• COST OF CAPITAL AS A BENCHMARK FOR INVESTMENT DECISIONS

A manager of a firm, with the responsibility for making investment decisions, uses a similar point of reference. This point of reference, the firm's required rate of return, is called the **cost of capital**. The firm must earn a minimum rate of return to cover the cost of generating funds to finance investments; otherwise, no one will be willing to buy its bonds, preferred stock, and common stock. The goal of a financial officer is to achieve the highest efficiency and profitability from assets and, at the same time, keep the cost of the funds that the firm generates from various financing sources as low as possible. In other words, the cost of capital is the rate of return (cost) that a firm must pay investors to induce them to risk their funds and purchase the bonds, preferred stock, and common stock issued by the firm.

Factors that determine the cost of capital include the riskiness of earnings, the proportion of debt exposure in the capital structure, the financial soundness of the firm, and the way investors evaluate the firm's securities. If expected earnings or cash flow is volatile, debt is high, and the firm lacks a sound financial record, investors will buy its securities only if high returns are paid to compensate them for taking the risk. In contrast, steadily growing earnings, low debt, and a good financial background will enable the firm to issue securities at low cost.

Clearly, the cost of capital is one of the major factors used in the determination of the value of the firm. In finance, the cost of capital is the same as the discount rate. High risk means a high cost of capital, while low risk means a low cost of capital. Moreover, a high cost of capital (high discount rate) usually means a low valuation for securities, and a low discount rate means a high value for the securities of a firm. Since the sale of these securities provides firms with funds for investments, the cost of financing increases when the value of securities is low, and it decreases when their value is high. The benchmark for determining whether the returns of a firm's securities are high or low is the cost of capital.

• COST OF CAPITAL AS A MEASURE OF PROFITABILITY

The role played by the cost of capital in the investment decision process can be explained in another way. When a firm issues securities, it promises to pay a return to its bond- and stockholders. This payment represents a cost. Funds raised by the issue of stocks and bonds are invested for the purpose of generating income for the firm. This income, usually referred to as cash flow, is measured by calculating the present values of the returns generated from investments and comparing them to the cost of the investments. The role played by the cost of capital in calculating the value and profitability of investments is illustrated below:

$$NPV = (PVCFAT_{(t)}) - I_0$$
$$IRR = (NPV = 0) \text{ or}$$
$$IRR = PVCFAT_{(t)} - I_0 = 0$$

where $PVCFAT_{(t)}=$ present value of cash flows after taxes generated from an investment

$NPV =$ profits from an investment

$IRR =$ internal rate of return (or when $NPV = 0$)

$I_0 =$ original cost of the investment

As discussed in Chapter 6, the profitability of an investment represents the *PV* of cash flows minus the cost of investment. When the present value of cash flows minus the cost of investment is brought down to zero, the **internal rate of return** (*IRR*) of the investment is obtained.

Since the *IRR* is the rate of return derived from an investment, it is easy to determine whether or not this investment is profitable just by comparing the *IRR* with the cost of capital. When the *IRR* exceeds the cost of capital, the firm gets a higher return than the costs it pays to borrow funds. Conversely, when the *IRR* of an investment falls below the cost of capital, it means that the rate of return of the investment is lower than the cost of acquiring funds, and the investment should not be undertaken.

In summary, there is a very simple relationship between the *IRR*, the cost of capital and the desirability of a project: When the *IRR* is greater than the cost of capital, the project is profitable; when it is lower than the cost of capital, it is unprofitable.

Example: Cost of Capital as a Measure of Profitability

Figure 9–1 shows how the cost of capital can be used to compare the relative profitabilities of projects. Project, or investment, A is profitable because its *IRR* is 20%, while the cost of capital is only 10%. By investing in this project a firm would make 10% (20% − 10%) more than its required rate of return. Project, or investment, B is unprofitable partly because its *IRR* is less than the cost of capital. This means that *NPV* is negative. Should the firm invest in Project B, it would lose 5% (5% − 10%), because while the cost of funds is 10%, those funds, once invested, would yield only 5%.

The cost of capital can also be viewed in terms of the risk premium that investors in the marketplace assign to a firm or to assets. A **risk premium** is the additional required rate of return that must be paid over and above the risk free rate. The higher the risk premium, the riskier the firm or the asset. Conversely, the lower the risk premium, the less risky the firm or asset.

As shown in Table 9–1, Firm C has been assigned a higher risk premium than Firms A and B. Obviously, the higher the risk premium, the higher the cost of issuing bonds and stocks.

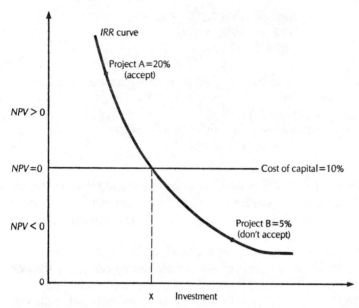

Figure 9–1 Comparing the *IRR*s of Investments to the Cost of Capital (CC)

When investors supply a firm with funds for investment purposes, they want to make sure that they are adequately paid for the risk they are taking. For instance, if the yield on an average-risk bond is 10%, a high-risk firm may have to pay investors 12% in order to sell its bonds. Many highly risky firms lack other attractive features, such as the prospect of making technological breakthroughs. They may have a low growth record or may be regarded as unsafe investments. Usually shares of such firms will be assigned a lower value than those of other, more stable companies. As a result, these firms would have to issue more shares to raise needed funds and would therefore incur a higher cost of financing. The reverse is true of a low-risk firm.

Although a firm has an average or overall cost of capital (CC), this does not mean that the profitability or net present value of each project or of each investment

Table 9–1.   Risk Premiums and the Cost of Capital (CC)

	Firm A	Firm B	Firm C
Cost of capital (CC)(%)	0.10	.08	0.12
Risk-free rate (%)	0.05	0.05	0.05
Risk premium (%)	0.05	0.03	0.07

decision should be evaluated with reference to that aggregate cost. Individual projects (or divisions) may require different discount rates than the firm's cost of capital, depending on how risky these projects are. This method of adjusting the cash flows of projects and decisions to reflect individual degrees of risk is called the *risk-adjusted discount-rate* approach (RADR). Unless this approach is used, the PV of returns or net present values of these risky projects would be subject to a bias, making them appear more or less profitable than they are. The determination of this adjustment is partly subjective. One way of calculating the RADR of risky projects (or divisions) is to find a publicly traded company that has similar characteristics to the project in question and to use that company's cost of capital as the appropriate RADR.

YOU SHOULD REMEMBER

The cost of capital is the required rate of return that a firm must achieve in order to cover the cost of generating funds in the marketplace. Based on their evaluations of the riskiness of each firm, investors will supply new funds to a firm only if it pays them the required rate of return to compensate them for taking the risk of investing in the firm's bonds and stocks. If, indeed, the cost of capital is the required rate of return that the firm must pay to generate funds, it becomes a guideline for measuring the profitabilities of different investments. When there are differences in the degree of risk between the firm and its divisions, a risk-adjusted discount-rate approach should be used to determine their profitability.

• *USING INTERNAL AND EXTERNAL SOURCES TO RAISE CAPITAL*

The funds available to a firm come from internal sources as well as from external ones. The origins of **internally generated funds** can be found on balance sheets and income statments, which report the amounts of funds generated from retained earnings and from depreciation.

These internally generated funds reduce the need for external financing. Because they are an alternative source of funds, they should be regarded as having an **opportunity cost**; without them, the firm would have to issue new shares of stocks or bonds, which would mean paying more dividends or more interest. In finance, it is usual practice to assign a cost to these internal sources of funds.

Since retained earnings are considered a proxy for common stock, financing the cost of retained earnings is the same as if new common stock were issued (without making an adjustment for flotation costs). Because depreciation is assumed to be a substitute for all types of financing, it is assigned the firm's cost of capital. As a result, depreciation does not enter into the computation of the overall cost of capital of the firm. Still, directly or indirectly, each internal source of funds plays an important role in determining the overall average cost of capital.

External sources of funds appear on the right-hand side of the balance sheet. The balance sheet indicates the relative importance of long- and short-term funds to the firm. All you have to do is compare the amounts generated from current debt (notes payable), long-term borrowings (mainly bonds), preferred and common stock.

RISK AND THE COST OF CAPITAL

The costs of capital to raise funds from short- or long-term sources are market determined. Investors analyze the degree of risk involved in supplying funds to firms. Obviously, if the risk is high, the return they demand—the firm's cost—will be high; if the risk is low, the cost will be low unless market rates are affected by extreme economic uncertainty.

There is also the uncertainty and risk of time. The longer the funds are invested, the higher the cost of capital because of time-related risks, including the risk of loss of principal through failure and default.

Table 9–2 presents a breakdown of current liabilities (notes payable) and long-term external sources of funds made available to the XYZ Co. This table presents the main entries that appear on the right side of the balance sheet, which includes current liabilities, long-term debt, and equity. In each case, the balance sheet tells you the origin of these funds, whether from a bank or from issuing new securities. For example, in most cases, external short-term funds can be assumed to come from bank credit made available to the firm, although trade accounts payable are also an important source. The balance sheet also indicates the external sources of long-term funds, whether these funds come from bank term loans or from issuing bonds or stocks, and internal sources such as retained earnings. Therefore, by referring to the balance sheet of the firm, you can determine the mix of external funds, the book values of these funds, and the importance of each source to the firm. Each source has its specific cost of capital. For example, Table 9–2 shows that new bond issues cost the firm 8%, while stock issues cost 13.5%. Also, note that the costs increase from 7% for short-term bank notes to 13.5% in the case of common stock equity.

A major reason for this increase is the time factor. Notes payable are usually short-term bank loans that are repaid within one year. The risk is small, and the cost of borrowing is usually lower than that for long-term sources. Long-term debt has the next lowest cost, because it comes due at a definite time and because bondholders are paid off before stockholders in case of bankruptcy. Finally, since

Table 9–2   XYZ Co.—External and Internal Sources of Funds Compared to the Cost of Capital

Source of Funds	Dollar Amount	Assumed Cost of Capital* for Each Source of Funds (%)	Percentage of Total Value of each Source (%)
External			
Current liabilities			
Notes payable	1,000,000	7.0	10
Long-term debt			
2,000 bonds @ $1,000 par value	2,000,000	8.0	20
Stockholders' equity			
Preferred stock			
50,000 shares @ $10 par value	500,000	10.0	5
Common stock			
1.0 million shares @ $5.00 par value	5,000,000	13.5	50
Internal			
Retained earnings	1,500,000	13.0	15
Total liabilities and stockholders' equity	$10,000,000		100

*These costs reflect the relative risk associated with each source of capital.

common stockholders invest funds for the entire life of the firm, their risk of losing principal is highest, the time involved is longest, and hence investors will claim a high rate of return to compensate them for taking these extra risks. Unlike lenders, however, stockholders participate in the growth, profitability, and wealth of the firm.

YOU SHOULD REMEMBER

Firms use the cost of capital as a break-even point, that is, the cost the firm must cover if it is to stay in business and remain profitable. This means that all projects with rates of return (*IRRs*) lower than the cost of capital are unprofitable, and that those investments with *IRRs* higher than the cost of capital are profitable. A firm cannot stay in business if it does not cover the costs of repaying bondholders. And the market value of the firm's stock will decline if it fails to provide stockholders with an expected rate of return.

A firm can generate capital from both internal and external sources. Because internal sources substitute for external sources, they should be assigned a cost. A firm's balance sheet tells you where funds originated, and it supplies most of the information necessary to calculate the cost of capital for each source. Usually, the lower the risk premium, the lower the cost of capital, and vice versa.

• COST OF LONG-TERM DEBT

One example of long-term debt is bonds, which are issued for specified lengths of time. Bonds have prescribed coupons, which usually come due semiannually and represent payments of interest to bondholders. These fixed-income securities have a **maturity date**, which is when the principal must be repaid. Bonds are usually issued at **par**, or face value, most commonly $1,000.

The cost of issuing bonds is determined by investors in the marketplace who evaluate the risks involved, assess the financial soundness of the firm, review its solvency record, and evaluate the chances of the firm's defaulting on its promised payments. The cost can also vary depending on whether market interest rates are high or low. When market rates are high, the cost of issuing bonds is greater than when market yields are low. Furthermore, longer maturity periods normally increase the cost of issuing bonds, partly because the chance of default increases with time, and partly because investors prefer short-term repayment dates over long-term repayment dates. In other words, a premium must be paid to overcome the reluctance of investors to commit funds for long periods of time.

MAKING A ROUGH ESTIMATE

The cost of issuing a bond is partly established by **rating agencies,** such as Standard and Poor's and Moody's rating services, which are the largest in this field. These agencies evaluate a company's financial status as well as its past record, and indicate the quality of its bonds by assigning a rating to these securities. These ratings provide measures for comparing the relative riskiness of different fixed-income securities. The two services named above usually—but not always—agree on a particular bond's rating.

Another way to find out what a bond will cost a firm is to examine bonds of companies with the same financial structure and risk characteristics. The going yield on long-term bonds can be found in almost any newspaper. If the bonds of similar companies yield 12% and the firm wishes to issue bonds at 12% or more, investors will probably purchase these bonds. However, an offer to pay a coupon rate of 10%, when bond buyers can get 12% for the same type of investment, would not be very successful.

INVESTMENT BANKERS AND FLOTATION COSTS

The stated coupon and corresponding yield on a bond is determined by investment bankers, who are responsible for sponsoring, distributing, and selling securities. These bankers are expert at determining fair prices for bond issues. They know the prevailing conditions in the market; they are familiar with the financial structure and status of the firm; and they have a fairly good idea, based on prior experience, of the cost or yield at which a bond will sell.

The process of issuing bonds through an investment banker or underwriting house also adds to the expense. The underwriter is a financial house that prepares a prospectus, lines up investors, and has a distribution network. A charge must be paid to the underwriter for this service. Since underwriters usually take risks by guaranteeing sales of the bonds, they want to be compensated. The combined charges for services and risk taking are called **flotation costs**. These costs reduce the receipts that a firm gets from the sale of bonds and stocks. Even though bonds are usually issued at par, the actual net amount paid to the firm is less than par. A firm with a flotation cost of 2% will receive $980 [$1,000(1 − .02)] instead of $1,000 per bond.

Because bonds pay interest that is deductible from the firm's income, the cost of issuing debt has to be adjusted for this tax benefit. As a result, the after-tax cost to the firm is always lower than the coupon rate. If the cost of debt is k_d, then the true cost of debt to the firm is

$$K_{dt} = K_d(1 - \text{tax rate})$$

A company with a tax rate of 40% that sells bonds to yield 11% will have a cost of debt equivalent to 6.6%, or .11(1 − .40). The tax benefit usually makes the cost of bonds lower than the cost of financing via other methods of raising funds.

CALCULATING THE COST OF DEBT

Taking all these factors into account, the calculation of the cost of debt to a firm is a relatively simple exercise. Having established the coupon and the annual interest payments that bondholders will receive, all you have to do is relate this coupon cost to the receipts obtained from a single bond:

$$\text{Cost of debt } (K_d) = \frac{\text{Annual coupon on new bond issue}}{\text{Principal}(1 - \text{flotation cost})}$$

There is, however, a distinction between the computation of the cost of debt for outstanding bonds and that for newly issued bonds. In the case of outstanding bonds, the cost principal is not adjusted for flotation costs. Thus, the formula for outstanding bonds is

$$K_d = \frac{\text{Annual coupon on outstanding bond}}{\text{Market value}}$$

Example: The Cost of Debt

A firm that issues a bond paying a $110 coupon per year and incurs a 2% charge for flotation costs would be assigned the following cost of debt:

Outstanding Bonds	Newly Issued Bonds
Cost of debt $= \dfrac{\$110}{\$1,000} = 11.0\%$	Cost of debt $= \dfrac{\$110}{\$1,000(1 - .02)} = 11.2\%$

The fact that receipts are lower because of flotation costs causes the firm to incur higher costs on newly issued bonds than on outstanding bonds. When the adjustment is made for taxes (assume a 40% rate), the effective cost of long-term debt becomes 6.6%, or $0.11(1 - .40)$, for outstanding bonds and 6.72%, or $0.112(1 - .40)$, for newly issued bonds. This is the cost the firm incurs when it raises funds by issuing bonds.

An alternative way to calculate the cost of capital uses the present value method discussed in earlier chapters. This approach solves for the unknown discount rate when all other factors are given. Therefore, a bond with a 10-year maturity date that sells at $887 and has a $100 annual coupon would have the following cost of capital:

$$\text{Bond price (\$887)} = \sum_{t=1}^{10} \frac{\$100}{(1 + R)^t} + \frac{\$1,000}{(1 + R)^{10}}$$

When the bond was originally issued, the yield was 10% ($100 ÷ $1,000). The current yield on the bond depends on market conditions and can change from the original yield. If market interest rates go up, the price, or value, of the bond will decline; if interest rates decline, the market price of the bond will increase and its yield will decrease. For example, if the bond declines to $887 and pays $100 annually, its yield is higher than the original 10%. More precisely, in the above example the aim is to determine the discount rate that will equate the present values of future coupon payments plus principal paid at maturity with the present price of the bond. A little figuring makes the solution clear:

Year		PVIF at 10%	Present Value	PVIF at 12%	Present Value
1 to 10	$ 100	6.145	$ 614	5.650	$565
10th	1,000	.386	386	.322	322
			$1,000		$887

As you can see, a discount rate of 10% is too low, but a 12% rate is about right. At 12%, the present values of the bond would just about equal the current price of the bond. This means that the cost of debt to a firm in a 40% tax rate bracket would be 7.2% [12% × .60(1 − .40)].

Since bonds represent the lowest cost of capital, why don't firms engage solely in debt financing? The answer is simple: Just as a baby gets indigestion from eating too much candy, a firm with too much debt runs into trouble. Up to a certain point, debt financing is beneficial. Beyond that point, however, the increased risk of insolvency makes further financing via the debt route an unsound practice. Too much debt raises the cost of capital and makes debt securities less marketable.

YOU SHOULD REMEMBER

The cost of debt is lower than the cost of equity. Debt cost increases or decreases in direct relationship to changes in market interest rates. When new bonds are issued, firms incur flotation costs, which raise the cost of debt. However, debt costs are reduced because the interest paid is tax deductible. Too much debt can increase the risk that the firm will become insolvent; it will force the cost of debt to increase and will ultimately make additional debt unmarketable.

• *COST OF PREFERRED STOCK*

Preferred stockholders have prior claim to the assets of a corporation over common stockholders. However, preferred stock has no maturity date; and, in the case of asset liquidation, the holders of preferred stock get paid only after short- and long-term debtholder claims are satisfied.

Whenever preferred stock is issued, there are usually a number of restrictions to ensure the owners that their dividends will be paid and that the company will strive to maintain a sound and liquid financial position. Although the firm commits itself to pay a fixed annual dividend, this payment need not, in most cases, be made if there are no earnings. If, however, the preferred stock is cumulative, as is usually the case, the dividend must be paid from future earnings before common-stock dividends are paid. Still, compared with bonds, the risk to the firm is less when it raises funds by issuing preferred stock. However, investors require a higher return on preferred stock than with the purchase of bonds.

The features of preferred stock include a fixed dividend payment or a stated percent return on the stock's value at the time of issue. The market plays an important role in establishing the dividend yield on preferred stock. Clues come from the yield that similar preferred issues, quoted on the exchanges, are returning. The underwriter, in consultation with the issuing firm, will finally decide on the terms to be offered.

DETERMINING THE COST OF PREFERRED STOCK

If preferred stock is issued at $100 per share, with a stated annual dividend of $12, the cost of the preferred stock to the firm is

$$\text{Cost of preferred } (K_p) = \frac{\text{Preferred dividend}}{(\text{Market price of preferred}) \, (1 \, - \, \text{Flotation cost})}$$

If the cost of floating the issue comes to 3%, then the actual cost of the preferred stock would be

$$\text{Cost of preferred } (K_p) = \frac{\$12}{\$100(1 \, - \, .03)} = 12.4\%$$

Unlike the situation with bonds, no adjustment is made for taxes, because preferred stock dividends are paid after a corporation pays income taxes. Consequently, a firm assumes the full market cost of financing by issuing preferred stock.

YOU SHOULD REMEMBER

In case of default, preferred stockholders get paid before common stockholders. Preferred stock is more costly to issue than bonds, but is less costly than common stock. Preferred stockholders receive a fixed dividend and usually cannot vote on the firm's affairs.

• COST OF COMMON STOCK

When individuals need money to pay debts, they can resort to several sources, any one of which may provide a limited amount of funds: they can borrow from banks or finance companies; they can hock their jewelry; they can ask a rich uncle for a loan. The same principle applies to firms—they do not have unlimited access to external funds from any one source. Also, if a firm were to issue only one type of security, it would lose out on the opportunities offered by other types of securities. In the case of bonds, the firm gains financial leverage, which is not available through stock financing. However, by issuing bonds the firm commits itself to fixed financial payments, which can prove dangerous when earnings decline. This implies increased risk. Because the firm strives to achieve an optimal capital structure, it seeks to finance at the most advantageous cost. At times, this calls for the issuing of common stock.

As owners of the firm, common stockholders normally have voting privileges and share in all the gains and losses—and risks—associated with the firm. When the firm makes no profits, stockholders may not be paid any return on their investments. Common stockholders are not guaranteed anything if the firm's assets are liquidated. On the other hand, although they cannot lose more than their original investment, they can gain substantial returns. Because common stockholders take bigger risks than holders of debt and preferred stock, their returns must be higher.

Common stockholders participate mainly in the future earnings of the firm, which translate into expected dividends and capital gains (or stock price appreciation). Since these earnings accrue in the future, the usual procedure is to discount them by a risk factor. The growth prospects of these earnings also affect the valuation of common stock shares. Moreover, the price of the stock reflects investor and market attitudes toward the risk and return prospects of the firm in years ahead.

DETERMINING THE COST OF COMMON STOCK

The cost of common stock, or its discount rate, is determined mainly by three factors: the price of the common stock, the dividends paid by the firm on common stock, and the growth rate of dividends. Chapter 5 indicates that the value of common stock (assuming constant growth of dividends) can be obtained from the following equation:

$$\text{Price of stock} = \frac{\text{Dividend } (1 + G)^1}{\substack{\text{Discount rate or} \\ \text{cost of capital } (K_s)} - \substack{\text{Constant} \\ \text{growth rate } (G)}} = \frac{D_1}{K_s - G}$$

The constant-dividend-growth model assumes that the growth rate of dividends remains the same to infinity. Consequently, current dividend need only be adjusted for one year's growth rate, or $D_0 (1 + G)^1 = D_1$. To obtain the cost of capital for common stock, all you have to do is to solve for K_s, or the discount rate.

By rearranging the terms in the above equation, the cost of newly issued common stock can be calculated by using this equation:

Cost of common stock

$$K_s = \frac{D_o (1 + G)^1}{\text{Price of stock } (1 - \text{Flotation costs})} + \text{Constant growth rate}$$

If the common stock is outstanding, all you have to do is eliminate the adjustment for flotation costs from the equation.

Where can you get the figures to calculate the cost of common stock? Stock quotation tables in *The New York Times* and other newspapers supply dividends and prices of stocks. The only other factor required to complete the calculation is growth. The growth of dividends can be obtained by looking up the dividends paid by the firm in the last 10 years and calculating the annual growth rate of these dividends.

Example: Calculating the Cost of Common Stock

Suppose the rate of growth for Firm A's dividends was 5% yearly, its stock price was quoted at $20, it paid $2 in dividends per share, and its underwriting costs were 3%. The cost can be easily calculated:

Cost of issuing common stock $(K_s) =$

$$\frac{\$2.00(1.05)^1}{\$20.00(1 - .03)} + .05 = \frac{\$2.10}{\$19.40} + .05 = 15.8\%$$

This 15.8% is not adjusted for taxes because the dividends on common stock are paid out after taxes are deducted.

Can the cost of issuing common stock for the firm differ from the 15.8% calculated above? Yes—if the growth rate and the risk associated with this firm are expected to change in the future. Faster growth, leading to higher dividends, will be reflected in a higher stock price and a lower cost of capital. Lower growth will be reflected in a lower stock price and a higher cost of capital.

It is easy to check the effects on the cost of common stock simply by changing the figures in the preceding example and observing the impact. For example, if the growth rate were raised from 5% to 10%, the cost of common stock would increase from its current level of 15.8% to 21.3%. It is also possible that investor expectations regarding the financial and operating outlook of the firm may become more optimistic. Should this happen, the price of the stock will be bid up and, correspondingly, the cost to the firm of issuing common stock will decline.

An alternate method for deriving the growth rate is to compute the product of return on equity (ROE) and the retention ratio. Therefore, if a firm's ROE is 10% and it usually retains 50% of its earnings, the growth of the firm is estimated to be 5% (.10 × .05).

YOU SHOULD REMEMBER

The cost of issuing new common stock is based on three factors: dividends, growth of dividends, and the market price of common stock. Common stock is the most costly security to issue of any long-term source of capital. It also does not generate a tax benefit as debt does because dividends are paid after taxes.

USING THE CAPM TO CALCULATE THE COST OF COMMON STOCK

The cost of common stock can also be computed by using the CAPM. Assume that you ascertained that the risk free rate was 5% and the average return of the market was 15%. The beta for a given stock, or the systematic sensitivity of the return of the firm's stock relative to the return of the market, is 1.0. The required rate of return, or the cost of common stock, can be calculated by using

$$RRR_s \text{ (or } K_s) = R_F + (\overline{R}_m - R_F) B_s$$

Inserting the figures given above into this formula, you get

$$K_s = 5\% + (15\% - 5\%)1.0 = 15\%$$

The cost of common stock found by using the CAPM in a perfect capital market, where there are no transaction costs or other impediments, should yield the same results obtained from the constant growth dividend model. Unfortunately, the CAPM runs into some difficulties. The assumptions are unrealistic, no one really knows which risk-free rate is the correct one at a given time, and the beta may not reflect the true systematic risk of the stock because no one has been able to develop a true market index. Consequently, the CAPM approach should be analyzed carefully before its results are accepted. It can, however, serve as a check against other methods of calculating the discount rate (K_s).

• COST OF RETAINED EARNINGS

Retained earnings are an internally generated source of funds. When dividends are deducted from net income, the funds left over are usually reinvested in the firm. There are no flotation costs associated with retained earnings. Retained earnings do, however, have a cost of capital associated with them. The reason is that, as a source of funds, the alternative to retained earnings would be to issue additional common stock. Consequently, the same cost of capital that applies to common stock applies to retained earnings.

Additionally, stockholders are the owners of the firm. When part of the earnings is retained by the firm, instead of being used to pay dividends, stockholders assume that these retained funds will earn the market-required rate of return on common stock. This market-required rate of return is the cost of common stock.

Because retained earnings are available after taxes, no tax adjustment is necessary. Also, as previously stated, these funds are internally generated and thus are not subject to the flotation cost associated with a new issue of securities.

DETERMINING THE COST OF RETAINED EARNINGS

The cost of retained earnings is the same as the cost of common stock without adjustment for flotation costs.

$$\begin{array}{l}\text{Cost of} \\ \text{retained} \\ \text{earnings}\end{array} = \frac{\begin{array}{c}\text{Dividends on} \\ \text{common stock}\end{array}}{\begin{array}{c}\text{Market value} \\ \text{of common stock}\end{array}} + \begin{array}{l}\text{Constant} \\ \text{growth of} \\ \text{dividends}\end{array} = \frac{D_1}{P_0} + G$$

Example: Calculating the Cost of Retained Earnings

PROBLEM   If a firm pays a $2.00 dividend, which is growing 5% annually, and the price of the stock is $20.00, what is the cost of the firm's retained earnings?

SOLUTION   Using the above equation you obtain:

$$\text{Cost of retained earnings} = \frac{\$2.00}{\$20.00} + 5\% = 15\%$$

The cost of retained earnings is generally a little lower than the cost of newly issued common stock, but is higher than the cost of debt or preferred stock.

In general, the cost of capital to a firm—no matter what kind of security is involved—reflects the annual payments made by the firm to investors relative to the amounts they invest. The cost of debt is less than the cost of common stock mainly because, in the case of default, creditors are paid before common stockholders. Therefore, investors who purchase debt securities from a firm are subject to less risk than stockholders. Also, common stock dividends, unlike interest on debt, provide no tax benefits.

YOU SHOULD REMEMBER

Retained earnings are considered to have the same cost of capital as new common stock. Therefore, their cost is calculated in the same way as for common stock, except that no adjustment is made for flotation costs.

MEASURING THE WEIGHTED AVERAGE COST OF CAPITAL (*WACC*)

When the cost of capital for different securities has been determined, the next step is to calculate the **weighted average cost of capital** for firms with a mixture of debt and stock in their capital structure. To understand this principle, consider how a hypothetical investor, Ms. Jones, might calculate the average return that she obtains from her investments. She keeps $10,000 invested in a time deposit at 5½% and $30,000 in a government bond that yields 10%. To find her weighted average return, it is necessary to determine how important each investment is in Ms. Jones's portfolio and then to assign weights to the returns, as shown below:

Investment	Value of Investment	Weight	Return	Weight × Return
Time deposit	$10,000	$\frac{\$10,000}{\$40,000}$ or .25	5.50%	1.38%
Gov't bond	$\frac{\$30,000}{\$40,000}$	$\frac{\$30,000}{\$40,000}$ or .75	10.00%	7.50%
		Weighted average return of Ms. Jones's portfolio =		8.88%

As you can see, the procedure for combining ānd averaging different costs of capital is relatively simple. All you have to do is look at a firm's balance sheet to find out the relative importance of each of the firm's sources of financing.

DETERMINING THE WEIGHTS TO BE USED

To simplify matters, assume that a firm generates funds solely from common stock, preferred stock, and long-term bonds. The balance sheet will show the book values of these sources of funds. As shown in Table 9–3, you can use the balance sheet figures to calculate book value weights, though it is more practicable to work with market weights. Basically, **market value weights** represent current conditions and take into account the effects of changing market conditions and the current prices of each security. **Book value weights**, however, are based on accounting procedures that employ the par values of the securities to calculate balance sheet

Table 9–3   Comparison of Book and Market Weights

Value	Dollar Amount	Weights* or Percentage of Total Value	Assumed Cost of Capital (%)
Book Value			
Debt			
2,000 bonds at par, or $1,000	2,000,000	40	10
Preferred stock			
4,500 shares at $100 par value	450,000	9	12
Common equity			
500,000 shares outstanding at			
$5.00 par value	2,500,000	51	13.50
Total value of capital	4,950,000	100	
Market Value			
Debt			
10,000 bonds at $900 (current			
price of bond)	9,000,000	29	10
Preferred stock			
20,000 shares at $90 (current			
price of stock)	1,800,000	6	12
Common equity			
400,000 shares at $50 (current			
price of stock)	20,000,000	65	13.50
Total value of capital	30,800,000	100	

*Weights are derived by dividing the value of each component by the total value of capital.

values, and represent past conditions. Table 9–3 illustrates the difference between book value and market value weights, and demonstrates how they are calculated.

The book values that appear on the balance sheet are usually different from the market values. Also, the price of common stock is normally substantially higher than its book value. This increases the weight of this capital component over other capital structure components (such as preferred stock and long-term debt). The desirable practice is to employ market weights to compute the firm's cost of capital.

Target weights can also be used. These weights indicate the distribution of external financing that the firm believes will produce optimal results. Some corporate managers establish these weights subjectively; others will use the best companies in their industry as guidelines; and still others will look at the financing mix of companies with characteristics comparable to those of their own firms. Generally speaking, target weights will approximate market weights. If they don't, the firm will attempt to finance in such a way as to make the market weights move closer to target weights.

COMPUTING THE WACC

In any event, whether book value or market value is used, the final goal is to compute the relative importance of each source of external funds in the capital structure of the firm. In other words, weights will show the extent to which each component contributes to the total value of the firm's capital structure.

Given the weights and the costs of capital for each source of financing, it is possible to obtain an average cost of capital of the firm using the following formula:

$$WACC\ (K_0) = K_{dt}\left(\frac{\text{Debt}}{D + P + S}\right)$$
$$+ K_p\left(\frac{\text{Preferred}}{D + P + S}\right) + K_s\left(\frac{\text{Common}}{D + P + S}\right)$$

where D = debt
P = preferred stock
S = common stock
K_0 = weighted average cost of capital $(WACC)$
K_{dt} = cost of debt [or $K_{dt} = K_d(1-T)$]
K_p = cost of preferred stock
K_s = cost of common stock
t = tax rate

The market weights and the cost of capital as calculated in Table 9–3 are used to compute the weighted average cost of capital of a firm, as shown in Table 9–4.

Table 9–4   Calculating *WACC* Based on Market Weights

Source of Financing	Cost of Capital (%)	Market Value Weight	Cost of Capital × Market Value Weight (%)
Debt (1 − *t*)*	6.00	29	1.74
Preferred stock	12.00	6	.72
Common equity	13.50	65	8.78
		Weighted average cost of capital =	11.24

*If the tax rate of the firm is assumed to be 40%, then the cost of debt equals 6.00% (10% × .60).

As you can see, the average cost of capital is influenced by changes in the weights or in the way the firm finances. Up to a certain point, the more debt that a firm issues, relative to common stock, the lower is the average cost of capital. Conversely, if more common stock financing is done, common equity becomes more and more important in the capital structure of the firm, and the average cost of capital increases. And when the cost of capital changes in each security, there will also be a change in the firm's overall cost of capital.

A shift in the weights of the various sources of financing—or a change in their respective costs of capital—can raise or lower the weighted average cost of capital. Clearly, excessive financing through one source can adversely influence the average cost of capital. This is especially true when the firm's debt becomes too high. If this occurs, rising fixed financial commitments may increase the risk of insolvency, causing the cost of debt and the firm's overall cost of capital to rise. The important point to remember is that the average cost of capital establishes the benchmark, or cutoff point, for determining whether or not an investment is profitable.

Although the average cost of capital is a crucial element in a firm's decision-making process, it is necessary to realize that the average cost of capital is only a starting point. It cannot be used indiscriminately to evaluate the profitability of all projects. Some projects are highly risky and require special treatment. In these cases, financial managers have to decide whether they should apply their subjective judgment and raise the discount rate to ensure that it not only reflects the average cost of capital but also includes an additional compensation for risk not taken into account by the *WACC*. The best course of action, especially when future cash flows are highly uncertain, is to use a risk-adjusted discount rate that makes the final assessment of the present values of expected returns more realistic.

YOU SHOULD REMEMBER

The WACC is calculated by determining the cost of each source of capital financing and weighting these costs according to the corresponding importance of that capital as a source of funds. It is better to use market weights when calculating the WACC, because they more accurately reflect market conditions. Book value weights tend to keep the weight assigned to common stock too low, causing a distortion in the WACC. Although the WACC is used as a guideline to judge the relative merits of individual investments, in many cases each project should be analyzed separately; and, if necessary, the discount rate applied to measure its profitability should reflect its own specific risk rather than that of the overall WACC.

MEASURING THE WEIGHTED MARGINAL COST OF CAPITAL (*WMCC*)

Corporations do not have unlimited sources of funds available for investment Investors in the marketplace are worried when corporations exceed their financial capabilities. The market, being an efficient mechanism, incorporates all information about each firm and then compares the financial merits of one firm against another. Since the market recognizes that resources are limited, investors will not make funds available to a firm beyond a certain limit. If a firm tries to extend its financing beyond such a market-determined limit, investor resistance increases, and more funds are made available only at higher and higher costs to the firm. The incremental cost of financing above a previous level is called the **weighted marginal cost of capital (WMCC)**.

How does a firm determine the point *beyond which* it will incur a higher cost when using a given source of external financing? One way is to consult with an investment advisor or banker who can assess market conditions and estimate how investors would respond to successively higher amounts of financing. The banker will present the firm with a series of ranges (see Table 9–5) showing the upper limit of financing from each source before the cost of capital increases. In other words, the banker calculates the incremental costs that the firm will incur when its financing passes the maximum limit in each range.

The weighted marginal cost of capital in any one of the ranges in Table 9–5 increases when its upper limit is breached by an individual source of financing. To illustrate,

Table 9–5   **Ranges of New Financing and Corresponding Levels of the Cost of Capital**

Range of New Financing (dollars)	Weighted Marginal Cost of Capital (%)
0 to 1,000,000	8.00
1,000,001 to 3,000,000	9.00
3,000,001 to 5,500,000	9.50
5,500,001 to 8,000,000	11.00
10,000,001 and over	11.90

the rise in the *WMCC* from 9.00% to 9.50% could be due to higher costs of issuing preferred stock, and the increase from 9.50% to 11.00% could occur because the limits for issuing both bonds and common stock were breached. The rising cost of capital reflects the increasing marginal cost of additional capital financing of specific components. This now becomes the cost benchmark against which the profitability of projects can be compared.

USING THE WMCC TO SELECT THE BEST PROJECTS

The most rational investment-decision approach is to select the projects with the highest profitabilities (*IRRs*) and then to move methodically down the profit scale to the ones yielding lower and lower *IRRs* until additional new projects fail to provide rates of return equal to the marginal cost of capital. The idea is based on the concept that the marginal productivity of capital—and, therefore, the profitability of projects—diminishes as more funds are invested. At the point where declining profitability and rising costs meet, investment should cease. This process is termed diminishing marginal productivity of capital or declining marginal efficiency of capital.

Take a look at how this works. The manager of a firm analyzes the merits of several projects and calculates their *IRRs*, or relative profitabilities. The investments required to implement these projects are then compared to the *IRR* of each project by ranking the *IRRs* in the order of their returns, as shown in Table 9–6.

This ranking procedure helps determine which projects are the best. It also indicates the amount of new financing required to implement the most profitable projects. Notice that, as more projects are added, their *IRRs* fall. Also, as more is invested in each project, more funds must be generated. This gradually leads to increased financing beyond the limits established by the investment banker and the market. Consequently, the *WMCC* will continue to increase with additional investments and additional financing. At some point, rising marginal cost and declining *IRR* will meet (*IRR* = *WMCC*). Beyond this point, additional financing becomes unprofitable and ceases.

Table 9–6   Ranking Projects by Profitability (*IRR*)

Project	IRR (%)	Investment in Project (dollars)	Cumulative Investment (dollars)
A	18.0	500,000	500,000
B	17.0	500,000	1,000,000
C	15.0	1,500,000	2,500,000
D	12.0	1,500,000	4,000,000
E	11.0	1,000,000	5,000,000
F	9.0	3,000,000	8,000,000
G	8.0	3,000,000	11,000,000

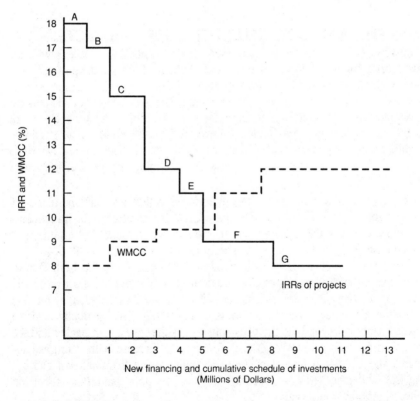

Figure 9–2 Determining Investment Limits Using IRRs and the WMCC

Figure 9-2 demonstrates this principle. The *WMCC* and the *IRR* curves are derived from the values in Tables 9-5 and, 9-6. An analysis of Figure 9-2 shows that all of the projects having *IRR*s equal to or higher than 9.5%—including Projects A, B, C, D, and E—will be financed. Total investment and new financing will be $5.0 million.

The *WMCC* principle provides a more realistic measure for choosing the most profitable projects. Because it implicitly recognizes the changing response of investors to increased financing requirements, it takes into account the limits imposed by the market on different levels of new financing. It also recognizes that money is a scarce resource, and that excessive financing leads to successively higher costs of capital.

The explanation for this phenomenon lies in the increased risk incurred by increased financing, especially when debt is issued. This limitation is the investors' response to growing illiquidity, rising risk of insolvency, and eventual deterioration of the value of the firm. As discussed in Chapter 4, this investors' response is an example of the risk/return tradeoff which calls for a higher return to compensate for increased risk.

YOU SHOULD REMEMBER

There is a point beyond which a firm cannot finance without incurring a higher marginal cost of capital. The weighted marginal cost of capital (WMCC) principle is useful in determining the total number of additional projects that can be financed because they are profitable. It is important to note that, as more projects are financed, the *IRR*s of these projects decline while the WMCC increases. Investment ceases when *IRR* = WMCC.

KNOW THE CONCEPTS

DO YOU KNOW THE BASICS?

1. List some factors that investors look at when assigning a cost of capital to a firm.

2. How is the value of a firm affected by a changing cost of capital?

3. In what sense does the cost of capital serve as a benchmark for determining the relative merits of projects? Give a graphical example.

4. Calculate the total risk of projects A and B if the risk-free rate is 5% and the risk premium is 3% for project A and 5% for project B. What does this imply?

5. If the maturity period of one bond is 5 years, and that of another bond 10 years, why is the cost of capital usually higher in the longer term bond?

6. What two adjustments are made to calculate the cost of newly issued debt?

7. What happens to a firm's cost of debt when market interest rates increase? Why does this occur?

8. Why is the cost of issuing preferred stock usually lower than the cost of issuing common stock?

9. All other things being equal, what happens to the value of common stock, when
   (a) the growth rate is expected to increase?
   (b) the volatility of earnings is anticipated to increase?

10. How does the calculation of the cost of retained earnings differ from the calculation of the cost of common stock?

11. What is the difference between book value weights and market value weights?

12. What happens to the marginal cost of capital when a firm exceeds its borrowing capacity, and how will this affect its investment decisions?

13. Why does the *IRR* of projects decline while the *WMCC* increases?

14. What does the term (D_1) imply in the constant-dividend-growth model?

15. Why is the risk adjusted discount rate (RADR) method used and assigned to different projects or divisions of a firm?

TERMS FOR STUDY

book value weights
cost of capital (*CC*)
expected return
external sources of funds
flotation costs
internally generated funds
marginal cost of capital (*MCC*)
market value weights

maturity date
opportunity cost
par value
rating agencies
required rate of return (*RRR*)
risk premium
weighted average cost of capital (*WACC*)

PRACTICAL APPLICATION

COMPUTATIONAL PROBLEMS

1. If a company issues a $1000 par value bond with a $90 coupon and a maturity date of 10 years, and flotation costs are 2% of the par value of the bond, calculate the cost of this debt issue.

2. If preferred stock has a dividend of $9 and an issue price of $100, and carries a flotation cost of $3 per share, calculate the cost of the stock.

3. Evaluate the cost of common stock if the current price is $50, the dividend is $2 per share, and dividends grew from $1 to $1.54 over the past 5 years.

4. Given a risk free rate of 7%, a market return of 12%, and a beta of 1.2, calculate the cost of common stock by using the CAPM. What would happen to the cost if beta was .8 instead of 1.2?

5. A finance company has the following values stated in its balance sheet: debt = $500,000 and common equity = $100,000. Compute the weights of this firm's capital structure. If its cost of debt is 10% and the cost of common stock is 12%, calculate its *WACC*.

6. The following are the IRR and the corresponding investments required by the projects listed below:

Project	IRR	Investment
A	10%	$1,000
B	12%	3,000
C	13%	2,000
D	9%	5,000
E	15%	9,000

The marginal cost of capital is 11%. Indicate which projects will be implemented and the total amount of financing, or investment, that will be required.

ANSWERS

KNOW THE CONCEPTS

1. The riskiness (volatility) of earnings, growth of profits, large or small exposure to debt obligations, financial soundness, and the attitude of investors toward management and the company (such as the P/E assigned to a stock).

2. If the cost of capital increases, the value of a firm will decline; if the cost of capital decreases, the firm's value will increase.

3. Rate of return (*IRR*)

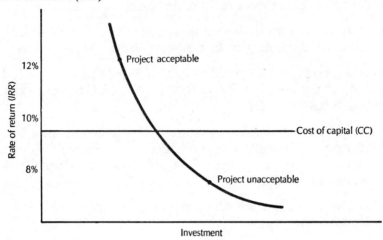

Any project having a rate of return (*IRR*) lower than the cost of capital (10%) will be rejected, and projects having an *IRR* higher than the (*CC*) will be accepted.

4. If total risk equals the risk free rate plus a risk premium, then Project A is less risky than Project B.

	Risk-free Rate	Risk Premium	Total Risk
Project A	5%	3%	8%
Project B	5%	5%	10%

To compensate for the higher risk premium, Project B has to have a rate of return 2% higher than that of Project A.

5. Because the 10-year bond has a longer maturity period, it has a greater chance of defaulting. As time increases, uncertainty increases. To compensate for this higher degree of uncertainty and increased chance of default, investors will require a higher return.

6. (a) Adjustment for flotation costs: (1 − flotation costs).
   (b) Adjustment for the tax benefits: $K_d(1 - $ tax rate).

7. If market interest rates increase, all rates move up in sympathy. The result will be a higher cost of issuing debt.

8. The cost of issuing preferred stock is lower than that of issuing common stock because investors are paid a stated dividend and are paid off before common stockholders in case of bankruptcy. This lower risk means that a lower return will be acceptable to investors.

9. (a) When G increases, the value of common stock increases.

   (b) When K_s increases, the value of common stock decreases.

10. The calculations are the same except that in the case of retained earnings the price of the stock is not adjusted for flotation costs.

11. Book value weights are based on the par values of stocks and bonds. Market weights reflect the current prices of common stock and outstanding bonds. Generally, market weights shift in favor of common stock.

12. The marginal cost of capital (MCC) increases when borrowing limits are reached, and the IRR decreases as more projects are financed. At some point, the MCC and IRR curves will meet ($MCC = IRR$). Beyond this point, investments become unprofitable.

13. The IRR of projects declines because of the diminishing marginal productivity of capital. MCC increases because the market, or investors, will not supply unlimited amounts of funds. Beyond a certain point, too much debt causes investors to become apprehensive, and they will ask for greater returns. Therefore, excessive borrowing can increase the chances of insolvency; excessive issue of stock leads to dilution of the earnings per share and possible loss of voting control. Hence, a higher cost of capital results.

14. The constant-dividend-growth model assumes that the growth rate remains the same (stays constant) to infinity. If so, the current dividend need only be adjusted upward by one year's growth rate $(D_0(1+G)^1)$.

15. The overall cost of capital of a firm does not fully reflect the degree of risk that should be assigned to each project or division. If the degree of riskiness is ignored, the NPV and the present values of cash flows after taxes will be biased. If the division is riskier than the firm, the profitability of its projects will turn out to be higher than they should be because the discount rate is too low. Thus, each project should be assigned its appropriate RADR in order for it to yield a realistic risk-adjusted NPV.

PRACTICAL APPLICATION

1. Company's cost of bonds $= \dfrac{\$90}{\$1,000(.98)} = \dfrac{\$90}{\$980} = 9.2\%$

2. Cost of preferred stock $= \dfrac{\$9}{\$100 - \$3} = \dfrac{\$9}{\$97} = 9.3\%$

3. Cost of common stock $= \dfrac{\$2.00}{\$50.00} + 9\% = .04 + .09 = 13\%$

4. RRR_s, or cost of common stock (K_s)

   Cost of common stock $= .07 + (0.12 - .07)1.2$

   $\qquad\qquad\qquad\qquad\quad = .07 + .06 = 13\%$

   A beta of .8 would yield an RRR_s of 11%

5.

		Weight (W)	Percentage Cost of Capital (CC)	W × CC
Debt	$500,000	.83	.10	8.3%
Equity	100,000	.17	.12	2.0%
	$600,000	1.00		WACC = 10.3%

6.

Projects	IRR (%)	Investment	Cumulative Investment
E	15	$9,000	$ 9,000
C	13	2,000	11,000
B	12	3,000	14,000
A	10	1,000	15,000
D	9	5,000	20,000

Projects E, C, and B will be undertaken, and since the marginal cost of capital is 11%, the total investment in these projects will amount to $14,000.

10
CAPITAL STRUCTURE

BASIC CONCEPTS

Capital structure is the financing mix of the firm. Itemized on the right side of the balance sheet, it represents major sources of external funds derived from financing. The capital structure of the firm consists of long-term debt, preferred stock; and common equity.

To simplify the presentation, only long-term debt and common equity will be considered in the following discussion of capital structure. When studying the capitalization (C) of a firm, it is important to calculate the ratio of debt (D) to total capitalization: D/C. The **debt/capitalization ratio** indicates the proportion of debt and equity issued by the firm. The firm must maintain a certain balance between debt and equity. Too much debt can increase the risk of the firm, making investors apprehensive about the ability of the firm to pay its creditors. This, in turn, may increase the cost of capital.

Up to a certain point, debt financing is beneficial to a firm because it provides financial leverage. The tax deductibility feature of interest paid to creditors enables a firm to achieve higher earnings per share when debt is issued than would be possible by issuing equity. In other words, by issuing debt, the firm achieves higher earnings per share as the return on borrowed funds exceeds the interest rate on these funds. This boost in earnings per share is called financial leverage.

• *FINANCIAL LEVERAGE*

Financial leverage relates to the practice of using debt securities to finance investments and consists of the relationship between EBIT (earnings before interest and taxes) and EPS (earnings per share). When debt is issued, the firm commits itself to pay interest and repay principal sometime in the future. Because this interest is a tax-deductible expense, more of the operating income flows through to investors.

However, the more debt a firm has in its capital structure, the greater the financial risk. This means that, regardless of the level of its operating income, the firm must continue to meet fixed coupon payments plus the payment of principal at maturity. Therefore, the more debt a firm issues, the more fixed financial costs it incurs and the greater the danger that it will not be able to meet these periodic fixed payments. As debt increases, interest payments rise—and although they provide financial leverage, there is an increasing financial risk that interest payments will become too large relative to EBIT. If business activity declines in a business contraction phase, EBIT will also decline, increasing the probability that the firm may not be able to cover the interest payments with existing operating profits. Remember, therefore, that financial leverage is a two-way street. Although it can be beneficial in a cyclical expansion period, it is detrimental in a cyclical contraction phase.

As debt increases, it tends to magnify the swings of EPS. As a result, the benefits of financial leverage must be weighted against the growing financial risk of insolvency. At some point, the tax-adjusted cost of increases in interest exceeds the EPS benefits derived from a smaller number of outstanding shares.

CHOOSING THE RIGHT CAPITAL MIX

Since capital structure influences the risk, the returns (EPS), and the valuation of the firm, financial managers are concerned with the impact of changes in the capital mix on the firm's value and wealth. If investors view debt as excessive, the firm may be prevented from borrowing at favorable terms.

Debt financing is fine—up to a certain point. The advantages of financial leverage disappear in a firm heavily laden with debt in its capital structure. Too much debt increases risk and raises the potential danger of default. Too much equity financing is not a good policy to pursue, either. It deprives the firm of the full advantages of financial leverage, and the weighted average cost of capital *(WACC)* becomes unnecessarily high. Furthermore, in some cases, issuing an excessive amount of common stock can lead to loss of voting control in the firm. As a result, an unbalanced capital mix (either too much debt or too much equity) can be detrimental to the valuation of a firm.

The primary goal of financial managers, then, is to establish a capital mix that will hold the costs of financing as low as possible, help maintain a stable dividend policy and good earnings record, and maximizes the wealth of stockholders. In other words, there is an optimum capital structure that minimizes the *WACC* while maintaining the firm's credit standing on a level at which it can attract new funds at reasonable terms.

```
YOU SHOULD REMEMBER
    Capital structure refers to the relationship between debt and eq-
uity. The more debt a firm has relative to equity, the greater its fi-
nancial leverage. Financial leverage can be beneficial up to a cer-
tain point, but too much debt can mean that the firm may not be able
to meet its fixed financial costs. On the other hand, too much com-
mon equity can sometimes mean loss of voting control and a higher cost
of capital. The goal of a financial executive is to achieve the right capital
mix.
```

CAPITAL STRUCTURE

The performance of financial managers is measured by the wealth of their firms. Consequently, these managers are concerned with the factors that affect the market value of the firm. In finance, the market value of the firm (V_f) in a no-growth state consists of the market value of debt plus capitalized earnings.

$$V_f = D + E$$

V_f = value of the firm

D = market value of debt

E = earnings after taxes divided by the required rate of return for equity

Funds from **long-term debt** originate in borrowings or from bondholders, and equity funds come from issuing stock. The value of the firm is determined by the way these funds are invested and by the amount of cash flow they generate. As a result, the total value of the firm is affected by the way the manager combines debt and equity. A change in the proportions of debt relative to equity can alter the value of a firm significantly.

The value of a firm is the sum of the value of its debt and its net income capitalized, or discounted, by a required rate of return. Therefore, if earnings are $91,000 and the required rate of return is 12%, the value of the firm's stock is $758,333 (91,000 ÷ 0.12). Given this definition, Table 10–1 indicates how the value of the firm changes when the D/C ratio changes in a firm having a total debt-plus-equity of $300,000 and an EBIT of $100,000.

By altering the debt-to-equity mix, but without changing the firm's total returns (EBIT), it becomes evident that the firm's value increases with a rising D/C ratio. At 67% debt and 33% equity, the firm's value is $866,677, compared to $848,333 when D/C equals 30%.

Table 10-1   Changes in the Value of a Firm, Given Different D/C Ratios (assuming no taxes)

Capital Structure	D/C Ratio		
	30%	50%	66²/₃%
Debt	$ 90,000	$150,000	$200,000
Equity	210,000	150,000	100,000
Total capitalization (C)	$300,000	$300,000	$300,000
EBIT	$100,000	$100,000	$100,000
Interest on debt at 10%	9,000	15,000	20,000
Earnings	$ 91,000	$ 85,000	$ 80,000
Value of firm (D + E)			
Debt (D)	90,000	150,000	200,000
Earnings capitalized at 12% (E)	758,333*	708,333*	666,667*
$V_f = D + E$	$848,333	$858,333	$866,667

*Note: $758,333 = $91,000 ÷ .12
$708,333 = $85,000 ÷ .12
$666,667 = $80,000 ÷ .12

THE EFFECT OF CAPITAL STRUCTURE ON A FIRM'S VALUE

Generally, when debt increases too much relative to common equity, investors tend to associate this with rising financial risk. Consequently, they assign a higher discount rate to future expected returns. In turn, the capitalized value of any given returns will produce a lower rather than a higher value for the firm. Why? The reason is that the growing risk of higher interest payments leads to a higher discount rate applied to earnings per share. Financial managers seek to adopt financing policies that will produce an optimal capital structure, thereby reducing the WACC to the lowest level possible and providing the firm with the maximum benefits from financial leverage.

Rising financial leverage can have magnifying effects. For example, should investors regard the risk/return trade-off that results from an increase in the D/C to 66²/₃% as favorable, the discount rate might decline to 11% and the value of the firm should increase to $927,273 ($200,000 + 727,273). If the move to a D/C of 66²/₃% is considered too risky, the discount rate may rise to 14% and the value of the firm $(D + E)$ will drop to $771,429 ($200,000 + $571,429).

Up to a certain point, increasing debt relative to equity in the capital structure can result in a higher EPS. But at some level, the debt to capitalization ratio will become excessive, making it more difficult for a firm to pay its debts. This will lead to a higher cost of generating external funds, and will increase the risk of owning stock.

It pays for managers to experiment with the capital structure mix because a reasonable amount of additional debt can help lower the firm's weighted average cost of capital.

Many managers study the capital structure of other companies in the same field and attempt to match their own *D/C* ratio with the company that has the lowest required rate of return.

Figure 10–1 shows the relationship between financial leverage, the costs of debt and equity, risk, expected returns, and the value of a firm's stock. Observe that after point *x,* the cost of debt, the cost of common stock, and the average cost of capital increase, partly because risk increases. Consequently, this produces a lower valuation

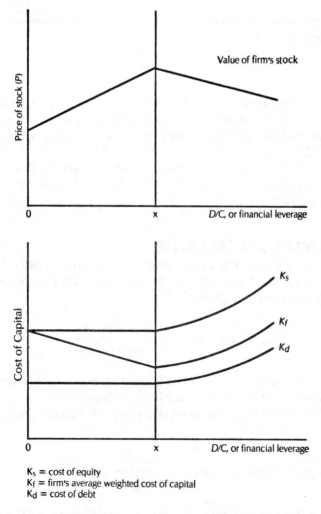

K_s = cost of equity
K_f = firm's average weighted cost of capital
K_d = cost of debt

Figure 10–1 Financial Leverage, Risk, and Value of Firm

Table 10–2   Financial Leverage and EPS

	Firm A (D/C = 0)	Firm B (D/C = 50%*)
EBIT	$100,000	$100,000
Interest on bonds (at 10%)	0	10,000
Earnings before taxes	$100,000	$ 90,000
Taxes (at 40%)	40,000	36,000
Net income	$ 60,000	$ 54,000
Shares outstanding	10,000	5,000
EPS (earnings per share)	$6.00	$10.80

*Debt equals $100,000 for Firm B.

for the firm. In other words, investors are willing to bear increased risks as long as leverage produces a substantial increase in earnings. When, however, financial leverage makes investors uncomfortable about the firm's ability to maintain solvency, they will sell the stock.

The effects of financial leverage on EPS can easily be seen in Table 10–2. Given the same EBIT, an increase in the D/C ratio from 0 to 50% produces an increase in EPS from $6.00 to $10.80.

MEASURING FINANCIAL LEVERAGE

If you accept the premise that the **degree of financial leverage** represents the lift that EPS receive from a given change in EBIT, this relationship can be expressed in the following way over *two points in time:*

$$\text{Degree of financial leverage} = \frac{\% \text{ change in EPS}}{\% \text{ change in EBIT}}$$

A major reason for investing more funds in a firm is to generate more income. Assume that, when a firm invests funds from newly issued bonds, EBIT increases 50% and EPS doubles. Under these conditions, the degree of financial leverage becomes

$$\text{Degree of financial leverage} = \frac{100\%}{50\%} = 2.00$$

This means that, given the financial structure of the firm, any change in EBIT will produce twice this change in EPS.

When calculating the degree of financial leverage of a firm at a point in time, the equation becomes

$$\text{Degree of financial leverage} = \frac{\text{EBIT}}{\text{EBIT} - I}$$

where I = interest expense
EBIT = earnings before interest and taxes

Example: Comparing the Financial Leverage in Two Firms

PROBLEM   Using the information provided in Table 10–2, calculate the degree of financial leverage for Firm A and Firm B.

SOLUTION   Firm B has a greater degree of financial leverage (DFL) than Firm A:

$$\text{DFL}_A: \quad \frac{\$100,000}{\$100,000 - 0} = 1.00$$

$$\text{DFL}_B: \frac{\$100,000}{\$100,000 - \$10,000} = 1.11$$

Because Firm A has no debt, a change in EBIT produces the same change in income. Firm B has a D/C ratio of 50%. For every change in its EBIT, net income increases by 1.11 times that change. This example illustrates how financial managers compare the effects of financial leverage in their firms relative to other firms.

Generally, the more debt there is, the higher the degree of financial leverage. However, leverage works in both directions. For example, when the degree of financial leverage has a value of 2.00, a 1% drop in EBIT will produce a 2% decline in EPS. Therefore, the more financial leverage, the more volatile EPS become—and the greater the risk associated with the firm.

YOU SHOULD REMEMBER

Up to a certain point, financial leverage tends to increase the value of the firm. When debt gets too high relative to equity, however, financial risk and the chances of **insolvency** (inability to repay debt) increase; consequently, the firm's market value is likely to decrease. The goal is to find the level of financial leverage (D/C) that does not produce large variations in the EPS of the firm and does not make investors apprehensive about the rising risks of insolvency.

• *THE EPS-EBIT APPROACH*

In the course of making decisions, financial managers have to choose the best way to finance new investments. The choice whether to finance investments by issuing bonds or by issuing stocks must take into consideration the estimated improvement in EPS. One method to help with this financing decision is called the **EPS-EBIT approach.**

This technique emphasizes maximization of EPS rather than optimization of the firm's wealth. It ignores changes in the degree of risk assigned to a firm by investors. However, as long as its limitations are taken into account, the EPS-EBIT method is a useful tool.

To facilitate the analysis, assume, as shown in Table 10–3, that only common stock or bond financing can be utilized to raise $100,000. Assume that the tax rate is 40% and that the cost of issuing debt is 10%. The additional $100,000 in financing is projected to increase EBIT from its current level of $30,000 to $60,000.

The next step is to see how the firm's income, or EPS, is affected by each type of financing. Calculate the EPS levels under each method of financing. As indicated in Table 10–4, given the existing capital structure, EPS are calculated at $1.20. New common stock financing will raise EPS to $2.00. The leverage effect of debt financing increases EPS to $2.40.

Then determine the levels of EBIT and EPS where the results are the same whether the firm issues debt or stock. Once this point of indifference is established, it becomes relatively easy to determine the merits of different financing vehicles. This point of indifference is called the break-even point for EBIT (BEP-EBIT). The equation for deriving this point is

$$\text{BEP-EBIT} = \left[\frac{(\text{EBIT} - I)(1 - t)}{N_s} = \frac{(\text{EBIT} - I)(1 - t)}{N_b} \right.$$

Table 10–3   EPS-EBIT Approach to Financing Decisions

	Existing Capital Structure	New Financing by Issuing $100,000 Common Stock	New Financing by Issuing $100,000 Bonds
Long-term debt (10%)	$100,000	$100,000	$200,000
Common Stock (at $20 par)	200,000	300,000	200,000
D + E	$300,000	$400,000	$400,000
Common shares outstanding	10,000	15,000	10,000

where I = interest expense
    t = tax rate
    N_s = number of common shares with stock financing
    N_b = number of common shares with bond financing
BEP-EBIT = level of EBIT that makes investors indifferent
           to either bond or stock financing

Inserting the values from Table 10–4, you can solve for the unknown EBIT.

$$\text{BEP-EBIT} = \left[\frac{(\text{EBIT} - \$10,000)(1 - .40)}{15,000 \text{ shares}} = \frac{(\text{EBIT} - \$20,000)(1 - .40)}{10,000 \text{ shares}}\right]$$
$$= \$40,000$$

The EBIT break-even point is $40,000.
Substituting this value of $40,000 in the above equations, you obtain $1.20 as the break-even point for EPS.

In other words, an EBIT of $40,000 produces $1.20 of EPS whether the firm finances by issuing debt or by issuing stock. Since this level of EBIT generates the same EPS, the firm is indifferent toward the type of financing it employs. For example:

Stock Financing

$$\text{BEP} - \text{EPS} = \frac{(\$40,000 - \$10,000) \times .60}{15,000 \text{ shares}} = \$1.20$$

Table 10–4 Income Statement under Different Capital Structures

	Estimated		
	Existing Capital Structure	New Common Stock Financing	New Debt Financing
EBIT	$30,000	$60,000	$60,000
Interest	10,000	10,000	20,000*
Earnings before taxes	20,000	50,000	40,000
Taxes (at 40%)	8,000	20,000	16,000
Earnings after taxes	$12,000	$30,000	$24,000
Shares outstanding	10,000	15,000	10,000
EPS	1.20	2.00	2.40

*Additional interest charges for new debt financing ($100,000 ×.10 =$10,000).

Debt Financing

$$\text{BEP} - \text{EPS} = \frac{(\$40,000 - \$20,000) \times .60}{10,000} = \$1.20$$

• USING EPS-EBIT TO CHOOSE BETWEEN STOCK AND BOND FINANCING

Having established the break-even, or indifference, point between EPS and EBIT, you can then proceed to find out whether bond or stock financing is most advantageous to the firm. This decision is simple: Choose the method which provides the higher EPS at any given level of EBIT. One way of doing this is shown in Figure 10–2.

You will note that, even when EBIT equals zero, the firm still incurs interest payments amounting to $10,000 when it issues new stock. These payments increase to $20,000 when it issues new debt. Connecting these two points on the horizontal scale with the corresponding break-even points for EBIT ($40,000) and EPS ($1.20), you obtain two straight lines that indicate which type of financing is more advantageous at a given level of EBIT.

New stock financing produces higher earnings at any EBIT level below $40,000; therefore, it is better to issue new stock. When EBIT exceeds $40,000, however, bond financing produces higher EPS and is more advantageous. As Table 10–4 indicates, debt financing yields EPS of $2.40, compared to $2.00 for stock financing since projected EBIT is higher than the BEP. Clearly, a bond issue is called for in this instance. In general, any EBIT above the break-even point favors bond financing over stock financing because of financial leverage effects.

The EPS-EBIT method does not tell you how much each type of financing adds to the firm's overall risk. Stock financing clearly means a lower degree of risk than

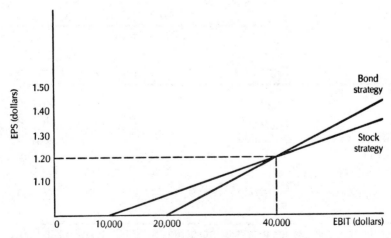

Figure 10–2 EPS-EBIT Decision to Issue Bonds or Stocks

bond financing, largely because it does not add to the firm's fixed financial charges, and also because greater debt produces greater volatility in EPS.

The decision whether to issue debt or stock is partly a judgmental one. Financial executives must weigh the benefits, the changing degree of risk, and the effects on EPS produced by changes in the capital structure before making a final financing decision.

YOU SHOULD REMEMBER

The EPS-EBIT method helps managers to decide whether to issue bonds or stocks. This method merely provides a starting point since the decision is based on the financing approach that yields the highest EPS. There are other considerations, such as risk, which must be taken into account before the firm can reach these financing conclusions. The best financing decisions take into account a combination of subjective and objective evaluations.

CAPITAL STRUCTURE CONTROVERSY

Researchers don't always agree on a given issue. This is a healthy condition, because it usually leads to a better understanding of various processes in the field of finance. Capital structure is an area that generated such a difference of opinion. One group of researchers claims that changes in capital structure produce a change in the firm's cost of capital. Another group argues that changes in financial leverage (D/C) or in capital structure do not affect the firm's cost of capital. Both groups have made important contributions to the development of the theory of capital structure.

Credit should be given to Modigliani-Miller (MM), who first developed a very important model on this subject. MM argue that changes in capital structure do not change the value of a firm because cheaper debt is exactly offset by the rising cost of equity. To prove their point, they introduce the concept of **arbitrage** (taking advantage of value differences between two markets), demonstrating that the value of two companies could not be different if the only difference was their capital mix. Should their values differ, investors would sell the overvalued firm and buy the undervalued firm until both firms had the same value.

This theory, however, was based on the assumption of no taxes or chance of bankruptcy. Once these two factors are introduced into the model, MM admit that financial leverage, up to a certain point, does result in a lower discount rate and a higher valuation for the firm. However, as debt increases further, the growing chances of bankruptcy and the loss of tax benefits result in a higher discount rate and a lower valuation for the firm. This MM Theory was a major breakthrough in finance and produced highly fruitful research on this subject, despite the restrictive nature of the assumptions underlying the model.

• *THE NET INCOME (NI) APPROACH*

The group of researchers who associate themselves with the **NI theory** provide a fairly traditional interpretation: they say that changes in capital structure influence the cost of capital and, consequently, the value of the firm. This occurs despite the fact that the costs of debt and of common stock remain constant, regardless of changes in financial leverage.

Because the cost of debt is adjusted for the tax benefits $(1 - t)$, however, it is lower than the cost of issuing common stock. Therefore, when the firm issues more debt, its average cost of capital is lowered, as shown in Table 10–5.

If this is what happens, the lower discount rate means a higher value for the firm's stock. Figure 10–3 illustrates this point. Note that the overall cost of the firm's capital declines as the D/C increases. When this happens, the lower discount rate raises the per-share price of the firm's stock.

Example: Calculating the Effect of a Change in the Discount Rate on Stock Value

PROBLEM   Assume that a firm (see Table 10–5) is not growing, and that its EPS are $1.00. What will be the effect of a rise in D/C from 50% to 67%?

SOLUTION   Each share will be worth $11.11 ($1.00 ÷ .09), when the D/C equals 50%. When the D/C ratio increases to 67%, the cost of capital decreases to 8% and the price of the firm's share increases to $12.50 ($1.00 ÷ .08).

Table 10–5   Capital Costs with Changing Capital Structures

Method of Financing	Capital Structure (D/C = 50%)			Capital Structure (D/C = 67%)		
	Weight (W)	Cost of Capital (K) (%)	W × K (%)	Weight (W)	Cost of Capital (K) (%)	W × K (%)
Common stock	.50	12	6	.33	12	4
Debt	.50	6	3	.67	6	4
WACC			9			8

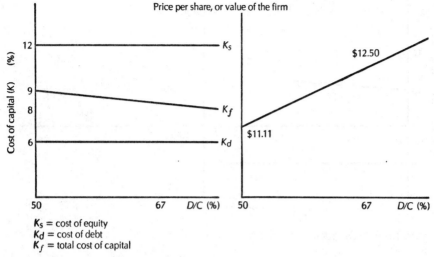

K_s = cost of equity
K_d = cost of debt
K_f = total cost of capital

Figure 10–3 NI approach and the Firm's Value

Although supporters of the NI concept correctly visualized the tax benefits of financial leverage, they failed to take into account the increased risk reflected in the cost of equity as the D/C ratio increases. This development was clearly considered by the supporters of the NOI thesis.

As Table 10–6 shows, even though there is a shift in financial leverage from a D/C of 50% to one of 67%, the weighted average cost of capital remains unchanged at 8%.

Figure 10–4 shows graphically what happens to the cost of capital and the price of the stock, given the NOI assumptions. The relative importance of lower cost debt, as a result of the shift to a 67% D/C, offsets the higher cost of common stock, so the average cost of capital remains unchanged. Given this condition, $1

Table 10–6   The Effect of NOI on the *WACC*

Method of Financing	Original Capital Structure (D/C = 50%)			New Capital Structure (D/C = 67%)		
	Weight (W)	Cost of Capital (K) (%)	W × K (%)	Weight (W)	Cost of Capital (K) (%)	W × K (%)
Common stock	.50	10	5	.33	12	4
Debt	.50	6	3	.67	6	4
WACC			8			8

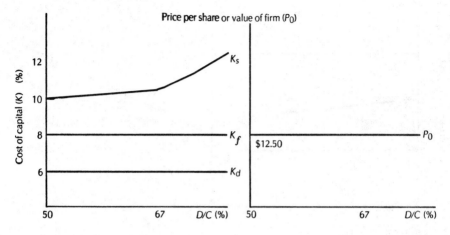

Figure 10–4 NOI approach and the Firm's Value

worth of earnings should produce a stock value of $12.50 ($1.00 ÷ .08) at a D/C of 50%, and the same dollar earnings capitalized by the same discount rate will, therefore, give rise to the same stock value of $12.50 ($1.00 ÷ .08) when the D/C ratio increases to 67%.

YOU SHOULD REMEMBER

The NI and NOI theories are based on many restrictive assumptions. They do not reflect the real world, but each approach enhances your comprehension of the effects of financial leverage on the value of the firm. It is up to the manager to use the insights provided by these theories to make better financial decisions.

• *A COMPROMISE SOLUTION*

The extreme positions of the NI and NOI approaches can be reconciled. Currently, the accepted view is that financial leverage adds tax benefits to a firm—up to a certain point—but too much debt has an adverse effect on the cost of capital and the value of the firm.

As Figure 10–5 and Table 10–7 show, an increase in the D/C ratio from 0 to 40% may help reduce the average weighted cost of capital simply because of the shift from higher-cost common stock to lower-cost debt $(1 - t)$. This indicates that a 40% D/C ratio is the optimal capital structure of the firm.

The benefits derived from financial leverage are reflected in a favorable attitude by investors toward a firm's stock. Investors recognize that up to a certain point

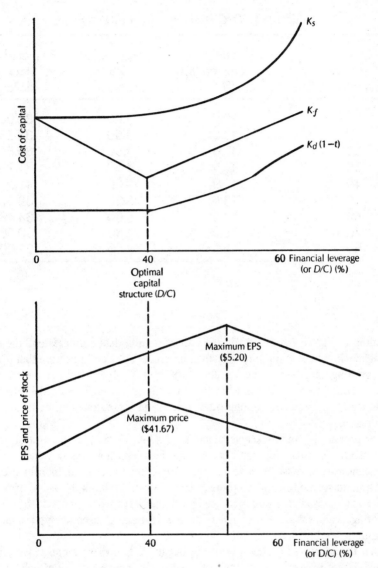

Figure 10–5 Effects of Financial Leverage on the Cost of Capital and Value of the Firm

an increasing D/C will increase EPS, which in turn will compensate them for the risk of higher financial leverage. Consequently, investors will probably be willing to purchase a firm's stock at higher prices. At some point, however, the D/C ratio becomes too high. Then the risks associated with increasing financial leverage are unacceptable, and, therefore, the price of the stock will decline.

When financial leverage (D/C) passes the optimal capital structure point, which

Table 10–7 D/C Ratio and Cost of Financing

Capital Structure (percentage D/C)	Estimated Cost of Common (K_s) (%)	Expected EPS (dollars)	Estimated Price of Stock (P_0)* (dollars)
0	10.0	3.00	30.00
10	10.5	3.50	33.33
20	11.0	4.00	36.36
30	11.5	4.50	39.13
40	12.0	5.00	41.67
50	13.5	5.20	38.52
60	14.5	5.00	34.48
70	16.0	4.80	30.00
80	18.0	4.50	25.00

$$*P_0 = \frac{EPS}{K_s}$$

according to Figure 10–5 is 40%, the cost of issuing debt increases and the cost of issuing stock increases more rapidly than before. This is an indication that investors are becoming more apprehensive about the ability of the firm to meet its fixed financial obligations, given available expected resources. As a result, the total cost of capital starts to increase. Among other factors, three reasons can be cited for this development.

1. The probability of *bankruptcy* increases. This means that there is a growing probability of incurring court costs, legal fees, and lower asset values.
2. *Agency costs* increase because managers are forced to devote an inordinate amount of time to search for ways to protect the claims of creditors in case of insolvency.
3. The *tax benefits* dissipate because the higher earnings, generated by financial leverage, are subject to a greater degree of risk. Consequently, risk-adjusted earnings tend to decline.

Given the increased probability of the occurrence of these events, investors will demand higher returns; this will be followed by an increasing cost of debt. Lenders will be less willing to buy bonds unless they receive a higher return, the advantage of shifting from stocks to bonds will disappear, and the overall average cost of capital for the firm will increase.

A D/C higher than 50% will lower EPS (see Table 10–7). Since the market is efficient, investors foresee this adverse trend in EPS. That is why the value of the stock reaches a peak at $41.67—when the D/C ratio reaches 40%, or before EPS reaches its peak.

If this is the condition facing the firm, financial managers will try to develop financing strategies leading to a capital structure that produces optimal results from financial leverage.

There are no specific rules that managers can use to determine the optimal capital structure of a firm. A great deal depends on how fast earnings are growing and how investors assess the financial soundness of the firm. This assessment can change from firm to firm because of varying investor attitudes toward different firms in regard to the quality of their management and their ability to cope with rising financial risk. Investor attitudes cannot be easily measured, and a great deal of judgment is required before managers sense the way a market will react to a changing capital structure. As you can see, the right financing mix or capital structure is difficult to pinpoint. The final decision represents a compromise. In the long run, all a manager can strive for is a reasonable wealth appreciation that is, if possible, better than that of the industry as a whole and of competing firms.

YOU SHOULD REMEMBER

The NOI and NI approaches have produced a compromise position. Academicians have come to recognize that, up to a certain point, financial leverage can produce a lower discount rate and a higher value for a firm. There is, however, a point beyond which the financial risks are too high and the value of the firm will decline because of the growing chances of bankruptcy and the adverse effects of high fixed financial cost on EPS. Theoretically, there is an **optimal capital structure** that will produce maximum wealth for a firm.

KNOW THE CONCEPTS

DO YOU KNOW THE BASICS?

1. What do relatively high fixed financial costs indicate about a capital structure, assuming it has no preferred stock, leases, and so forth?

2. Why can debt produce benefits from financial leverage?

3. What happens to the value of a firm and its cost of capital when it achieves an optimal capital structure? Explain why this occurs.

4. List the factors that make up the total capitalization of a firm.

5. When a firm's D/C ratio gets too high, what is the investors' reaction to risk and their attitude toward the stock?

6. In what way can the EPS-EBIT approach help a financial manager reach a financing decision?

7. Name two problems associated with the EPS-EBIT approach.

8. In broad terms, explain the concepts developed by the NI and the NOI theorists.

9. What is the current synthesis of capital structure theory?

10. As a financial manager, what factors would you look at to determine whether a firm's D/C ratio is acceptable to investors?

11. Name two industries that have high D/C ratios and two that have low debt-to-equity ratios. Generally speaking, why do these differences exist?

12. What should a manager do to develop a capital structure that will produce the best results?

13. What reasons can you supply to explain why the cost of issuing debt, common stock, and the overall cost of capital of a firm increases after the *D/C* ratio exceeds the optimal capital structure point?

TERMS FOR STUDY

arbitrage
capital structure
debt/capitalization (D/C) ratio
degree of financial leverage
EPS-EBIT approach
financial leverage

insolvency
long-term debt
NI theory
NOI theory
optimal capital structure

PRACTICAL APPLICATION

COMPUTATIONAL PROBLEMS

1. If the EBIT of a company were to increase from $100,000 to $200,000, and its EPS increased from $1.00 to $2.50, calculate the degree of financial leverage of the company and explain what this means.

2. A firm's debt is $100,000, and the value of its equity is $200,000. K_s is 12%, K_d is 10%, and the tax rate is 40%. Calculate the weighted average cost of capital of this firm.

3. The break-even levels of EPS-EBIT are $2.00 (EPS) and $100,000 (EBIT). What kind of bond or stock financing would a firm decide on if the new EBIT were $200,000 and stock financing produced EPS of $3.00 and debt financing yielded EPS of $3.50? Explain your answer.

4. Assume EBIT = $10,000; debt is $10,000, with an assigned coupon rate of 8%; the cost of common stock (K_e) or required rate of return is 10%. Calculate the value of this firm, whose tax rate is 40%.

5. If a firm's EPS changes from $2.00 to $2.50 per share between 1989 and 1990, and if its EBIT goes up from $500,000 to $600,000, calculate the degree of financial leverage implied by these figures and interpret the results.

ANSWERS

KNOW THE CONCEPTS

1. The firm's capital structure has a high proportion of debt.

2. The benefits are derived from the fact that more EBIT filter down to earnings per share because of a lower number of shares. Financial leverage, up to a certain point, helps the firm to reduce its overall cost of capital.

3. A firm attains its highest value when the optimal capital structure is achieved. This occurs when the WACC is lowest, which is also the time at which the firm's capitalized value of EBIT is highest.

4. The factors that make up the total capitalization of the firm are long-term debt, preferred stock, and common equity.

5. When D/C is too high, investors find that the volatility of earnings per share usually increases and the chances of default rise. This increased risk means the assignment of a higher discount rate to dividends or future returns of the firm. As a result, the present value of these returns declines.

6. The EPS-EBIT approach tells managers when it is advantageous to issue stocks or bonds. EBIT below the EBIT indifference point call for a decision in favor of issuing stock because EPS generated via this method of financing will be higher than those obtained by issuing bonds. Conversely, EBIT higher than the indifference point yield higher EPS when bonds are issued instead of stocks; therefore, bonds should be issued.

7. The EPS-EBIT approach ignores risk. It also does not consider the fact that there is a limit beyond which it is unsafe to issue more debt.

8. The NI theorists say that financial leverage reduces the cost of capital of the firm, thereby increasing the value of its shares. The NOI theorists say that, no matter how the capital structure of the firm is changed, its cost of capital and the value of its stock will remain unchanged.

9. The current synthesis draws from the contributions made by the NI and NOI theorists and says that, up to a point, financial leverage helps to reduce the cost of capital of a firm. Beyond this point, tax benefits vanish and the chances of bankruptcy increase. Overall risk increases, and the WACC will also increase.

10. Look at the D/C of the firm versus the industry's D/C. Compare the firm's D/C and financial structure to the financial structure of the best firm in the industry. Ask investment bankers whether the firm's D/C is high or low, and how they feel the market or investors would react to a given capital structure. Finally, try to keep the D/C at a conservative level to avoid association with excessive financial risk.

11. Two industries with high D/C ratios are utilities and railroads. Two industries with low D/C ratios are drugs and travel agencies. (See Morris Associates' data.)

12. Financial managers should avoid excesses. They should study the most successful companies in the industry and try to keep a balance between debt and equity. At all costs, they should avoid debt that increases fixed obligations beyond a reasonable level. To do this, they should calculate the worst situation, such as a recession, and observe whether the payments occasioned by a given debt level could be met. The goal is to maintain a conservative capital structure which yields the lowest possible risk and the best (not necessarily the optimal) value of the firm's common stock.

13. The cost of capital increases when the D/C ratio exceeds its optimal point because the probability of incurring bankruptcy costs increases—that is, there is a growing chance of incurring legal costs, court costs, and asset losses. Agency costs increase because of the increased cost of protecting creditor claims. Also, the value of risk-adjusted EPS deteriorates because the discount rate increases faster than the increase in earnings.

PRACTICAL APPLICATION

1. Degree of financial leverage $= \dfrac{150\%}{100\%} = 1.5$. This indicates that a 1% change in EBIT will produce a 1.5% change in the EPS of the firm.

2.

Capital Structure		Weight (W)	K	(K × W)
Debt	$100,000	.33%	.06	2.0%
Equity	200,000	.67%	.12	8.0%
		100%		WACC = 10.0%

3. The firm would decide to issue bonds because more debt would produce a higher level of EPS ($3.50) at the $200,000 EBIT level, compared to EPS of $3.00 if it financed by issuing stock.

4. $V_f = D + E$

EBIT	$10,000
I	800
EBT	$ 9,200
Taxes @ 40%	3,680
EAT	$ 5,520

$$E = \frac{\text{EAT}}{\substack{\text{Discount} \\ \text{rate}}} = \frac{\$5,520}{.10} = \$55,200$$

Value of firm is $65,200 ($10,000 + $55,200).

5. The degree of financial leverage is:

$$\frac{25\%}{20\%} = 1.25$$

Every 1% change in EBIT translates into a 1¼% change in EPS.

11
DIVIDEND POLICY

KEY TERMS

dividend a return on an investment, usually in the form of cash or stock

par value the face value of a share of stock or a bond

stock dividend a dividend in the form of additional shares of stock, issued in lieu of a cash dividend

stock split the issuing of more shares of stock to current stockholders without increasing stockholders' equity.

• *SIGNIFICANCE OF DIVIDEND POLICY*

Dividend policy plays an important role in determining the value of a firm. Stockholders visualize dividends as signals of the firm's ability to generate income. A large number of analysts employ dividends to calculate the intrinsic value of stocks. The returns used to compute the beta of a stock include dividend yields as one of the factors. Consequently, dividends are an important component for calculating the value and the beta of a stock.

Although some academicians argue that the decision to pay dividends is independent of investment decisions, dividends can indirectly influence the external financing plans of financial managers. For example, a decision to pay high dividends will leave less internal funds for reinvestment in the firm. This could force the firm to generate funds from new stock or bond issues. In turn, external financing can change the firm's capital structure and cost of capital. Accordingly, financial managers try to strike a balance between paying a reasonable dividend to stockholders (to maintain their loyalty) and reinvesting earnings (to achieve future growth and maximize the price of the firm's shares).

One of the key theories to be discussed in this chapter states that dividends should be paid only after all financing and investment requirements are satisfied. Another theory claims that dividends do not affect the price of shares. Yet others argue that dividends are important for measuring the value of a firm.

Each of these theories helps managers understand the role played by dividends. A study of each theory will provide better guidelines for finding the best dividend policy for any firm.

ROLE OF DIVIDENDS

To the investor, **dividends** represent a return which can be compared to other investment opportunities. This return is called the **dividend yield.** It is the relationship between the dividend payment and the price of a share of stock.

$$\text{Current dividend yield} = \frac{\text{Current dividend}}{\text{Current price of stock}}$$

If a company pays $10 in dividends per share, and its stock is selling for $100, the dividend yield is 10% ($10 ÷ $100). This yield can then be compared with the yields of other stocks or the rates of return offered by bonds and other assets.

Dividends provide a basis for calculating the cost of issuing common stock (K_s) as well as the value of a firm's shares. Theoretically, this can be done by employing the *constant-dividend-growth model.* This model assumes that current dividends (D_0) will continue to grow (G) at the same rate each year to infinity. If so, to calculate the value of the firm's common stock (V_s), [or its price (P_0)], one must estimate the growth rate of dividends and the required rate of return or discount rate. The final step is to adjust (D_0) for one year's growth, or $D_0 (1 + G)^1$. The appropriate equations to determine the discount rate and the value of a share of stock are:

$$P_0 = \frac{D_1}{K_s - G}$$

where:

$$K_s = \frac{D_1}{P_0} + G$$

Example: Use Dividends to Derive the Value of a Share of Common Stock.

The calculation of each component of the above dividend model is shown below:

D_0 = Look up this value in any financial service or the *Wall Street Journal.*

G = Can be derived in two ways.

FIRST APPROACH:

G = *ROE* × retention ratio.

Where:

$$ROE = \text{Return on equity} = \frac{\text{Net income}}{\text{Equity}}$$

$$\text{Retention ratio} \quad = \quad \frac{\text{Retained earnings}}{\text{Net income}}$$

Therefore, if ROE = 20% and retention ratio = .50, then

$$G = .20\ (0.50) = .10$$

SECOND APPROACH

Calculate the growth of dividends for the most recent 5 years from two terminal dates.

Years	Dividends Per Share
1984	$3.11
1985	3.42
1986	3.75
1987	4.13
1988	4.55
1989	5.00

$$\text{Growth rate, 1984 to 1989} = \frac{3.11}{5.00} = .622\ (\text{PVIF})$$

Look up this factor in the present-value table and you get the annual growth rate for the past 5 years, which is equal to 10% per year. Note that this growth rate is the same as the rate computed by the first method.

Having calculated G, the next goal is to estimate K_s. One way is:

$$K_s = \frac{D_1}{P_0} + G$$

The current price of a stock is quoted in the daily financial pages (assume the quote is $55.00 per share). D_1 is equal to $D_0\ (1 + G)^1$, which means raising current dividends ($5.00) by one year's growth, already estimated to be 10%. Therefore, substituting the appropriate values in the above equation, you obtain an answer:

$$K_s = \frac{\$5.00\ (1 + .10)^1}{\$55.00} + .10 = \frac{\$5.50}{\$55.00} + .10 = 20\%$$

Another method for calculating K is to use the SML equation of the CAPM model. Assume you know that the beta of the stock (B) is 1.5, the return of the market (K_m) is 15%, and the risk-free rate is 5%, then:

$$K_s = R_F + (K_m - R_F)\ B_s$$

Solving this equation:

$$K_s = .05 + (.15 - .05)\ 1.5 = 20\%$$

This 20% is the same figure derived by employing the first method.

Having calculated the factors required by the constant-dividend-growth model, it is time to demonstrate how dividends help to determine the intrinsic value of a firm's stock (P_0) by using the following equation:

$$P_0 = \frac{D_1}{K_s - G}$$

Substituting previously calculated values, you obtain:

$$P_0 = \frac{\$5.00\ (1 + .10)^1}{.20 - .10} = \frac{\$5.50}{.10} = \$55.00$$

In other words, a stock that is paying $5.00 in dividends, growing at 10%, and has an assigned discount rate of 20% is worth $55.00.

PAYOUT RATIO

The **payout ratio** is another important aspect of dividend policy. It is found by taking dividends per share and relating them to earnings per share.

$$\text{Dividend payout ratio} = \frac{\text{Dividends per share}}{\text{Earnings per share}}$$

Assume Company A pays a $5.00 per share dividend and Company B pays $3.00. Also, Company A's EPS are $10.00 and those of Company B are $4.00.

Using this equation, the payouts of two companies can easily be compared:

$$\text{Payout ratio of Company A} = \frac{\$5.00}{\$10.00} = 50\%$$

$$\text{Payout ratio of Company B} = \frac{\$3.00}{\$4.00} = 75\%$$

Company A pays out 50% of its earnings in dividends, while Company B's payout is 75%.

The payout ratio is useful for calculating the price/earnings ratio (P/E) of a stock. This can be done as follows:

$$P/E = \frac{\text{Payout ratio}}{K_s - G}$$

Therefore, if a company's average payout is .50 and its discount rate is 20% while its growth is 10%, it should be assigned a P/E of 5 times earnings per share.

$$P/E = \frac{.50}{.20 - .10} = \frac{.50}{.10} = 5 \text{ times}$$

The payout ratio varies from industry to industry and from company to company. Fast-growing companies need all the funds they can get. Therefore, their payout is usually low. Electric utilities, who have highly dependable earnings growth, are known to pay out a high percentage of earnings as dividends.

The payout ratio does not indicate anything about the stability of earnings and dividends. As a matter of fact, payout ratios may be misleading: During business contraction phases, the payout ratio may increase sharply, even though earnings are falling because a firm may attempt to pay the same dividends as in good economic periods. However, a steady dividend payout policy telegraphs a message. It tells investors that they can rely, within reason, on the company to maintain its dividends. This message generally attracts a loyal following. Erratic dividend payments create uncertainty. This raises the discount rate and a lower valuation of a stock. Companies often adopt conservative policies that provide investors with reasonable assurances of receiving stated dividends in good and bad times.

There are several things a manager should do when establishing a dividend policy:

1. Determine the potential growth of future earnings.

2. Find out how sensitive earnings are during various phases of the business cycle.

3. Determine the yields and payouts of other firms in the industry.

These and other considerations provide a basis for setting a dividend policy. The wise course of action is to keep dividend payments fairly low, raising them only when there is an ample earnings cushion. Firms whose earnings are volatile might consider paying a low but steady dividend, accompanied by extra dividends when earnings and times are good. The ultimate goal is to assure the investor that dividend payments will be maintained.

Any break in this dividend policy can damage the firm's image and the value of its stock.

YOU SHOULD REMEMBER

Financial managers must pay considerable attention to dividend policy because it influences both investor attitudes toward the firm's stock and the firm's cost of financing investments. The most acceptable policy is determined by judgment and comparison with policies adopted by other companies in the industry.

• NONCASH DIVIDEND PAYOUTS

Instead of paying cash, firms may decide to make noncash payments to stockholders. Basically, these types of dividend payments include stock dividends and stock splits. What are these dividends like, and how do they influence the value of the firm?

STOCK DIVIDENDS

Stock dividends—that is, dividends in the form of additional shares—may be paid instead of cash dividends to keep stockholders happy when a firm wishes to conserve cash for investment purposes. As long as these stock dividends are small (about 2% to 5%), they do not have any major dilutive effects on earnings. Although stockholders may feel better psychologically when they receive more shares, they don't really gain anything when a stock dividend is declared because the price of the stock declines by the same percentage as the stock dividend.

Example: Calculating the Effects of Stock Dividends on the Value of Stock

PROBLEM   A stock can be purchased for $50 before a 5% stock dividend is declared.

     a. What is the effect on a parcel of 100 shares bought before the dividend was declared?

     b. What can a share of stock be bought for after the sale?

SOLUTION   a. Calculate the value of 100 shares before the stock dividend: $50 × 100 shares = $5,000. After the dividend is paid, the parcel contains 105 shares but is still worth $5,000 ($47.62 × 105).

     b. Use the information from the first part of the question, and you see that the stock can be purchased for $47.62 ($5,000 ÷ 105) when the stock goes ex-dividend.

STOCK SPLITS

Stock splits are similar to stock dividends, but they usually involve the issuance of even more shares. When a firm states that it will split its stock 2-for-1, it is saying that a stockholder who owns 100 shares of the firm's stock will receive another 100 shares. A 3-for-2 split means that 50 additional shares would be issued to a stockholder who owns 100 shares.

• EFFECTS OF DIVIDENDS ON THE BALANCE SHEET

Cash and stock dividends produce different changes in the balance sheet of a firm.

Cash dividends, for instance, result in a reduction of cash in the balance sheet and a corresponding reduction in retained earnings.

The effects of *stock dividends* are illustrated in Table 11–1.

If the market price of the stock is $20, then the value of the new shares amounts to $2.0 million (100,000 shares × $20). This $2.0 million is divided into $500,000 going to common stock ($100,000 shares × $5 par value), and the remaining $1.5

Table 11–1   Balance Sheet Changes Resulting from a 10% Stock Dividend

	Stockholders' Equity	
	Before Stock Dividend	After Stock Dividend
1.0 million old shares at $5 par value	$ 5,000,000	
1.1 million new shares at $5 par value		$ 5,500,000
Paid-in capital surplus in excess of par*	$10,000,000	$11,500,000
Retained earnings	6,000,000	4,000,000
Total stockholders' equity	$21,000,000	$21,000,000

*Market value of a share of stock = $20.00. 100,000 additional shares (1,000,000 × .10)

million ($2,000,000 − $500,000) goes into capital surplus. The $2.0 million comes out of retained earnings, leaving $4,000,000 ($6,000,000 − $2,000,000) to retained earnings. Total stockholders' equity, however, remains unchanged.

In the case of a stock split, the numbers in the capital account do not change. The only changes are a reduction of par value and an increase in the number of outstanding shares as seen in Table 11–2. Therefore a stock split of 2 for 1 does not change the total value of stockholders' equity. However, the par value is reduced from $5 to $2.50, and the number of outstanding shares doubles to 2.0 million.

As indicated, these accounting changes do not change the ownership positions of stockholders in the firm. These payments do, however, allow the firm to keep cash. Also, stockholders are often happier owning more shares than fewer shares. For these reasons, and because of the greater number of shares after a split, the market's response to stock splits and stock dividends is usually favorable.

Table 11–2   Balance Sheet Changes Resulting from 2-for-1 Stock Split

	Stockholders' Equity	
	Before Stock Split	After Stock Split
1.0 million old shares at $5 par value	$ 5,000,000	
2.0 million new shares at $2.50 par value		$ 5,000,000
Paid-in capital in excess of par value	$10,000,000	$10,000,000
Retained earnings	6,000,000	6,000,000
Total stockholders' equity	$21,000,000	$21,000,000

INTERNAL AND EXTERNAL RESPONSES

In the case of small stock dividends, investors seem to ignore the dilution. As a result, the prices of shares tend to hold up well despite the stock dividend. In the case of stock splits, the anticipation of a dividend increase, for example, usually results in an improving market value of the shares before the stock split. However, if a higher dividend is not declared on the ex-dividend date, there is an unfavorable impact on the price of the shares.

Firms benefit from noncash payments for several reasons. Their shares are more widely distributed, which can facilitate future financing via rights or convertible issues. The firms retain funds internally for investment purposes. Also, although stock dividends or splits cost more to process than cash dividends, they ultimately tend to increase the supply of shares among more shareholders—and this can dampen stock price fluctuations in thinly distributed markets.

In the final analysis, remember that, although these forms of dividend payments provide some temporary flexibility, they are no substitute for a sound long-term dividend policy.

YOU SHOULD REMEMBER

If a firm can't pay dividends, there are noncash payments that can be temporarily substituted for cash dividends. Stock dividends change the balance sheet by increasing the total value of common stock par, raising the paid-in capital surplus, and reducing retained earnings. Stock splits reduce par value but do not affect the common equity part of the balance sheet. These noncash dividends are sometimes used to widen the distribution of the stock ownership, but aside from the psychological benefits to investors, they do not change the value of the firm.

• LIMITATIONS ON DIVIDEND PAYMENTS

There are financial restrictions on the payment of dividends that vary from firm to firm, and there may be legal contractual limitations to the payout of dividends. The main purpose of these restrictions is to conserve liquidity and protect creditor claims in case of insolvency. Payment of high dividends can reduce the amount of funds available to creditors when a firm is liquidated.

FINANCIAL RESTRICTIONS

Financial restrictions are related to a firm's need to maintain a sound financial base, to avoid high costs of financing, and to limit the chances of **insolvency**. The fact that a firm generates good profits does not necessarily mean that it has ready cash to pay dividends to stockholders. Therefore, when a firm considers a dividend policy, it must take into account the investments required to achieve its targeted growth in earnings. Growing firms require substantial amounts of funds. They cannot continually go to the market to generate these funds, because the marginal cost of capital will increase. The best course of action is to control the dividend payout in order to minimize external financing.

Dividend payments must also take a back seat to liquidity considerations. If a firm is short of cash and has inadequate net working capital, it may have problems covering its short-term liabilities. Creditors are not easy to get along with when they don't get paid on time. Therefore, prudent managers must make sure—before they make a dividend commitment—that cash and marketable securities are available to cover bills coming due. Financial managers must be concerned with the future potential payment of dividends. Their plans should include projections of earnings so they can establish a long-term policy of stable dividend payments. Remember: companies that maintain stable and steadily growing dividends can expect a stockholder following and a favorable market response.

Stockholders study a firm's past record of dividend payments. Stable and gradually increasing dividends raise investor confidence, reduce uncertainty, and help maintain a high valuation for a firm's stock.

LEGAL RESTRICTIONS

External legal commitments must also be taken into account when the firm develops a dividend policy. In most states, the **capital impairment rule** limits the payment of cash dividends drawn from capital stock or from the par value of the firm. These restrictions are designed to ensure that there is ample equity to protect the claims of creditors.

Dividend payment is, by the same token, restricted to the total of a firm's present and past earnings. Again, the goal is to protect creditors in case of insolvency or liquidation. When a firm cannot meet its liabilities, the law prohibits the firm from paying cash dividends. Otherwise, creditors would suffer and could sue the firm to recover these dividends.

The Internal Revenue Service (IRS) enters the picture when firms accumulate excess earnings. It looks on this strategy as a ploy to avoid paying ordinary income taxes on dividends. Although the value of a firm's shares may increase because of this earnings accumulation, its stockholders will not pay capital gains taxes until they sell their shares. The IRS frowns on this policy, and will investigate a firm which accumulates excessive earnings in the form of cash and marketable securities. It will also penalize such a firm unless it pays out more dividends.

CONTRACTUAL RESTRICTIONS

In addition to these legal constraints on dividends, there are also **contractual obligations** that restrict the payment of dividends. For example, when bonds are issued, the firm may have to promise not to pay dividends if the current ratio, the interest coverage, or other ratios fall below certain levels. Other contracts can require that the amount of dividends paid be limited to a percentage of earnings.

These contractual restraints exist to protect creditors. Any disregard of these obligations can provide grounds for immediate repayment of loans to creditors.

YOU SHOULD REMEMBER

Many states impose restrictions on the payment of dividends to protect the claims of creditors. Creditors are lenders whose positions are protected by contractual promises or covenants in loan agreements to ensure repayment of the loans. There are also financial restrictions that a firm may impose on itself in order to hold the costs of financing as low as possible, to induce lenders to supply more funds, and to limit the chances of insolvency. These self-imposed restrictions ensure readily available sources of external financing. All these constraints on dividends are designed to maintain the firm's ability to meet its fixed financial obligations.

DIVIDEND POLICY AND THE PRICE OF STOCK

There are those who claim that the value of a firm is unaffected by dividends or changes in dividend policy. Modigliani and Miller (MM) are the leading proponents of this theory. It should be pointed out that MM present a theoretical argument based on the assumption of perfect capital markets and no taxes. Obviously, they realize that taxes and other factors are real-world conditions that can make dividends an important aspect of valuation. Their argument is important, however, in that it produces a fruitful dialogue on an important subject.

Others feel that dividend policy does matter, and that it has an important effect on stock valuation. Myron Gordon is one of the well-known academicians who supports this thesis. As always, different theories and interpretations provide a better basis for understanding the process of valuation.

DIVIDENDS ARE NOT IMPORTANT?

Those who claim that dividends are not relevant to stock valuation argue that dividends do not enter into a firm's decision to invest, and do not influence the outcome of earnings generated from investment strategies. Their contention is that dividends are a residual payment after all decisions have been made. Because earnings and the cost of common stock do not change when dividend policy changes, it can be said that the value of the firm does not change. Also, it is assumed that the firm should reinvest all retained earnings, as long as the return is at least equal to or higher than any return the stockholders can get in the market.

At the foundation of their theory, MM postulated that a condition of equilibrium existed between returns from reinvested earnings and the marginal cost of capital

($K_e = MCC$). As long as $K_e > MCC$, it would be inappropriate for a firm to pay dividends mainly because this payment would prevent it from maximizing its value and the wealth of the stockholders. Why? Because when returns from reinvested earnings exceed MCC, Net Present Value is positive. As long as NPV is positive, paying dividends would preclude the firm from maximizing the value of its stock.

The MM theory evolved in a period when the capital gains tax rate was lower than ordinary tax rates. In that tax environment, many stockholders would prefer allowing the stock to appreciate in value as opposed to receiving cash dividends (which were subject to higher taxes). Today, there is no difference in the two tax rates. As a result, this argument is not valid unless President Bush and Congress lower the current capital gains tax again, below ordinary rates.

In their proof, Modigliani and Miller neutralize the influence of dividends on stock valuation by assuming that, if dividends are included in the valuation of a firm, they can easily be offset by issuing more stock or debt to cover the exact value of these dividends, $D(t)$. In a simplified form, the equation for the value of a firm, V_f, under the MM model (assuming no debt and taxes) is

$$V_f = \frac{D(t) + \text{EBIT}_t - \text{Value of newly issued shares}}{\text{Discount rate } (K_0)}$$

Since dividends minus the value of newly issued shares is equal to zero, these two factors drop out of the equation. The value of the firm is therefore determined by investments and the discounted earnings they generate:

$$V_f = \frac{\text{EBIT}_t}{K_0}$$

This highly sophisticated and theoretical presentation by MM is designed to show that the firm's decision-making process is based mainly on the evaluation of the relative merits of investments and their profitability. Dividends are a separate policy and do not enter into this decision because they are a derivative of these factors. In neutralizing the role of dividends, MM are merely demonstrating that in the real world the valuation process involves complex strategies. By presenting the theory in this manner, MM pave the way for understanding more clearly the valuation-decision process.

DIVIDENDS ARE IMPORTANT?

Another group of academicians says that dividends *do* count in determining the value of a firm. They claim that, if you look at the real world, dividends are important to stockholders, and since that is the case, they play a role in the valuation process.

Supporters of this position indicate that there are three main reasons why investors prefer dividends and why the value of the firm is affected by dividend payments.

First, there is the *"bird in hand"* concept. Current cash dividends are worth more than future cash derived from reinvesting retained earnings. When a firm pays cash dividends, it reduces investor uncertainty. This lowers risk, which, in turn, lowers the discount rate (K_s). In other words, the discount rate assigned to dividends ($K_{dividends}$) is lower than the discount rate assigned to future retained earnings ($K_{retained\ earnings}$):

$$K_{dividends} < K_{retained\ earnings}$$

If the value of a stock is determined by discounting the future stream of returns, the lower discount rate assigned to dividends will influence the value of shares favorably.

Second, the *informational content* is another important factor that makes dividends relevant in stock valuation. By paying dividends, a firm signals to investors that it expects to generate the earnings to pay these dividends in the future. Conversely, when a firm *stops* paying dividends, it is letting investors know that something is wrong.

Any alteration in dividend policy will influence investors' attitudes toward a firm, and this will affect the market price of its stock. The important thing is to know why this change occurred. Sometimes a firm reduces dividends to maintain its liquidity base, and it may convince investors that the reinvested earnings will produce substantially higher dividends in the long run. If investors are convinced that this represents a good deal, the market value of the shares of the firm may remain unchanged or even increase.

Furthermore, some investors cannot interpret changes in earnings as easily as changes in dividends. They react to dividend changes more easily than to changes in earnings because of lack of financial sophistication or inability to understand how earnings are generated. That part of the decision-making process is left to security analysts. Ordinary investors want to know whether dividends will be paid and whether the firm is doing well. The signals given by the firm's dividend policy produce investor reactions, which lead to changes in valuation.

Third, the *clientele effect* implies that some investors need or prefer current income to future income. This is especially true of low or moderate income investors, who are less concerned with the higher returns that may be paid at some future date. This group of dividend followers gravitates toward stocks that pay steady dividends and offer high dividend yields. They search for stocks that provide a return close to that of other assets. Consequently, these stockholders become apprehensive when a company reduces its dividend, and are likely to dispose of the stock, thereby adversely affecting its value.

As you can observe, these three reasons, among others, make dividends important in the determination of stock valuation. Supporters of both the irrelevance and the relevance theses have something to contribute toward our understanding of the investment and valuation process. The answer probably lies between these two extreme views.

A COMPROMISE POSITION

In the world of theory, it is possible to establish a controlled environment and to present a good case in support of a given position. Theoretically, the decision to invest and to make plans to achieve a certain growth in earnings is independent of dividend policy. After all, dividend policy takes place after the earnings are generated and is a residual decision. The payment of dividends, therefore, should not affect the value of a firm. Realistically, however, investors prefer current gains or dividend income. As long as the potential return that a firm makes available to stockholders is greater than the returns they can receive from outside sources, it is logical to reinvest the earnings. Since there are no flotation costs associated with reinvested earnings, the cost of these funds is lower than the cost of issuing new stock.

But it is not always advantageous for investors to have a firm reinvest all retained earnings. In periods of high inflation, investors may receive a higher return from reinvesting cash dividends in assets other than in the firm in question. Also, during some periods of the business cycle it may be advantageous to pay dividends and finance investments with low-cost debt than by issuing common stock. Hence the argument for irrelevancy does not apply in all cases.

Enough evidence has been presented to indicate that dividends play a role in determining the value of a firm. Analysts and investors do pay a great deal of attention to the way firms invest and generate earnings, but the market also takes into account dividend signals issued by the firm. In the real world, some investors prefer current income and are less concerned with future income. They prefer stocks that pay steadily rising dividends and stocks that provide a good yield. Dividends supply information on the future course of the firm and play a role in the final valuation of the firm. Generally speaking, you should recognize that investment decisions may be completely independent of dividend policy. However, both the independent investment and dividend decisions influence the value of stocks.

YOU SHOULD REMEMBER

Some academicians say dividends are irrelevant, and others say they are relevant, to stock valuations. It all depends on one's interpretation. Some investors prefer the current income of dividends, while others prefer the future income of reinvested earnings. The information value and preference for current income make dividends attractive to some investors, and this in turn influences the value of stocks.

• *THE NET RESIDUAL APPROACH*

Assuming that all firms seek to achieve an optimal capital structure at the lowest cost of capital, their dividend policies should be influenced by these considerations. This means that dividends should be paid only after all profitable investment opportunities have been undertaken. In adopting a net residual approach to dividend policy, a firm should evaluate how its cost of capital will change as a result of new financing. It should compare this to the returns (*IRR*s) obtained from different projects. Any funds left over can be used to pay dividends. Under these circumstances, the goal is to achieve the lowest cost of capital, which, in turn, will maximize the value of the firm.

$$\frac{\text{Highest EBIT}}{\text{Lowest discount rate}} = \text{Maximum value of firm}$$

Given this scenario, those who support the *net residual dividend principle* claim that a firm should reinvest internally generated funds and not pay dividends, as long as there are profitable opportunities for such investment. Their assumption is that the firm maximizes its value when it has achieved an optimal capital structure. This optimal financing mix should be maintained. To do so, the firm first draws on its retained earnings. Once these are used up (and assuming that there are additional profitable investment opportunities because IRR>MCC), then it will have to engage in external financing.

Since the goal is to maintain the present capital structure, it will continue to issue debt and stock in the same proportion as its present mix. Therefore, if the firm's optimal capital structure is 30% stock and 70% debt, and it has profitable (NPV is positive) opportunities amounting to $10 million, the financing will be divided into $3 million worth of stock and $7 million worth of debt. Because dividends are paid to stockholders, these funds should come from surplus funds available to the firm or from retained earnings and not from externally generated (borrowed) funds. Once retained earnings are exhausted, no dividends should be paid if this forces the firm to engage in additional equity financing. Only that part of profitable investment originating from new stock issue is important in the decision either to pay or not to pay dividends.

An example should help to clarify this point. Assume an optimal capital structure of 30% common stock, 70% debt, and retained earnings equal to $4 million. Given profitable investment opportunities of $10 million, new financing will be split into $3 million for equity financing and $7 million for debt. Since there are $4 million in retained earnings, then $1 million ($4 million − $3 million) is the amount of dividends that can be paid to stockholders. If retained earnings were only $3 million and $1 million of dividends were declared, additional equity financing would be required, causing the capital structure mix to move away from its optimal level and thus preventing the firm from maximizing the value of its stock.

Advocates of the residual thesis claim that the rate of return (K_s) that investors require to justify their investment in a stock remains unaffected by a firm's dividend policy. In fact, you have seen that the firm financed more funds than it required, and as a result it could have done with less. What this illustrates is that what works

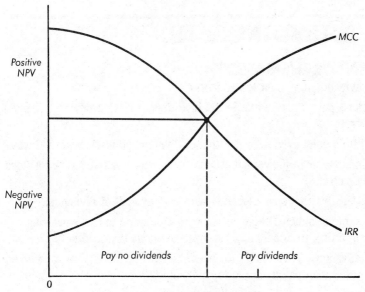

Figure 11-1 Residual Dividend Policy and the Relationship Between *IRR* and *MCC* Curves

well in theory may not work well in practice. There are many other considerations that enter into the determination of dividend policy. The firm's responsiveness to investor attitudes toward dividends is one factor. The return offered by competing assets and similar types of stocks is another. The process is more complicated than simply advocating a residual policy. The fact remains that, in actuality, dividends play a role in stock valuation and should be taken into consideration along with other factors in the final analysis of stock pricing.

YOU SHOULD REMEMBER

In the final analysis, some dividend policies are more effective than others. Financial managers should aim for a stable dividend policy to reduce uncertainty. It should be conservative enough to ensure steady payments without periodic interruptions. Companies whose earnings are highly cyclical and volatile should institute a low dividend payment policy, accompanied by extras when earnings and economic conditions are favorable.

The main goal is to set up a dividend policy that will be accepted by investors as being sound, that will provide them with reasonable returns, and that will result in the highest possible price for the stock of a firm.

KNOW THE CONCEPTS

DO YOU KNOW THE BASICS?

1. Why are dividends important to investors?
2. Does dividend policy play a role in the investment decision process? Explain your answer.
3. From the firm's point of view, what kind of dividend policy is best, and why?
4. What changes occur in the capital account when stock is split? When a stock dividend is paid?
5. Name two legal restrictions associated with the payment of dividends.
6. What are some contractual agreements with creditors, and in what way can they prevent a firm from adopting the most favorable dividend policy?
7. What tax advantage is available to investors who permit a firm to *reinvest* earnings, rather than pay them out to stockholders?
8. How do Modigliani and Miller explain the irrelevance of dividends in stock valuation?
9. Give three reasons why dividends may be relevant to stock valuation.
10. Explain how the residual dividend policy works.
11. What kind of dividend policy is the best one for a firm?

TERMS FOR STUDY

capital impairment rule	net residual principle
contractual obligations	par value
dividend	payout ratio
dividend yield	stock dividend
ex-dividend	stock split

PRACTICAL APPLICATION

COMPUTATIONAL PROBLEMS

1. Firm A's dividend payment is $7, and the price of its stock is $40. Compute the dividend yield. If Firm B's dividend yield is 10%, discuss what this difference in yield means.
2. Calculate the dividend payout ratio of a firm with earnings of $10 per share and a dividend payment of $3 per share.
3. A firm declares a 2-for-1 stock split. Its stock before the split is selling at $50 and has a par value of $10. Indicate the price of the stock and its par value after the split takes place.

4. Firm A reported the following figures on its balance sheet:

	Millions of Dollars
Common stock shares outstanding (5.0 million at $10 par value)	50.0
Paid-in capital surplus in excess of par	140.0
Retained earnings	100.00

Indicate what changes would occur to the above figures if the firm paid a 20% stock dividend and the value of its stock is $40.

5. Using the Myron Gordon dividend model, compute the value of Company X's stock if its earnings grew from $2.00 to $4.00 per share in the past 9 years, the payout ratio is 50%, and the discount rate is 15%. Remember to add 1 year's growth to current dividends.

6. The optimal capital structure of a firm is 35% equity and 65% debt. Retained earnings are $6 million, and shares outstanding equal 100,000. This firm follows the net-residual-dividend principle in paying dividends to stockholders. Assuming it has a total of $15 million in new profitable investments forthcoming, what is the maximum amount of dividend per share the firm will pay to common stockholders?

ANSWERS

KNOW THE CONCEPTS

1. Dividends are important because they signal to investors the firm's ability to generate income. They serve as a basis for calculating the value of stocks and are used also to calculate the returns of stocks.

2. Investment decisions are independent of a policy to pay dividends. However, the payment of dividends can indirectly influence external financing plans and the cost of capital. In this way, dividends play a role in the decision process of the firm.

3. The best dividend policy is one that attracts investors and maximizes the value of a firm's stock. The main thing is to apply a policy that leads to the payment of stable dividends, and that investors will interpret as less risky than volatile dividend payments.

4. A stock split does not change the capital structure of the firm. The higher number of shares is counterbalanced by a commensurate decline in the par value of the common stock. A stock dividend increases the number of outstanding shares, reduces retained earnings, and raises both the common stock par value and paid-in capital surplus in excess of par value.

5. Two legal restrictions associated with the payment of dividends are (1) in most states cash dividends are prohibited when the firm is insolvent, and (2) payment is restricted in cases where dividends are paid out of a firm's equity, thereby reducing the protection given to creditors.

6. There are loan agreements and certain constraints required by creditors, such as limiting the payment of dividends when earnings and/or net working capital fall below certain levels.

7. Prior to 1987, investors could gain by a lower tax rate by allowing reinvested earnings to be reflected in a higher price of the stock. In some countries, the capital gains tax rate on the capital appreciation of stocks is lower than the tax rate applied to current dividends.

8. Modigliani-Miller say that dividends are a residual. If it is assumed that

$$\text{Return of firm} \geq \text{Return of investor}$$

then it is logical to reinvest earnings. Also, these theorists neutralize the impact of dividends on the valuation of the firm by assuming that dividend payments are offset by issuing an equivalent value of shares. In other words, no matter what dividend policy is adopted, dividends do not play a role in generating income or in determining the value of the firm. Consequently, dividends are irrelevant in the determination of the value of stocks.

9. Three reasons why dividends are relevant to stock valuation are (1) the "bird in hand" principle, (2) the clientele effect, and (3) informational content.

10. The net residual dividend policy says that if a firm has extra funds after it has invested in all profitable projects or assets, and if these funds do not raise the firm's costs of capital, then cash dividends should be paid to stockholders.

11. Most managers believe the best dividend policy is one that minimizes the weighted average cost of capital. This policy should provide stable payments, maintain investor confidence, and give good signals to investors about the ability of the firm to maintain and increase its wealth. It should be conservative enough to hold the uncertainty of future payments to a minimum. Cyclical firms should pay low dividends regularly, and an "extra dividend" when economic conditions are favorable and profits are high.

PRACTICAL APPLICATION

1. Dividend yield $= \dfrac{\$7}{\$40} = \$17.50\%$

A 10% yield would mean that an investor interested in getting a high return—assuming both firms have the same risk level—would buy the stock of Firm A

However, if Firm A is very risky, the investors may look for the safety offered by stock B. Also, Firm B might be a fast-growing firm which prefers to reinvest a large portion of its earnings. As indicated, yield is not in itself a sufficient basis upon which investment decisions are made. Investors must look at many other factors.

2. Dividend payout $= \dfrac{\$3}{\$10} = 30\%$

3. Stock value after the split equals $25, and the par value is reduced to $5 per share.

4. The following are the changes that would appear on the balance sheet after Firm A paid a 20% stock dividend:

	Stockholders' Equity	
	Before Stock Dividend	After Stock Dividend
Common stock shares outstanding (5.0 million at $10 par value)	$ 50,000,000	
Common stock shares outstanding (6.0 million at $10 par value)		$ 60,000,000
Paid-in capital surplus in excess of par value	140,000,000	170,000,000
Retained earnings	100,000,000	60,000,000
Total stockholders' equity	$290,000,000	$290,000,000

5. The Myron Gordon dividend valuation formula is:

$$V_s = \frac{D_1}{K_s - G}$$

Given the appropriate figures, the value of Company X's stock is equal to:

$D_0 = \$2.00$ ($\$4.00 \times .50$)

$G = \dfrac{\$2.00}{\$4.00} = .50$ (look up this value in the present-value table for 9 years and you find that $G = .08$.)

$D_1 = \$2.00 (1 + .08) = \$2.16$

$V_s = \dfrac{\$2.16}{.15 - .08} = \dfrac{\$2.16}{.07} = \$30.86$

6. Financing in equity = (.35 × $15,000,000)
   = $5.25 million

$6,000,000	Retained earnings
5,250,000	Equity financing
$ 750,000	Residual or surplus

$$\text{Maximum dividends per Share} = \frac{\$750,000}{100,000} = \$7.50$$

LONG-TERM CAPITAL

12
LEASES

KEY TERMS

equivalent purchasing cost the discount rate that makes the present value of lease payments and lost tax benefits equal to the purchase price of an asset

lease a legal contract under which the owner of an asset gives another party the right to use an asset for a certain period of time in return for specified periodic payments.

lessee the user of an asset that is leased from another party

lessor the owner of an asset that is leased to another party

BASICS OF LEASING

A **lease** is a legal contract between two parties, the **lessor,** who owns the asset, and the **lessee,** who uses the asset. The lessor gives the lessee the right to use the asset for a specified period of time. In return, the lessee agrees to pay a certain amount of rent during the lease period. Commonly leased items are computers, equipment, cars, apartments, and offices. Lessors and lessees can be people or companies. Commercial banks, automobile dealers, and lease companies are major lessors in today's market.

The procedure to lease an asset is basically the same as that for borrowing money, though with some significant differences. After selecting the equipment (or other asset), the lessee contacts a leasing company and applies for lease financing. Following the receipt of the lease application, the lessor carefully evaluates the lessee's credit record, prepares a description and determines the cost of the asset to be leased. Once the application has been approved, the lessor informs the lessee how much the annual rental payments are, the dates when payments are due, the arrangements for the maintenance of the equipment, and other rights and obligations of the lessee during the lease period. If the lessee finds the terms and conditions acceptable, a lease contract is signed and the equipment is delivered to the lessee. At the end of the lease period, the leased equipment is returned to the lessor.

The contract may contain a clause giving the lessee the option to purchase the asset during, or at the end of, the contract period. At the end of the lease period, should the lessee decide to exercise this option, he/she will make an additional payment to the lessor, as stipulated by the contract, and the lessee then becomes the new owner of the asset.

ADVANTAGES OF LEASING

There are a number of advantages to leasing equipment rather than borrowing money to purchase it.

Leases place fewer restrictions on the lessee than on the borrower. Since the title of the leased equipment is in the name of the lessor, a lease is like financing with collateral. In simple terms, if the lessee fails to pay the annual or periodic rent, the lessor can easily reclaim the equipment because it legally belongs to the leasing company. The leasing company does not have to impose many restrictions on the lessee. Applications for leases are usually approved faster, and with more relaxed credit standards, than those for borrowing.

A lessee does not have to raise capital by issuing bonds or new common stock. When issuing bonds and common stock, a firm must follow certain procedures required by regulatory agencies, and investment bankers, such as Merrill Lynch. On the other hand, leasing is a straight-forward arrangement between the lessor and the lessee.

Another main advantage of a lease is that the lessee passes the risk of obsolescence (the risk that the equipment becomes outdated) to the lessor. In the business environment today, innovative ideas and products can become outdated quickly. Even the best equipment today may become obsolete in a short time. Borrowing a lot of money and buying risky equipment may not be an economically sound investment, since the value of this investment will drastically decline if new and more efficient equipment is brought to the market a few years after the purchase. This is especially true in the case of high-technology products, such as computers and precision instruments. In such cases, leasing can be a good alternative to buying the equipment.

Leasing, unlike purchasing, does not require a large initial investment. Lease expenses are paid over a period of time, so there is less financial burden on the lessee. Also, since the lessor receives a tax advantage on the leased equipment, the lease offer may be cheaper than the price charged by a supplier. In other words, the lessor may share the tax benefits with customers who regularly lease equipment, and in most cases the annual lease payments are tax deductible.

DISADVANTAGES OF LEASING

The disadvantages of leasing should also be considered whenever there is a choice between leasing and purchasing. A lessee, unlike the buyer of an asset, cannot depreciate the asset, so the tax benefit of depreciation will be lost. The loss of this depreciation benefit can be very costly for a solvent company with a large taxable income and only a small amount of debt.

Another disadvantage is that the lessee has to return the equipment after a certain period. What happens if the lessor decides not to renew the lease contract when the lessee badly needs the equipment to continue the operations of the firm? Because of this possibility, leasing with an option to buy should be considered.

When equipment is leased rather than owned, any major modification to improve the efficiency of the equipment needs the approval of the lessor. Getting the lessor's approval for technical modifications during the period of the lease contract may not be easy. This means that the lessee does not have complete control over the use of equipment that an owner would enjoy.

Another obvious disadvantage of a lease is the loss of salvage value. Salvage value of a purchased asset increases the cash inflow of the company if the asset is sold at the end of the last year. This advantage is lost if the asset is leased.

YOU SHOULD REMEMBER

A lease is a contract between two parties: the lessor, who owns the asset, and the lessee, who uses it. From the viewpoint of a lessee, leasing is flexible financing. Since there is no initial investment in a lease, the lessee is not concerned about raising capital and its effect on the company.

TYPES OF LEASES

There are four well-known types of leases:

1. Operating or service lease
2. Capital or financial lease
3. Sale-and-leaseback lease
4. Leveraged lease

An *operating lease* has a life span of no more than 5 years. All maintenance and repairs are the responsibility of the lessor. These leases are cancellable at the option of the lessee. They are written for periods that are shorter than the economic life of the asset.

A *financial lease* is a long-term contract between the lessee and the lessor and is noncancellable. The asset is usually fully amortized. Maintenance and repairs are the responsibility of the lessee.

In a *sale-and-leaseback* arrangement, the owner of an asset sells the asset to another company and leases it back for a specified period of time. The original owner of the asset now becomes the lessee. This arrangement allows a company to raise capital and still retain use of the asset. At the end of the contract, the lessee buys back the asset. This type of leasing is a form of temporary borrowing of funds.

Leveraged leasing involves four parties:

1. Lessor
2. Lessee
3. Lender
4. Trustee

The lessor puts up part of the purchase price of the asset, let us say about 20%. The remaining 80% of the purchase price is provided by other lenders, who receive a first mortgage secured loan collateralized by the leased asset. A trustee holds title to the lease contract, and the periodic rental payments are sent to this person. In turn, the trustee pays the interest and principal to the lenders, and the residual is sent to the lessor as a rental payment. When the lease ends, the trustee pays off the creditors and the lessor gains ownership of the asset.

The Financial Accounting Standards Board (FASB) has reviewed this aspect of leasing carefully. Their decision is that an operating lease does not have to be included in the balance sheet. Most companies report these leases in a footnote. In doing so, they avoid putting these leases on the books, so that there is a distortion in some debt and profit ratios—they are inflated.

According to FASB rule #13, the present value of a capital lease must be reported as both an asset and a liability on a company's balance sheet. Therefore, the "Board" recognizes that a financial lease is similar to the borrowing of funds or an outright purchase of an asset. To be considered a financial lease for accounting purposes, the FASB rule #13 stipulates that:

- The lessee has an option to purchase the property.

- The contract is for three quarters (or more) of the life of the property.

- The present value of lease payments is 90% (or more) of the purchase price of the property.

All lease payments are deducted from revenues as annual expenses.

• IS A LEASE AN ASSET OR A LIABILITY?

There has been a great deal of discussion among accountants whether or not a lease should be reported on a balance sheet as an asset. One argument is that the equipment leased is an asset, because it is continuously used by the lessee—like any other asset in the company. An opposite argument is that the lessee actually borrows the equipment and uses the leased equipment on a temporary basis; therefore, the lease is a current expenditure like other rentals. If this argument is accepted, a lease should not be reported on the balance sheet and cannot be depreciated. Instead, annual lease payments should be reported as current expenses on the income statement.

YOU SHOULD REMEMBER

In the case of a capital lease, the lessee should estimate the present value of lease payments, reporting that figure both as an asset and as a liability on the balance sheet. If the property is an operating lease, the accounting treatment is more straightforward. At the end of each year, total lease payments are deducted from revenue—like other annual expenses on the income statement.

CASH FLOWS OF A LEASE

Lease payments are somewhat like an annuity in which the first payment is made before the lease starts. In other words, lease payments are made at the beginning of each time period rather than the end. Since lease payments are made at the beginning of the time period, the lessee usually does not receive a tax benefit in the first period. The IRS does not allow deductions of lease payments covering a period of time before the leased equipment is actually used.

Example: Cash Flows of a Lease

Suppose the ABC Co., which is in the 40% tax bracket, leases equipment for 5 years with annual lease payments of $10,000 starting in January 1985.

In 1985, the ABC Co. pays $10,000, but no tax benefit accrues in that year. The cash outflow of the lease in the first year is $10,000, paid in the beginning of the year. The first tax benefit of $4,000 (40% × $10,000) is realized in the following year, reducing the effective lease payment of 1986 to only $6,000. This $6,000 is the cash outflow of the lease, or the actual cost of the lease after the tax benefit is deducted. The cash outflow of the lease is $6,000 each year from 1986 to 1989. In 1990, the lease contract expires and no further lease payment is due. However, the ABC Co. has claimed tax benefits for only 4 years, from 1986 to 1989, and has not received the tax benefit of the last lease payment in 1989. Therefore, in 1990 the ABC Co. claims the $4,000 tax credit which was not taken before.

Table 12–1   Cash Flow of the Lease for the ABC Co.

Year	Lease Payment	Tax Benefit	Cash Outflows of Lease
1985	$10,000	0	− $10,000
1986	10,000	$4,000	− 6,000
1987	10,000	4,000	− 6,000
1988	10,000	4,000	− 6,000
1989	10,000	4,000	− 6,000
1990	0	4,000	+ 4,000

The preceding example shows that tax benefits can be a major motivation for leasing assets. In reality, though, a company that doesn't have a great deal of taxable income cannot immediately enjoy the tax benefit of a lease. This company can, however, try to find a bank or financial institution with a considerable net income and tax liability. Such a bank has good motivation to purchase an asset and lease it to the company. Once the bank (the lessor) purchases the equipment, it can depreciate the asset and reduce its tax liability. At the same time, the company (the lessee) will expect the bank to share the tax benefits through favorable lease payments and more flexible terms.

Since lease contracts offer a great opportunity for reducing taxes, many lessors are wealthy individuals and profitable corporations with substantial tax liabilities. Congress has tried to weaken the tax motivation of lease contracts. One objective of the Economic Recovery Tax Act of 1981 was to reduce the depreciation lives of various types of assets to make the purchase of an asset more attractive than a lease because of faster depreciation. However, leases are widely used in many industries, and there is no evidence that the growth of this popular form of financing will decline in the future.

• CALCULATING ANNUAL RENTAL CHARGES

A lessor must determine the annual payment to charge a lessee. To do this, one must establish the following:

1. Cost of purchasing the leased asset
2. Present value of the benefits derived from outright ownership.
3. Net cost = Cost of leased asset minus PV of benefits.

Example:

The cost of the leased payment is $2.0 million. The life of the asset is 3 years. The discount rate is (K_{dt}) 9%, and depreciation is based on the ACRS schedule (.33, .44, .23). Calculate the before-tax annual rental of the equipment.

The value of the benefits is assumed to be depreciation only. The equipment has no salvage value at the end of the contract. The PV of benefits of owning are:

Period	Depreciation	Depreciation (T) @ .40	PVIF @ 9%	PV
1	$660,000	$264,000	.917	$242,088
2	880,000	352,000	.842	296,384
3	460,000	184,000	.772	142,048
				$680,520

*Note: First-year depreciation = $660,000 ($2,000,000 × .33)
Second-year depreciation = $880,000 ($2,000,000 × .44)
Third-year depreciation = $460,000 ($2,000,000 × .23)

Net cost to lessor = $2,000,000 − $680,520 = $1,319,480

Since the lease payment is an annuity (or equal rentals over 3 years), it is necessary to obtain the $(PVIFA_{k,n})$ $(1 + k)$ for 3 years at a discount rate that permits the lessor to obtain a given required rate of return. The term $(1 + k)$ is added to the annuity factor because this is an annuity due that includes a payment right after the contract is signed.

The before-tax lease payments are calculated as follows, if the lessor's required rate of return is 12%:

$$\text{Annual lease payment} = \frac{\text{Net cost to lessor}}{(PVIFA_{k,n})\,(1\,+\,k)}$$

In other words, given $k = 12\%$ and $n = 3$ years, the annual lease payments will amount to:

$$\begin{array}{l}\text{Annual lease payments} \\ \text{charged to lessee}\end{array} = \frac{1{,}319{,}480}{(2.402)(1\,+\,.12)} = \frac{1{,}319{,}480}{2.690} = \$490{,}513$$

Another method for determining the annual rental of an equipment is called equivalent purchasing cost (EPC).

• *EQUIVALENT PURCHASING COST (EPC)*

The **equivalent purchasing cost (*EPC*)** of a lease offers a practical method to determine the cost of leasing an asset. A lessee not only pays an annual lease, but also loses the tax benefit of depreciation because the lessee is not the owner of the asset. The *EPC* is a discount rate that makes the present value of lease payments and lost tax benefits equal to the purchasing price of an asset. The calculation of the *EPC* is similar to that for the internal rate of return. A numerical example makes the idea and the calculation of the *EPC* easy to understand.

Example: Calculating the EPC *of a Lease*

PROBLEM Suppose a company has an offer to lease equipment, at an annual cost of $20,000 after taxes, for the next 5 years. To make the example simple, assume that lease payments, like an ordinary annuity, are paid at the end of each year. Additional information (purposely simplified to make the calculation of the *EPC* more easily comprehensible) is as follows:

- The purchase price of the equipment is $80,000.

- There is no salvage value after 5 years.

- In the case of outright purchase, the equipment is depreciated on a straight-line basis.

Calculate the *EPC* of the lease.

SOLUTION To find the *EPC*, divide the purchase price of $80,000 by the annual total cash flow of $26,400 to get 3.03. Looking up this value in the present value annuity table, you find a discount rate of 20%. By definition, 20% is called the equivalent purchasing cost of the lease.

In Table 12–2, the first column is the lease payment after tax. In addition, the company loses a 40% tax benefit on an annual deprecia-

Table 12–2   The Equivalent Purchasing Cost of a Lease

Year	Lease Payments after Tax (1)	Loss of Depreciation Benefit (2)	Total Cash Outflow (1) + (2)
1	$20,000	$6,400	− $26,400
2	20,000	6,400	− 26,400
3	20,000	6,400	− 26,400
4	20,000	6,400	− 26,400
5	20,000	6,400	− 26,400

tion of $16,000 ($80,000 ÷ 5 years), which amounts to $6,400. The total cash flow each year is the after-tax lease cost of $20,000 plus the loss of a $6,400 tax benefit (because the lessee cannot depreciate the equipment). This cash outflow of $26,400 each year for 5 years should be discounted at 20% to make its present value equal to the purchase price at $80,000, as stated below:

$$\$26,400 \times \text{Present value annuity at 20\% for 5 years (3.00)}$$
$$= \$79,200$$

The rate of 20% is the *EPC* of the lease. This 20% cost of the lease includes not only the annual lease payments, but also the tax benefit of depreciation lost in the lease option.

Now that the lessee knows how to calculate the payments necessary to lease the equipment, the primary concern is to find out whether it is cheaper to lease or to buy the equipment outright. That decision depends on the nature of the outflows. If the net outflows (or costs) are higher for leasing, it makes sense to borrow money to buy the equipment rather than lease it.

YOU SHOULD REMEMBER

When an asset is leased, the risk that the asset will become out-dated remains with the lessor. However, the lessee loses the tax benefit of depreciation. Since there are both advantages and dis-advantages to a lease, its cost should be calculated and compared to the purchase option before signing a lease contract.

• LEASE VERSUS PURCHASE: AN NPV APPROACH

Business owners and managers are often faced with the question whether to lease or purchase an asset. When an asset is leased, the lessee does not have to be concerned about raising capital, since the lessor is responsible for financing the project. On the other hand, the lessee loses both the tax savings of depreciation and the salvage value. The loss of these benefits should not be ignored when a comparison is made between the cost of a lease and the cost of a purchase.

In making the final decision whether to lease or to purchase, financial analysts try to pick the less expensive alternative. Since most expenses, such as lease payments, and most benefits, such as tax benefits, occur in the future, a good way to evaluate the lease and purchase options is to compare the net costs of both alternatives in terms of present dollars. This is where the net present value (*NPV*) technique can be helpful.

In other words, the question whether to lease or purchase can be answered if the present values of the expenses for leasing are compared to the purchase price. Using this technique, the approach is similar to a capital budgeting problem. However, there is a major difference between capital budgeting problems and lease problems. In capital budgeting, the project with the *higher NPV* is the preferred one, whereas in the case of lease versus purchase, the option with the *lower* present value of expenditure should be selected. Below is a step-by-step procedure necessary to make a lease/purchase decision:

Calculating Present Values of Leasing and Purchasing Costs

1. Determine the present value of the lease:
   a. Obtain the figures for annual lease payments (these are usually given).
   b. Calculate the annual tax benefits of lease payments.
   c. Subtract b from a to get the annual cost of the lease after taxes.
   d. Multiply c by the present value interest factor for each year.
   e. Add up the present values in d to get the total present value of the lease expenditure.

2. Determine the present value of the purchase expenditure:
   a. Obtain the figures for the annual repayment of the loan (these are usually given).
   b. Find out the interest portion of the annual repayment of the loan.
   c. Find out the annual depreciation of the asset to be purchased.
   d. Add b and c, and calculate the tax benefit of these two deductible items.
   e. Subtract the tax benefits (d) from the annual repayment of the loan.
   f. Multiply e by the present value factor for each year. Add up the figures to get the total present value of the purchase expenditure.

3. Compare the present value of the lease expenditure (from step 1) with the present value of the purchase expenditure (from step 2). Select the option with the lower present value.

Example: Choosing Between Leasing and Purchasing

PROBLEM   XYZ Inc. plans to buy an electronic precision tool. Its depreciation policy is straight-line, has a life of 5 years, and costs $50,000. There are two ways that the new tool can be financed. The first alternative is to borrow $50,000 at 12% and pay $13,800 annually for interest and principal for 5 years. Assume that the annual interest expense is $3,000. The second alternative is to lease the equipment for an annual payment of $11,000 for 5 years.

Suppose this company is in the 40% tax bracket, and there is no salvage value if the equipment is purchased. Is a purchase or a lease the better alternative?

SOLUTION   As explained before, the alternative with the lower present value of expenditure is the preferred one. Table 12–3 shows the cash flows and the present value of the lease option.

The tax benefit of lease payments in column 2 of Table 12–3 is calculated by multiplying the lease payments in column 1 by the 40% tax bracket. The cash flow in column 3 is the lease payment minus the tax benefit. The present value factor at 7% is used to discount the cash flow. Note that this 7% is the after-tax cost of borrowing at 12% (12% × (1 − 40%) = 7.2%). The reason for using the after-tax cost of borrowing of 7% is that the figures for cash flows include the tax benefit. To avoid counting the tax benefit twice, cash flows should always be discounted at an after-tax rate, which in this example is about 7%. The total present value of the lease expenditure is $30,215.

The next step is to compare this figure with the present value of the purchase expenditure, which is computed in Table 12–4.

Table 12–3   Present Value of the Lease Expenditure

Year	Payment (1)	Tax Benefit (2)	Cash Outflows (3) = (1) − (2)	PVIF at 7% (4)	Present Value of Cash Outflows 5 = (3)(4)
0	$11,000	0	$11,000	1.000	$11,000
1	11,000	$4,400	6,600	.935	6,171
2	11,000	4,400	6,600	.873	5,762
3	11,000	4,400	6,600	.816	5,386
4	11,000	4,400	6,600	.763	5,036
5	0	4,400	(4,400)	.713	(3,137)
			Present value of lease expenditure =		$30,218

Table 12–4 Present Value of the Purchase Expenditure

Year	Loan Repayment (1)	Interest (2)	Depreciation* (3)	Deductible Expenses: Interest + Depreciation (4) = (2) + (3)	Tax Benefit at 40% (5)	Loan Repayment After Tax (6) = (1) – (5)	Present Value Factor at 7% (7)	Present Value of Loan Repayment After Tax (8) = (6)(7)
1	$13,800	$3,000	$ 7,500	$10,500	$4,200	$9,600	.935	$8,976
2	13,800	3,000	11,000	14,000	5,600	8,200	.873	7,159
3	13,800	3,000	10,500	13,500	5,400	8,400	.816	6,854
4	13,800	3,000	10,500	13,500	5,400	8,400	.763	6,410
5	13,800	3,000	10,500	13,500	5,400	8,400	.713	5,989

Present value of purchase expenditure = $35,388

*Annual depreciation, computed on the ACRS basis, is 15%, 22%, 21%, 21%, and 21% in years 1 through 5, respectively.

In Table 12–4, column 1 is the annual loan repayment from which the tax benefit of interest and depreciation should be deducted. The tax benefit, as reported in column 5, is computed by multiplying the interest and depreciation expenses by the tax rate of 40%. By subtracting the tax benefit from the annual loan repayment, the loan repayment after tax is calculated in column 6. In column 8, the present value of loan repayments has been determined, using the present value factor at 7%, to obtain a total value of $35,388.

Since the present value of the lease expenditure ($30,218) is lower than $35,388, the lease option is more economical. Broadly speaking, XYZ Inc. would save $5,170 in current dollars by leasing rather than purchasing the equipment ($35,388 − $30,218 = $5,170). Without this analysis, the firm might have decided to borrow $50,000 from a bank, purchased the equipment, and lost the opportunity to save $5,170 through the lease option. *Always work out a step-by-step comparison before making a final decision whether to lease or purchase.*

YOU SHOULD REMEMBER

The equivalent purchasing cost of a lease is a discount rate that makes the present value of lease payments and lost tax benefits equal to the purchasing price of an asset. A step-by-step comparison, using the net present value approach, is recommended to determine which alternative—lease or purchase—is more economical. Unless these analytical techniques are used to study the options available, a firm can pay more than it should.

KNOW THE CONCEPTS

DO YOU KNOW THE BASICS?

1. What is a lease?
2. What is a major difference between an operating lease and a financial lease?
3. Is a lease an asset or a liability?
4. What are the main advantages of leasing?
5. Define the equivalent purchasing cost of a lease.

TERMS FOR STUDY

equivalent purchasing cost
capital lease
financial lease
lease
lessee

lessor
leverage leasing
operating lease
sale and leaseback
service lease

PRACTICAL APPLICATION

COMPUTATIONAL PROBLEMS

1. The XYZ Co., which is in the 40% tax bracket, leases new equipment for 5 years at an annual lease payment of $10,000, due at the beginning of each year. Determine the annual cash outflows of the lease.

2. Using the following data, calculate the equivalent purchasing cost (*EPC*) of a lease option:

   • Annual lease cost is $18,000 after taxes.

   • The equipment can be purchased for $75,000.

   • There is no salvage value.

   • The straight-line depreciation method is used.

   • The depreciable life of the equipment is 5 years

3. Would you recommend lease financing in Problem 2 if the after-tax cost of borrowing is 10%? Why? or Why not?

4. George and Associates are planning to buy a machine that costs $80,000. The machine can be purchased or leased. The company is in a 40% tax bracket. If the machine is leased, the company will make equal payments of $19,810 at the beginning of each year. The lease will be for 5 years. If the firm borrows money to buy the machine, it has to pay 15% to issue debt. Annual payments on the loan will be $23,302, and the machine will be depreciated over a period of 5 years under the ACRS. ACRS Factors = 15%, 22%, 21%, 21%, 21%. The salvage value is expected to be $10,000.

   (a) Determine the cash flow of the lease option.
   (b) Determine the cash flow of the purchase option.
   (c) Determine the present value of cash flow in part a.
   (d) Determine the present value of cash flow in part b, and state which option is preferable

5. The initial cost of a machine to a lessor is $60,000. The lessor's required rate of return on the lease is 15% annually. Assuming that lease payments are made

at the beginning of the period (ordinary annuity) and ignoring taxes, determine the lease payments that should be charged to the lessee. Assume a lease period of 5 years in your calculation.

ANSWERS

KNOW THE CONCEPTS

1. A lease is a legal contract in which the lessor gives the lessee the right to use an asset. The lessee agrees to pay a certain amount of rent each year (period) and to return the asset when the lease contract has expired.

2. An operating lease is an agreement usuaslly for less than 5 years, whereas a financial lease is a long-term contract for longer than 5 years. In an operating lease, the lessor is responsible for maintenance, insurance, taxes, and so on. These expenses are the lessee's responsibilities in a capital lease.

3. A lease is both an asset and a liability. The value of a Financial Lease equals the present value of its future cash outflows and is included on the balance sheet as an asset and a liability.

4. The main advantages of leasing are 100% financing, avoiding the risk that the asset will become obsolete, and flexible financing.

5. The equivalent purchasing cost (*EPC*) provides a practical method to determine the cost of an asset. The *EPC* is a discount rate that makes the present value of lease payments and lost tax benefits equal to the purchasing price of an asset.

PRACTICAL APPLICATION

1. Year	Payment	Tax Benefit	Cash Outflows
0	$10,000	$ 0	$10,000
1	10,000	4,000	6,000
2	10,000	4,000	6,000
3	10,000	4,000	6,000
4	10,000	4,000	6,000
5	0	4,000	(4,000)

2. Year	Lease Payment after Tax	Loss of Depreciation Benefit	Total Cash Flow
1 to 5	$18,000	$6,000	$24,000

This is like an annuity. If a tax rate of 40% is assumed, the loss of tax benefit is $\dfrac{\$75,000}{5 \text{ yr}} \times 40\% = \$6,000$.   The annuity is a $24,000 annual cash flow. Dividing $75,000 by $24,000, you get 3.125. A present value annuity table for 5 years shows that the equivalent purchasing cost in this problem is about 18%.

3. No, because the annual cost of leasing is 18% (compared to the after-tax cost of borrowing at 10%).

4. (a) Cash outflows of lease

Year	Cash Outflows
0	$19,810
1–4	$11,886
5	($7,924)

Year	Beginning Balance	Interest	Principal
1	$80,000	$11,200	$12,102
2	67,898	9,506	13,796
3	54,102	7,574	15,728
4	38,374	5,372	17,930
5	20,444	2,862	20,440

(b) Cash flow of purchase

Year	Loan Payment (1)	Interest (2)	(ACRS) Depreciation (3)	Total (4) = (2) + (3)	Tax Savings (5) = .40(4)	Cash Outflow (6) = (1) − (5)
1	$23,302	$11,200	$12,000	$23,200	$ 9,280	$14,022
2	23,302	9,506	17,600	27,106	10,842	12,460
3	23,302	7,574	16,800	24,374	9,750	13,552
4	23,302	5,372	16,800	22,172	8,869	14,433
5	23,302	2,862	16,800	19,662	7,865	15,437

(c) Present value of lease payments discounted at 9%* = $19,810 + $11,886(3.240)** − $7,924(.650) = $53,170

*9% is the after-tax cost of debt $\left[.15 \times (1 - .40)\right]$
**3.240 is PVIFA at 9% for 4 years.

(d) Present value of cash flow of purchase

Year	Cash Outflows (1)	PVIF at 9%* (2)	PV of Outflows (if machine is purchased) (3) = (1)(2)
1	$14,022	.917	$12,858
2	12,460	.842	10,491
3	13,552	772	10,462
4	14,433	.708	10,219
5	15,437	.650	10,034
		Present value of cash outflow =	$54,064

*Note: The after-tax cost of debt is 9%. Therefore, cash outflows of purchase are discounted at an after cost of 9%.

Since cash outflow of the lease option has a lower present value, the lease option is recommended over the purchase.

5. $$\$60,000 = x + \frac{PVIFA(x)}{15\%,\ 4\ \text{years}}$$

where x = annual lease payment

Then $60,000 = $x + 2.855x$

$60,000 = 3.855x$

$$x = \frac{\$60,000}{3.855}$$

$x = \$15,564$

13

WARRANTS, CONVERTIBLES, AND OPTIONS

WARRANTS AND CONVERTIBLE BONDS

Warrants and convertibles give investors the right to purchase common stock at a predetermined price. For this privilege, investors make certain concessions: they agree to accept a lower return on the securities they purchase, and usually they agree to accept less protection than is given to straight bondholders in the case of bankruptcy.

Firms find these securities an attractive source of funds because of their lower cost of capital. Convertibles also provide a certain degree of financing flexibility by allowing a firm to postpone issuing stock until a more advantageous time. Also, in the case of warrants, a firm generates more funds when the warrants are exercised. These forms of financing have become popular, and they play an important role in a firm's financing decisions.

Whether financing is done via warrants or convertibles, the firm gains certain benefits. Also, these securities can successfully be used as "sweeteners" to make a merger more palatable to a target company.

• *WARRANTS*

Warrants ordinarily have a limited lifespan, usually 3 to 5 years, although some warrants are issued in perpetuity. For the purpose of this discussion, warrants are assumed to have a specified expiration date. A **warrant** gives the buyer of a bond or preferred stock the option to purchase a number of shares of common stock at a pre-established price, the **exercise price**. This exercise price is generally 15% to 20% above the current price of the stock. Therefore, if the current stock price is $50, the firm may say to the investor: "When you buy one bond, we will allow you to purchase our shares of common stock, within a specified time (let us say over a 3-year period), at $60." Should the price of the stock rise to $70, the bondholder can exchange, or exercise, the warrants and pay $60 for the stock. The result is a net gain of $10 per share. Obviously, investors will not exchange their warrants for stock before the price passes the exercise price, since they can purchase the stock more cheaply in the open market.

The terms of exchange can vary over time. Sometimes a firm will raise the exercise price after several years. For example, it may say to investors that they can exercise the warrants at $60 for the next 3 years, but that thereafter the investors have to pay $65 for the stock.

The terms set by the firm indicate how many shares can be purchased at a stated price with one warrant. Some firms will say one warrant is good for the purchase of one share of stock. Other firms may say one warrant can purchase two shares of stock, and so forth. Generally, warrants are detachable. This means that once they are issued to the bond or preferred stock buyer, they can be sold independently, without reference to the security they came with. These warrants trade separately on the stock exchange or over the counter.

VALUE OF WARRANTS

A warrant derives its value from investors' anticipation that the price of the stock will increase beyond the exercise price, thereby giving them the opportunity to make a profit. If this expectation did not exist, warrants would be worthless, and no one would want to own them. It is also assumed that the firm's earnings will grow in the future, leading to higher dividends. When the dividends are high enough, they will make ownership of the common stock an attractive proposition.

The value of a warrant is simply derived by taking the difference between the price of the common stock (P_0) and the exercise price (E_{xp}), and multiplying this residual by the terms of exchange (N). This is called the **theoretical value of the warrant** (TV_w).

$$TV_w = N \times [\text{Current price of common } (P_0) - \text{Exercise price } (E_{xp})]$$

Therefore, if a company assigns an exercise price of $60 to the warrants, the current price of its stock is $65, and the exchange terms are two shares for one warrant, the theoretical value of the warrant (or lowest price) is

$$TV_w = 2(\$65 - \$60) = \$10$$

The theoretical value of a warrant is the lowest price at which it will sell. If the market value of the warrant were to fall below the theoretical value, arbitrageurs would buy the warrants, exercise them, and then sell the stock. As more warrants are purchased, the market value would rise to the theoretical value, and arbitrage would cease.

Warrants have greater leverage than their stocks. A given percentage change in the price of the stock will produce a higher percentage change in the value of the warrant.

$$\text{Leverage of a Warrant} = \frac{\% \, \Delta \text{ price of warrant}}{\% \, \Delta \text{ price of stock}}$$

Example: Warrants Have Greater Leverage Than Stock

Suppose the market price of a warrant (MV_w) moves dollar for dollar with the price of its stock. (This often happens after a substantial price move in the stock.) And suppose you are given the following information:

Current price of stock:	$70
Exercise price:	$65
Exchange ratio or terms:	2 shares for 1 warrant

Then,

$$TV_w = 2(\$70 - \$65) = \$10$$

Assume an investor buys the warrant at the current market price of $10 and the stock for $70. Thereafter, the price of the stock increases to $75. The market value, or theoretical value, of the warrant will increase to $20 [2($75 - $65)]. The value of the warrant increased 100% ($10/$10) whereas the value of the stock appreciated about 7% ($5/$70).

To calculate the fair value of a warrant, it is necessary to know

Stock price, (P_0)
Risk free rate, (R_F)
Time to expiration date, (t)
Standard deviation of stock's returns, (σ)
Exercise price (X_p)

The mathematical calculations involve determining the relationship between $\alpha(t)$ and $P_0/X_p \div e^{RF,t}$. In other words, the value of a warrant depends on two relationships

1) the volatility of a stock's returns (α) and the time to expiration (t).

2) the position of the price of the stock (P_0) relative to its exercise price (X_p).

Generally speaking, it can be seen that the higher the standard deviation and the more time left to expiration the higher the value of the warrant. Also, the higher the price of the stock relative to the exercise price the higher the value of the warrant.

Example:
Assume you have, or calculate, the following values:
$$P_0 = \$50$$
$$\alpha(t) = .35$$
$$P_0/X_P \div e^{RF,t} = 1.00$$

Look up the amount which corresponds to the above coordinate values in a special option table and you will find it equals 0.1389. Take the current price of the stock and multiply it by this value and you will get the **fair** value of a warrant, $6.94 ($50 × 0.1389).

This is a short cut method for obtaining the value of a warrant. Note, the **fair** value of a warrant is usually higher than the theoretical value mainly because it reflects investors' expectations that the price of the stock will increase above the exercise price of the stock.

BENEFITS TO THE FIRM

What are the effects of a combination bond/warrant issue to a firm? First, the firm obtains more money in addition to the funds it received from the original issue of bonds, because investors have to pay for the stock when they exercise the warrant. Second, the firm gains by being able to sell the bond at a lower cost of capital than is incurred by selling straight bonds. Third, there is some dilution of EPS when warrants are exercised because of the increase in the number of outstanding shares. Fourth, both the par value and the capital surplus of the firm increase. Fifth—and very important—the debt stays on the balance sheet.

• CONVERTIBLE BONDS

A **convertible bond** is a security that gives its owner the option to exchange it for a specified number of shares of common stock. It normally has a call feature that enables the issuing company to force investors to turn over, or return, the security at a specified price. For example, suppose a convertible bond is issued at a par value of $1,000. If the call price is set at 10% above par, the 10% call premium will enable the firm to call in their convertible bonds when they reach or exceed a price of $1,100.

A convertible bond has several attractive features. Even though the firm can issue the debenture at a lower cost of debt than a nonconvertible bond, it still retains some of the characteristics of a straight bond. Therefore, a convertible is like a bond, but has a feature that allows the holder to participate in the growth of the stock. Although convertible bonds may be called in at a given **call price**, this type of security also has a maturity date—like any other bond. Thus, if convertible bonds are not called in or are not converted, they will mature after a specified time period. A 20-year convertible means that the firm will pay the owners of this debenture par value ($1,000) at the end of the twentieth year. In the interim years, of course, the firm agrees to pay a stated coupon on these bonds.

VALUE OF CONVERTIBLES

To understand the way convertibles are valued, it is necessary to examine some of the general features that make up this value. Suppose a firm issues a convertible bond when the current price of its stock is $35; the price at which the bond can be exchanged for stock is set at $40. This price of $40 is called the **conversion price**. The difference between the current price of the stock and its conversion price is the **conversion premium**, or $5 ($40 − $35). This premium means that the convertible owners will have to wait until the price of the stock reaches $40 before they can consider converting the bond into stock.

The **conversion ratio** is the number of shares received in exchange for a convertible bond when it is turned in.

$$\text{Conversion ratio} = \frac{\text{Par value of convertible security}}{\text{Conversion price}}$$

Using the above figures the conversion ratio is:

$$\text{Conversion ratio} = \frac{\$1,000}{\$40} = 25 \text{ shares}$$

This means the firm issues 25 shares of common stock when each bond is converted.

Conversion value is a very important feature, because it tells you the underlying stock value of the convertible.

$$\text{Conversion value} = \text{Current market price of the stock} \times \text{Conversion ratio}$$

Using the figures in the previous example once more, you get

$$\text{Conversion value} = \$35 \times 25 \text{ shares} = \$875$$

This equation for finding the conversion value makes clear that part of the bond's value originates in the value of the stock. Therefore, par value minus the conversion value ($1,000 − $875), or $125, represents the premium paid by an investor for the option to convert into stock.

Conversion value is the minimum stock value that an investor can receive for a convertible debenture. For instance, should the price of the stock drop to $30, the minimum value behind the convertible debenture is $750 ($30 × 25). In other words, should investors convert into common stock, the least amount they could receive is the conversion value of the bond, or $750. Given that $1,000 was the initial price paid for the bond, you can see clearly why it does not pay to convert until the price of the stock reaches $40 or more. At $35, investors would receive only $875 out of the $1,000 they originally paid. Conversion would result in a loss of $125; hence, it would not pay to convert. At $40, investors would get their $1,000 back ($40 × $25). At $50 the convertible would have a value of $1,250 ($50 × 25), and investors would have a profit of $250 ($1,250 − $1,000).

Since conversion value is the minimum value at which the debenture will sell, a profit can be made by investors when the market value of the convertible bond falls below its conversion value. All they have to do is buy the bond, convert it immediately, and then sell the stock. For example, suppose the market value of a convertible is $1,100 and its conversion value is $1,150. When its holders convert, they get stock worth $50 more than the value of the bond. This imperfection in the market does not last very long. Investors see it as a chance to make an easy profit, and they will continue to purchase the convertible (and make a profit by converting it), putting upward pressure on the market value of the convertible until it rises to, or above, the conversion value of the debenture.

In addition to having a conversion value, a convertible bond has a floor value, or **investment value,** equivalent to that of a straight bond. This is the price at which the convertible security would sell in the absence of its conversion feature. Consequently, convertible bonds offer more protection than stocks because, while the price of a stock can decline sharply, the market value of a convertible is unlikely to decline below its straight bond value.

The calculation of this value is easy enough. You have, in fact, already done this in Chapter 3 when you found how to obtain the present value of a bond. All you have to do is find a straight bond having the same characteristics and issued by a firm with the same financial structure as that of the issuer of the convertible. The yield to maturity of that straight bond will then serve as a discount rate. The familiar formula for determining the value of a straight bond is

$$\text{Bond value} = \sum_{t=1}^{N} \frac{\text{Coupon}_t}{(1 + R)^t} + \frac{P_n}{(1 + R)^n}$$

This formula also works for determining the straight bond value of a convertible.

Example: Calculating the Straight Bond Value of a Convertible

PROBLEM A newly issued $1,000 convertible bond pays an annual coupon of $80 and will mature in 10 years. The straight bond of a comparable company has a yield to maturity of 10%. What is the straight bond value of the newly issued convertible?

SOLUTION

Years	Payment	PVIF at 10%	Present Values
1–10	$80 interest	6.145*	$492
10th	$1,000 par value	.386	386
		Bond value =	$878

*(PVIFA) 10%, 10 yrs

The present value method shown above for calculating the straight bond value of a convertible can be expressed as a formula:

$$\text{Bond value} = \sum_{t=1}^{N} \frac{80(t)}{(1 + .10)^t} + \frac{\$1,000}{(1 + .10)^{10}} = \$878$$

When market rates increase, the straight bond value of a convertible declines; when market yields decline, the straight bond value increases. The market value of the convertible will not decline below the straight bond value of $878 regardless of any drop in the price of the underlying stock. All these convertible bond features can be more readily visualized in Figure 13–1.

After the price of the stock increases beyond a certain point, say $50, expectations of further price advances in the stock diminish, and the market value curve collapses toward the conversion value, as seen in Figure 13–1. The leverage of the convertible bond disappears. Also, at $50 the convertible has a value of $1,250, which gives investors little protection, since the bond can be called in at $1,100. The more the stock increases, the less investment protection the convertible bondholders have— and the more willing they are to convert.

What other factors induce investors to convert? Sometimes a firm's original agreement states that after a few years the conversion ratio will be lowered. Since this means that investors will receive fewer shares than with the initial conversion ratio, they will be induced to convert before that date so they will not be penalized. Suppose the conversion ratio changed after 3 years from 25 to 23 shares, and

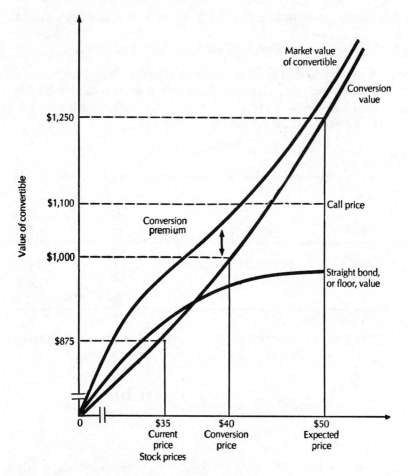

Figure 13–1 Features of Convertible Bonds

the price of the stock reached the $40 conversion price in this period. Since investors would realize only $920 instead of $1,000 (based on a conversion ratio of 23 shares per bond), they would be forced to convert before the change in the conversion ratio occurred. Conversion may also take place when the dividend yield on the common stock is higher than the return obtained from the convertible. Another reason for converting arises from the fact that, as the price of the stock increases, the investor receives less and less protection from the straight bond value. Also, the danger that the bond will be called at a lower price than the conversion value will induce investors to convert the bond into common stock to avoid a potential loss of profit.

BENEFITS TO THE FIRM

Besides being able to raise funds at a cost of capital lower than a straight bond or common stock issue, a firm knows when it issues a convertible that the debt will disappear from the balance sheet upon conversion. Also, after conversion, the par value and capital surplus increase, although the increased number of shares causes dilution in the earnings per share.

When the price/earnings (P/E) ratio of a firm's common stock is too low, it is not advantageous to issue new stock. In this case, the use of convertibles is convenient because they help defer common stock financing to a more advantageous time. The firm can raise a large amount of funds via the convertible bond route, and the final dilutive effects will be less than in the case of common stock financing. From the point of view of investors, a convertible bond is a chance to participate in the growth of the common stock. It provides them with a greater degree of protection against losses because convertibles have a floor investment value. Also, while investors have the option of making capital gains by converting, convertible bonds still provide some hedge against the downside risk associated with variability in the price of the stock.

One major disadvantage must be mentioned: Claims of convertible owners are subordinate to those of straight bondholders. In other words, if the firm defaults, the claims of its convertible bondholders will be paid only after the claims of straight debtholders are satisfied.

YOU SHOULD REMEMBER

Warrants and convertibles, which give their holders the right to exchange them for their underlying stock, represent two major alternative sources of financing.

Bonds issued with these "sweeteners" cost less than issues of straight debt. When convertibles are exchanged for stock, although no additional funds are made available to the firm, the debt is wiped from the balance sheet. Conversely, though debt remains part of the capital structure when warrants are exercised, additional funds are generated. Basically, while warrants increase the marketability of bonds, convertibles allow firms some financing flexibility.

The value of warrants to investors is based on the expectation that the stock price will increase. Because of the low price of warrants relative to stocks, they provide substantial leverage.

The market value of a convertible bond will not decline below its investment value, which is equivalent to the value of a straight debt issue with similar characteristics.

• DIFFERENCES BETWEEN WARRANTS AND CONVERTIBLE BONDS

Warrants don't earn interest and are more risky investments than convertibles because they are highly leveraged. They are worthless at their expiration date and when the price of their stock declines to very low levels. Convertibles, on the other hand, have a floor investment value; they provide investors with a steady interest income and pay a stated par value at maturity. The cost of capital for issuing a bond/warrant package is a little higher than for a convertible bond. More importantly, when warrants are exercised they provide additional funds to the firm, whereas the conversion of convertible debentures does not. However, when convertibles are exchanged for stock, the debt is wiped off the books. When warrants are exercised, the debt stays on the balance sheet.

OPTIONS

Corporations sometimes offer stock purchase **options** to key management officials as an inducement to keep them with the firm. Conversely, options can also be offered to attract new management skills to a firm. The right to exercise an option is given for a specified period of time. Since the IRS requires a 3-year holding period for stock options to qualify for long-term capital gains, many firms establish expiration periods longer than 3 years.

Example: Executive Options

Suppose a firm's stock is currently selling for $10. The firm agrees to give key executives the right to buy a certain number of shares at $14 per share. Assume that the price of the stock increases to $20. The executives can then borrow funds, buy the stock from the firm at $14, and sell these shares in the market at $20—making a profit of $6 on each share.

The additional shares issued to executives have a corresponding dilutive effect on the firm's earnings per share. Since the executives don't have to put up any money, the only loss they might incur is one of opportunity—or the inability to exercise and make a profit should the price of the stock fail to exceed $14 per share within the specified period.

Other options of interest to institutional investors and financial managers include stock calls, stock puts, stock index options, and stock index futures. Because many financial officers have the responsibility of supervising, either directly or indirectly, the management of pension and other corporate funds, they should be knowledgeable about the features of these instruments. These securities can be used to reduce portfolio risk and for hedging purposes. Option strategies can be adopted to protect the value of security investments or to increase returns by writing options. Some studies show that options can also influence the volume of trading in the firm's shares and enchance the liquidity of the stock. For these reasons a brief introduction to the way this market operates is in order.

Investors buy and sell options for several reasons. They may want to defer buying a stock until a certain date or price is reached. If the stock declines in price, they will buy at the market price and give up the premium they paid. If the price increases, however, the shares can be purchased at the striking price set by the option writer.

Also, investors may wish to speculate, but may be unwilling to buy or sell a stock outright because of the large investment involved. An option costs much less than the stock, and if the price moves differently than anticipated, the only loss will be the premium paid for the right to exercise the option.

• *STRATEGIES: CALL OPTIONS AND PUT OPTIONS*

There are two main types of options:

- • Call options
- • Put options

Call option buyers, who purchase the right to buy a security at a specified price, gamble that the price of the underlying stock will increase. **Put option buyers**, who purchase the right to sell a security at a specified price, gamble that the price will decline. The option sellers, or **option writers**, require payment for this right and, for their part, hope that the price of the stock involved will remain unchanged or move in the opposite direction from what the buyers want.

A contract between buyer and writer establishes a price at which the call buyer can buy the stock from a writer, or at which the put buyer can sell the stock to the writer.

Example: How Call and Put Options Work

Assume you are given the following information:

	Call Option	Put Option
Current price of stock	$ 90	$110
Exercise price of option	100	100
Expected future price of stock	120	80
Premium paid	10	10

Call buyers will purchase a call option at an exercise price of $100. They will not exercise this right as long as the price of the stock is less than $100. Why? Because it is not rational to pay $100 for a stock when one can buy it at less than $100 in the market. However, should the price of the stock rise to $120, the call buyers can ask the writer to deliver stock at the $100 price. When this happens, the buyer can sell the stock at $120, recovering the original $10 premium and making a $10 profit.

Put buyers anticipated that the price of the stock would decline, and it did. They can now buy the stock on the exchange for $80, sell the stock at $100 to the writer, and make a $10 profit after deducting the original $10 premium paid to the option writer.

This simple explanation does not take into account the many different ways of dealing with options. Writers, for example, can sell calls and puts on either a covered or a naked basis. "Writing naked," as opposed to "covered," means that the writer does not own the underlying security. Even if the price of a stock rises to very high levels, the writer is still obligated to deliver the stock at the stated, or exercise, price. Needless to say, the writer of naked calls and puts engages in a highly risky transaction.

To avoid this risk, writers protect themselves by either buying the stock outright, in the case of a call, or selling the stock short, in the case of a put. Should the stock price move in the wrong direction (up in the case of calls and down in the case of puts), the maximum loss incurred by the writer would be the premium. Any price change beyond the exercise price plus the premium would be covered by having the stock ready for delivery at any time the buyer requests it.

Also, there are numerous "strategies" whereby investors buy and sell options of the same type, hoping to profit on the difference between the premiums as market conditions change.

One problem facing a call or put buyer is the time limitation. Calls and puts usually have a maximum life of 9 to 12 months, and they become worthless upon the **expiration date.** Accordingly, the risk of time has a relationship to the premium paid. The more time there is before the expiration date, the greater the chance that the price of the stock will move favorably for the buyer of calls and puts. Therefore, the more time, the higher the premium, and the less time (or the closer to expiration date), the lower the premium.

FACTORS AFFECTING THE VALUE OF OPTIONS

The relationship between the value of a call option, its exercise price (Xp), and the underlying price of the stock can be visualized in Figure 13–2.

When the stock price is below the exercise price (Xp), the call option is out of the money. When it exceeds the exercise price, it is in the money. The premium paid for an in-the-money option is greater than for an out-of-the-money option. Also, the theoretical value (minimum price of a call option) is zero when the stock price is less than the Xp. It becomes positive when the stock price exceeds the Xp. Note that the market value premium on a call increases as the price of the stock moves toward the Xp, then declines as the price of the stock passes or exceeds the Xp. Why? Because investors' expectations of further stock price increases diminish.

These are some basic features of options. Some sophisticated models have been developed to determine the fair value of options.

These models have borrowed heavily from techniques developed to price warrants. One of the better known stock option valuation models is the Black and Scholes model. The other option valuation models are similar in nature to the Black and Scholes method, though with some variations. Although the underlying theories and mathematics are quite complicated, modern computers make the task of calculating the fair values of these options quite simple.

A short cut method used to calculate the value of a call option entails taking into account (see explanation of actual warrant price determination) the relationship between standard deviation and time to expiration compared to the price of the stock relative to its exercise price. This relationship can be more easily translated into the value of an option by referring to a special option table. This table indicates what part of the stock price is represented by the option.

Example:

Assume you are given the price of the stock and the two other factors with reference to a call option

$$Po = \$100$$
$$\alpha\ (t) = .40$$
$$Po/Xp \div e^{RF,t} = .92$$

Looking up these two values of .40 and .92 in the call option table you obtain a value of .1255. The approximate value of a call that has the above risk, time and exercise price relative to the stock price is $12.25 ($100 × 0.1225).

Generally speaking, most option pricing models include the following factors:

- Current stock price relative to exercise price
- Time to expiration
- A risk-free rate
- A risk measure, such as standard deviation
- Exercise price
- Dividend payment on the stock

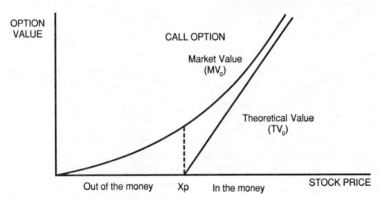

Figure 13-2 Call option relationship

In solving these models, the value of a call option or its premium will be high if the current price of the stock is above the exercise price, if the standard deviation is large, if time to expiration is long, if the riskless rate is high, and if dividend payments are small.

As you can see, option pricing models allow corporate managers to understand how various factors interact and influence the value of options. Understanding the way these factors change and how they influence the value of options can help those seeking to hedge against the risks of individual securities and portfolios to make the right kind of investment decisions.

Many option models provide financial managers with insight into the forces that determine the value of corporate assets and the securities held or managed by corporations. The importance of stock options and financial futures is growing steadily, and corporate officers in charge of handling funds must become knowledgeable about the advantages offered by these instruments.

YOU SHOULD REMEMBER

The owner of a call option is given the right to purchase stock at a stated exercise, or striking, price. Some companies use stock options to provide employees and key management with incentives to stay with the firm and to become more productive. Sometimes options are employed to attract new executive talent.

There are two basic types of options: calls and puts. The call buyer gambles that the price of the underlying stock will go up, and the put buyer gambles that the price of the underlying stock will decline. The writer of an option hopes that the price of the stock will move in the opposite direction expected by call and put buyers. Usually, to guard against large losses occasioned by big moves in the price of the stock, the writer will buy the stock outright when selling a call and will sell the stock short when selling a put. Selling options without this protection is called writing naked options.

Several well-known models can be used to calculate the fair value of an option. This value helps the investor determine whether an option is priced correctly or whether it is over- or undervalued.

Out-of-the-money options sell at lower premiums than in-the-money options. This premium increases as the stock price moves up to the exercise price. It moves toward the theoretical value after the stock price exceeds the exercise price.

These instruments can also be employed to minimize portfolio losses. Options have expanded the horizons of the investment community and play a key role in establishing intelligent risk/return strategies.

KNOW THE CONCEPTS

DO YOU KNOW THE BASICS?

1. Give several reasons why a firm might choose to issue warrants and convertibles instead of straight debt or common stock.

2. What kind of advantages does an investor receive with a warrant? With a convertible bond?

3. In what way is the capital structure of a firm affected by the exercise of a warrant or the conversion of a convertible into stock?

4. What happens to interest and earnings per share when warrants are exercised or when convertible bonds are converted into stock?

5. If the market price of a warrant falls below its theoretical value, what will happen in the marketplace to correct this imbalance?

6. What is meant by the leverage derived from a warrant?

7. Why would a convertible bondholder want to convert into common stock? Include dividends, conversion price, and stock price in your answer.

8. In addition to the conversion value, what other investment feature does a convertible have that is not available with warrants?

9. If the yield to maturity on a straight bond increases, what will happen to the value of the convertible, and what does this mean to the investor?

10. If all other things remain unchanged, how would the value of a call option change when the following changes occur in related factors:
    (a) There is a reduction of dividends per share.
    (b) The risk-free rate declines.
    (c) The price of the stock is expected to decline.
    (d) The standard deviation of the stock price declines.
    (e) There is a decline in the life of the call.

11. What is the definition of an in-the-money call option?

TERMS FOR STUDY

call option buyers	expiration date
call price	investment value of convertibles
conversion premium	option
conversion price	option writer
conversion ratio	put option buyer
conversion value	theoretical value of a warrant
convertible bond	warrant
exercise price	

PRACTICAL APPLICATION

COMPUTATIONAL PROBLEMS

1. Calculate the straight bond value and the conversion ratio of a convertible if the current price of the stock is $60, its conversion price is $70, and it matures 5 years from now. Also, a straight bond with similar features has a yield to maturity of 10%, compared to an 8% coupon for the convertible. (Assume par value of the bond is $1,000.)

2. The premium paid to buy a call is $5, the price of the stock is $50, and the striking price is $40. How much profit or loss would a call buyer make by exercising the option?

3. Calculate the theoretical value of a warrant when the current price of the stock is $50 and the exercise price is $45. The exchange ratio is 3 shares for each warrant.

4. A firm has $10 million of outstanding convertible bonds. The coupon on these convertibles is $100 per bond, and each bond is convertible into common stock at a conversion price of $25. What will happen to the income statement and EPS when all bonds are converted, if the income statement of the firm before conversion was as follows and EBIT remained at $6.0 million after conversions? (Assume the firm originally paid $2.0 million in interest on other outstanding debt before the convertible was issued.)

	Millions of Dollars Before Conversion
EBIT	6.0
Interest (at 10%)	−3.0
Earnings before taxes	3.0
Taxes (at 40%)	−1.2
Earnings after taxes	1.8
Shares outstanding (millions)	1.0
EPS	$1.80

5. A convertible bond has a call price of $1,100. Its underlying stock is selling at $60 per share, and the conversion price is $50. If owners of the convertible bond convert and sell the stock, how much profit or loss will they make on each bond if the convertible is called by the company, given the above conditions?

ANSWERS

DO YOU KNOW THE BASICS?

1. Warrants and convertible securities provide a firm with financing flexibility and a lower cost of capital. However, investors usually agree to less creditor protection in case of bankruptcy when they buy convertible bonds instead of straight bonds.

2. A buyer of a warrant participates in the capital appreciation of the stock. An investor can share in the dividends paid to stockholders when the warrant is exercised. Some investors buy warrants for the substantial leverage they provide when the price of the stock increases.

   Investors in convertibles get an interest income, just as they would from a straight bond, and still have downside price protection because of the investment value of convertible bonds. Convertible bond investors have the option to participate in the future growth of the stock and the rising dividend yield paid to stockholders when they decide to convert.

3. When a warrant is exercised in exchange for stock, the debt remains on the balance sheet. When convertible bonds are converted into stock, the debt is wiped off the balance sheet. The D/E decreases when the warrant is traded for stock; equity increases while debt remains the same. The warrant is not actually *exchanged* for stock; it entitles the holder to exchange money for stock. However, the D/E remains at a higher level when warrants are exercised, whereas it declines when convertible bonds are converted.

4. When warrants are exercised, interest on the income statement remains unchanged but the number of shares increases, causing dilution in EPS. When convertible bonds are converted into common stock, the interest from the convertible bonds disappears from the income statement and the number of shares increases, causing dilution in EPS.

5. The warrant will be purchased and exercised, and the stock will be sold at a profit. This arbitrage will continue until the $MP_w = TV_w$.

6. Leverage of a warrant, or $\dfrac{\% \, \Delta \text{ Price of warrant}}{\% \, \Delta \text{ Price of stock}}$, means that for any given percentage change in the price of the stock, the percentage change in the price of the warrant is greater. In other words, investors receive a bigger gain or loss for any dollar invested in warrants than they receive from investing in the underlying stock.

7. A convertible bondholder will convert into common stock when the dividend yield on the stock exceeds the yield from the convertible, when the conversion value and the market price are substantially above the call price, and when the price of the stock moves substantially above the conversion price. At that point, expectations of a further increase in the price of the stock diminish, and the straight bond value protection weakens substantially.

8. A convertible security yields a return, whereas a warrant is only an option to buy stock at a stated price, and thus provides no income.

9. If the yield to maturity increases, the discount factor increases and the investment value of the convertible bond will decline. The investor will find that the straight bond value of a convertible will appreciate when interest rates decline, usually during a recession. A decrease in the yield to maturity may also mean that, because the market value of the convertible bond increases (assume conversion value remains unchanged), it becomes vulnerable to a call by the issuer. Hence, the investor may wish to convert.

10. The value of a call option would decline with any of the changes listed.

11. An in-the-money call option is a condition that arises when the price of the stock exceeds the exercise price.

PRACTICAL APPLICATION

1. Conversion ratio $= \dfrac{\$1,000}{70} = 14.29$ shares

This means that investors receive 14.29 shares of stock when they exchange the convertible for common stock.

Straight bond value of a convertible:

Years	Payment	PVIF at 10%	
1 to 5	$80	3.791	$303
5th	$1,000	.621	621
		Straight bond value of convertible bond =	$924

2. Assume the call is for 100 shares of stock. Then:

Current value of shares ($50 × 100 shares)	$5,000
Value of shares at striking price ($40 × 100 shares)	−4,000
Net change	$1,000
Cost of call ($5 × 100)	−500
Net profit	$ 500

3. The theoretical value of the warrant is

$$3(\$50 - \$45) = \$15$$

4.	Millions of Dollars before Conversion	Millions of Dollars after Conversion
EBIT	6.0	6.0
Interest	−3.0	−2.0
Earnings before taxes	3.0	4.0
Taxes (at 40%)	−1.2	−1.6
Earnings after taxes	1.8	2.4
Shares outstanding (millions)	1.0	1.4
EPS	$1.80	$1.71

Note: The interest declines by $1.0 million because 10% ($100 coupon) of $10 million is $1.0 million and the original $2.0 million stays on the income statement after conversion. Also, the conversion ratio equals 40 shares ($1,000 ÷ 25). This produces 400,000 additional shares on conversion, and a dilution of 9¢ in earnings per share (from $1.80 before conversion to $1.71 after conversion).

5. Conversion ratio = $\dfrac{1,000}{50}$ = 20 shares

Conversion value = 20 × $60 = $1,200

$1,200	conversion value of convertible bond
1,100	call price of convertible bond
$ 100	loss to owners on each bond

INTRODUCTION TO FINANCIAL ANALYSIS

14 FINANCIAL PLANNING

KEY TERMS

cash cycle the number of days between the purchase of raw materials and the collection of sales proceeds from finished goods

cash turnover the number of times a firm's cash is collected in a year

financial planning the process of estimating a firm's fund needs and deciding how to finance these funds

liquidity management the process of ensuring adequate cash for the operation of a firm

---

THE IMPORTANCE OF FINANCIAL PLANNING

Financial planning is the process of estimating the amount of financing required to continue a company's operations, and of deciding when and how the needed funds should be financed. Without a reliable procedure to estimate financing needs, a company may run out of sufficient funds to pay obligations such as interest on loans, suppliers' bills, rental expenses, and the cost of utilities. A company is in default if it is unable to pay its contractual obligations, such as interest on loans. Therefore, the lack of sound financial planning may cause lack of liquidity and then bankruptcy—even when total assets, including nonliquid assets, such as inventory, plant, and equipment, are well in excess of liabilities.

The success and solvency of a firm cannot be guaranteed merely by profitable projects and increasing sales. "Liquidity crisis," that is, a shortage of cash to pay financial obligations, always threatens a company. Since the problem is more critical when credit is limited, small and medium-sized firms are in greater danger of possible cash shortages than larger corporations, which usually have a wider range of financing alternatives. This does not mean that large firms never have liquidity problems. A good example is the Chrysler Corporation, which suffered badly from a shortage of cash in the 1970s.

Be aware that even accounts receivable don't have liquidity unless they are readily convertible into cash. A supernormal growth rate of sales does not protect a firm from possible bankruptcy, either. Management has to do regular financial planning to estimate future financing needs. The timing of different types of financing is also critical to financial planning. For instance, in a time of rising interest rates, a long-term, fixed-rate loan is preferred to a short-term loan. When the interest rate is expected to decline, however, a financial officer is better off borrowing temporarily, and then refinancing the loan at a lower rate once the interest rate has fallen.

Financing sources include short- and long-term debt, preferred and common stock, and retained earnings. Retained earnings, which are accumulated profits after tax and dividends, are an especially desirable source of financing. The ability to expand business operations by using retained earnings is a sign of financial solvency, because these funds make the firm financially self-sufficient. In the absence of adequate retained earnings, however, management has a more difficult decision to make, and needs to find the best combination of debt and equity. In the following sections, the emphasis will be on the methods used to estimate financing needs and the analysis of sources and uses of funds.

YOU SHOULD REMEMBER

Financial planning is referred to as the process of estimating future financing needs and identifying how previous funds were financed and for what purposes they were spent. Through financial planning and control, the management of a company can evaluate whether the existing patterns of financing and spending funds are in line with the overall goals of the company. The timing as well as the amount of required funds can be determined through financial planning techniques.

METHODS TO ESTIMATE NEEDS

There are several methods to estimate the financial needs of a firm. Although none of the methods can predict future needs precisely, a financial manager must use some method to roughly estimate the amount of cash required for at least 1 year ahead. The basic methods for this purpose are discussed below.

PERCENT-OF-SALES METHOD

The purpose of the percent-of-sales method is to show how financing needs for working capital can be calculated. The percent-of-sales method assumes that changes in sales affect the amount of assets to be maintained in a company. By definition, an asset that changes as a result of increases or decreases in sales is called a **spontaneous asset**. In other words, sales or revenue basically determines how much financing is required to run a business. There is a logical connection between expected sales and various types of assets. For instance, if sales are expected to rise, the company needs more cash and inventory and should expect more accounts receivable to accumulate. On the other hand, if sales are predicted to decline, inventory levels should be reduced. Sales also determine the amount of liabilities, or debt, a company maintains. As sales go up, the company increases its trade debt and borrows more money to purchase goods and raw materials to ensure that the level of inventory is sufficient. Accounts payable and short- and long-term debts will then tend to increase, enabling the company to acquire more assets and expand operations.

By looking into previous financial statements, a financial analyst can determine the ratios of different types of assets and liabilities to sales. Suppose the ratio of changing assets to sales is 60% and the ratio of changing liabilities is 40%. These ratios indicate that when sales increase by $100, assets and liabilities of the company will probably go up by $60 and $40, respectively. Subtracting 40% from 60%, you get 20% net assets as percent of sales. In simple words, if the company plans to expand its sales by $100, it needs $20 in new financing, part of which can be financed internally—through expected profits—though the rest must be raised from outside. For instance, if the firm can generate $5 in net earnings after dividends, $15 must be financed through borrowing and by issuing preferred or common stock. On the basis of the above line of reasoning, the following equation to determine the external financing needs of a company is easily developed:

$$\text{External required financing} = \frac{A}{S}(\Delta S) - \frac{L}{S}(\Delta S) - rS$$

where A = assets that change with sales
  ΔS = expected change in sales forecast for the year
  L = liabilities that change with sales
  r = ratio of net profits after dividends to sales

Example: Percent-of-Sales Method

PROBLEM   The historical ratio of assets that spontaneously change with sales is 70% for the ABC Co. The ratio for liabilities is 30%. Sales are expected to increase by $200,000 in the next year. The company has historically maintained 3% of its sales revenue as net earnings after dividends. Assuming that expected sales are $1,000,000, predict the amount of external required financing for the next year.

SOLUTION   Inserting the given information into the equation gives

$$\begin{aligned}
\text{External required financing} &= 70\%(\$200,000) - 30\%(\$200,000) \\
&\quad - 3\%(\$1,000,000) \\
&= \$140,000 - \$60,000 \\
&\quad - \$30,000 = \$50,000
\end{aligned}$$

Therefore, the ABC Co. has to arrange for external financing of $50,000 if it plans to increase sales by $200,000, as assumed in this case. Without that external financing, the company will be unable to buy more inventory, acquire other assets and meet its sales target.

CASH BUDGET METHOD

A major part of financial planning is liquidity management. In simple terms, the purpose of **liquidity management** is to ensure that the company will never run out of cash. The cash budget technique is commonly used to achieve this objective.

Using this technique, a financial analyst compares future cash receipts with future cash payments on a monthly basis and determines the financing surplus or deficit for each month. The result is a cash budget through which future financing of the firm can be predicted. Table 14–1 shows a format that can be used to estimate the required cash.

In Table 14–1, net monthly cash flow is determined by subtracting estimated payments from estimated receipts, as shown in column 3. The amount of cash at the end of each month, found by adding the cash at the beginning of each month to the net cash flow, is reported in column 5. Column 6 is the minimum cash reserve that a company maintains to avoid running out of cash. Adding the minimum cash reserve to the ending cash reported in column 5 gives the estimated cash surplus or deficit. If there is a surplus in column 7, the company may think of investing the excess cash in an interest-bearing security. Should column 7 show a deficit, the company must plan in advance to determine how and where to borrow the money needed to cover the deficit. Note that the cash surplus/deficit computed in column 7 is different from the expected earnings or losses reported in an income statement. Despite a substantial amount of earnings, a company may run into cash deficit problems if accounts receivable are not properly collected. Therefore, cash budgeting is absolutely necessary to forecast and arrange for future financing.

This method of projecting cash flow is very popular in practice. However, the estimated cash flow is reliable only if receipts and payments are correctly estimated. Cash receipts result mainly from cash sales; collection of accounts receivable, interest, and dividends (from investments); the sale of old equipment; and lease revenues. The major components of cash payments are cash purchases and payments of accounts payable, wages, salaries, taxes, interest charges, rental expenses, insurance premiums, cash dividends, and other operating expenses. By looking into both old and current data for receipts and payments, a financial analyst can prepare a cash budget similar to that shown in Table 14–1 to get a clear idea about the future cash requirements of the firm.

Table 14–1   A Format to Estimate Required Cash

Month	Receipts (1)	Payments (2)	Net Monthly Cash Flow (1) – (2) (3)	Beginning Cash (4)	Ending Cash (3) + (4) (5)	Cash Reserve (6)	Cash Surplus or Deficit (5) + (6) (7)
January							
February							
March							
April							
May							
June							
July							
August							
September							
October							
November							
December							

CASH TURNOVER METHOD

In the cash turnover method, the minimum amount of cash needed by a company to run its operation is determined by the use of the following equation:

$$\text{Minimum cash required} = \frac{\text{Annual operating expenditures}}{\text{Cash turnover}}$$

This equation assumes that there are no significant changes in operating expenditures from one period to another. Annual operating expenditures are defined here as total cash expenditures, or expenditures such as purchases of goods and raw materials and payment of salaries, wages, interest, and dividends.

Cash turnover is the number of times that a firm's cash is collected, or turned over, in a year. Cash turnover is calculated as follows:

$$\text{Cash turnover} = \frac{360 \text{ days}}{\text{Days between purchase of raw materials and collection of sales proceeds}}$$

or, simply,

$$\text{Cash turnover} = \frac{360 \text{ days}}{\text{Cash cycle}}$$

Note that **cash cycle** refers to the number of days that pass between the purchase of raw materials and collection of sales proceeds.

Example: Using the Cash Turnover Method

PROBLEM   Suppose the cash cycle of a company is 72 days. Assuming that the company has annual expenditures of $600,000, determine the minimum required cash of the company.

SOLUTION   Using the equation given above, calculate the cash turnover:

$$\text{Cash turnover} = \frac{360 \text{ days}}{72} = 5$$

To determine the minimum cash required, you divide the annual expenditures of $600,000 by the firm's cash turnover:

$$\text{Minimum cash required} = \frac{\$600,000}{5} = \$120,000$$

Therefore, the firm must keep a minimum cash balance of $120,000 throughout the year to maintain its liquidity. Keeping a balance below $120,000 will create a shortage of cash and possibly lead to bankruptcy. On the other hand, maintaining a balance significantly above the level of $120,000 would be costly to the company, since interest has to be paid on borrowed funds. Note that this method is recommended only if the flow of funds is maintained at a steady, even pace.

YOU SHOULD REMEMBER

The three basic methods to estimate future cash needs are the percent-of-sales method, cash budget method, and cash turnover method.

ANALYSIS OF SOURCES AND USES OF FUNDS

In financial planning and control, it is essential to understand how funds have been generated and where they have been used. This study is called the **analysis of sources and uses of funds**. Without a good understanding of the sources and uses of funds, and of the changes that occur in these sources and uses, management cannot evaluate what the company has done or in what direction it is going. A thorough analysis of the sources and uses of funds will determine the extent to which the company is relying on debt or equity. It also gives a good indication whether generated funds are being used effectively to maintain sufficient cash, purchase inventories, expand fixed assets, reduce liabilities, pay dividends, and so on.

Once the sources and uses of funds have been determined, management can decide whether or not the sources are reliable and what changes must be made to ensure future cash inflows. It can also be determined whether or not the uses of funds are consistent with the overall objectives of the firm, and, if not, corrective measures can be taken.

Sources of Funds

a. *A decrease in assets*, such as the sale of assets.

b. *An increase in liabilities*, such as borrowing money.

c. *An increase in capital*, such as reinvestment of profits.

Uses of Funds

a. *An increase in assets*, such as the purchase of new equipment.

b. *A decrease in liabilities*, such as the payment of debts.

c. *A decrease in capital*, such as the payment of dividends and various expenses.

Table 14–2 illustrates how a change in a balance-sheet account could be either a source or a use.

Table 14–2 Sources and Uses of Funds

Transaction	Source	Use
If asset ↑		✓
If asset ↓	✓	
If liabilities ↑	✓	
If liabilities ↓		✓
If capital ↑	✓	
If capital ↓		✓

Example: Analyzing Sources and Uses of Funds

PROBLEM The balance sheets of the Brown Company are given for 2 consecutive years in Table 14–3. Analyzing the sources and uses of funds, determine how the funds were generated and for what purposes they were spent.

SOLUTION The analysis in Table 14–3 indicates that the sources of funds for the Brown Company were cash, marketable securities, accounts receivable, depreciation, long-term debt, and retained earnings. The generated funds were spent to acquire more inventories and fixed assets and to repay accounts payable, notes payable, and accruals. Note that depreciation has a negative sign, which means that the value of assets has decreased. Since depreciation is a decrease in asset value and a noncash expenditure offset in retained earnings, it is viewed as a source of funds.

Table 14–3 Balance Sheets of the Brown Company (values in thousands of dollars)

	Year 1	Year 2	Source	Use
Assets				
Cash	12	7	5	
Marketable securities	30	20	10	
Accounts receivable	20	15	5	
Inventories	15	55		40
Fixed assets	140	180		40
Accumulated depreciation	−40	−80	40	
Total assets	177	197		
Liabilities				
Accounts payable	8	7		1
Notes payable	17	7		10
Accruals	13	11		2
Long-term debt	47	67	20	
Preferred stock	14	14		
Common stock	50	50		
Retained earnings	28	41	13	
Liabilities and capital	177	197		

With further analysis, you can pinpoint which accounts absorbed most of the funds and which accounts contributed most to the generated funds. This can be done by calculating the percentage of the total for each source and use, as in Table 14–4.

To determine the relative significance of each account in generating or using funds, the sources and uses in Table 14–4 are then ranked—based on their percentages—as shown in Table 14–5.

Table 14–5 is very informative, as it clearly reveals the main sources and uses of funds. For instance, in the case of the Brown Company, depreciation generates 43% of the total sources. Second to depreciation as a main source of funds is long-term debt, which contributes 22% of all generated funds. Note that depreciation, long-term debt, and retained earnings together account for 79% of the total funds and, therefore, are the major sources of funds on which the financing of Brown Company relies. If the management thinks that any of these major sources are not very reliable for future operations, the company should take corrective actions and arrange for new sources of financing in advance.

Table 14–4 Percentages of Sources and Uses of Funds
for the Brown Company

	Dollar Amount	Percentage
Sources		
Cash	5	5
Marketable securities	10	11
Accounts receivable	5	5
Depreciation	40	43
Long-term debt	20	22
Retained earnings	13	14
	93	100
Uses		
Inventories	40	43
Fixed assets	40	43
Accounts payable	1	1
Notes payable	10	11
Accruals	2	2
	93	100

Table 14–5 Ranking of Sources and Uses of Funds for the Brown Company

Rank	Source	Percentage	Rank	Use	Percentage
1	Depreciation	43	1	Inventories	43
2	Long-term	22	2	Fixed assets	43
3	Retained earnings	14	3	Notes payable	11
4	Marketable securities	11	4	Accruals	2
5	Cash	5	5	Accounts payable	1
6	Accounts receivable	5			

Table 14–5 also indicates that the generated funds are spent mainly to increase inventories (63%), purchase new assets (63%), and pay outstanding notes payable (11%). If this pattern of spending funds is not a desired one, management should correct the situation before the shortage of funds for other purposes becomes a problem. Because it can reveal such vital information, the analysis of sources and uses of funds is an integral part of any sound financial planning and control system. The final results of such analysis are also needed to prepare and present the financial sections of the annual reports of publicly held companies.

YOU SHOULD REMEMBER

Analysis of sources and uses of funds reveals how a firm has been financed and how its resources have been spent. This analysis is an integral part of financial planning and control.

Decreases in assets, increases in liabilities, and increases in capital are the sources of funds. Increases in assets, decreases in liabilities, and decreases in capital are the uses of funds.

KNOW THE CONCEPTS

DO YOU KNOW THE BASICS?

1. What are the main purposes of financial planning and control?
2. Name three techniques of financial planning used to estimate external financing needs.
3. What information is required before you can make an analysis of the sources and uses of funds?
4. Give an example of an actual company that suffered badly from lack of financial planning in the past.
5. How do you determine cash surplus/deficit in the cash budget method?
6. How do you determine the required external financing in the percent-of-sales method?

TERMS FOR STUDY

cash cycle	liquidity management
cash turnover	sources and uses of funds analysis
financial planning	spontaneous asset

PRACTICAL APPLICATION

COMPUTATIONAL PROBLEMS

1. Using the following information, determine the amount of external financing required by the MBO Co.

Estimated sales for the next year	$400,000
Current sales	$350,000
Ratio of net profit after dividends to sales	3%
Assets that change with sales have a ratio of 80% of sales	
Liabilities that change with sales have a ratio of 40% of sales	

2. Using the following data, compute the sources and uses of funds and interpret your results:

Balance Sheets of the ABC Co.

	Year 1	Year 2
Assets		
Cash	100	200
Marketable securities	50	110
Accounts receivable	40	42
Inventories	80	110
Fixed assets	90	95
Depreciation	(30)	(34)
	330	523
Liabilities		
Accounts payable	45	46
Notes payable	45	45
Long-term debt	20	210
Common stock	100	100
Retained earnings	120	122
	330	523

3. Determine the minimum cash required if a firm's total annual expenditures are $2,000,000 and the cash cycle is 60 days.

4. Determine the cash surplus/deficit for a particular month, given the following information: receipts, $100,000; payments, $60,000; beginning cash, $10,000; and cash reserve, $5,000.

ANSWERS

KNOW THE CONCEPTS

1. The main purposes of financial planning and control are estimating future financing needs, deciding how to finance, identifying sources and uses of funds, and taking corrective actions as to how funds are allocated.

2. Percent-of-sales method, cash budget method, and cash turnover method.

3. To make an analysis of the sources and uses of funds, you will need the balance sheets and income statements for at least the past 2 years.

4. The Chrysler Corporation in the 1970s.

5. The equation is

$$\text{Cash surplus/deficit} = \text{Ending cash} + \text{Cash reserve}$$

where

$$\text{Ending cash} = \text{Net cash flow} + \text{Beginning cash}$$
$$\text{Net cash flow} = \text{Receipts} - \text{Payments}$$

(See Table 14–1.)

6. The equation is

$$\text{External required financing} = \frac{A}{S} (\Delta S) - \frac{L}{S} (\Delta S) - rS$$

where A = assets that change with sales
ΔS = expected change in sales forecast for the year
L = liabilities that change with sales
r = ratio of net profits after dividends to sales

PRACTICAL APPLICATION

1. The equation is

$$\frac{A}{S} (\Delta S) - \frac{L}{S} (\Delta S) - rS$$

Using the given values, you have

$$80\%(\$50,000) - 40\%(\$50,000) - 3\%(\$400,000) = \$8,000$$

2.

Account	Source	Use
Cash		100
Marketable securities		60
Accounts receivable		2
Inventory		30
Fixed assets		5
Depreciation	4	
Accounts payable	1	
Notes payable	0	
Debt	190	
Retained earnings	2	
	197	197

This company borrows heavily to have inventory and liquidity.

3. Step 1. Cash turnover $= \dfrac{360 \text{ days}}{\text{Cash cycle}} = \dfrac{360 \text{ days}}{60} = 6$

    Step 2. Minimum cash required $= \dfrac{\text{Annual expenditures}}{\text{Cash turnover}}$

$$= \frac{\$2,000,000}{6}$$

$$= \$333,333$$

4. Net cash flow $=$ Receipts $-$ Payments

                          $= \$100,000 - \$60,000 = \$40,000$

   Ending cash $=$ Net cash flow $+$ Beginning cash

                          $= \$40,000 + \$10,000 = \$50,000$

Cash surplus/deficit $=$ Ending cash $+$ Cash reserve

                          $= \$50,000 + \$5,000 = \$55,000$

The company has a cash surplus of \$55,000 in that month.

MANAGING WORKING CAPITAL

FINANCING
WORKING CAPITAL

NET WORKING CAPITAL

By definition, **net working capital** is the amount of money left after current liabilities have been subtracted from current assets:

$$\text{Net working capital} = \text{Current assets} - \text{Current liabilities}$$

Therefore, net working capital can also be thought of as the portion of current assets that should be financed through long-term borrowing or owners' equity.

If current liabilities remain the same, net working capital rises as current assets increase. Between two firms in the same industry and with equal amounts of assets, the one with higher net working capital is more liquid, because more liquid assets are available to cover short-term debts. Because of this line of reasoning, net working capital is often viewed as an indicator of liquidity in working capital management.

MANAGING CURRENT ASSETS

Current assets usually fluctuate from month to month. During months when sales are relatively high, firms usually carry a lot of inventory, accounts receivable, and cash. The level of inventory declines in other months when there is less selling activity. The timing of high and low inventory levels basically depends on the nature of the product. For example, sporting goods stores will generally have larger inventories of ski equipment in November than in July. These inventory fluctuations mean that the current asset values of the firms also vary.

Management should be aware of the expected minimum and maximum levels of current assets each year. The minimum level can be viewed as the permanent portion of current assets, while the difference between the minimum and maximum levels is called the seasonal portion. For instance, if the highest level of current assets from January to December is $50,000 and the lowest level is $30,000, by definition the permanent portion of current assets is $30,000 and the seasonal portion is $20,000 ($50,000 − $30,000). These figures play a large part in financing decisions. Since the fixed portion of $30,000 remains on the book for a relatively long period of time, it should be financed like a fixed asset, through long-term debt or equity. On the other hand, the seasonal requirement of $20,000 can be financed by short-term borrowing.

Example: Calculating Permanent and Seasonal Financial Needs

PROBLEM   The total value of current assets of the XYZ Co. fluctuates: $80,000 in February; $100,000 in April; $140,000 in June; $40,000 in August; $60,000 in October; and $90,000 in December. The company's fixed current assets are estimated to be $50,000 from January to December. How should the company's assets be financed?

SOLUTION   To solve this problem, you should break the total financing into two portions: **permanent financing** and **seasonal financing**. The permanent portion is the minimum level of current assets plus fixed assets. The seasonal portion is the amount of current assets exceeding the minimum level. The following equations help illustrate these relationships:

Permanent financing = Minimum level of current assets
+ Current fixed assets

Seasonal financing   = Current assets
− Minimum level of current assets

Table 15–1   Analysis of Financing Assets for the XYZ Co.

	Feb.	April	June	Aug.	Oct.	Dec.
Current assets (A_c)	$80,000	$100,000	$140,000	$40,000	$60,000	$90,000
Minimum level of current assets (M)	−40,000	−40,000	−40,000	−40,000	−40,000	−40,000
Seasonal financing ($A_c − M$)	40,000	60,000	100,000	-0-	20,000	50,000
Current fixed assets (A_f)	50,000	50,000	50,000	50,000	50,000	50,000
Permanent financing ($M + A_f$)	90,000	90,000	90,000	90,000	90,000	90,000

Table 15–1 shows both the permanent and seasonal financing needs of the XYZ Co. Follow the calculations column by column. For instance, the value of current assets in April is $100,000. When the minimum level of $40,000 is subtracted, the April seasonal financing requirement is $60,000. The seasonal requirement goes up to $100,000 in June, then drops to zero in August, and so on. Since these financing needs are not permanent or stable, they are usually arranged through short-term bank loans. In contrast, the permanent financing requirement of $90,000 in Table 15–1 should be provided through a combination of long-term debt and equity. If the $90,000 permanent needs were borrowed for a short period, the lender might not renew the loan at maturity, and the company would face liquidity problems and possibly bankruptcy.

RISK AND PROFIT: CHOOSING THE RIGHT MIXTURE

The decision whether to finance assets with short-term or long-term loans is a choice between minimizing risk and maximizing profits. Under normal economic situations, long-term loans are more costly than short-term loans. The reason is that lenders who extend credit for a longer period are faced with more uncertainty than lenders who collect their original loans after a short period of time. The risk of default and inflation is usually more significant for long-term loans, since the loss of principal investment is greater for loans of longer maturity if the interest rate rises. An increase in interest rate produces a bigger discount in the value of a long-term bond because the time to maturity is relatively long. Therefore, the higher costs of long-term loans are partly a compensation for risk. Another reason for costly long-term financing is that the borrowers are assured of being able to use the funds for a long period of time without having to renew the loans from year to year. Remember that, if short-term loans are not rolled over on time, the firm may run out of cash, and business activities may be disrupted. Long-term financing, although very costly, is a conservative approach to ensure the continuous liquidity of the firm. On the basis of this line of reasoning, conservative financial managers meet most future financial needs through long-term loans, borrowing only a very limited amount of funds through short-term loans.

Figure 15–1 illustrates three different approaches to financing: very conservative, conservative, and aggressive. In a very conservative approach, fixed current assets, the minimum level of current assets, and a portion of seasonal requirements are all financed through long-term loans and equity. Only a portion of seasonal requirements is financed by short-term loans. As a result, the cost of this type of financing may be high, but the risk of running out of cash is minimal. In a **conservative approach,** long-term loans and equity are used to finance fixed assets and the minimum level of current assets. The seasonal requirement is financed through short-term loans. In an **aggressive approach,** fixed assets and only part of the minimum level of current assets are financed by long-term debt and equity. All seasonal requirements, plus a portion of the minimum level of current assets, are provided through short-term financing. Therefore, the cost of financing is minimal but the risk of running into liquidity problems is relatively high. (See the graphic illustrations in Figure 15–1.)

Depending on the attitude of financial managers toward risk, each firm takes a specific approach to finance its assets. If a firm is confident that its short-term loans are easily renewed, an aggressive approach will save considerable interest expense. On the other hand, if there is no assurance that loans will be available in the future, a conservative approach, or sometimes a very conservative approach, may be a better solution.

YOU SHOULD REMEMBER

In a very conservative approach to financing working capital, fixed assets, the minimum level of current assets, and a portion of seasonal requirements are all financed by long-term debt and equity. In a conservative approach, equity and long-term debt are used to cover fixed assets and the minimum level of current assets. In an aggressive approach, fixed assets and only part of the minimum level of current assets are financed by long-term sources; the rest are arranged through short-term funds.

MANAGING ACCOUNTS RECEIVABLE

The volume of accounts receivable is basically determined by the credit standards of the company. If these standards are rigid, fewer customers are qualified for credit, sales decrease, and, as a result, accounts receivable decline. On the other hand, if credit standards are relaxed, more customers are attracted to the firm, sales increase, and higher accounts receivable are generated. Relaxing credit standards to increase accounts receivable has both advantages and disadvantages. The advantages are increases in sales and profits. The disadvantages are reflected in the probability of more bad debts and the additional financing cost of accounts receivable.

Accounts receivable are like interest-free loans to customers, because sellers must pay interest expenses as long as their capital is tied up in accounts receivable. Before making a decision to lower credit standards, the cost of additional accounts receivable and the benefit of more sales should be compared. If the result of this cost/benefit analysis is a net profit, the firm should relax credit standards.

Example: Managing Accounts Receivable

PROBLEM   Jones Electronic Manufacturing has current sales of 100,000 units of electronic signal devices. Each unit is sold for $50. The variable cost per unit is $40; therefore, the contribution margin is $10. (**Contri-**

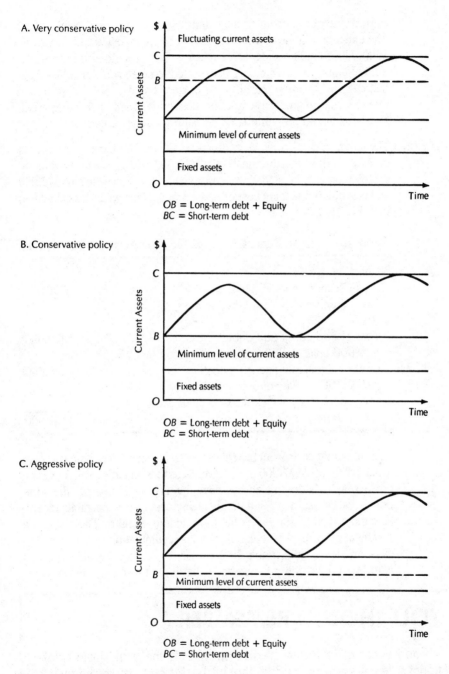

Figure 15–1 Financing Approaches

bution margin is equal to the selling price minus the variable cost.) The existing volume of accounts receivable is expected to increase by $500,000 if credit standards are relaxed. Sales should also increase by 30,000 units, from which 5% is expected to be an additional loss from bad debts. Assuming that the cost of goods sold is 80% of sales and that the cost of financing is 12%, determine whether relaxing credit standards would be a profitable decision for Jones Electronic.

SOLUTION The solution is a simple cost/benefit analysis. The benefits are profits of $300,000 from additional sales (30,000 additional units sold × contribution margin of $10); the costs are additional bad debts of $75,000 and a $48,000 financing cost of new accounts receivable, as calculated in Table 15–2.

Table 15–2   Cost/Benefit Analysis for New Accounts Receivable

Benefits	
Profits from additional sales	$300,000
(30,000 units × $10 contribution margin)	
Costs	
Cost of additional bad debts	(75,000)
[(30,000 units × $50 unit price) × (5% bad debt)]	
Cost of additional financing costs	(48,000)
[($500,000 additional accounts receivable × 80% cost	
of goods sold) × (12% cost of financing)]	
Net profit	$177,000

Subtracting costs from benefits shows that Jones Electronic will earn a net profit of $177,000 if it lowers credit standards. But lowering credit standards doesn't always have this effect. Sometimes the additional cost of bad debts and the financing cost of new accounts receivable more than offset the profits from additional sales. The result is a combination of new receivables and an accumulation of old ones because of slower collections. In that case, of course, the right decision is to leave the credit policy alone—that is, not to relax standards.

YOU SHOULD REMEMBER

The benefit of lowering credit standards is the profit from additional sales; the costs are additional bad debts and greater financing costs for additional accounts receivable.

The benefits of raising credit standards are reduction of bad debts and lower financing costs for accounts receivable; the cost is reduction of profits from sales.

MANAGING INVENTORY

The main purpose of **inventory management** is to determine and maintain the level of inventory that will ensure that customer orders are satisfied in sufficient amounts and on time. However, holding inventory is costly because it ties up money on which no interest or income is generated. In other words, the cost of inventory precludes other profitable opportunities for investment. If there is an opportunity to make 15% profit on an investment, maintaining a level of inventory at $10,000 costs $1,500 annually. Put another way, the firm would make $1,500 profit if it could invest $10,000 rather than using it to purchase inventory. Understanding this concept is essential in solving a number of problems in the area of inventory management.

WHEN TO INCREASE INVENTORY

The level of inventory should be increased if the added benefits will be greater than the cost of maintaining additional inventory. Suppose a company saves $10,000 in ordering goods if the average inventory is increased from $450,000 to $600,000. If the firm has an opportunity to earn 16% on its money, is the proposal to raise the level of inventory acceptable? In answering this question, you would compare the additional profits of $10,000 against the lost opportunity to earn profit on the money tied up in the additional inventory of $150,000.

Since the $24,000 cost of additional inventory (16% × $150,000) exceeds the savings of $10,000, the decision should be to *not* increase the level of inventory. If inventory is increased to a new level of $600,000, the company would have a net loss of $14,000 ($24,000 loss − $10,000 savings). The firm may also decide to decrease the level of inventory if savings of inventory cost outweigh profits.

ECONOMIC ORDER QUANTITY (EOQ)

The **economic order quantity**, better known as **EOQ**, is the quantity of an item that, when ordered regularly, results in minimum ordering and storage costs. Costs of ordering include salaries and wages paid to full- and part-time employees working in the purchasing department and the cost of computer time and supplies to prepare purchase orders. The more frequently orders are placed, the more costly is the ordering process. Ordering costs will be minimal if annual requirements are all ordered at one time in the beginning of the year. Figure 15–2 shows the general relationship between order quantity (number of units in each order) and ordering cost.

Storage costs include the various expenses associated with warehouse operations and stocking items. As the number of units in each order increases, storage costs rise. Therefore, storage cost is maximum when the annual consumption is requested through a single order. By the same token, storage cost declines as items are ordered in smaller amounts. The relationship between storage costs and the order quantity (number of units in each order) is illustrated in Figure 15–3.

The economic order quantity (*EOQ*) can be determined if Figures 15–2 and 15–3 are projected side by side, as shown in Figure 15–4.

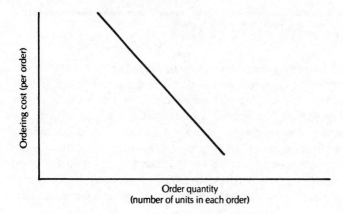

Figure 15–2 Ordering Cost and Order Quantity

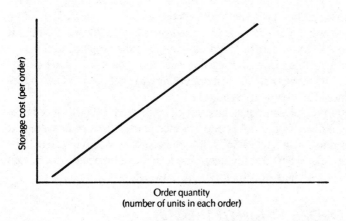

Figure 15–3 Storage Cost and Order Quantity

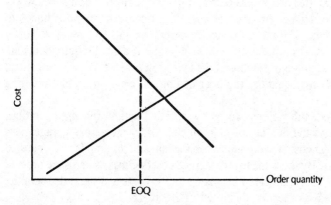

Figure 15–4 The Economic Order Quantity (EOQ)

The EOQ can also be determined by the use of the following equation:

$$EOQ = \sqrt{\frac{2RO}{W}}$$

where R = required number of units in each time period
O = ordering cost per order
W = cost of warehouse/storage

Example: Calculating the EOQ

The annual consumption of an item is 10,000 units, the ordering cost per order is \$120, and the storage cost per unit is \$4. Under these assumptions, the EOQ can quickly be found with the given equation:

$$EOQ = \sqrt{\frac{2RO}{W}} = \sqrt{\frac{(2)(10,000)(120)}{4}} = \sqrt{600,000}$$

$$= 774 \text{ units}$$

The firm will minimize the total cost of ordering and storage if 774 units are requested with every purchase order. Since the annual consumption is 10,000 units, the firm should order 13 times, each time requesting 774 units:

$$\text{No. of orders per year} = \frac{\text{Annual consumption}}{\text{EOQ}} = \frac{10,000}{774} = 12.91, \text{ or 13 times}$$

YOU SHOULD REMEMBER

The economic order quantity (EOQ) is the quantity of an item that, when ordered regularly, results in minimum ordering and storage costs.

The purpose of inventory management is to determine and maintain the level of inventory that will ensure satisfaction of customer orders in sufficient quantity and on time. To operate economically, management should increase the level of inventory if the resulting benefits will exceed the cost of maintaining the additional inventory.

MANAGING ACCOUNTS PAYABLE

Accounts payable can be viewed as free loans from suppliers. In the absence of accounts payable, the firm has to borrow money or use its own equity to pay suppliers' bills. Therefore, the benefit of accounts payable is in the saving of interest expenses that would have to be paid if credit weren't given by the supplier. However, accepting credit and using accounts payable are not always in the best interests of the purchasing company. Suppliers usually offer generous cash discounts if bills are paid either on delivery or within a few days after the receipt of an invoice. In this case, a crucial question is whether to take the cash discount and pay immediately or to purchase on credit and use accounts payable. If the cash discount is taken, the advantage is the cash discount itself and the disadvantages are the cost of borrowing money to pay cash and the loss of a free loan. The cash discount offer should be accepted if the benefit exceeds the cost.

Example: Managing Accounts Payable

PROBLEM   ABC Co. is eligible for a 3% cash discount if a merchandise bill of $100,000 is paid in cash immediately. However, the company also has the option of using its credit and paying the bill within 60 days. ABC Co. has contacted its local bank and learned that money to pay the bill can be borrowed at a rate of 14%, which would allow ABC Co. to take advantage of the 3% cash discount offer. Which option is more economical: using the cash discount or paying through accounts payable?

SOLUTION   Table 15–3 compares the benefit of taking the cash discount, which amounts to $3,000, versus the cost of the cash discount, $2,263.

Table 15–3   Using Cash Discounts or Accounts Payable

Benefit of cash discount	$3,000.
(3% cash discount × $100,000 bill)	
Cost of cash discount	− 2,263
(Interest expenses on $97,000 for 60 days at 14%	
interest rate: $97,000 × $\left(14\% \times \frac{60\ days}{360\ days}\right)$	
Net benefit	$ 737

Note: Since the 3% cash discount is used, the company has to borrow only $97,000, rather than $100,000.

Using accounts payable rather than taking the cash discount, in this case, is somewhat similar to rejecting a free cash offer of $737 from the supplier.

Since the net result is a saving of $737, ABC Co. should take the cash discount. Taking the cash discount of 3% requires an immediate payment of $97,000, which must be borrowed or taken from existing funds.

The benefit of a cash discount can also be calculated using standard terms like 2/10 net 30. This means that a buyer can receive a 2% cash discount if the bill is paid within 10 days; otherwise, the full amount—without discount—is due in 30 days. If the bill is paid immediately, the benefit of this cash discount is 2% for 30 days and approximately 24% in 1 year (2% × 12 months). In the preceding example, the cash discount should be accepted if the borrowing rate is less than 24%, since the benefit of the cash discount would outweigh the cost of borrowing to pay the bill within 10 days.

There is a precise formula by which the cost of not using the cash discount (the benefit of the cash discount) can be calculated·

Cost of not using cash discount

$$= \frac{\text{Cash discount}}{1 - \text{Cash discount}} \times \frac{360 \text{ days}}{\text{Days credit outstanding} - \text{Discount period}}$$

According to this formula, the precise cost of not using the cash discount is 36.7%:

$$\left(\frac{2\%}{1 - 2\%}\right) \times \left(\frac{360 \text{ days}}{30 - 10}\right) = 36.7\%$$

YOU SHOULD REMEMBER

A cash discount is an acceptable offer if its benefit (or the cost of not using the cash discount) exceeds the cost of borrowing. If, however, the benefit of the cash discount is less than the cost of borrowing, the firm is better off using accounts payable and paying the bill at a later time.

KNOW THE CONCEPTS

DO YOU KNOW THE BASICS?

1. Give two definitions of net working capital.

2. What is the difference between seasonal and permanent working capital?

3. Describe a conservative approach to financing working capital.

4. Under what conditions should a cash discount offer be accepted?

5. What does the term 3/10 net 45 mean?

6. What does the EOQ strive to minimize, and what does it strive to maximize?

TERMS FOR STUDY

aggressive approach	inventory management
conservative approach	net working capital
contribution margin	permanent financing
economic order quantity (EOQ)	seasonal financing

PRACTICAL APPLICATION

COMPUTATIONAL PROBLEMS

1. Management at Brown Mfg. has determined that relaxing credit standards would add $14,000 to profits, but that the average investment in accounts receivable would increase by $20,000. As a result of lowering the credit standards, the cost of bad debts is expected to increase from $5,000 to $13,000. The required return on investment is 14%. Determine whether a policy to relax credit standards should be recommended.

2. The Ajax Co. has the following options: (a) borrow at 15%, pay the purchase invoice of $100,000 immediately, and take a 3% cash discount; or (b) use accounts payable and pay after 90 days. Which option is more economical?

3. LI Bolts and Nuts purchases 10,000 units of a particular item per month. The monthly storage cost per item is $0.10, and each order costs $50. Determine the EOQ of this company.

4. Determine the average level of inventory and the number of orders per month in Problem 3.

5. Determine the precise cost of not using a cash discount under the terms 3/10 net 40.

ANSWERS

KNOW THE CONCEPTS

1. Two definitions of net working capital are: (a) Current assets − Current liabilities, and (b) the portion of current assets financed by long-term sources.

2. The minimum level of current assets is "permanent," whereas the amount over the minimum level is "seasonal."

3. A conservative approach would be to finance permanent current assets and a good portion of seasonal working capital through long-term debt or equity.

4. A cash discount offer should be accepted if its benefit (the amount of discount) is greater than the cost of borrowing to be able to pay cash.

5. The customer is entitled to a cash discount of 3% if the bill is paid within 10 days of receipt of the invoice. Otherwise, the customer must pay the full price within 45 days.

6. The EOQ strives to maximize order quantity while minimizing ordering and storage costs.

PRACTICAL APPLICATION

1. Additional profit from new sales $14,000

Cost of investment in accounts receivable	(2,800)
Additional bad debts because of new sales	(8,000)
Net profit	$ 3,200

The proposal should be recommended because it leads to additional profit.

2. Benefit   3% ($100,000) = $3,000
   Cost   15% ($97,000 borrowed) (3 months/12) = $3,637
   The cost of borrowing is greater than the benefit of discount. Obviously, option (b) is preferable.

3. $EOQ = \sqrt{\dfrac{2(10,000)(50)}{.10}} = 3,162$

4. Average level of inventory $= \dfrac{3,162}{2} = 1,581$

   No. of orders per month $= \dfrac{10,000}{3,162} = 3$ orders

5. Cost of not using cash discount $= \left(\dfrac{3\%}{1 - 3\%}\right)\left(\dfrac{360}{40 - 10}\right) = 37\%$

16
FINANCIAL STATEMENTS AND RATIOS

KEY TERMS

balance sheet an accounting statement that displays the assets, liabilities, and equity of a firm

current ratio current assets divided by current liabilities (a liquidity measure)

debt/equity (D/E) ratio debt divided by equity (a financial leverage measure)

income statement an accounting statement of a firm's sales, operating costs, and financial charges

net profit margins the rate of return obtained from sales calculated by dividing net income by net sales

return on investment (ROI) ratio net profits divided by assets (a measure of overall effectiveness)

times interest earned ratio EBIT divided by annual interest expense. (a measure of how well the firm meets its fixed interest payments)

FINANCIAL STATEMENTS

There are several ways to evaluate the performance of a firm. One approach is to analyze its financial statements. You can accomplish this in three ways:

1. Study the contents of the income statement and the balance sheet.

2. Compare sources and uses of funds from one period to another.

3. Examine the relationship between the income statement and the balance sheet by engaging in ratio analysis.

The ultimate purpose of analyzing financial statements by these three procedures is to help managers achieve sound planning. By studying income and balance sheet statements, managers can spot areas of weakness in financial operations and take appropriate remedial action. It is through the analysis of these statements that managers can establish a more effective way of allocating funds and resources. They can also control the future direction of the firm's operations and help maximize its wealth.

INCOME STATEMENT

Income statements report the flows of receipts generated by a firm and the flows of expenses incurred to produce and finance company operations. An abbreviated version of an income statement appears in Table 16–1. It starts by reporting the sales generated from the assets and liabilities reported in the balance sheet. The company then incurs certain expenses. These expenses include cost of goods sold (including labor and materials to produce salable products) and other operating expenses, mainly depreciation, selling, and administrative expenses. By deducting these expenses from sales, operating profits are found. Beyond this point, the income statement shifts and considers financial costs, such as interest and taxes. Subtracting these financial costs from operating profits gives net profits and retained earnings. As a generalization, then, income statements provide a picture of the sales, costs, and profitability generated by a firm during a certain period of time.

Table 16–1   Typical Income Statement for Year Ending December 31

Sales	$20,000,000
Less cost of goods sold	16,000,000
Depreciation ($500,000)	
Gross profits	4,000,000
Less operating expenses	2,000,000
Other ($1,500,000)	
Operating profits	2,000,000
Less net interest (at 10%)	44,000
Profit before taxes	1,956,000
Less taxes (at 40% rate)	782,400
Profits after taxes (NI)	1,173,600
Less common stock dividends	588,000
Retained earnings	$ 588,000
Number of outstanding shares	300,000
Earnings per share $\left(\dfrac{\text{NI}}{\text{Number of shares}} \text{ or } \dfrac{\$1{,}173{,}600}{300{,}000}\right)$	$3.91

It is customary to translate net income into earnings per share (EPS) (outstanding shares of the firm divided into net income) because this measure informs stockholders and investors how much profit is behind a share of stock and helps to establish a common basis for deriving the valuation (P/E) and price of one company's share versus another's.

BALANCE SHEET

The **balance sheet** is a statement of assets, liabilities, and stockholders' equity. As of a certain date, the left side of this statement shows a breakdown of current assets in the form of cash and other assets that constitute the working capital of the firm. Fixed assets are mainly long-term investments, including plant and equipment.

The right side of the balance sheet shows current liabilities, consisting of accounts payable, notes payable, and other short-term liabilities. From this point on you continue to find long-term debt, which has a maturity date of over 1 year. This part of the balance sheet may also include the capitalized value of financial leases. After you deduct the liabilities from the assets, the remaining value is the net worth or stockholders' equity on the firm. The components of net worth include the par value of common stock outstanding, paid-in capital surplus, and retained earnings accumulated from previous profits generated by the firm after the deduction of dividend payments. If the firm were to be liquidated and all creditors' claims paid off, the net worth is what would be left over for distribution to stockholders.

As a statement of assets and liabilities, a balance sheet allows investors to observe the mix of these components and to decide whether the allocation is sound. By deducting current assets from current liabilities, you can find out something about the liquidity of the firm; and by matching profits against the assets invested in the firm, you can gain some idea of how effectively the firm has utilized assets to generate profits.

Table 16–2 Typical Balance Sheet

Assets		Liabilities and Common Stockholders' Equity	
Cash	$ 40,000	Accounts payable	$ 150,000
Marketable securities	50,000	Notes payable	50,000
Accounts Receivable	320,000	Other current assets	20,000
Inventory	250,000	**Total current liabilities**	**220,000**
Total current assets	**660,000**	Long-term debt	440,000
Net fixed assets	550,000	Common stock	350,000
		Retained earnings	200,000
Total assets	**$1,210,000**	**Total liabilities and equity**	**$1,210,000**

• USES OF FINANCIAL STATEMENTS

One important use of financial statements is to determine the efficiency of a firm's cost control or profit production. This can be done by comparing the income statement of the firm to the income statement of the industry or to the best firm in the industry.

Income statements can also tell you how a firm's profits are affected by changes in its fixed charges like interest, depreciation, and fixed costs. Balance sheets help managers of firms find out if certain assets and liabilities are utilized effectively. For example, assume that a firm has higher inventories than are usual for its industry. This might indicate that it is carrying too much stock and is incurring excessive carrying costs. Or the analysis of the balance sheet might indicate that the firm's net fixed assets are too high for the sales it generates. This might mean that it has excess capacity or that it uses assets inefficiently. Also, the firm may be carrying excess liabilities, which would make it vulnerable to insolvency.

In summary, financial statements lend themselves to a great deal of analysis, and they can reveal the operating and financial strengths and weaknesses of a firm. It is up to the firm's manager to properly interpret the figures in the financial statements and to institute corrective actions when required. Two ways of facilitating this process are:

- Analyzing the sources and uses of funds of the firm.

- Engaging in the analysis of financial ratios.

• SOURCES AND USES OF FUNDS

Most funds come from profits, depreciation, equity, and long-term debt, while increases in accounts receivable, marketable securities, and fixed assets are the major uses of these funds. Spotting where the funds come from and where they go is highly useful, because it helps financial managers find the best ways to generate and use those funds.

To calculate sources and uses of funds, you apply the simple rules listed below:
Sources of cash occur when:

1. There is a decrease in assets from one period to the next.

2. There is an increase in liabilities from one period to the next.

3. There are depreciation charges in the income statement in the latest year.

4. A firm sells stock.

5. A firm earns net income in the latest period.

Uses of funds occur when:

1. Assets increase from one period to the next.

2. Liabilities decrease from one period to the next.

3. The firm incurs income losses in the latest period.

4. The firm pays out cash dividends.

5. The firm repurchases or retires stock.

Using these guidelines, you can proceed to determine the sources and uses of funds for 1989 to 1990 from the balance sheet and selected income statement figures for a firm that will be called Company X.

This has been done in Table 16–3, where you will observe that a decrease in inventories resulted in a source of funds. Increases in marketable securities, ac-

Table 16–3   Calculating the Sources and Uses of Funds Based on Selected Balance Sheet and Income Components for Company X (1989–1990) (all values in thousands of dollars)

	1989	1990	Sources	Uses
Assets				
Cash	450	530		80
Marketable securities	80	110		30
Accounts receivables	1,500	1,650		150
Inventories	1,400	1,390	10	
Gross fixed assets				
Net fixed assets	4,170	4,570		400
Less accumulated depreciation	(1,000)	(1,345)		
Total assets	6,600	6,905		
Liabilities and Equity				
Accounts payable	550	650	100	
Notes payable	150	130		20
Other current liabilities	100	150	50	
Long-term debt	1,700	1,760	60	
Common stock	1,500	1,505	5	
Paid-in capital	1,600	1,610	10	
Retained earnings	1,000	1,100	*	*
Total liabilities and stockholders' equity	6,600	6,905		
Income Statement Components				
Net profits after taxes			300	
Depreciation			245	
Dividends				100
Total sources			780	
Total uses				780

*Changes in retained earnings are not classified as sources or uses of cash.

counts receivables, inventories, and gross fixed assets represented a use of funds. Declining notes payable also produced a use of funds, whereas the remaining components of current liabilities increased and gave rise to sources of funds. Higher common stock and paid-in capital surplus also gave rise to additional sources of funds. Profits after taxes and depreciation are considered sources of funds, while the payment of dividends is a use of cash.

Analysis of sources and uses of funds can help financial managers to determine whether there are excesses or imbalances in the way the firm generates and allocates funds. It can also reveal to the firm whether it can rely on internal sources, or whether it should tap outside sources, to finance its operations.

You can readily see from Table 16–3 the importance of each balance sheet and income statement category as a source or use of funds. Also, uses of funds must always equal sources of funds. This approach facilitates the analysis of financial statements and makes it easier to perceive how effective the mix of internal and external financing has been. By studying these figures, managers can make better judgments regarding ways to generate new and cheaper sources of funds and to improve the use of these funds.

YOU SHOULD REMEMBER

The balance sheet and income statement provide important information on the way a firm allocates its resources and produces profits. Analysis of these statements should help the firm to spot areas of financial weakness and strength. One way of interpreting these financial statements is to construct a table of sources and uses of funds.

FINANCIAL RATIOS

Responsible management of a firm requires constant monitoring of operations. For example, financial executives have to know whether or not they have enough liquidity; that is, they must ensure that sufficient funds are available to pay liabilities on time. Firms also establish guidelines regarding acceptable amounts of debt and fixed financial commitments.

Accordingly, managers are concerned about trends and degrees of their firms' efficiency and profitability. One way to measure the liquidity, debt position, and profitability of a firm is to engage in financial ratio analysis. This analysis can serve as a basis for financial planning and can provide a tool for monitoring performance.

• *USES AND TYPES OF RATIOS*

Ratio analysis helps to reveal the overall financial condition of a firm. It helps analysts and investors spot whether a firm is subject to the risk of insolvency and whether the firm is doing well compared to its industry or its competitors. Investors look at ratios to help them evaluate a company's performance and growth. Accordingly, poor financial ratios generally lead to higher financing costs, while good ratios usually mean that investors will be willing to make funds available to the company at more reasonable costs. Banks use ratios to help determine how much credit to grant a firm.

Creditors worry when a firm does not generate enough earnings to make periodic payments of interest on outstanding debt. They also become concerned about firms that are top-heavy in debt, since a downward trend in business activity may lead to insolvency. Security analysts constantly monitor different financial ratios of the companies they follow by using ratio spreadsheets. By this analysis they can detect strengths and weaknesses in different companies.

Managers use financial ratios to monitor operations, to make sure their firms are using available resources effectively, and to avoid insolvency. The idea is to find out whether the firm's financial and operating status is improving over time and whether its overall ratios are better or worse than the ratios of competing companies. When these ratios fall below certain standards, it is the responsibility of the manager to regain control before serious problems arise.

Ratio analysis allows you to better understand the relationship between the balance sheet and the income statements. For instance, to compute a firm's return on investment, you need the total assets figure from the firm's balance sheet and the net income from its income statement. In addition, some ratios can indicate how effectively assets are being used and whether the liability mix is a good one. Clearly, the use of financial ratios is an important tool in modern financial planning.

Although there are a substantial number of individual ratios, they are usually lumped into four major categories:

- Liquidity ratios.
- Activity ratios.
- Debt ratios.
- Profitability ratios.

LIQUIDITY RATIOS

An asset's degree of liquidity depends on how quickly that asset can be converted into cash without incurring a substantial loss. Liquidity management consists of matching debt claims with asset maturities and other cash flows in order to avoid technical insolvency. The measurement of liquidity is important. The main question, therefore, is whether or not a firm can generate sufficient cash to pay its suppliers and creditors.

In essence, liquidity ratios test a firm's degree of solvency. Two well-known ratios used to measure the liquidity of a firm include the current and the acid-test (quick) ratios.

CURRENT RATIO

The **current ratio** is the relationship between current assets and current liabilities:

$$\text{Current ratio} = \frac{\text{Current assets}}{\text{Current liabilities}}$$

Example: Current Ratio

A firm with $20 million in current assets and $10 million in current liabilities is said to have a current ratio of 2.0 times:

$$\text{Current ratio} = \frac{\$20,000,000}{\$10,000,000} = 2.0 \text{ times}$$

The current ratio roughly indicates the margin of safety available to a firm to meet short-term liabilities. The ratio can vary, depending on the industry and the type of company. A ratio of 2.0 times or better may be good for a manufacturing firm, while a ratio of 1.5 may be acceptable for a utility, because of its highly predictable cash inflow and small current liabilities.

The current ratio does not measure a firm's flexibility. Obviously, if a firm has large cash reserves and marketable securities, it is more liquid than a firm with large inventories. A more refined ratio to deal with the asset mix problem would eliminate the component in current assets that is the least liquid.

ACID-TEST RATIO (QUICK RATIO)

By eliminating the less certain value of inventory and concentrating on easily convertible assets, the **acid-test** (or **quick**) **ratio** determines whether a firm could meet its creditor obligations if sales were to drop catastrophically.

$$\text{Acid-test ratio} = \frac{\text{Current Assets} - \text{Inventories}}{\text{Current liabilities}}$$

Example: Acid-test Ratio

In the preceding example, current assets were valued at $20 million. But what if $5.0 million were tied up in inventories?

$$\text{Acid-test ratio} = \frac{\$20,000,000 - \$5,000,000}{\$10,000,000} = 1.5 \text{ times}$$

This figure might tell you that the firm can easily meet its short-term obligations because it would have no trouble generating cash from other current assets. On the other hand, this firm might have some doubtful receivables or be in a very highly sensitive industry in which creditors get paid quickly. Thus, this firm might require a quick ratio of 2.0 times, and the 1.5 times ratio would indicate that the firm should attempt to either reduce inventories or raise the value of its other liquid assets.

> The intelligent use of ratios requires that you apply them in association with other information.

ACTIVITY RATIOS

Activity ratios determine the speed with which a firm can generate cash if the need arises. Clearly, the quicker a firm can convert inventories and accounts receivable into cash, the better off it is. The following ratios and computations assume that a year has 360 days.

AVERAGE COLLECTION PERIOD

Finding the **average collection period** of a firm will tell you how long that firm must wait before receivables are translated into cash. Note that cash sales are excluded from total sales.

$$\text{Average collection period} = \frac{\text{Accounts receivable}}{(\text{Annual credit sales}/360 \text{ days})}$$

Example: Average Collection Period

If a firm's balance sheet shows an accounts receivable figure of $700,000 and its income statement shows credit sales of $5,500,000, then

$$\text{Average collection period} = \frac{\$700,000}{(\$5,500,000/360 \text{ days})} = 45.8 \text{ days}$$

As with other ratios, the average collection period must be examined against other information. If this firm's policy is to extend credit to customers for 38 days, then a period of 45.8 days implies that the firm has trouble collecting on time and should review its credit policy. Conversely, if the firm's usual policy is to set a 55-day collection period for customers, then the 45.8-day average indicates the firm's collection policy is effective.

Remember that the average collection ratio is only *an average*, which can be misleading. For example, consider Firm A and Firm B, which have the same amount of accounts receivables but different collection schedules.

Table 16–4   Time Needed to Collect Payment

	% Collected within 10 Days	% Collected within 30 Days	% Collected within 60 Days
Firm A	10	30	60
Firm B	60	30	10

Table 16–4 shows the percentage of the two firms' accounts receivable collected in each time period. Clearly, Firm B is in a better position since 60% of its receivables are collected within 10 days, compared to only 10% for Firm A. If Firm A and Firm B have the same number of customers and the same amount of receivables, their average collection periods will be the same. But the *distributions* of collections, a factor not shown in the ratio, clearly favor Firm B. Again (because this bears repeating), *financial ratios are useful, but you have to be careful how you interpret them.*

AVERAGE PAYMENT PERIOD

The counterpart to accounts receivable is accounts payable. To find out the **average payment period** for accounts payable, you simply do the same thing you did for accounts receivable—that is, divide annual purchases into accounts payable:

$$\text{Average payment period} = \frac{\text{Accounts payable}}{(\text{Annual credit purchases}/360 \text{ days})}$$

However, annual credit purchases are not reported in a financial statement. To obtain this figure, estimate the percentage of cost of goods sold that are purchased on credit.

Example: Calculating the Average Payment Period

PROBLEM   Assume an accounts payable figure of $275,000. If cost of goods sold is $3,000,000 and it is estimated that 80% of these goods are purchased on credit, what is the average payment period?

SOLUTION   The figure to use for annual credit purchases is $2,400,000 ($3,000,000 × .80). The average payment period for accounts payable can now be computed:

$$\text{Average payment period} = \frac{\$275,000}{(.80 \times \$3,000,000/360 \text{ days})} = 41.3 \text{ days}$$

The average payment period (for accounts payable) of the firm is 41.3 days. Anything lower might mean that sellers give a discount or that they consider the firm a poor risk and therefore hold it to stricter terms. Anything higher might indicate that the firm can receive good credit terms, or that it is "a slow payer"—that is, it is using suppliers as a source of financing.

Sellers—who generally want their money as soon as possible—calculate this ratio to obtain an idea of how long it may take to collect from a firm. And since delaying payment is usually beneficial to the firm, the manager who controls payments is placed in the position of having to strike a balance between the two extremes.

If the industry average exceeds the firm's ratio, the manager may want to find out why the credit that the firm receives is limited and what can be done to obtain better or longer credit terms from suppliers.

INVENTORY TURNOVER

Inventory turnover is important to a firm because inventories are the most illiquid form of current assets. Since the firm must tie up funds to carry inventories, it is advantageous to sell inventories as quickly as possible to free cash for other uses. Generally, a high inventory turnover is considered to be an effective use of these assets.

The **inventory turnover ratio** is calculated as follows:

$$\text{Inventory turnover} = \frac{\text{Cost of goods sold}}{\text{Average inventory}}$$

Example: Inventory Turnover

If a firm's annual cost of goods is $3,000,000 and an average inventory value is $300,000, then the firm's inventory ratio is 10 times.

$$\text{Inventory turnover} = \frac{\$3,000,000}{\$300,000} = 10 \text{ times}$$

This figure must be compared with the industry average before any interpretations can be made, since reasonable ratios can vary widely between industries. Companies selling perishable goods, such as vegetables, will normally have a high turnover rate, while a bulldozer manufacturer's inventory turnover will be much lower. If a firm's ratio is lower than its industry average, however, the manager should probably investigate why inventories are moving so slowly.

Be careful when interpreting the inventory turnover figure. A high turnover ratio does not necessarily imply that a firm is effective in moving inventories. A high ratio can occur when a firm continually runs out of stock because it does not produce or purchase enough goods. In this case, a high ratio actually implies poor planning or control of inventories. As a result, unless the inventory policy of a firm is studied in detail, this ratio alone does not provide enough information about the ability of that firm to generate cash from inventories.

DEBT STATUS OF THE FIRM

A firm may borrow money for short-term purposes, mainly to finance working capital, or for long-term reasons, mainly to buy plant and equipment. When a firm borrows for the long run, it commits itself to make periodic payments of interest—and to repay the principal at maturity. To do this, it has to generate sufficient income to cover debt payments. One way to find out the debt position of a firm is to analyze several debt ratios.

DEBT RATIO

The debt ratio indicates the percentage of total assets that is financed by debt. The lower the debt ratio, the less financial leverage; the higher the debt ratio, the greater the financial leverage.

$$\text{Debt ratio} = \frac{\text{Total liabilities}}{\text{Total assets}}$$

Example: Debt Ratio

If a firm's balance sheet shows liabilities at $1,000,000 and assets of $5,000,000, then

$$\text{Debt ratio} = \frac{\$1,000,000}{\$5,000,000} = .2, \text{ or } 20\%$$

A high ratio tends to magnify earnings and a low ratio could mean inefficient use of debt.

DEBT/EQUITY (*D/E*) RATIO

A more familiar debt ratio involves the relationship between long-term debt and stockholders' equity. This is called the **debt/equity ratio:**

$$\text{Debt/equity } (D/E) \text{ ratio} = \frac{\text{Long-term debt} + \text{value of leases}}{\text{Stockholders' equity}}$$

Thus, if long-term debt and leases on the balance sheet is $2,000,000 and stockholders' equity is $5,000,000, the debt/equity ratio is ($2,000,000 ÷ $5,000,000), or 40%. Electric utilities, which have steady inflows of receipts, can safely afford to have high D/E ratios, wheras cyclical companies usually have lower ones. In other words, the customers of electric utilities make periodic payments to these companies. Since these utilities know just about how much they will be paid and are allowed to raise customer charges when their rates of return fall below a certain level, they can estimate profits fairly well. Knowing this, they feel more confident about issuing bonds because the income they will generate in the future will ensure that they can meet interest and principal payments without much danger of default. Cyclical companies, on the other hand, enjoy high operating profits in good economic periods but must endure low operating profits in periods of economic contraction: If they issue substantial debt, they may not be able to cover interest payments when profits deteriorate. As a result, these companies must adopt a more conservative debt policy and issue more equity which does not require payment of dividends in bad business periods.

LONG-TERM DEBT/TOTAL ASSET (LD/TA) RATIO

The long-term debt/total asset ratio (LD/TA) relates debt to the total assets of a firm, and can provide useful information regarding the degree to which that firm finances its assets with long-term debt.

$$LD/TA \text{ ratio} = \frac{\text{Long-term debt}}{\text{Total assets}}$$

This ratio can serve as a proxy for evaluating financial leverage.

TIMES INTEREST EARNED RATIO

It is also important to find out how well a firm can pay its interest. For this purpose, you can use the **times interest earned ratio.** This ratio measures how well a firm's interest payments are covered by the operating income of the firm (EBIT). It indicates how well a firm can meet its interest payments. Obviously, the higher the rates, the better situated the firm is to pay off its creditors.

$$\text{Times interest earned ratio} = \frac{\text{EBIT}}{\text{Annual interest expense}}$$

Example: Times Interest Earned Ratio

If EBIT is $8,000,000 and annual interest charges are $3,000,000, then

$$\text{Times interest earned ratio} = \frac{\$8,000,000}{\$3,000,000} = 2.67$$

In other words, income is 2.7 times higher than interest charges.

A low interest coverage indicates a dangerous position because a decline in economic activity could reduce EBIT below the interest a firm must pay, thus leading to default and ultimate insolvency. This danger, however, is mitigated by the fact that EBIT is not the only source of coverage. Firms also generate cash flows from depreciation, which can be used to pay off interest. What a firm should aim for is a big enough cushion so that it is in a position to pay its creditors.

The interest earned ratio is deficient because the denominator does not consider other fixed payments such as principal repayments, lease expenses, and preferred dividends.

OVERALL COVERAGE RATIO

To deal with the problems associated with the times interest earned ratio, an overall coverage ratio can be computed:

Overall coverage ratio

$$= \frac{\text{Cash inflows}}{\text{Lease expenses} + \frac{\text{Interest}}{\text{charges}} + \left(\frac{\text{Debt repayment}}{1 - t}\right) + \left(\frac{\text{Preferred dividend}}{1 - t}\right)}$$

All charges in the denominator are fixed and must be taken into account. Obviously, a firm and its investors would like to see the highest coverage possible, but this depends partly on the profitability of the firm.

When debt ratios get out of line, the firm may find that its cost of capital increases. The value of its stock may also deteriorate in response to the higher degree of risk associated with the firm. Therefore, financial managers must be careful to avoid carrying excessive debt in their capital structures. Important sources of industry data related to interest coverage and overall coverage can be found in the SEC quarterly financial statements of manufacturing, retail, and mining industries. You can also refer to Dun and Bradstreet, Moody's, and Standard and Poor's reports for similar composite industry figures.

PROFITABILITY RATIOS

Investors, stockholders, and financial managers pay a great deal of attention to the profitability of firms. Profit analysis begins with an examination of the way the asset mix of a firm is employed. Good managers make efficient use of their assets. Through increased productivity, they are able to reduce or control expenses. The rates of return achieved by any firm are important if its managers expect to attract capital and to engage in successful financing for the firm's growth.

If the rates of return for a given firm fall below an acceptable level, the P/E and the value of the firm's shares will decline—which is why the measure of profit performance is crucial to any firm.

GROSS PROFIT MARGINS

Gross profit margins show how efficiently a firm's management uses material and labor in the production process.

$$\text{Gross profit margin} = \frac{\text{Sales} - \text{Cost of goods sold}}{\text{Sales}}$$

Example: Gross Profit Margin

If a firm has $1,000,000 in sales and cost of goods sold amounts to $600,000, its gross profit margin would be

$$\text{Gross profit margin} = \frac{\$1,000,000 - \$600,000}{\$1,000,000} = 40\%$$

When labor and material costs increase rapidly, they are likely to lower gross profit margins unless the firm can pass these costs on to customers in the form of higher prices. One way to find out whether these costs are out of line is to compare the margins of comparable companies. If the margins of competitors are higher, the firm should realize that it must do something to gain better control over labor and material costs.

OPERATING PROFIT MARGINS

Operating profit margins show how successful a firm's management has been in generating income from the operation of the business.

$$\text{Operating profit margin} = \frac{\text{EBIT}}{\text{Sales}}$$

The numerator of this ratio represents earnings calculated after deducting the cost of goods sold and operating expenses from sales (EBIT).

Example: Operating Profit Margin

If EBIT amounted to $200,000 compared to sales of $1,000,000, the operating profit margin would be

$$\text{Operating profit margin} = \frac{\$200,000}{\$1,000,000} = 20\%$$

This ratio is a rough measure of the operating leverage a firm can achieve in the conduct of the operational part of its business. It indicates how much EBIT is generated per dollar of sales. High operating profits can mean effective control of costs, or they can mean that sales are increasing faster than operating costs. It behooves managers to trace the causes of high or low operating profit margins so that they can determine whether a firm is operating efficiently or inefficiently, or whether its prices have increased faster or slower than costs.

NET PROFIT MARGINS

Net profit margins are those generated from all phases of a business. In other words, this ratio compares net income with sales.

$$\text{Net profit margin} = \frac{\text{Net profits after taxes}}{\text{Sales}}$$

Example: Net Profit Margin

If a firm's after-tax earnings are $100,000 and its sales are $1,000,000, then

$$\text{Net profit margin} = \frac{\$100,000}{\$1,000,000} = 10\%$$

Some firms have high profit margins of over 20%, and others have low profit margins of around 3% to 5%. The level of these margins varies from industry to industry. Usually, the better managed companies record higher relative profit margins because they manage their resources more efficiently. From an investor's point of view, it is advantageous for a firm to hold profit margins above the industry average and, if possible, to demonstrate an improving trend. Also, the more effectively a firm holds its expenses down—at any level of sales—the higher its net profit margin ratio will be.

RETURN ON EQUITY (*ROE*) RATIO

The **return on equity (*ROE*) ratio** measures the rate of return to stockholders. Security analysts, as well as stockholders, are especially interested in this ratio.

Generally, the higher the return, the more attractive the stock. This ratio is one way of assessing the profitability and the rate of returns of the firm, which can be compared to those of other stocks. The ratio is computed as follows:

$$ROE = \frac{\text{Net profits after taxes}}{\text{Stockholders' equity or tangible net worth}}$$

RETURN ON INVESTMENT (ROI) RATIO

The **return on investment (*ROI*) ratio** was developed by the Du Pont Company for its own use, but is now used by many major firms as a convenient way to measure the combined effects of profit margins and total asset turnover.

$$ROI = \frac{\text{Net income}}{\text{Sales}} \times \frac{\text{Sales}}{\text{Total assets}} = \frac{\text{Net income}}{\text{Total assets}}$$

The purpose of this formula is to compare the way a firm generates profits, and the way it uses its assets to generate sales. If assets are used effectively, income (and *ROI*) will be high; otherwise, income (and *ROI*) will be low.

YOU SHOULD REMEMBER

Financial statements can be interpreted by calculating financial ratios, which are divided into four major categories: liquidity ratios, activity ratios, debt ratios, and profitability ratios. Creditors pay close attention to these ratios in order to assure themselves that a firm can meet its short-term and long-term fixed interest and principal obligations. Bank lending policies are based heavily on the evaluation of relevant ratios, and financial analysts use them to compare the relative merits of different companies.

Liquidity ratios tell you how easily a firm can pay its short-term liabilities. *Activity ratios* indicate how fast the firm collects its accounts receivable or pays its bills, and the speed with which accounts payable, inventories, and accounts receivable are turned over. The faster it collects and the slower it pays, the better off the firm is— within certain limits. *Debt ratios* reveal what the financial leverage of the firm is and whether debt is becoming too top-heavy. Debt ratios can alert management to the need for altering the firm's financing mix before insolvency problems develop. *Profitability ratios* reveal how effectively a firm uses its assets to produce sales, to keep costs in line, and to generate net income.

• *USING RATIOS FOR ANALYSIS*

Each of the ratios just discussed provides some insight into the effective way a firm is run. As you know, however, financial analysis is most meaningful when you have some standards against which a firm's ratios can be measured. Not only do you want to find out whether a firm's profitability, liquidity, debt positions, and activity relationships are high or low, and whether they are improving or deteriorating, you should also determine how well a firm is performing relative to competitors, the industry, or the best firm in the industry.

Although the manager of a firm can compute the ratios of other companies, this information is readily available from published sources, such as *The Almanac of Business and Industrial Financial Ratios, Dun and Bradstreet Key Business Ratios, Value Line Service,* and *Standard and Poor's Corporation Financial Sheets.* These sources provide industry and individual company ratios to be used for comparison purposes. The *Robert Morris Associates Standard Ratios* even breaks down these ratios by sizes of firms.

These industry and company ratios can be compared with a firm's ratios to see whether there are differences or similarities. One way this can be done is illustrated in Table 16–5, where several hypothetical financial ratios for a firm and its industry are compiled.

Table 16–5 Comparing Firm and Industry Ratios

Ratio	Firm 1978	Firm 1985	Industry 1978	Industry 1985
Current ratio	2.0 times	2.5 times	1.8 times	1.9 times
Average collection period	51.3 days	60.0 days	43.0 days	45.2 days
Debt / equity ratio	30%	45%	40%	38%
Times interest earned ratio	4.1 times	3.8 times	3.0 times	3.0 times
Net profit margin	6.2%	8.3%	5.1%	6.0%
Return on investment	12.3%	13.4%	10.4%	11.0%
Coefficient of covariation $\left(\frac{\sigma}{\varepsilon}\right)$	.90	.81	.90	.90
Growth rate of earnings (7-year avg.)	—	.09%	—	.09%
Price/earnings ratio	10.5 times	10.0 times	8.0 times	8.0 times

At a glance, the figures in Table 16–5 tell you that over the 7-year period, the improvement in the liquidity and profitability of the firm was greater than that for the industry as a whole. The firm's times interest earned ratio declined, partly because the *D/E* ratio increased sharply, but was still higher than the industry level. Also, you find that, generally speaking, the levels of liquidity, profitability, and interest coverage were better than those for the industry. Somewhat less favorable was the change in the firm's financial leverage (*D/E*), which rose to 45% and in 1985 was noticeably higher than financial leverage in the industry. This indicates that in the future it might be advisable to issue stock rather than debt to bring the *D/E* ratio in line with the industry. Table 16–5 also indicates that although the firm's growth rate is the same as the industry's, its *P/E* ratio is higher — probably because the overall liquidity and soundness of the firm is better than that of the industry. However, the firm's risk/return trade-off in 1978 was the same as its industry's, as revealed by the coefficient of covariation. Investors apparently viewed the increase in the *D/E* ratio with alarm; consequently, the price/earnings ratio declined from 10.5 in 1978 to 10.0 in 1985. The industry's *P/E* remained unchanged in this period of time.

Breakdowns of ratios similar to those presented in Table 16–5 help firms pinpoint areas of strength and weakness in their operations. As a result, the analysis of these ratios provides managers with tools for improving the overall performances of their firms.

YOU SHOULD REMEMBER

Financial ratios are more meaningful when they are compared with the averages of competitors, an industry, or the best companies in the industry. Industry and other external ratios provide the benchmark measures for determining whether or not a firm is better off financially or more profitable than others, at one particular moment or over a period of time.

By monitoring changes in these ratios, managers can spot developing areas of strength and weakness and can take appropriate action.

• *LIMITATIONS OF RATIO ANALYSIS*

Financial ratios supply only part of the information necessary to evaluate the overall performance and efficiency of a firm. Other statistical measures—such as risk—should be taken into account to obtain a full picture of a firm's financial status.

Furthermore, comparisons of ratios can be misleading on several counts. A firm may have adopted new accounting standards; that is, it may have shifted from a

FIFO to a LIFO valuation of inventories. It may have changed from a straight-line method to an **accelerated method of depreciation.** Through mergers, the firm may be identified with a new industry. Also, the value of the firm's assets may be understated because of high inflation. Some industry figures may also be distorted, especially if the averages include many small firms with specific financial weaknesses.

You should be careful to determine the type of debt incurred by the firm you're studying. If funds were raised by issuing convertible debentures that are due to be called or may be converted soon, the interpretation of the D/E ratio will be different than when the debt represents straight bond issues. Also, some companies finance their investments with short-term leases. As a result, several financial ratios will be understated as a result of these financial arrangements. This is especially true in the case of *ROI*.

Also be wary when using reported data, because industry figures sometimes represent only the best and most financially sound companies. In addition, the classification of specific companies into an industry is difficult, because most companies have diverse product lines. This problem may distort the comparison of the firm's ratios with industry ratios.

In addition, watch out for companies that try to manipulate their figures by selling assets or by understating certain replacement costs. Although the accounting profession attempts to deal with some of these problems, there are different interpretations and methods for compiling financial statements which can mask the true strengths or weaknesses of a company. Therefore, when engaging in financial statement and ratio analysis, it is necessary to realize that interpretations can vary among managers and analysts. All in all, be careful when analyzing a firm on the basis of financial ratios. Make allowances for the limitations associated with these ratios.

YOU SHOULD REMEMBER

Make sure that ratios are consistent and comparable. Some firms employ different inventory valuation methods or depreciation policies. Other firms may report on a different fiscal basis. Industry averages could be biased in favor of small or large companies.

Therefore, to ensure that ratio comparisons are as representative as possible, make a careful analysis of the accounting interpretations of standards and the different methods employed by firms to calculate charges (e.g., using straight-line depreciation or accelerated depreciation methods) in their financial statements. *This must include a careful reading of the footnotes that follow these statements.*

KNOW THE CONCEPTS

DO YOU KNOW THE BASICS?

1. Describe the information you can get from reading the income statement and the balance sheet.

2. What can the analysis of sources and uses of funds tell you about the financial activity of a firm?

3. Define cash flow, and explain its contribution as a source of funds.

4. Indicate whether the following changes represent sources or uses of funds:

Increases	Decreases
Accounts receivable	Accounts payable
Long-term debt	Notes payable
Marketable securities	Inventories

5. How do you compute a firm's average collection period? If it turns out to be 40 days, while the industry average is 30 days, what does this mean?

6. How is it possible for a firm to incur a loss even when sales increase?

7. How will profits and cash flow in a firm that employs straight-line depreciation differ from those of another firm that uses accelerated depreciation?

8. What does a times interest earned ratio of 1.0 mean?

9. If a firm's D/E ratio is too high compared to the ratios of its industry and competing companies, what may you conclude about this firm? What should the financial manager attempt to do?

10. What things should an analyst look for in financial statements to ensure that the financial ratios they compute are as accurate as possible?

11. What are several problems to consider when using industry ratios as norms?

12. Explain the difference between *ROI* and net profit margins.

TERMS FOR STUDY

accelerated method of depreciation	income statement
acid test or quick ratio	inventory turnover ratio
average collection period	net profit margins
average payment period	operating profit margins
balance sheet	return on equity (*ROE*) ratio
current ratio	return on investment (*ROI*) ratio
debt/equity ratio (*D/E*)	times interest earned ratio

PRACTICAL APPLICATION

COMPUTATIONAL PROBLEMS

1. If a firm's current assets are $1,000,000 and its current liabilities $500,000, calculate its current ratio. What does this ratio tell you?

2. You are given the following balance sheet and income statement for 1988 and 1989:

Table A   Balance Sheet for 1988 and 1989
(all values in thousands of dollars)

	1988	1989
Assets		
Cash	200	300
Marketable securities	300	200
Receivables	800	1,000
Inventory	1,200	1,000
Fixed assets	3,300	3,700
Total assets	5,800	6,200
Liabilities and common equity		
Accounts payable	300	200
Notes payable	200	300
Other current liabilities	1,000	800
Long-term debt	1,000	1,200
Common equity	3,300	3,700
Total liabilities and common equity	5,800	6,200

Table B   Income Statement for 1989

Sales	$1,000,000
Operating and other costs	− 700,000
EBIT	300,000
Interest	− 100,000
Profits before taxes	200,000
Tax at 40% rate	− 80,000
Profits after taxes	120,000*

*Depreciation amounts to $50,000 in 1989.

Using the financial information given in Table A, calculate the changes that occurred to assets, liabilities, and equity from 1988 to 1989, and indicate whether these changes were sources or uses of funds.

3. Using the financial information presented in Table A of Problem 2, calculate the following ratios for 1983:
   (a) The current ratio.
   (b) The debt/equity ratio.
   (c) The acid test or quick ratio.
   State what each ratio might imply.

4. Analyzing both the income statement (Table B) and the balance sheet (Table A) in Problem 2, calculate the following ratios for 1984:
   (a) Times interest earned ratio.
   (b) Net profit margins.
   (c) Return on investment.

5. If the firm in Table A (Problem 2) had 100,000 common shares outstanding, its stock sold for $20 per share, and it paid $0.50 per share in dividends, calculate its EPS, *P/E,* and dividend payout ratio (dividend ÷ net income).

6. Selected financial ratios for a firm and its industry are as follows:

	Firm Ratio	Industry Ratio
Current ratio	2.5	3.0
Debt/equity ratio	30%	40%
Times interest earned ratio	3.0	2.0
Net profit margins	10%	8%
Average collection period	45 days	35 days
Return on investment	5%	3%
Inventory turnover ratio	10 times	12 times
Average payment period	30 days	40 days

Compare the financial ratios of the firm and the industry, and discuss their strengths and weaknesses.

ANSWERS

KNOW THE CONCEPTS

1. When you read an income statement, you find out the sales generated by the firm, the cost breakdown of the business. By deducting all costs—including interest and taxes—from sales, you obtain the net income available for common stockholders. The income statement also reveals the dividends paid by the firm and the amount of profits available for reinvestment.

   The balance sheet records the mix of current and fixed assets. It indicates the liabilities incurred by the firm in the form of short-term and long-term obligations. This statement also reveals the net worth, or common stockholder's equity in the firm (assets − liabilities).

   In short, the income statement indicates the profitability of the firm, and the balance sheet indicates the sources of funds and the assets into which these sources are invested.

2. Analysis of sources and uses of funds helps a firm control the costs of obtaining funds. It provides a basis for determining the most efficient allocation of scarce funds.

3. Cash flow is defined broadly as net profits after taxes plus depreciation. Depreciation charges permit the firm to reduce tax payments and thus retain more funds in the firm for investment purposes. The more cash flow, the easier it is for the firm to finance investments from internal sources and the less funding it has to generate from external sources.

4.

Increases*	(S) or (U)	Decreases*	(S) or (U)
Accounts receivable	U	Accounts payable	U
Long-term debt	S	Notes payable	U
Marketable securities	U	Inventories	S

    *(S) Sources; (U) Uses.

5. The average collection period is computed by dividing accounts receivable by (annual credit sales ÷ 360). If the industry has a 30-day collection period versus 40 days for a particular firm, generally speaking, the firm's customers are not paying their bills as fast as the customers of other firms in the industry. A longer collection period could be due to the fact that the firm has a more liberal customer payments policy, or it could mean that the firm has trouble collecting accounts receivable. A long collection period usually leads to higher interest costs and bad debt write-offs for the firm.

6. An increase in sales does not guarantee a profit. This increase may occur at a time when capacity is limited; as a result, substantially higher costs can be

incurred by the firm to supply customers with goods or services. In this case, the increase in costs may be so high that it produces losses.

7. All other things being equal, profits will be higher in the early years and lower in later years with straight-line depreciation. Higher depreciation does, however, mean lower tax payments. From a present value point of view, accelerated depreciation is more valuable to a firm than the straight-line method.

8. An interest earned ratio of 1.0 indicates that the firm barely generates enough EBIT to cover its fixed financial obligations. Any small decline in EBIT would put the firm in danger of becoming insolvent, unless it found some reserves or other sources of funds to match debt payments in the short run.

9. If the firm's D/E ratio is greater than the ratios for the industry and competing companies, investors may feel that it is out of line, and the cost of capital of the firm may increase. When this situation arises, the firm may want to change its capital structure by issuing more common stock, by merging with a company that has a lower D/E ratio, or by retiring (buying back) some of its debt.

10. Analysts should seek to adjust for differences in inventory policy (LIFO vs. FIFO), differences in methods of depreciating assets, differences in charging off research and development costs, and differences in leasing policies. Also, analysts should examine the composition of industry averages used for comparison purposes.

11. Industry ratios may include factors that can produce an upward or downward bias in the ratios. For example, the liquidity ratios may be better if the industry average gives a greater weight to large, well-run companies. If, on the other hand, the averages are heavily weighted in favor of small companies, the liquidity ratio may have a downward bias.

12. *ROI* provides a measure of how effectively the firm uses assets to produce income. Net profit margins indicate how well a firm controls its costs and how much it benefits from financial leverage. In some industries, like services, the asset base is small compared to other factors. Therefore, in those cases, net profit margins are a more meaningful measure of profitability and efficiency than *ROI*.

PRACTICAL APPLICATION

1. Current ratio $= \dfrac{\$1,000,000}{\$500,000} = 2.0$ times

This current ratio indicates that the firm can meet its current, or short-term, obligations because it has twice the amount of cash from liquid assets as it does current liabilities.

2.   **Table A**   **(all values in thousands of dollars)**

	1988	1989	Sources	Use
Assets				
Cash	200	300		100
Marketable securities	300	200	100	
Receivables	800	1,000		200
Inventory	1,200	1,000	200	
Fixed assets	3,300	3,700		400
Total assets	5,800	6,200		
Liabilities and common equity				
Accounts payable	300	200		100
Notes payable	200	300	100	
Other current liabilities	1,000	800		200
Long-term debt	1,000	1,200	200	
Common equity	3,300	3,700	400	
Total liabilities and common equity	5,800	6,200	1,000	1,000

Note that in 1989 combined cash flow [Depreciation ($50,000) + Profits after taxes ($120,000)] amounted to $170,000, and this sum represents a source of funds.

3. (a) $\dfrac{\text{Current ratio}}{\text{(for 1988)}} = \dfrac{\text{Current assets}}{\text{Current liabilities}} = \dfrac{\$2,500}{\$1,500} = 1.67 \text{ times}$

This implies that the company has inadequate working capital to cover its liabilities. The ratio should be more than 2 times.

(b) $\dfrac{\text{Debt equity ratio}}{\text{(for 1988)}} = \dfrac{\text{Long-term debt}}{\text{Common equity}} = \dfrac{\$1,000}{\$3,300} = 30\%$

This seems to be a reasonable mix between debt and equity for a manufacturing corporation, but electric utilities will allocate much higher proportions to debt than 30%.

(c) $\dfrac{\text{Acid test ratio}}{\text{(for 1988)}} = \dfrac{\text{Current assets} - \text{Inventories}}{\text{Current liabilities}} = \dfrac{\$1,300}{\$1,500} = .86 \text{ times}$

The current asset coverage in this case is inadequate, suggesting that the company needs to generate more current assets, excluding inventories.

4. (a) Times interest earned ratio =

$$\frac{\text{EBIT}}{\text{Annual interest expense}} = \frac{\$300,000}{\$100,000} = 3.00 \text{ times}$$

(b) Net profit margins $= \dfrac{\text{Net profits after taxes}}{\text{Sales}} = \dfrac{\$120,000}{\$1,000,000} = 12\%$

(c) Return on investment $= \dfrac{\text{Net income}}{\text{Total assets}} = \dfrac{\$120,000}{\$6,200,000} = 1.9\%$

5. EPS $= \dfrac{\text{Net income}}{\text{Outstanding shares of common}} = \dfrac{\$120,000}{100,000} = \$1.20$

$P/E = \dfrac{\text{Price per share of stock}}{\text{Earnings per share}} = \dfrac{\$20}{\$1.20} = 16.67$

Dividend payout ratio $= \dfrac{\text{Dividends per share}}{\text{EPS}} = \dfrac{\$0.50}{\$1.20} = 41.7\%$

6. The *industry current ratio* is better than the firm's indicating that the firm is less liquid than some of its competitors. Nevertheless, a 2.5 ratio indicates a satisfactory level of liquidity. The firm has a lower *D/E ratio* than the industry, indicating an opportunity to issue more debt without incurring too much financial risk, especially since its times interest earned ratio is 3.0 versus 2.0 for the industry.

The *times interest earned ratio* is better than the industry's, probably because of the lower debt/equity ratio. The firm appears to have ample coverage of interest expense and less danger of defaulting than the industry, on average.

Net profit margins are better for the firm than for the industry, indicating either that the firm may have more effective cost controls, better salesmen or that it charges higher prices because of a differentiated product line.

Average collection period for the firm appears too high, suggesting that the firm should institute discount policies or other collection procedures to get customers to pay their accounts receivable earlier.

The firm's *return on investment,* like its net profit margins, is higher than the industry's, indicating that it is making more effective use of available resources or assets.

The firm has a slower *inventory turnover rate* than the industry, suggesting that it is carrying too much inventory. However, if this extra inventory is helpful in satisfying customer needs and in enabling the firm to charge slightly higher prices, it may be worth the additional investment.

The firm's *average payment period* of 30 days indicates that the firm is paying its accounts payable faster than the industry at large. The firm might consider having suppliers provide it with longer credit terms so that it can retain this source of funds longer and thereby reduce its borrowing requirements at banks. This lower payment period could also be due to the fact that the firm is paying its bills faster because it is getting a higher discount for doing so.

SPECIAL TOPICS

17 MERGERS

KEY TERMS

book value (of a firm) assets minus liabilities

economies of scale the increasing returns derived from spreading output over a fixed amount of assets, capacity, or investment

merger a combination of two firms, with one firm maintaining its identity

synergism economies and other gains created by the combination of companies in a merger

tender offer an offer from an acquiring firm or other source to purchase a number of shares from stockholders at a stated price per share

---

WHY COMPANIES MERGE

There are almost as many reasons why companies merge as there are mergers. Some firms do so because they believe that the combination will bring faster and steadier growth of earnings per share for both companies. This growth can often be achieved with less cost and with less risk than by starting from scratch. If an attractive buy is available which can provide new products and new capacity, the merger may quickly produce the desired results.

A firm may have a high D/C ratio and may want to bring better balance to its capital structure. A quick way to adjust the capital structure of the firm is to acquire a firm with a low debt base so as to lower the D/C ratio to a more acceptable level.

There are also advantages in acquiring other companies for certain managerial skills not available in your own firm. Also, the cost of setting up new regional distribution systems may be prohibitive. Therefore, why not acquire a successful firm operating in the region into which you wish to expand? Not only do you gain a good sales force, but you also eliminate head-on competition with the acquired firm and achieve immediate access to additional plant capacity.

Some benefits that originate from a merger are referred to as *synergistic* effects. These synergistic gains indicate that the value of the merged firm exceeds the sum of the value of each separate firm. If the value of a firm (V_F) is equal to $V_F = D + E$, then synergism produces:

$$V_{A+T} = V_A + V_T + V_S$$

where

V_{A+T} = value of acquiring firm (A) plus value of acquired or target firm
V_A = value of acquired firm
V_T = value of target or acquired firm
V_S = gain from synergistic effects

Assume that V_F for the acquiring firm and the target firm are determined separately by summing up the value of debt plus the capitalized value of earnings. Now add to these values the gains from synergistic effects and you get

$$
\begin{aligned}
V_A &= \$1,000,000 \\
V_T &= 500,000 \\
V_S &= \underline{100,000} \\
V_{A+T+S} &= \$1,600,000
\end{aligned}
$$

This synergism usually can arise, in part, as a result of economies of scale. That is, the bigger the merged firm, the lower the unit costs, partly because of favorable operating leverage effects and partly because the duplication of functions is eliminated.

This means that the merged company benefits from a larger fixed-cost base, which may help to lower unit costs. For example, the computer and accounting departments of the two companies can be consolidated into one unit. This can eliminate duplication and should lead to lower per-unit costs of operation. Extra employees and administrative functions can be eliminated, and savings may be generated at the corporate headquarters level.

In addition, a merger may unintentionally reduce the volatility of earnings. For example, consolidating the operations of two companies whose earnings are subject to different co-movements can lower the overall variability in earnings. This steadier earnings pattern is likely to be recognized by investors which could mean a lower discount rate and a higher value for the firm's stock. A firm with a low *ROI* and a low *P/E* may seek to improve its image and valuation by acquiring another firm with a higher *ROI* and a higher *P/E*.

• *TAX BENEFITS OF MERGERS*

Sometimes a merger will occur because of tax considerations. A company with a large **tax-loss carry-forward** may be acquired by a firm with substantial profits. In this case, the losses can be used to reduce taxable profits.

The tax benefits of a merger can be shown more clearly in the following example.

Example: Tax Benefits of Mergers

Company T has incurred $600,000 in tax losses during the past 4 years. Company A has achieved earnings of $400,000 in each of the past 4 years. As a result, Company A acquires Company T to gain the tax benefit. Table 17–1 shows what happens to the income of Company A once it acquires Company T.

Table 17–1   Sample Tax Benefits of a Merger

Year	Earnings before Taxes	Taxes before Merger (Taxes at 40%)	Tax-Loss Carry-Forward	Taxable Income	Taxes after Merger (Taxes at 40%)
1	$400,000	$160,000	$400,000	0	0
2	400,000	160,000	200,000	$200,000	$ 80,000
3	400,000	160,000	0	400,000	160,000
4	400,000	160,000	0	400,000	160,000
Total taxes		$640,000			$400,000

The tax benefits from this merger should be evident. Whereas Company A would have paid a total of $640,000 before the merger, it pays only $400,000 after the merger.

These tax advantages play a role in the search for suitable merger candidates. In the final analysis, however, tax reduction features are short-term considerations, and should not be the only factor influencing the decision of whether or not to merge. The success of a merger depends on many considerations, not the least of which is the price paid for the acquisition—in terms of money *and* personnel.

YOU SHOULD REMEMBER

The merger movement in the United States has produced some good and some bad experiences. In general, you might conclude that it is difficult to generate growth internally, since only a few firms such as Kodak, Polaroid, Du Pont and IBM can compete by engaging in heavy internal research to promote overall growth. A large part of the growth in other companies stems from mergers and acquisitions.

Some of the reasons why these mergers take place are to avoid paying taxes, to eliminate competition, to increase the liquidity of the acquiring firm, to diversify into new product lines, to reduce risk, to expand into new regional markets, to bring a better balance to the acquiring company's debt/equity structure, to infuse new managerial skill into a stodgy company, and to achieve economies of scale. The marketability of the merged company stock may improve because of the increased number of shares outstanding. However, even if a merger produces some dilutive effects in its early years, this should not be a problem as long as the firm is able to show a steady improvement in its long-term growth potential.

SOME MERGER CONSIDERATIONS

It is easy to focus only on the balance sheet when trying to decide whether or not to merge with another firm, but you must also consider how management will be affected. After all, good management plays a major role in any company's success.

Unless the managers of the two companies can get along, key personnel may be lost. This is especially a problem when the acquiring company's executives attempt to run the newly acquired firm or to "second-guess" its management. Although the extremely complex field of management cannot be summarized in a few paragraphs, this factor should be considered along with the balance sheet.

In many cases, successful mergers include firms that have compatible product lines and problems of a similar nature. Why? Because the management of both acquiring and target company understand, and have a good appreciation of, and are responsive to, each others' needs. A less desirable fit, such as would generally occur when a steel company merged with a food company, creates more problems than it solves.

• METHODS OF ACQUISITION

The acquisition of a firm entails the evaluation of key variables such as earnings per share, market prices of shares, book value, and operating and financial risks of the target company. The idea is to assess the risk associated with the merger so that a discount rate can be assigned to the future flows of these returns. In addition, some attempt must be made to predict the future trend of these variables and their effect on the merged company.

Given the required information on these variables, the acquiring company can employ several techniques to evaluate the merits of a merger. The acquiring company can buy the target company by making a cash payment and can exchange common stock in a tax-free transaction. Cash is paid to acquire other companies, especially when the acquiring firm has a sizable liquid base that cannot be put to very profitable use. Conversely, when firms are on the brink of insolvency they will often sell out for the value of their assets, rather than go through the expense and trouble of bankruptcy. In this way, they may get a better price than the liquidation value of their assets.

Some acquiring companies employ a form of mixed payments, which can include a combination of one of the above techniques plus some form of financial incentive, such as issuing preferred stock or convertible securities. Management of the acquired company may also be induced to stay on by the use of options. Some of these acquisition approaches are discussed below.

• *THE NEGOTIATING RANGE*

Successful mergers depend partly on how well an acquiring company does its homework. After all, the ultimate goal is to determine whether the target company will be a profitable acquisition. Once this has been established, the acquiring firm should determine the *negotiating range*. This range is simply the minimum price the acquiring company has to pay for the target firm and the maximum price beyond which it will not go.

The minimum price is the actual price of the target company's stock, as quoted in the market, times the number of its shares outstanding. Although the target company sells in the marketplace at this price, most of its stockholders would not part with their shares for that price. If the acquiring company tries to purchase shares in the open market, it would drive the target's stock price upward. The minimum price, however, represents the lowest value in the negotiating range and furnishes a starting point.

Estimating the maximum price an acquiring company is willing to pay for a target company involves the use of **normal capital budgeting techniques** and the following steps:

1. The goal is to compute the net present value of the target company.
2. This is done by:
   a. estimating cash flows after taxes (CFAT) that can be expected to be generated by the target company within a given stated number of years (i.e., 5 years).
   b. estimating the growth of CFAT beyond the 5-year period.
   c. employing the constant dividend growth model to project the value of the target company after the fifth year to infinity.
   d. determining a discount rate reflecting the risk of the target company and calculating the present value of the cash flows.
   e. finding out the total liabilities of the target company and computing NPV = Present value CFAT − Liabilities. This is the maximum price an acquiring company should pay for a target company.

Example:

Assume that the discount rate assigned to the target company is 12%. Cash flows after taxes are estimated as shown below, and the growth of these cash flows after the fifth year is 5% annually. The target company's liabilities equal $1,258,950, and it has 100,000 shares outstanding. The acquiring company has 200,000 shares outstanding.

Period	CFAT	PVIF @ 12%	PV
1	$100,000	.893	$ 89,300
2	150,000	.797	119,550
3	200,000	.712	142,400
4	250,000	.636	159,000
5	300,000	.567	170,100
5−	4.500,000	.567	2,551,500
			$3,231,850

$$\text{Value of the target firm after 5 years} = \frac{\$300,000 \ (1+.05)}{.12 - .05}$$

$$= \frac{\$315,000}{.07} = \$4,500,000$$

Maximum Price of target company = PVCF − liabilities
= $3,231,850 − $1,258,950 = $1,972,900 (maximum price)

If the target company has 100,000 shares outstanding and the current price of its stock is $10 per share, then the minimum price the acquiring firm must pay is $1,000,000 (100,000 × $10).

You now have the negotiating range, which is:

Minimum Price	Maximum Price
$1,000,000	$1,972,900

The final acquisition price will depend on the bargaining strength of the target company relative to the acquiring firm. If the target company is strong financially and unwilling to settle except for a higher premium over the minimum price, its final acceptance will be closer to the maximum price.

The acquiring company's offer will consist of the lowest possible price within the negotiating range. In this case, the maximum premium over the current price of the target company is 97% ($1,972,900 ÷ $1,000,000) − 1. Assume the final agreement is for a premium of 60% over the current price. The acquiring firm would pay $1,600,000 ($1,000,000 × 1.60) in cash for the target company. That means that the stockholders of the target company would get $16 per share ($1,600,000 ÷ 100,000) in a straight cash deal.

PAYMENT BY EXCHANGE OF STOCK

When a merger involves the exchange of stock, the crucial factor to be determined is how many shares does the acquiring company offer the target company to induce its stockholders to surrender their original holdings? In the bargaining process, the acquiring company attempts to give up the minimum number of shares, and the company being acquired tries to get as many shares as possible of the acquiring company. This difference is generally resolved through negotiations in which the company with the greater wish to consummate the merger should be willing to make concessions.

One way of determining the number of shares to be exchanged is to calculate the *exchange ratio*. Going back to the previous example, let us assume that the current price of the acquiring company is $20. Obviously, the acquiring company will not be willing to make an even swap (or share for share) for the target company stock because its stock is selling for twice the current price of the target company stock. The exchange ratio in a stock transaction can be calculated as follows:

$$\text{Share exchange ratio} = \frac{\text{Price per share offered to target company}}{\text{Price per share of acquiring company}}$$

Referring to the previous computations and example, the negotiated and settlement price offered and accepted by the target company was $16 per share. The exchange ratio will tell us how many shares target stockholders will receive in exchange for all their shares.

$$\text{Exchange ratio} = \frac{\$16}{\$20} = .8$$

This means that to consummate the merger, the acquiring company will give up .8 shares of its own stock for each share of the target company. The total number of shares received by the target company will be 80,000 (100,000 × .8). Since the acquiring company had 200,000 shares outstanding, the merged company will have a total of 280,000 shares (200,000 acquiring + 80,000 target) outstanding.

THE MODIFIED EPS APPROACH

What if the two merger parties are privately held or the target company has no publicly owned stock? In either case it may be necessary to apply the modified EPS approach. Some analysts compare the earnings per share of both companies to obtain an exchange ratio. Unfortunately, a simple comparison of EPS is subject to several flaws. It assumes that the growth rate, the timing of cash flows, and the risks of the target and acquiring companies are roughly the same. Should the two companies have disparate growth and risk characteristics, one way of resolving these differences (and to give these factors adequate consideration) would be to employ a constant growth dividend model.

$$V_A = \frac{EPS_A \, (1 + g)^1}{ks - g}$$

$$V_T = \frac{EPS_T \, (1 + g)^1}{ks - g}$$

Once these values are calculated, the exchange ratio would then be:

$$\text{Modified EPS exchange ratio} = \frac{V_T}{V_A}$$

Example:

You are given the following:

	Target Company	Acquiring Company
EPS	3.95	5.25
ks	.10	.12
g	.05	.08

Based on these factors, the EPS of each company becomes adjusted for growth and risk:

$$V_T = \frac{3.95 \, (1.05)^1}{.10 - .05} = \frac{\$4.15}{.05} = \$83.00$$

$$V_A = \frac{5.25 \, (1.08)^1}{.12 - .08} = \frac{\$5.67}{.04} = \$141.75$$

The current value of the target company as computed above (V_T) represents its current intrinsic value. A premium is usually paid above this value. Through negotiations, both parties might agree to a premium of 25% above the current value. That means an offer price of \$103.75 (\$83 × 1.25) per share for the target company. This would make the modified EPS exchange ratio equal to

$$\text{Modified EPS exchange ratio} = \frac{V_T}{V_A}$$

$$= \frac{\$103.75}{\$141.75} = .73$$

That is, the acquiring company would exchange .73 of its shares for each share of the target company. The modified EPS approach provides an alternate method for determining the exchange ratio.

AFTER-MERGER EPS

A concise formula for estimating the after-merger EPS of the combined company's earnings is shown below:

$$\text{After-merger } EPS_{A+T} = E_{a+T} \Big/ \left(N_a + \frac{P_T \times N_T}{P_a}\right)$$

where,

EPS_{A+T} = the sum of the current earnings per share of the target and acquiring companies plus any synergistic gains

E_{A+T} = combined earnings of target and acquiring companies

N_a = acquiring company's outstanding shares

P_T = offered price for target company

N_T = number of target company's outstanding shares

P_A = current price of acquiring company's stock

Example:

Looking up the prices of stock quoted on the Exchange, it is discovered that the share price of the acquiring company is $20 and the price offered to the target company is $16 per share. Total earnings of the merged company are estimated at $920,000 plus estimated synergistic gains of $100,000, occasioned by several cost reductions. Using the figures given in the example on pages 318–319, the after-merger EPS_{A+T} is equal to:

$$EPS_{A+T} = \frac{1{,}020{,}000}{\left(100{,}000\right) + \left(\dfrac{16 \times 100{,}000}{\$20}\right)}$$

$$= \$1{,}020{,}000/180{,}000 = \$5.67$$

Merger negotiations don't always work out as neatly as outlined above, however. In some cases, a good merger candidate may get a bid from a second firm that is higher than the offer of the first firm. Many times the bidding gets out of hand, so that the price paid for the shares of the target company bears little relationship to the **intrinsic value** of the target firm's stock.

MIXED PAYMENT

Financial arrangements other than the payment of cash or exchange of common stock may be agreed upon by the merging companies. While some stockholders of a target company prefer common stock because they wish to participate in the growth of the merged firm, other stockholders are concerned with interest and dividend income. In addition, cash payment of shares held may result in substantial tax payments by some target shareholders to the Internal Revenue Service. Therefore, to avoid taxes and to retain certain options for the future, some target firms ask for a package deal involving some cash and the rest in convertible preferred stock or convertible bonds. These convertible securities provide steady income and leave the door open for the target stockholders to participate in the future growth of the merged company. This arrangement also has the advantage of reducing the dilutive effect that occurs when common stock is the medium of exchange.

Other inducements used to get target companies to agree on a merger include issuing options to management which can be exercised to purchase stock at a stated price. Some target officials may be offered bonuses or profit-sharing arrangements when the earnings of the target subsidiary exceed a certain level. These so-called **contingency payments** are offered to overcome the reluctance and resistance of target company management toward the merger. In a way, this is not a bad strategy for assuring both continuity of management and continued productivity of target company officials. Moreover, these special inducements are especially important to target companies that relies on a few key individuals. Unless these individuals can be induced to stay on, the future of those target companies may be in jeopardy.

A takeover must not generate bad feelings, which usually lead to the defection of key personnel and, sometimes, to increased competition from those who leave to start competing businesses.

• OTHER CONSIDERATIONS IN MERGER DEALS

In the process of evaluating the relative merits of a merger, other factors are taken into consideration. One of these might be the difference in the prices of the stock. For example, suppose two firms have the same earnings per share, but the acquiring firm's stock is quoted in the market at $65, compared to $40 a share for the firm being acquired. This indicates that there are other favorable factors the market is taking into account, which is why a higher P/E may be assigned to the acquiring than to the target firm. Under these conditions, the merger terms are influenced by this difference in valuation. Given this situation, the more appropriate guideline for establishing an exchange ratio is found in the prices of the two stocks. As a result, negotiations might begin with a ratio of .62 ($40 ÷ $65), which indicates that the acquiring company would be willing to exchange .62 share for each share of the target company. Reaching a final exchange ratio will obviously depend in part on the willingness of each side to make concessions.

Book value is another factor to consider. **Book value** per common share is obtained by dividing total assets, minus the sum of liabilities and preferred stock, by the number of outstanding common shares of the firm. This measure becomes relevant in negotiations when the book value is higher than the quoted price of a share. In other words, if the market price per share of the target company is $50 and its book value per share is $60, this indicates that an acquiring company can buy the shares of the target company at a bargain. As long as book value exceeds market value, the merger favors the acquiring company.

Another factor that might be considered in a merger is the net current assets of the firm being acquired. This measure of liquidity could help determine the bargaining positions of the two firms. A target company with substantial net working capital would make an important contribution to the liquidity of the acquiring firm. For example, marketable securities would be an important source of funds to the acquiring firm and might be used to reduce debt.

In the merger process, the acquiring company cannot overlook the costs involved. In addition to the costs of searching for the proper candidate, there are legal fees for determining potential antitrust actions or court costs associated with target company stockholders who object to the merger. Many times, instead of utilizing direct negotiations, the firm uses an investment banker to perform the search, carry on the negotiations, and consummate the final deal. There are, of course, paperwork expenses, costs of transactions in issuing new shares and registering stock in the name of new stockholders, and expenses incurred for handling other financial matters. Parties entering into negotiations should be serious about their intentions; otherwise, they will incur useless expenditures of time and money.

YOU SHOULD REMEMBER

The final merger terms or agreement will depend on the bargaining power of each participant in the negotiations. The initial basis for arriving at a value depends on the method of payment. Usually, a cash payment entails the use of capital budgeting techniques to determine the present value of expected returns to be derived from the target company over a stated number of years. Obviously, if the present value exceeds the cash payment, the merger is a feasible one.

The exchange of common stock is another method employed to consummate a merger. In this case, the two companies involved in the merger could employ the modified constant growth dividend model to calculate an exchange ratio, which indicates how many shares the target company shareholders will receive in exchange for their own shares. When there is a substantial difference in the *P/E* between the two companies, the parties to a merger may also calculate the exchange ratio by comparing the stock prices of the two negotiating companies.

Whatever the terms, the acquiring company will usually pay a premium over the existing value of the target company to induce target stockholders to turn over their stock. Attractive terms, however, don't always determine whether a target company is willing to merge. Consideration must also be given to whether the two companies are compatible, whether the two managements can work together, and whether the acquiring company can assure the target company managers that their jobs will not be in jeopardy after the merger is consummated.

ACCOUNTING ASPECTS OF MERGERS

There are two main methods of dealing with the accounting aspects of mergers:

1. The pooling of interest method.

2. The purchase acquisition method.

The **pooling of interest method** is used when an exchange of stock takes place on a tax-free basis. The accounting treatment consists simply of combining the values in the balance sheets of the two companies. For example, assume Firm A acquires Firm B. The merged company balance sheet is shown in Table 17–2. For postmerger total assets and liabilities, see column (3).

When an outright purchase occurs, accountants use the **purchase acquisition method**. If the purchase price equals the net worth (assets—liabilities) of the target company, the consolidated balance sheet will look the same as when the pooling of interest method is used. However, when the price paid exceeds the net worth of the acquired company, it is assumed that two things will happen: There will be an upward valuation of assets and an additional adjustment will be made to cover an appreciation of

Table 17–2   Balance Sheet for the Pooling of Interest and Purchase Acquisition Methods (all values in thousands of dollars)

			Merged Company	
	Firm A (1)	Firm B (2)	Pooling of Interest A + B (3)	Purchase A + B (4)
Current assets	$100	$50	$150	$150
Fixed assets	100	60	160	170
Goodwill	0	0	0	10
Total assets	$200	$110	$310	$330
Debt	$ 80	$ 30	$110	$110
Common equity	150	50	200	220*
Total liabilities and net worth	$230	$ 80	$310	$330

*This $220 figure includes $10,000 of goodwill and $10,000 worth of upwardly revalued assets.

intangible assets called goodwill. Therefore, in the consolidated balance sheet statement, the asset and the equity values are raised to take these changes in valuation into account. If the price paid for a target company is $70,000 and its book value is $50,000, the additional value is $20,000 ($70,000 − $50,000). The accountants will figure out how the $20,000 is divided between assets and goodwill. Table 17-2 shows how these changes in values are allocated when the division is half ($10,000) for revaluation of assets and half ($10,000) for goodwill.

The income statement is also adjusted when these valuation changes occur. The upward revaluation of fixed assets gets depreciated as do any other assets—by applying the depreciation schedules used by the firm. That means that if the firm used a 10-year straight-line depreciation policy, the additional depreciation charge would be $1,000 per year. Goodwill can be amortized over a period not to exceed 40 years. Because goodwill is a nontaxable item, it is written off after net income is determined in the income statement. It does, however, dilute the net earnings of a merged firm as well as its EPS. Assuming the firm decides to amortize goodwill over a 5-year period, then the income statement will show a deduction of $2,000 yearly from net earnings.

This is a simplified explanation of the accounting techniques employed in consolidating the balance sheets of merged firms when the pooling of interests or the purchase acquisition method is used by the acquiring company.

NEGOTIATING THE DEAL

If the negotiations are friendly, there is little problem in arriving at mutually satisfactory terms. The actual negotiations may take place directly between the two management teams.

A friendly takeover involves a negotiated exchange ratio and acceptance by the target company of certain financial policy changes after the merger. When the two parties agree, they present the terms to the stockholders and ask for their approval.

At other times, the target company may feel that a merger will not be in the best interest of its management or stockholders, and negotiations may break down. This may also occur when the acquiring company tries to exert too much pressure and impose too many conditions. Sometimes target company management may become apprehensive about job security and put up a fight to remain independent. In this case, it will appeal to its own stockholders for support or may look for a more suitable partner.

Generally, when a target company is faced with an unfriendly takeover attempt by an acquiring company, it employs several defensive tactics. These measures, generally referred to as *poison pills,* are designed to make the buyout less attractive. They may include selling a highly profitable division and giving the proceeds to stockholders, paying the stockholders a large cash dividend, thereby reducing the liquidity of the target firm; agreeing to pay large compensation packages to senior managers.

To thwart an unfriendly takeover, the target company may seek a *white knight*. This means finding another more friendly company (whose compatible management would make a better fit) that would be willing to merge with the target company.

In cases involving unfriendly mergers, either the negotiations are terminated or the acquiring company makes a direct appeal to the stockholders of the target company in the form of a **tender offer.** The goal is to gain controlling interest of the target company. A successful tender offer consists of offering a premium above the current price of the target company's stock. Stockholders are told of this offer through direct mail or by newspaper announcements. When this happens, the price of the target company will generally rise to the newly offered price. If the target company's shareholders continue to balk, the price offering may be raised even further. Should financial institutions have large blocks of target company stock, they may offer the acquiring firm a buyout at attractive terms—with the acquiring firm getting the company it wants, and the sellers of the stock receiving a nice profit—without transaction costs.

A tender offer does not require approval by the target company management. Because of certain abuses, legislation has been enacted that requires the acquiring company to notify the target company and the Securities Exchange Commission in advance that it intends to make a tender bid. Some target companies then resort to state courts to block tender offers, in the hope that the legal delays will prove too costly and cumbersome for the acquiring company.

Being too persistent in seeking a tender of stock from a target company's stockholders, then, can backfire, leaving the acquiring company in the unenviable position of having bought overpriced stock in an amount insufficient for control. This may pose a problem for the acquiring company when it attempts to dispose of these shares in the market. Obviously, if the price of the stock is bid too high—even if this does lead to a merger—the initial advantages for having entered into the merger negotiation will have been lost.

FINANCING MERGERS

Over the years, investment bankers and other institutions have come up with many innovative ways of financing acquisitions. In the 1980s, the most notable development was the widespread use of junk bonds. These bonds are low in quality, unsecured debentures, usually assigned a Baa or lower quality rating, and yield 3% to 5% more than high-quality bonds. Because acquiring firms don't have sufficient collateral to buy out the target company, they issue large amounts of these low-quality bonds. All too often, their debt-to-capitalization ratio increases to dangerously high levels. The classical example of a brokerage house involved in this type of financing is Drexel Burnham Lambert under the direction of Michael Milken, who was indicted for violations of federal securities laws in 1989.

These junk bonds tend to weaken the position of existing creditors and sometimes lead to unexcusable excesses. Investors in fixed-income securities have thus begun to require firms to introduce protective clauses in the indentures of new bond issues. Some creditors may even forbid junk bond financing unless they receive appropriate protection. Recent experience shows that some firms have relied on junk bond financing and have overextended their fixed financial commitments. The major test for these firms will come in a recession, when many will be faced with reduced cash flows. Will these firms be able to meet the interest payments on the debt when economic activity is contracting?

Some of the financing of mergers takes place via *leveraged buyouts,* whereby part of the debt is financed and paid by selling off some of the target company's divisions or assets. In a leveraged buyout, the acquiring firm merely puts up a small percentage of the total purchase price. The remainder of the financing is arranged through financial institutions which agree to assume the debt in exchange for a piece of the action, namely, the right to receive a substantial stake in the ownership of the merged firm.

And then, there are the *Employee Stock Ownership Plans* (ESOP). These plans call for a firm to tender its own stock, paying for it by borrowing at a bank. The firm then repays the loan from the employee stock fund. Avis and Polaroid engaged in this type of financing. Because of several special tax advantages, these types of financing are attractive. They are also used to increase controlling stock ownership, hence, prevent hostile takeovers.

Another practice involves a corporate raider purchasing a large stake in a target company and threatening a takeover. Often the directors of such a company will succumb to greenmail, signing a repurchase agreement whereby the greenmailer sells his stock to the firm at a price far higher than he paid for it. In addition, the greenmailer agrees not to purchase shares of the target company for a stated period of time. This fictitious increase in the price of the stock is unsupported by any change in the financial or asset structure of the firm. The greenmail arrangement is a dubious practice that is likely to be curbed by future government legislation.

All in all, the financing of many mergers leaves a great deal to be desired because it allows acquiring firms to issue huge amounts of debt that cannot be fully backed by the resources available to the acquiring company. In addition, there are many abuses involving special concessions with large compensation packages, labeled *Golden Parachutes.* They involve large awards to the senior managers of target companies, who insist on being protected against adverse developments arising from a merger. Payments include large salaries, options on stocks, bonuses, and pre-established long-term payments. Some companies go so far as to assume the tax payments for the managers who reap the benefits of these golden parachutes.

The payment in the leveraged buyout of RJR Nabisco to F. Ross Johnson, the company's chief executive officer, included a package amounting to $53.8 million. Gerald Tsai, chairman of Primerica, was guaranteed a total of $46.8 million in case of a takeover. One wonders whether these arrangements are in the best interest of stockholders.

YOU SHOULD REMEMBER

There are two ways to negotiate a prospective merger. The acquiring company can approach the target company's management directly and negotiate terms, or it can appeal to stockholders via a public tender offer. If negotiations are friendly, the ultimate result is a merger by cash payment or exchange of securities. When the negotiations are unfriendly, the cost of fighting a takeover via mail, newspaper advertising, or court action can be substantial. Some target firms raise dividends or tell their stockholders not to sell to the acquiring company. Recent legislation requires that advance notice be given to the Securities Exchange Commission and to the target company.

THE FUTURE OF MERGERS

Are mergers a fad or are they here to stay? Recently, there was a surge of activity by large firms acquiring other large firms and large firms acquiring small, fast-growing, and innovative companies. The justification for many of these mergers was less than sound, and the conglomerate wave of the 1960s left many companies in a fragmented state without the means to deal effectively with different unrelated businesses.

In theory, mergers are supposed to generate **synergism**—that is, the value of a merged firm is greater than the sum of the two separate firms. If this argument is carried to the extreme, the conclusion might be that there should be only one firm in the economy, and that this would be the most efficient system. In reality, the large size of the firm can create management problems. The early success of many small firms comes from entrepreneurs who manage and control them efficiently. When these small firms are acquired, their managers may lose the drive and incentive needed to compete aggressively in the marketplace because they feel protected by the umbrella of the greater resources available from the acquiring firm. They no longer feel the pressure or need to struggle for survival and may not operate as successfully as they did when they were on their own.

Also, the management of an acquired company may become demoralized or disenchanted by directives from the top that put restraints on former methods of operation. This can lead to the eventual departure of the best managers or to loss in the motivation needed to maintain the acquired firm's efficiency. The urge to retire or leave grows, especially when generous golden parachutes are available to the target firm's managers.

A combination of many small companies into a large company may pose additional problems of fragmentation. Top management does not usually have the expertise or time to monitor each individual small company, and this can lead to poor control over costs and profitability.

A merger should be based on long-term considerations. Management should consider whether or not the merger will result in a favorable future growth trend for the merged company, whether it leads to a healthy diversification of product lines and lower risk, whether it improves the capital structures of the firm, and whether it results in wealth maximization for the merged firm.

Recent mergers have produced a number of successes and many failures. Some mergers make sense, whereas others seem to be mere power plays to become bigger rather than better. There are indications that merged companies in related fields have produced superior results, partly because the two managements work together and understand what has to be done to run a successful business. For example, it made sense for Pepsi Co. to acquire Frito-Lay; both are in the snack business. Heinz and Weight Watchers had a common interest—food. Typical examples of incompatible partnerships are the acquisition of Montgomery Ward by Mobil Oil and Exxon's takeover of Reliance Electric. Some mergers took place on the basis of wrong forecasts, as in the acquisition of mining companies by large firms who thought commodity prices would continue to increase indefinitely. A case in point is Atlantic Richfield's purchase of Anaconda.

In many cases, even after it becomes evident that a merger was a mistake, the acquiring company (partly because of the inability of some executives to admit errors of judgment) continues to infuse large amounts of money into the acquired company in a vain attempt to keep it afloat. Often, the results are disastrous. Exxon's acquisition of Vydec Corporation in an attempt to penetrate the office automation field is a good example of poor decision making. After investing $500 million over a 10-year period, Exxon finally conceded that this merger was a failure. Part of the reason for the disaster was Exxon's persistent misunderstanding of the office automation market and its persistent inability to accept defeat.

You can see that diversification just for the sake of changing the product mix is not a very good reason for merging. Some companies pay too much for a target company and also fail to investigate fully the problems they will face after the two companies are combined. Once a merger takes place, some acquiring companies use the bulldozer effect (as in the case of Schlumberger and Fairchild Camera and Instrument Corp). Schlumberger's exploitation of Fairchild caused key personnel to leave and profits to shrink. This is why mergers in related fields are more likely to succeed.

It is evident that certain lessons can be learned from recent merger experiences. Usually, when both companies share information about their strengths and weaknesses, when they carefully evaluate their future expected cash flows, and when they are satisfied that they can benefit each other in different ways, the outcome is likely to be good.

As stated earlier, one of the more worrisome trends in the merger field has been the issuing of junk bonds to finance these transactions. Junk bonds per se are not the problem; rather, it is the high debt created by this type of financing that is of significance. It indicates a diminishing concern with financial soundness and could create problems for merged firms in the future. The jury is still out on this one, but the test will come during a business recession, when earnings decline and interest coverage becomes a problem. Historically, excesses of this kind seem irrelevant until a crisis emerges. As in the case of the savings and loan associations, current merger excesses may come to roost in the 1990s unless more fiscally and financial sound practices are adopted in future consolidations.

Mergers are here to stay, but the mistakes of many large companies in the recent past should provide acquiring companies with food for thought. No doubt there will still be chief executives who seek personal aggrandizement through mergers, but in many cases they will regret their actions later. When seeking a merger candidate, an acquiring company must determine how both companies will work out the future patterns of geographic distribution, the technological base, and their management skills. The two companies should complement each other to make the merger work. Attempts to interject corporate politics and to override each other's decisions can lead only to frustration and poor results.

There are no standard rules on which to base mergers. In most cases, success comes from careful analysis, advance planning, and the application of modern decision-making techniques to calculate a fair exchange of values and long-run benefits for the combined company.

YOU SHOULD REMEMBER

Mergers have produced mixed results in the past. Some experiences have been good, others less than satisfactory. The trend seems to show a continued movement toward mergers. It is hoped that more careful attention will be given to the goal of maximizing the wealth of both participants in the merger deal.

KNOW THE CONCEPTS

DO YOU KNOW THE BASICS?

1. Give five major reasons why firms merge.
2. What is meant by the term *synergism?*
3. When a firm buys another firm for cash, what technique does it use to appraise the value of the acquired firm?

4. Will the calculated exchange ratio determine the ultimate terms of a merger? What other factor plays a key role in the final negotiations?

5. Why do some target companies ask for convertible securities as a condition for a merger?

6. When does book value become a significant factor in negotiations, and why?

7. How does the debt/capitalization ratio play a role in the selection of a likely merger candidate by an acquiring company?

8. Besides cash and common stock, what methods of exchange can be used to consummate a merger? Why are these methods attractive to management and stockholders?

9. Indicate some of the ways a target company can attempt to thwart a merger with an unfriendly acquiring firm. What are these practices called?

10. What should the parties to a merger expect in terms of short-range results from the merged firm?

11. What are the tax benefits of acquiring a firm with tax losses?

12. Define the negotiating range and how would you calculate the upper and lower limits of the range?

TERMS FOR STUDY

book value (of a firm)   merger exchange ratio
contingency payments   negotiating range
economies of scale   poison pill
golden parachute   pooling of interest method
goodwill   purchase acquisition method
greenmail   synergism
intrinsic value   tax-loss carry-forward
junk bond   tender offer
merger   white knight

PRACTICAL APPLICATION

COMPUTATIONAL PROBLEMS

1. The expected cash flow of a target company is $10,000 for the next 10 years; the corresponding discount rate is 15%; and the growth rate of cash flow is 10% after the tenth year. Also, the target company's liabilities are $80,000. The outstanding shares of the target company equal 1,000, and the price of its stock is $10. Calculate the minimum and maximum negotiating range.

2. The acquiring firm's stock price is $30, and the target company's stock price is $20. Calculate the exchange ratio and state what the results mean.

3. An acquiring company has agreed to an exchange ratio of 1.75 for 100,000 shares of the target company.

    a. How many shares will the acquiring company exchange for the target company's shares?

    b. What will be the total price paid for the target company if the acquiring stock is selling in the market at $60 per share?

4. You are supplied with the following financial data:

	Target Company	Acquiring Company
Earnings	$100,000	$200,000
Outstanding shares	10,000	20,000
Price of stock	$24 (offered to merge)	$50

Calculate the EPS of the merged company when the merger is consummated.

5. Firm A acquires Firm B. The exchange ratio is 2 shares of Firm B's stock for 1 share of Firm A's stock. You are given the following·

	Firm A	Firm B
Earnings available to common stockholders	$200,000	$100,000
Number of shares outstanding	100,000	50,000

    (a) Calculate EPS of the merged company.

    (b) If the exchange ratio was 5 for 1, what would the combined EPS of the merged company be?

6. Firm A purchases Firm B for $1,600,000 in cash. Given the following premerger balance sheets of the two firms, indicate how the merged firm's balance sheet will look and what happens to the income statement.

Balance Sheet (all values in thousands of dollars)

	Firm A	Firm B
Current assets	$ 850	$ 975
Fixed assets	1,500	1,200
Total assets	2,350	2,175
Debt	1,000	800
Equity	1,350	1,375
Total liabilities and net worth	2,350	2,175

Assume that goodwill is amortized over 25 years.

ANSWERS

KNOW THE CONCEPTS

1. Here are five major reasons why companies merge:
   (a) To achieve synergistic effects.
   (b) To gain tax advantages.
   (c) To reduce the overall risk of the firm.
   (d) To improve the capital structure of the firm.
   (e) To acquire talent or managerial skills.

2. Synergism relates to economies of scale derived from mergers, among other things. The synergistic effects obtained from a merger can result in lower unit costs; elimination of duplication (e.g., combining two accounting and two computer departments into one); and elimination of superfluous jobs.

3. When acquiring for cash, the acquiring firm usually analyzes book value versus market price, and the present value of the cash flows of the target company are compared to the cost of acquiring the company.

4. The exchange ratio represents a starting point for negotiations. The final terms depend on the respective bargaining powers of the two negotiating firms. If the target company is eager to merge, it will accept a lower exchange ratio than it would if it were reluctant to merge. A great deal depends on market conditions, the relative *P/E*s of the two companies, their comparative growth, and their comparative stock prices.

5. Some target companies prefer convertible securities as a condition for a merger because the stockholders want the income from these securities. They also want the option of investing in the stock of the merged firm at a future date, should the merger prove successful.

6. Book value becomes especially important when it exceeds the market price of the target company's stock. In this instance, the net worth of the target company is higher than its market value. The price of the target company is a bargain since its shares can be purchased for less than its book value or net worth.

7. The candidate's debt/capitalization ratio may help the acquiring company to modify its capital structure. For example, assume that the acquiring company's *D/C* ratio is too high by its industry and all other standards. In that case it may seek to acquire a company with a low *D/C* ratio to bring its own ratio down to a more acceptable level.

8. The acquiring firm can issue convertible securities, or options to purchase its stock. Contingency payments may be arranged to permit the target company management to share in the profits of the merged company.

9. To stop an unfriendly merger, the target company can appeal to state courts to block the tender offer. It can sell out to a friendlier partner, or so-called white knight. It can also raise the dividend so that shareholders will be reluctant to

tender their stock. In a poison pill defense, the target company can make its stock much less attractive to a takeover specialist by creating a new class of stock or requiring special dividends in the event of a buyout.

10. In the short run, it is possible that the growth of the merged company's EPS could fall below the premerger growth rate of the acquiring firm. It takes time for the merged companies to work out their differences. Also, the initial payment to the firm's stockholders may have been high. The acquisition can only be justified over the long run. Merging for short-term gains will not result in wealth maximation of the postmerged company.

11. The taxes paid by the postmerged company can be reduced when the acquiring company has profits and the target company has carry-forward losses.

12. The negotiating range is the minimum and the maximum price an acquiring company is willing to consider in discussion with a target company. The minimum price is calculated as the current price of the stock times the outstanding shares of the target company. The maximum range is the present value of discounted cash flows (plus a value of the target company to infinity) minus all liabilities of the target company.

PRACTICAL APPLICATION

1. $\$10,000 \times 5.019 = \$50,190$

$$\frac{\$10,000(1.10)}{.15 - .10} = \frac{\$11,000}{.05} = \$220,000(0.247) = \$54,340$$

$\$54,340 + \$50,190 = \$104,530$ *PVCF*

$$
\begin{aligned}
NPV &= PVCF - L \\
&= \$104,530 - \$80,000 = \$24,530 \quad \text{Maximum price} \\
&= 1,000 \times \$10 = \$10,000 \quad \text{Minimum price}
\end{aligned}
$$

2. $\dfrac{\$20}{\$30} = .67$ Exchange ratio

This means that the acquiring company will give up .67 of each share of its stock for each share of the target company.

3. a. $1.75(100,000) = 175,000$

The acquiring company will exchange 175,000 of its shares for 100,000 of the target company's shares.

b. $175,000 \times \$60 = \$10,500,000$

The target company is acquired for a total price of $10,500,000.

4. $\text{Earnings}_A = \$200,000$

$\text{Earnings}_T = \underline{100,000}$

$\text{Earnings}_{A+T} \; \$300,000$

$$EPS_{A+T} = E_{A+T}/[N_a + (P_T \times N_T)/P_A]$$
$$= \$300{,}000 \,/\, [200{,}000 + (\$25 \times 100{,}000)/\$50]$$
$$= \$300{,}000 \,/\, (200{,}000 + 50{,}000)$$
$$= \$1.20 \text{ (earnings per share of merged company)}$$

5. (a)

	Firm A	Firm B	Merged A + B
Earnings available for common stockholders	$200,000	$100,000	$300,000
Number of outstanding shares	100,000	50,000	
Original EPS	$2.00	$2.00	
Merger exchange ratio is 1 share of A for 2 of B			$2.40*
(b) 1 share of A for 5 of B			$2.73†

*The number of shares outstanding after the merger would be 125,000.
†The number of shares outstanding after the merger would be 110,000.

6. Since the purchase price exceeds the net worth of Firm B, goodwill is created in the amount of $225,000 ($1,600,000 − $1,375,000). The balance sheet of the merged company will be as follows:

Balance Sheet (all values in thousands of dollars)

	Firm A	Firm B	Merged A + B
Current assets	850	975	1,825
Fixed assets	1,500	1,200	2,700
Goodwill			225
Total assets	2,350	2,175	4,750
Debt	1,000	800	1,800
Equity	1,350	1,375	2,950*
Total liabilities and net worth	$2,350	2,175	4,750

*Includes $225,000 of goodwill. The income statement will show a goodwill write-off of $9,000 ($225,000 ÷ 25) each year for the next 25 years.

18
BASICS OF INTERNATIONAL FINANCE

KEY TERMS

arbitrage taking advantage of temporary differences in market prices to make a profit

balance of payments a document showing all payments and receipts of a country vis-à-vis the rest of the world for a year

Eurodollars U.S. dollars traded outside U.S. borders

foreign exchange rate the price at which the currency of one country can be bought with the currency of another country

multinational corporation a firm with significant operations outside its national borders

---

INTRODUCTION TO INTERNATIONAL FINANCE

An **international firm** can be defined as a company that is involved in the export/import of goods and services, or a company that has at least a business branch (subsidiary) in a foreign country for business purposes. An international firm with substantial operations (usually over 30% of its total activity) in one or more foreign countries is called a **multinational corporation (MNC).** There is no universal definition for an MNC. Some academicians argue that the term "multinational" is misleading unless the firm is actually owned and managed by people or institutions of more than one country. According to this view, a true multinational is a firm that has international operations, international management, and international ownership. Since this is not a realistic definition, we refer to any firm with significant operations outside its national borders as a multinational company. Therefore, a multinational corporation is the outgrowth of an international firm. For the sake of simplicity in this chapter, the term "international firm" refers to any company with some type of business outside its home country.

Among the unique problems of international firms are fluctuation of the U.S. dollar and foreign currencies, international taxation laws, political events outside the home country, and, most important, the need to understand and respect foreign cultures. If we lived in a world where there was only one international currency, no export and import barriers, and no taxation, the main differences between domestic business and international business would be reduced to cultural factors. The reality is that we are in a complex world with different national currencies, export and import regulations, and tax laws, and diverse cultural and political systems. Therefore, knowledge of domestic finance is not sufficient to cope with the problems of international finance. You need to understand how the value of a foreign currency is determined and why it fluctuates from day to day. You need to learn about the balance of payments, which shows the payments and receipts of a country in relation to the rest of the world. Understanding of international financial markets such as the Eurodollar market, the Eurobond market, futures markets, and option markets is essential to an international financial officer. In view of this need, the basic principles of international finance are explained in this chapter to supplement foregoing discussion of corporate finance.

UNDERSTANDING FOREIGN CURRENCY

A currency is a financial asset that has a value, or price. The holder of a foreign currency has a financial claim against the assets of its issuing country. Stated differently, the issuing government has a financial liability to the holder of its currency. The value of a currency such as the U.S. dollar is expressed in terms of other currencies such as the deutsche mark (DM), Japanese yen, and Italian lira. For example, to express the value of a dollar in terms of another currency, we write DM 1.90/$. This means that a dollar is worth 1.90 deutsche marks. If we take the reciprocal of 1.90 (1 divided by 1.90), we get .53, indicating that one deutsche mark is worth 53 cents. We write this relationship as $ .53/DM. When we define the value of a foreign currency in terms of a domestic currency, we call it a direct quotation (e.g., $ .53/DM). The value of a domestic currency in terms of a foreign currency is an indirect quotation (e.g., DM 1.90/$). *The Wall Street Journal* publishes the prices of different currencies both directly and indirectly. European countries, except England, use a direct quotation system, quoting foreign currency price in terms of local currency.

WHAT DETERMINES THE VALUE OF A FOREIGN CURRENCY?

Like any other asset, the value of a foreign currency is determined by demand and supply. For instance, if the total of U.S. imports from Japan go up, we need more Japanese yen to pay our import bills. Since our demand for that currency goes up, its value must go up also. On the other hand, if the Japanese buy more U.S. goods, their demand for dollars goes up and they have to sell local currency to obtain dollars. This would lead to more supply of their currency in the market. An increase in the supply of Japanese yen will bring its price down.

The price of a currency, where demand equals supply, is called the market price of a currency (see Figure 18.1). This market mechanism works in the existing currency system, where the values of major international currencies are continuously floating. That is why the current system is called a floating system. Since governments periodically intervene in the market to control drastic fluctuations, however, it is more precise to call the existing system a managed floating system. This system has been in effect since the early part of the 1970s.

From the end of World War II up to the early 1970s, a different system, called a

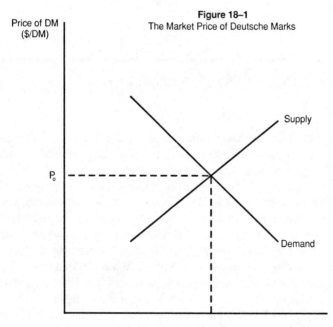

Figure 18–1
The Market Price of Deutsche Marks

fixed currency system, was in effect throughout most of the world. In the fixed system, the values of currencies were connected to the value of the U.S. dollar, which was, in turn, defined in terms of a fixed quantity of gold (1 oz. of gold = $35.00 U.S.). The U.S. government could print as many dollars as it wanted, but it had an obligation to convert dollars into gold for other governments that were holding dollars. By the late 1960s, however, the Vietnam War and other monetary expansion policies had created a huge supply of dollars both domestically and overseas. Clearly, there was not nearly enough gold to back up all of these "wandering dollars." The French government was among the first to suspect the true state of affairs and claimed redemption of gold in exchange for their dollars. Other countries began to follow suit. Washington had benefited from free credit, printing as many dollars as the demand called for in the 1950's, but now the bills were coming due, and there was not enough gold in vaults to honor the obligations. The situation can be imagined as if a major bank was unable to pay back the money of its own depositors.

This was a very unsettling experience for the United States in international markets because a currency system (like any credit system) is based on full faith and trust. And trust in the U.S. dollars was significantly diminished in the late 1960s and early 1970s. Consequently, in 1972, the fixed monetary system, which had been operating according to the Bretton Woods agreement of 1944, collapsed. A new mechanism, the managed floating system, which still exists, replaced the old system. Thus, the values of major currencies are now determined by supply and demand and by periodic government interventions. Indeed, there is every indication that this existing system, which basically lets the markets set the rates, within limits, will continue to operate for many years to come.

YOU SHOULD REMEMBER

A currency is a financial asset, and its value is expressed in terms of another currency. If a foreign currency is quoted in terms of local currency, we call it a direct quotation. If the domestic currency is quoted in terms of foreign currencies, we call it an indirect quotation. The market price of a currency is its value when supply and demand are equal. After the collapse of the fixed exchange rate system in 1972, the current managed floating exchange rate system emerged and replaced the old one.

TERMINOLOGY AND CONCEPTS

In this section, we define five important terms and then explain four major concepts in international finance:

1. The spot rate is the price of a currency for immediate delivery.

2. The forward rate is the price for delivery in the future. When you buy a currency in a forward market, you sign a paper but nothing is exchanged until the specified delivery time.

3. The nominal interest rate is the actual rate and includes a premium based on the rate of inflation. The rate you receive on your certificate of deposit and the interest rate you pay on your mortgage are examples of nominal interest rates

4. The real interest rate is a more accurate measure of the value of interest payments because it excludes inflation. Once you subtract the rate of inflation from the nominal interest rate, you arrive at a real interest rate. Thus, if the rate of inflation is 5% and you receive 9% on your certificate of deposit, the real interest rate you enjoy is approximately 4% (9% − 5%).

5. A currency is said to be at premium if its forward rate is higher than the spot rate; if the forward rate is lower, the currency is at discount. Let us explain it differently. Currencies that are more expensive for future than for immediate delivery are called "at premium." If it is cheaper to buy and wait for future delivery, usually three, six, or nine months in future, the currency is "at discount."

Read the above five terms again before you continue. Once you know these terms, you are ready to understand the following four major concepts:

1. *The purchasing power parity:* According to this theory, there is a relationship between inflation rates and the values of currencies in different countries. If the U.S. rate of inflation is 5% more than that of Japan, the U.S. dollar should lose value (depreciate) by approximately 5%. If two countries have equal rates of inflation, the values of their currencies, relative to each other, should remain the same. This theory suggests that currencies fluctuate because rates of inflation change. The higher the rate of a country's inflation, the less valuable would be its currency in the international currency markets. Why? Because inflation erodes the value, or purchasing power, of money.

2. *Interest rate parity:* Generally speaking, the difference between interest rates in two countries is equal to the premium or discount of their currencies. For example, if the interest rate in the U.S. is 2% more than that in another country, the U.S. dollar should be sold at 2% discount compared to the other currency. Note that according to this theory, the country with a higher interest rate must bear a discount on its currency, and vice versa. In other words, what you gain as an extra interest rate in X country is offset out by a discount on its currency when you sell it in the currency market. This is partly consistent with the concept of market efficiency, which suggests that investors cannot beat the market.

3. *International Fischer relation:* Between two countries, the one with a higher rate of inflation must have a higher interest rate. If the rate of inflation in England is 2% more than that of the U.S., banks in England must pay approximately 2% more on deposits.

4. *Foreign exchange expectation:* According to this theory, the forward rate of a currency is the same as what we expect the currency to be worth in the future. If you want to get a sense of what will happen to the value of the U.S. dollar 6 months from now, simply look up the six-month forward rate of the U.S. dollar, published daily in *The Wall Street Journal*. This theory suggests that the forward rate reflects the future value of a currency. Why? Because future is basically a realization of what people expect today.

• BALANCE OF PAYMENTS

The **balance of payments** of a country is a document that shows all payments and receipts of the country vis-à-vis the rest of the world for a year. Table 18–1 illustrates a numerical example of a balance of payments reported in the local currency, P, of an imaginary country named Parsland.

A balance of payments has five major accounts: trade account, service account, current account, capital account, and overall account. Each account is described separately in the following sections.

TRADE ACCOUNT

The **trade account** shows the difference between the exports and the imports of goods and services of a country in its local currency. Other, equivalent terms for the trade account are merchandise balance and external gap or surplus. In Table

Table 18–1   Country: Parsland
Balance of Payments for the Year 1989
(Figures in Millions of P)

Export of goods	+100	
Import of goods	− 80	
Trade account		+20 P
Export of services and other intangibles	+ 40	
Import of services and other intangibles	− 10	
Service account		+30
Current account		+50 P
Export of long-term capital	+ 20	
Import of long-term capital	− 40	
Export of portfolio and other short-term capital	+ 30	
Import of portfolio and other short-term capital	− 20	
Capital account		−10
Overall account		+40 P
Foreign exchange inflow		−30
Gold inflow		−10
Total inflow of funds		−40 P

18–1, Parsland has a surplus of 20 million P in the trade account, which means that the country exported 20 million P more than it imported in 1989. As a result of this surplus, Parsland has generated 20 million P worth of foreign currencies in the economy. In other words, the country has a claim, equal to 20 million P, against other countries that purchased goods from Parsland.

SERVICE ACCOUNT

Technical know-how, financial services, trade and military aids, gifts, and other intangible items are reported in the **service-and-other-intangible account.** Countries around the world not only export and import goods, but actively trade services as well. The plan and design of manufacturing facilities, consultations for military affairs, permission to copy patents (licensing), financial services (including arrangements to borrow from foreign banks or to issue bonds and stocks in foreign markets) marketing research, and various other similar activities are all reflected in the service account. A country that renders more services than it receives ends up with a surplus in this account. In Table 18–1, Parsland has generated a surplus of 30 million P in the service-and-other-intangible account.

CURRENT ACCOUNT

The **current account** is the algebraic sum of the trade account and the service account. Because of the combined effect, a negative trade account may completely or partially offset a surplus balance of the service account. For instance, a negative trade account of $100 and a surplus service account of $100 lead to a zero balance in the current account. In the case of Parsland, both the trade account and the service account are positive; therefore, the balance of the current account, +50 million P, is derived from adding the +20 million of the trade account and the +30 million of the service account.

CAPITAL ACCOUNT

The **capital account** shows the net inflows and outflows of various types of capital, such as direct investment and portfolios. **Direct investment** refers to over-10% ownership of an investment in a foreign country. Ownership of a foreign project by less than 10% is called **portfolio investment.** For instance, if General Motors invests in 40% of a $100 million project to manufacture cars in Brazil, the capital account of the U.S. balance of payments would reflect a $40 million outflow in the form of direct investment overseas. Meantime, the capital account would include $1 million worth of foreign portfolio if U.S. residents buy 1% of the project in the form of the Brazilian stock. Capital also may be imported or exported by short- and long-term borrowings between two countries. French corporations may use the U.S. market to issue bonds, American or Japanese firms may use the Swiss financial market to raise funds, and so on. All these lending and borrowing activities are reported in the capital account of each country's balance of payments. Borrowing from other countries generates an inflow of funds, while lending to other countries creates a cash outflow in the balance of payments of the lending country.

OVERALL ACCOUNT

The **overall account** is the net of all other accounts in the balance of payments. In a simple form, the overall account is the sum of the current account and various capital accounts. For instance, Parsland has an overall account of +40 P, derived from the 50-P surplus in the current account and the 10-P deficit in the capital account. The overall account reflects the net inflow or outflow of funds as a result of various short- and long-term transactions of a country with the rest of the world. In Table 18–1, Parsland receives its surplus overall account in the form of foreign exchange and gold. Precisely speaking, Parsland received 30 P in foreign exchange and 10 P in gold, resulting in a 40 P surplus in its overall account. Note that a surplus overall account is always equal to the total inflow of funds, and that a deficit overall account is always equal to the total outflow of funds. Inflow and outflow of funds may occur in the form of foreign currencies, gold, or special drawing rights (SDRs).

• SPECIAL DRAWING RIGHTS (SDRs)

In the late 1960s, neither gold nor major foreign currencies were available in sufficient quantities to support the growing volume of international transactions. In 1967, therefore, an agreement was reached among the industrial and developing countries to create an artificial currency named Special Drawing Rights (SDRs). **SDRs** are credits extended to importing countries, and are monitored by an international organization called the International Monetary Fund (IMF), located in Washington, D.C. Each country has a credit quota depending on the volume of its exports and imports. SDRs are exchanged only among central banks and are convertible into other currencies. Although there are currently over $30 billion (U.S.) worth of SDRs outstanding in international transactions, they constitute—excluding gold—less than 8% of world international reserves.

The value of an SDR was initially determined by sixteen major currencies, each of which had a different weight depending on its volume in international trade. The method of valuation was changed in 1981, and the value of an SDR now is basically the weighted average of five currencies: the U.S. dollar, deutsche mark, French franc, Japanese yen, and U.K. pound sterling. The U.S. dollar has the most influence, with a weight of over 40% in the valuation of the SDR.

YOU SHOULD REMEMBER

The balance of payments of a country reports all payments and receipts of the country, in a given year, in relation to the rest of the world. The balance of payments has five major accounts: trade account, service account, current account, capital account, and overall account. The overall account is the net of all other accounts, and its balance equals the total inflow or outflow of funds.

An agreement was reached among the industrial and developing countries to create Special Drawing Rights (SDRs) in 1967. The purpose of the SDRs is to increase liquidity in world financial transactions.

UNDERSTANDING FOREIGN EXCHANGE

In recent years, the foreign exchange rate has experienced sharp fluctuations as a result of the increased volatility of relative currency values and the increased volume of world trade. The two major types of foreign exchange risk consist of transaction risk and translation risk.

Transaction risk exists when future foreign currency cash flow is exposed to a possible adverse currency movement before the transaction can be completed. For instance, suppose a U.S. exporter has export proceeds in Italian lire to be collected 6 months from now. In this case the U.S. exporter has transaction risk because she may lose part of the credit if the Italian lire depreciates in value vis-à-vis the U.S. dollar.

Translation risk arises from the need to translate the assets and liabilities of a foreign subsidiary, expressed in local currency, into the currency of the home country. This is necessary for consolidating the financial statement of the subsidiary with that of its parent company.

Many foreign exchange transactions arise in connection with the importation or exportation of goods or raw materials. However, such transactions are also performed for numerous other purposes, including acquisition of foreign facilities, financing of operations of foreign subsidiaries, repayment of foreign borrowings, pursuit of attractive short-term investment opportunities, and diversification of securities holdings.

There is no organized exchange to establish a market for these rates. The market in foreign currencies exists in every large financial center in the world and consists primarily of trading by the world's international banks. Foreign exchange rates are established through instantaneous communication facilities, and as a result these rates tend to be very similar worldwide. However, when dispersion occurs, traders in foreign currency will quickly bring rates back into alignment.

Foreign currency rates involving the U.S. dollar may be quoted in one of two ways: as the cost of the foreign currency in U.S. dollars, or as the cost of the U.S. dollar in the stated foreign currency. In the U.S. interbank market, exchange rates for most currencies are quoted in U.S. dollars.

• INSTRUMENTS OF FOREIGN EXCHANGE

Instruments available to traders of foreign exchange consist of spots, forwards, futures, and options. In addition, a method employed strictly by corporations to avoid currency losses is a direct swap with a foreign business. The precise arrangements are widely varying and complex, but the principle is simple: Instead of buying and selling currencies directly, corporations locate a foreign business with opposite needs and work out a set of loans to each other.

THE SPOT MARKET

The **spot market** establishes the current price of a specific foreign currency. This rate is the underlying basis for evaluating forwards, futures, and options.

Spot rates of the currencies of the major industrial countries are determined mainly by supply and demand. If an excess amount (in comparison to demand) of domestic currency is offered, the value of that currency will tend to decline. Conversely, when demand for a certain currency exceeds the supply, the value of that currency will increase.

The demand for a country's products and raw material plays a principal role in determining the demand for its currency—and, subsequently, its exchange rate. In other words, a country's balance of payments has an important impact on the value of its currency. Factors affecting the level of demand for a country's products include its supply of raw materials, the efficiency of its manufacturing facilities, the size and skills of its labor force, and the price levels of its products. The level of investment in foreign plants and financial assets also has an impact on the exchange rate. If foreign facilities are acquired by a country, that country's demand for foreign currencies may increase. The fiscal and monetary policies of a government also are important determinants of exchange rates because of their effects on inflation, interest rates, and income levels. With a sharp increase in the money supply unaccompanied by comparable growth in the gross national product (GNP), inflationary conditions can be created that will lower the value of the currency.

Short-term rates are affected by additional factors, and because of the complex interrelationships and unpredictability of these factors, forecasting short-term exchange rates is very difficult.

FORWARDS

In a **forward transaction,** the seller sells any specified amount of foreign currency, at a fixed rate, for delivery on a future date. The exchange rate is fixed when the transaction is agreed upon, just as it is in spot transactions. The buyer and seller determine the dollar size of the contract because there are no standardized amounts. Forward delivery dates are computed as the number of months from the spot delivery date. "Spot" indicates delivery at the time of transaction. In practice, "forward" is counted after "spot"; for example, 3 months forward means 3 months after spot. Contracts providing for delivery in 1 month, 3 months, 6 months, 9 months, or 12 months are the most common; however, contracts with maturities of more than a year can be obtained in the major currencies. Forward contracts normally require no cash outlay until the delivery date. If the creditworthiness of a customer is in doubt, a deposit of cash or other collateral may be required.

FUTURES

Foreign currency futures are different from forward contracts. Futures contract prices are determined by open auction markets. The sizes of these contracts are also standardized. Each German mark contract is for 125,000 marks; each British pound contract, for 25,000 pounds; each Canadian dollar contract, for 100,000 Canadian dollars; each Japanese yen contract for 12,500,000 yen; and each Swiss franc contract, for 125,000 Swiss francs. In addition, delivery dates are standardized.

An active futures market exists for a few major currencies on the International Monetary Market (IMM). Futures contracts differ from forward contracts in that transactions are made through a clearinghouse. The clearinghouse becomes the buyer to every seller, and the seller to every buyer, in the futures market. As a result, a trader is not concerned about the creditworthiness of the other party, and foreign currency futures-contract positions can be closed out more easily than can foreign currency forward contracts. Most futures contracts are liquidated by an offsetting purchase or sale and never reach delivery. If delivery occurs, the procedure is identical to that used in the interbank market.

OPTIONS

Foreign currency options give their buyer the right—but not the obligation—to buy (or sell) a fixed amount of currency at a fixed rate, or **strike price,** on or before an expiration date. The right to buy the currency is known as a call, and the right to sell is a put. The two parties to a currency option contract are called the option buyer and the option writer.

The time period for delivery of foreign currency option contracts is limited to several weeks or a month. This type of option is merely a variation of a foreign currency forward contract.

There are two types of currency options: call options and put options. **A call option** gives the right to buy, and a **put option** gives the right to sell.

PROFIT AND LOSS IN OPTION TRANSACTIONS

BUY A CALL

The investor who thinks a foreign currency's price is likely to rise may want to buy a call. As the foreign currency price rises, the buyer of a call will have capital gains. If the foreign currency price decreases, only the premium is lost. Because the call buyer invested only the amount of the writer's premium, a large rate of return on the investment can be realized if the price of the foreign currency rises substantially.

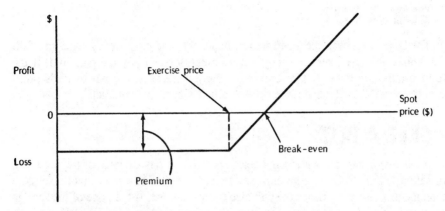

Figure 18-2 Buy a Call

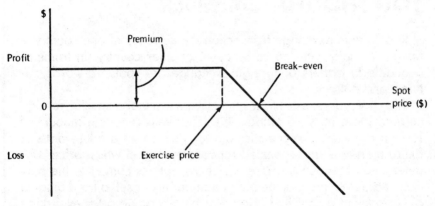

Figure 18-3 Sell a Call

In Figure 18-2 the call option buyer has a loss, equal to the premium paid, up to the point where the exchange rate rises above the exercise price. When the exchange rate exceeds the exercise price by enough to cover the premium, the option buyer's profit is zero. If the currency price rises still further, the buyer makes a profit.

SELL A CALL

A speculator who expects the value of a foreign currency to fall may wish to sell a call. The writer of a call has a profit graph opposite to that of a call buyer. Profit is limited to the premium received from the call buyer, and risk is unlimited (see Figure 18-3).

BUY A PUT

The buyer of a put, like a call writer, hopes the foreign currency price will fall. But unlike the call writer, the buyer has limited losses (only the premium) if the foreign currency rises. If the foreign currency price falls, the put owner's profit cannot exceed the exercise price times the unit size of the contract.

SELL A PUT

An investor who feels a foreign currency will rise has a choice of buying a call or selling a put. If the foreign currency falls, the writer of a put cannot lose more than the exercise price times the unit size of the contract. If the price of the foreign currency rises, the writer gains no more than the premium.

YOU SHOULD REMEMBER

In a foreign exchange transaction the currency of one country is bought or sold with the currency of another country. Instruments available to traders of foreign exchange are spots, forwards, futures, and options.

The spot market establishes the current price of a specific foreign currency. In a forward market, the seller sells a certain amount of foreign currency at a specific rate for delivery at a future date. A future market is an organized forward market in which prices are determined by open auctions. Currency options convey to the purchaser the right (but not the obligation) to buy or sell a fixed amount of currency at a specified rate on or before a particular expiration date.

• *THE FUTURE CURRENCY MARKET*

The International Monetary Market (IMM) in Chicago is a typical future currency market. In the IMM, an American exporting firm with future income in foreign currencies can sell those foreign currencies at a certain rate with the promise of delivery at a certain time. On the other hand, an importing company needing foreign currencies to pay its import bills may buy those foreign currencies for future delivery. Through this technique, both the exporting and importing firms are hedged (protected) against an unfavorable currency fluctuation.

Example: The Future Currency Market

The ABC Export Co. is supposed to collect £100,000 from a British firm 6 months from now. At the present rate, 1 British pound (£) = $1.20. However, there is a possibility that the value of the British pound will decrease.

By using the future currency market, the ABC Export Co. sells its £100,000 at the rate of £1 = $1.15. After 6 months, the company will collect $115,000 (£100,000 × $1.15/£) and deliver £100,000 to the other party of the contract. Regardless of what occurs to the value of the British pound during the next 6 months, the total income of the company is guaranteed, by a forward contract, for $115,000. The actual cost of this contract that locks the exporting company into a certain rate is $0.05 per British pound. The reason is that the British pound was undersold by $0.05 for future delivery ($1.20 − $1.15 = $0.05). Another way to look at the cost of this arrangement is that the actual cost depends on the value of the British pound after 6 months. If the value of the pound rises to $1.25 by the time of the delivery, the export company has lost $.10 per pound, because the contract rate of $1.15 is $.10 below the market value of the British pound. According to this line of reasoning, the company saves money, rather than pays costs, if the value of the British pound falls below the contract rate of $1.15 at the time of delivery.

The *Wall Street Journal* and the financial sections of *The New York Times* and many other daily journals are good sources of information about the rates of major foreign currencies in different future markets.

• *ARBITRAGE*

Arbitrage means taking advantage of temporary differences in price. The person who does arbitrage is called an arbitrageur. Arbitrage in foreign currencies can take different forms. A simple form of arbitrage is **geographical arbitrage,** which exploits the difference in the price of a foreign currency between two markets at the same time. If transaction costs allow, an arbitrageur can buy the foreign currency in the market at a lower price and sell it immediately at a higher price in the other market. The **spread** (the difference between the selling price and the buying price), after the transaction cost has been subtracted, is the net benefit of the arbitrage. This kind of opportunity rarely exists in practice because of transaction costs and market efficiency. **Market efficiency** means that information about prices of foreign currencies is transmitted across the borders so quickly that differences between prices disappear before a person or an institution can take advantage of them.

Arbitrage may also become possible if there is a difference between the interest rates in two countries, and if there is a difference between the spot rate and the future rate of their currencies.

Example: Arbitrage

Suppose interest rates in the United States and England are 8% and 10%, respectively, and the U.S. dollar is sold at a 4% premium over the British pound in the future market. In this case arbitrageurs can borrow British pounds in London at 10%, invest in U.S. dollars at 8%, and then sell their future dollar proceeds at a 4% premium. The result is a 2% net profit, as shown in Table 18–2. This kind

Table 18–2   Procedure for Arbitrage

Transaction	Cost/Benefit
Borrow British pounds in London at 10%	−10%
Convert British pounds into U.S. dollars and invest in U.S. dollars at 8%	+8%
Sell dollar proceeds for British pounds in the future market at 4% premium	+4%
Net benefit	**2%**

of arbitrage could also become unprofitable in practice because of transaction costs, market efficiency, and the difference between the investment rate and borrowing rates.

YOU SHOULD REMEMBER

Arbitrage takes place when there are temporary differences in price between two markets at the same time. Arbitrage is also possible if there is a difference between the interest rates in two countries and a difference between the spot rate and the future rate of a currency.

The International Money Market (IMM) in Chicago is an active market where contracts for future delivery of foreign currencies are purchased and sold.

• *INTERNATIONAL FINANCIAL MARKETS*

The term "international financial markets" refers to various financial institutions around the world in which multinational firms and governments participate to borrow money or invest their surplus funds. The two major international financial markets are the Eurodollar market (Euromarket) and the international bond (Eurobond) market.

THE EUROMARKET

The Eurodollar market offers short-term and intermediate loans denominated in the U.S. dollar. The maturity date of Eurodollar loans is usually less than 5 years. **Eurodollars,** by definition, are U.S. dollars traded outside U.S. borders. The Eurodollar market is an alternative to domestic banks for financing the business operations of international firms. Instead of using commercial banks in the United States, an American firm may find it cheaper and easier to borrow dollars outside this country to finance its foreign or domestic subsidiaries. Borrowing through the Euromarket has become very popular because the banking procedure is not controlled by the host governments and credit terms are more flexible and sometimes cheaper than those for domestic loans These flexible and relatively cheaper terms are sometimes attributed to greater availability of funds and more efficiency in the Euromarket as compared to domestic banking.

THE INTERNATIONAL BOND MARKET
Whereas the Euromarket deals with short-term and intermediate loans, the international bond market lends long-term funds outside the country of the borrower. For instance, a firm in Brazil may issue long-term bonds denominated in the U.S. dollar in European countries. Such bonds, denominated often in most major currencies and issued outside the borrowing country, are called **international bonds** or Eurobonds.

HOW EURODOLLARS ARE CREATED
Eurodollars are created when deposit holders in the United States transfer their deposits outside the country and maintain the denomination in the U.S. dollar. Suppose the XYZ Corporation in New York decides to transfer $50,000 of deposit from Citibank in New York to Westminster Bank in London. If this deposit is maintained in terms of the U.S. dollar, the XYZ Corporation becomes the owner of 50,000 Eurodollars. As a result, Westminster in London becomes liable to the XYZ Corporation, and Citibank to Westminster. Note that Eurodollars, despite being traded outside the United States, keep their origin with a bank in this country.

Another characteristic of Eurodollars is that they may continuously create more credit. To illustrate, the Westminster Bank in London may lend the 50,000 Eurodollars obtained in the above example to a firm in or outside England. Suppose the borrowing firm is located in France, and it decides to keep the loan in the form of a deposit with Credit Lyonnais in Paris. What happens in the United States is simply a change in liability of the Citibank from Westminster to Credit Lyonnais. As long as deposits are maintained in the U.S. dollar, Eurodollars may grow without limit in the form of new loans. The reason is that Eurodollar banks need not maintain reserve requirements. The absence of reserve requirements could be a major reason for the substantial growth of Eurodollar loans in the last decade.

The beginning of Eurodollar markets can be traced to the late 1940's, after World War II. Many scholars believe that the Soviet Union and some Eastern European governments were among the first active participants in this market; the Soviet Union placed its dollar deposits with Soviet banks in Europe, and these banks rechanneled the deposits in the form of loans to other European banks. Substantial growth of the Eurodollar and international bond markets occurred in the mid-1970s, when American and European commercial banks aggressively started to lend the deposits of the OPEC countries to both developed and developing countries.

Although the Eurodollar market has served the financial needs of both American and non-American firms, some scholars argue that it was responsible for the double-digit inflation rates in the 1970s. The spectacular growth of Eurodollars led to a significant increase in the money supply in that period, which, in turn, raised price levels both domestically and overseas. Although this economic reasoning makes sense to some extent, proof would require thorough empirical research.

YOU SHOULD REMEMBER

International financial markets consist of various financial centers around the world in which governments and international firms participate to raise capital or invest money. The international bond market and the Eurodollar market are the two major categories of these markets.

Eurodollars are U.S. dollars traded outside the geographical boundaries of the United States. Eurodollars are created when a deposit is transferred outside the United States and maintained in U.S. dollars. The origin of Eurodollars always remains with a bank in this country. Eurodollars may grow continuously as long as Eurodollar loans are not converted into other currencies.

KNOW THE CONCEPTS

DO YOU KNOW THE BASICS?

1. Define a multinational corporation.
2. List some of the problems unique to firms operating in an international environment.
3. Define the balance of payments, and list its major accounts.
4. What is the difference between direct and indirect quotations of foreign currencies?
5. What obligation could the U.S. government not fulfill in the previous fixed currency system? What happened next?
6. Fill in the missing words:
   a. Approximately, nominal interest rate minus the rate of inflation equals
      _____.
   b. If the forward rate exceeds the spot rate, the currency is at _____.
   c. If you want to "lock in" a certain currency rate for a future delivery, you can buy the currency in the _____.

7. Fill in the missing words:
   a. Purchasing power parity connects _____ and _____.
   b. Interest rate parity connects _____ and _____.
   c. International Fischer effect connects _____ and _____.
   d. The forward rate reflects _____.

8. Define a currency option, and explain the major difference between it and a future contract.

9. What is arbitrage?

10. What is the difference between a portfolio investment and a direct investment?

11. In what forms does a surplus overall balance flow into an economy?

12. What is the maximum loss/gain of a call option buyer?

13. What is the maximum loss/gain of a put option seller?

14. What is the cost of hedging in a future currency market?

TERMS FOR STUDY

arbitrage	international firm
balance of payments	international Fischer effect
call option	multinational corporation
capital account	overall account
current account	portfolio investment
direct investment	purchasing power parity
Eurodollars	put option
foreign currency futures	SDRs (Special Drawing Rights)
foreign currency options	service-and-other-intangible account
foreign exchange rate	spot market
forward rate	spread
forward transaction	strike price
geographical arbitrage	trade account
interest parity theorem	transaction risk
international bonds	translation risk

ANSWERS

KNOW THE CONCEPTS

1. A multinational corporation is a firm with substantial operations (usually 30% of its total activity) in a foreign country.

2. Some of the problems unique to firms operating internationally are foreign currency fluctuations, tax laws of different countries, political events outside the home country, and the need to understand and respect foreign cultures.

3. The balance of payments report is a document showing all receipts and payments, in 1 year, of a country in relation to the rest of the world. Major accounts are the trade account, current account, service account, capital account, and overall account.
4. In a direct quotation, the value of a foreign currency is expressed in terms of a local currency; in an indirect quotation, the value of the local currency is defined in units of a foreign currency.
5. The United States did not have enough gold to support and pay for dollars. As a result, in the early 1970s the fixed currency system collapsed.
6. a. the real interest rate
   b. premium
   c. forward market
7. a. inflation and currency fluctuations
   b. interest rate and currency premium/discount
   c. inflation and interest rates
   d. the value of a currency in the future (the trend of a currency)
8. A currency option is the right, with no obligation, to buy or sell a certain amount of foreign currency at a certain rate on or before a certain date. In a future contract, the buyer has the obligation to buy or settle the account as determined in the contract.
9. Arbitrage involves taking advantage of different prices of the same commodity or currency, in two markets at the same time, to make a profit.
10. Investment in a project with over 10% ownership is direct investment.
11. Investment with less than 10% ownership is portfolio investment.
12. The maximum loss that can be incurred by a call option buyer is the premium paid when the option was purchased. There is no maximum gain.
13. The maximum loss that can be incurred by a put option seller is the value of the currency. The maximum gain is the premium collected when the option was sold.
14. The cost of hedging in a future currency market is the difference between the spot rate and the future rate. Another possible answer is the difference between the actual future price and the spot rate.

APPENDIX

TABLES

Table A-1   Future Value Interest Factor

Period	1%	2%	3%	4%	5%	6%	7%	8%	9%	10%
1	1.010	1.020	1.030	1.040	1.050	1.060	1.070	1.080	1.090	1.100
2	1.020	1.040	1.061	1.082	1.102	1.124	1.145	1.166	1.188	1.210
3	1.030	1.061	1.093	1.125	1.158	1.191	1.225	1.260	1.295	1.331
4	1.041	1.082	1.126	1.170	1.216	1.262	1.311	1.360	1.412	1.464
5	1.051	1.104	1.159	1.217	1.276	1.338	1.403	1.469	1.539	1.611
6	1.062	1.126	1.194	1.265	1.340	1.419	1.501	1.587	1.677	1.772
7	1.072	1.149	1.230	1.316	1.407	1.504	1.606	1.714	1.828	1.949
8	1.083	1.172	1.267	1.369	1.477	1.594	1.718	1.851	1.993	2.144
9	1.094	1.195	1.305	1.423	1.551	1.689	1.838	1.999	2.172	2.358
10	1.105	1.219	1.344	1.480	1.629	1.791	1.967	2.159	2.367	2.594
11	1.116	1.243	1.384	1.539	1.710	1.898	2.105	2.332	2.580	2.853
12	1.127	1.268	1.426	1.601	1.796	2.012	2.252	2.518	2.813	3.138
13	1.138	1.294	1.469	1.665	1.886	2.133	2.410	2.720	3.066	3.452
14	1.149	1.319	1.513	1.732	1.980	2.261	2.579	2.937	3.342	3.797
15	1.161	1.346	1.558	1.801	2.079	2.397	2.759	3.172	3.642	4.177
16	1.173	1.373	1.605	1.873	2.183	2.540	2.952	3.426	3.970	4.595
17	1.184	1.400	1.653	1.948	2.292	2.693	3.159	3.700	4.328	5.054
18	1.196	1.428	1.702	2.026	2.407	2.854	3.380	3.996	4.717	5.560
19	1.208	1.457	1.753	2.107	2.527	3.026	3.616	4.316	5.142	6.116
20	1.220	1.486	1.806	2.191	2.653	3.207	3.870	4.661	5.604	6.727
21	1.232	1.516	1.860	2.279	2.786	3.399	4.140	5.034	6.109	7.400
22	1.245	1.546	1.916	2.370	2.925	3.603	4.430	5.436	6.658	8.140
23	1.257	1.577	1.974	2.465	3.071	3.820	4.740	5.871	7.258	8.954
24	1.270	1.608	2.033	2.563	3.225	4.049	5.072	6.341	7.911	9.850
25	1.282	1.641	2.094	2.666	3.386	4.292	5.427	6.848	8.623	10.834
30	1.348	1.811	2.427	3.243	4.322	5.743	7.612	10.062	13.267	17.449
40	1.489	2.208	3.262	4.801	7.040	10.285	14.974	21.724	31.408	45.258
50	1.645	2.691	4.384	7.106	11.467	18.419	29.456	46.900	74.354	117.386

Period	11%	12%	13%	14%	15%	16%	17%	18%	19%	20%
1	1.110	1.120	1.130	1.140	1.150	1.160	1.170	1.180	1.190	1.200
2	1.232	1.254	1.277	1.300	1.322	1.346	1.369	1.392	1.416	1.440
3	1.368	1.405	1.443	1.482	1.521	1.561	1.602	1.643	1.685	1.728
4	1.518	1.574	1.630	1.689	1.749	1.811	1.874	1.939	2.005	2.074
5	1.685	1.762	1.842	1.925	2.011	2.100	2.192	2.288	2.386	2.488
6	1.870	1.974	2.082	2.195	2.313	2.436	2.565	2.700	2.840	2.986
7	2.076	2.211	2.353	2.502	2.660	2.826	3.001	3.185	3.379	3.583
8	2.305	2.476	2.658	2.853	3.059	3.278	3.511	3.759	4.021	4.300
9	2.558	2.773	3.004	3.252	3.518	3.803	4.108	4.435	4.785	5.160
10	2.839	3.106	3.395	3.707	4.046	4.411	4.807	5.234	5.695	6.192
11	3.152	3.479	3.836	4.226	4.652	5.117	5.624	6.176	6.777	7.430
12	3.498	3.896	4.334	4.818	5.350	5.936	6.580	7.288	8.064	8.916
13	3.883	4.363	4.898	5.492	6.153	6.886	7.699	8.599	9.596	10.699
14	4.310	4.887	5.535	6.261	7.076	7.987	9.007	10.147	11.420	12.839
15	4.785	5.474	6.254	7.138	8.137	9.265	10.539	11.974	13.589	15.407
16	5.311	6.130	7.067	8.137	9.358	10.748	12.330	14.129	16.171	18.488
17	5.895	6.866	7.986	9.276	10.761	12.468	14.426	16.672	19.244	22.186
18	6.543	7.690	9.024	10.575	12.375	14.462	16.879	19.673	22.900	26.623
19	7.263	8.613	10.197	12.055	14.232	16.776	19.748	23.214	27.251	31.948
20	8.062	9.646	11.523	13.743	16.366	19.461	23.105	27.393	32.429	38.337
21	8.949	10.804	13.021	15.667	18.821	22.574	27.033	32.323	38.591	46.005
22	9.933	12.100	14.713	17.861	21.644	26.186	31.629	38.141	45.923	55.205
23	11.026	13.552	16.626	20.361	24.891	30.376	37.005	45.007	54.648	66.247
24	12.239	15.178	18.788	23.212	28.625	35.236	43.296	53.108	65.031	79.496
25	13.585	17.000	21.230	26.461	32.918	40.874	50.656	62.667	77.387	95.395
30	22.892	29.960	39.115	50.949	66.210	85.849	111.061	143.367	184.672	237.373
40	64.999	93.049	132.776	188.876	267.856	378.715	533.846	750.353	1051.642	1469.740
50	184.559	288.996	450.711	700.197	1083.619	1670.669	2566.080	3927.189	5988.730	9100.191

Period	21%	22%	23%	24%	25%	26%	27%	28%	29%	30%
1	1.210	1.220	1.230	1.240	1.250	1.260	1.270	1.280	1.290	1.300
2	1.464	1.488	1.513	1.538	1.562	1.588	1.613	1.638	1.664	1.690
3	1.772	1.816	1.861	1.907	1.953	2.000	2.048	2.097	2.147	2.197
4	2.144	2.215	2.289	2.364	2.441	2.520	2.601	2.684	2.769	2.856
5	2.594	2.703	2.815	2.932	3.052	3.176	3.304	3.436	3.572	3.713
6	3.138	3.297	3.463	3.635	3.815	4.001	4.196	4.398	4.608	4.827
7	3.797	4.023	4.259	4.508	4.768	5.042	5.329	5.629	5.945	6.275
8	4.595	4.908	5.239	5.589	5.960	6.353	6.767	7.206	7.669	8.157
9	5.560	5.987	6.444	6.931	7.451	8.004	8.595	9.223	9.893	10.604
10	6.727	7.305	7.926	8.594	9.313	10.086	10.915	11.806	12.761	13.786
11	8.140	8.912	9.749	10.657	11.642	12.708	13.862	15.112	16.462	17.921
12	9.850	10.872	11.991	13.215	14.552	16.012	17.605	19.343	21.236	23.298
13	11.918	13.264	14.749	16.386	18.190	20.175	22.359	24.759	27.395	30.287
14	14.421	16.182	18.141	20.319	22.737	25.420	28.395	31.691	35.339	39.373
15	17.449	19.742	22.314	25.195	28.422	32.030	36.062	40.565	45.587	51.185
16	21.113	24.085	27.446	31.242	35.527	40.357	45.799	51.923	58.808	66.541
17	25.547	29.384	33.758	38.740	44.409	50.850	58.165	66.461	75.862	86.503
18	30.912	35.848	41.523	48.038	55.511	64.071	73.869	85.070	97.862	112.454
19	37.404	43.735	51.073	59.567	69.389	80.730	93.813	108.890	126.242	146.190
20	45.258	53.357	62.820	73.863	86.736	101.720	119.143	139.379	162.852	190.047
21	54.762	65.095	77.268	91.591	108.420	128.167	151.312	178.405	210.079	247.061
22	66.262	79.416	95.040	113.572	135.525	161.490	192.165	228.358	271.002	321.178
23	80.178	96.887	116.899	140.829	169.407	203.477	244.050	292.298	349.592	417.531
24	97.015	118.203	143.786	174.628	211.758	256.381	309.943	374.141	450.974	542.791
25	117.388	144.207	176.857	216.539	264.698	323.040	393.628	478.901	581.756	705.627
30	304.471	389.748	497.904	634.810	807.793	1025.904	1300.477	1645.488	2078.208	2619.936
40	2048.309	2846.941	3946.340	5455.797	7523.156	10346.879	14195.051	19426.418	26520.723	36117.754
50	13779.844	20795.680	31278.301	46889.207	70064.812	104354.562	154942.687	229345.875	338440.000	497910.125

Period	31%	32%	33%	34%	35%	36%	37%	38%	39%	40%
1	1.310	1.320	1.330	1.340	1.350	1.360	1.370	1.380	1.390	1.400
2	1.716	1.742	1.769	1.796	1.822	1.850	1.877	1.904	1.932	1.960
3	2.248	2.300	2.353	2.406	2.460	2.515	2.571	2.628	2.686	2.744
4	2.945	3.036	3.129	3.224	3.321	3.421	3.523	3.627	3.733	3.842
5	3.858	4.007	4.162	4.320	4.484	4.653	4.826	5.005	5.189	5.378
6	5.054	5.290	5.535	5.789	6.053	6.328	6.612	6.907	7.213	7.530
7	6.621	6.983	7.361	7.758	8.172	8.605	9.058	9.531	10.025	10.541
8	8.673	9.217	9.791	10.395	11.032	11.703	12.410	13.153	13.935	14.758
9	11.362	12.166	13.022	13.930	14.894	15.917	17.001	18.151	19.370	20.661
10	14.884	16.060	17.319	18.666	20.106	21.646	23.292	25.049	26.924	28.925
11	19.498	21.199	23.034	25.012	27.144	29.439	31.910	34.567	37.425	40.495
12	25.542	27.982	30.635	33.516	36.644	40.037	43.716	47.703	52.020	56.694
13	33.460	36.937	40.745	44.912	49.469	54.451	59.892	65.830	72.308	79.371
14	43.832	48.756	54.190	60.181	66.784	74.053	82.051	90.845	100.509	111.119
15	57.420	64.358	72.073	80.643	90.158	100.712	112.410	125.366	139.707	155.567
16	75.220	84.953	95.857	108.061	121.713	136.968	154.002	173.005	194.192	217.793
17	98.539	112.138	127.490	144.802	164.312	186.277	210.983	238.747	269.927	304.911
18	129.086	148.022	169.561	194.035	221.822	253.337	289.046	329.471	375.198	426.875
19	169.102	195.389	225.517	260.006	299.459	344.537	395.993	454.669	521.525	597.625
20	221.523	257.913	299.937	348.408	404.270	468.571	542.511	627.443	724.919	836.674
21	290.196	340.446	398.916	466.867	545.764	637.256	743.240	865.871	1007.637	1171.343
22	380.156	449.388	530.558	625.601	736.781	866.668	1018.238	1194.900	1400.615	1639.878
23	498.004	593.192	705.642	838.305	994.653	1178.668	1394.986	1648.961	1946.854	2295.829
24	652.385	783.013	938.504	1123.328	1342.781	1602.988	1911.129	2275.564	2706.125	3214.158
25	854.623	1033.577	1248.210	1505.258	1812.754	2180.063	2618.245	3140.275	3761.511	4499.816
30	3297.081	4142.008	5194.516	6503.285	8128.426	10142.914	12636.086	15716.703	19517.969	24201.043
40	49072.621	66519.313	89962.188	121388.437	163433.875	219558.625	294317.937	393684.687	525508.312	700022.688

Table A-2 Future Value Interest Factor Annuity

Period	1%	2%	3%	4%	5%	6%	7%	8%	9%	10%
1	1.000	1.000	1.000	1.000	1.000	1.000	1.000	1.000	1.000	1.000
2	2.010	2.020	2.030	2.040	2.050	2.060	2.070	2.080	2.090	2.100
3	3.030	3.060	3.091	3.122	3.152	3.184	3.215	3.246	3.278	3.310
4	4.060	4.122	4.184	4.246	4.310	4.375	4.440	4.506	4.573	4.641
5	5.101	5.204	5.309	5.416	5.526	5.637	5.751	5.867	5.985	6.105
6	6.152	6.308	6.468	6.633	6.802	6.975	7.153	7.336	7.523	7.716
7	7.214	7.434	7.662	7.898	8.142	8.394	8.654	8.923	9.200	9.487
8	8.286	8.583	8.892	9.214	9.549	9.897	10.260	10.637	11.028	11.436
9	9.368	9.755	10.159	10.583	11.027	11.491	11.978	12.488	13.021	13.579
10	10.462	10.950	11.464	12.006	12.578	13.181	13.816	14.487	15.193	15.937
11	11.567	12.169	12.808	13.486	14.207	14.972	15.784	16.645	17.560	18.531
12	12.682	13.412	14.192	15.026	15.917	16.870	17.888	18.977	20.141	21.384
13	13.809	14.680	15.618	16.627	17.713	18.882	20.141	21.495	22.953	24.523
14	14.947	15.974	17.086	18.292	19.598	21.015	22.550	24.215	26.019	27.975
15	16.097	17.293	18.599	20.023	21.578	23.276	25.129	27.152	29.361	31.772
16	17.258	18.639	20.157	21.824	23.657	25.672	27.888	30.324	33.003	35.949
17	18.430	20.012	21.761	23.697	25.840	28.213	30.840	33.750	36.973	40.544
18	19.614	21.412	23.414	25.645	28.132	30.905	33.999	37.450	41.301	45.599
19	20.811	22.840	25.117	27.671	30.539	33.760	37.379	41.446	46.018	51.158
20	22.019	24.297	26.870	29.778	33.066	36.785	40.995	45.762	51.159	57.274
21	23.239	25.783	28.676	31.969	35.719	39.992	44.865	50.422	56.764	64.002
22	24.471	27.299	30.536	34.248	38.505	43.392	49.005	55.456	62.872	71.402
23	25.716	28.845	32.452	36.618	41.430	46.995	53.435	60.893	69.531	79.542
24	26.973	30.421	34.426	39.082	44.501	50.815	58.176	66.764	76.789	88.496
25	28.243	32.030	36.459	41.645	47.726	54.864	63.248	73.105	84.699	98.346
30	34.784	40.567	47.575	56.084	66.438	79.057	94.459	113.282	136.305	164.491
40	48.885	60.401	75.400	95.024	120.797	154.758	199.630	259.052	337.872	442.580
50	64.461	84.577	112.794	152.664	209.341	290.325	406.516	573.756	815.051	1163.865

Period	11%	12%	13%	14%	15%	16%	17%	18%	19%	20%
1	1.000	1.000	1.000	1.000	1.000	1.000	1.000	1.000	1.000	1.000
2	2.110	2.120	2.130	2.140	2.150	2.160	2.170	2.180	2.190	2.200
3	3.342	3.374	3.407	3.440	3.472	3.506	3.539	3.572	3.606	3.640
4	4.710	4.779	4.850	4.921	4.993	5.066	5.141	5.215	5.291	5.368
5	6.228	6.353	6.480	6.610	6.742	6.877	7.014	7.154	7.297	7.442
6	7.913	8.115	8.323	8.535	8.754	8.977	9.207	9.442	9.683	9.930
7	9.783	10.089	10.405	10.730	11.067	11.414	11.772	12.141	12.523	12.916
8	11.859	12.300	12.757	13.233	13.727	14.240	14.773	15.327	15.902	16.499
9	14.164	14.776	15.416	16.085	16.786	17.518	18.285	19.086	19.923	20.799
10	16.722	17.549	18.420	19.337	20.304	21.321	22.393	23.521	24.709	25.959
11	19.561	20.655	21.814	23.044	24.349	25.733	27.200	28.755	30.403	32.150
12	22.713	24.133	25.650	27.271	29.001	30.850	32.824	34.931	37.180	39.580
13	26.211	28.029	29.984	32.088	34.352	36.786	39.404	42.218	45.244	48.496
14	30.095	32.392	34.882	37.581	40.504	43.672	47.102	50.818	54.841	59.196
15	34.405	37.280	40.417	43.842	47.580	51.659	56.109	60.965	66.260	72.035
16	39.190	42.753	46.671	50.980	55.717	60.925	66.648	72.938	79.850	87.442
17	44.500	48.883	53.738	59.117	65.075	71.673	78.978	87.067	96.021	105.930
18	50.396	55.749	61.724	68.393	75.836	84.140	93.404	103.739	115.265	128.116
19	56.939	63.439	70.748	78.968	88.211	98.603	110.283	123.412	138.165	154.739
20	64.202	72.052	80.946	91.024	102.443	115.379	130.031	146.626	165.417	186.687
21	72.264	81.698	92.468	104.767	118.809	134.840	153.136	174.019	197.846	225.024
22	81.213	92.502	105.489	120.434	137.630	157.414	180.169	206.342	236.436	271.028
23	91.147	104.602	120.203	138.295	159.274	183.600	211.798	244.483	282.359	326.234
24	102.173	118.154	136.829	158.656	184.166	213.976	248.803	289.490	337.007	392.480
25	114.412	133.333	155.616	181.867	212.790	249.212	292.099	342.598	402.038	471.976
30	199.018	241.330	293.192	356.778	434.738	530.306	647.423	790.932	966.698	1181.865
40	581.812	767.080	1013.667	1341.979	1779.048	2360.724	3134.412	4163.094	5529.711	7343.715
50	1668.723	2399.975	3459.344	4994.301	7217.488	10435.449	15088.805	21812.273	31514.492	45496.094

Period	21%	22%	23%	24%	25%	26%	27%	28%	29%	30%
1	1.000	1.000	1.000	1.000	1.000	1.000	1.000	1.000	1.000	1.000
2	2.210	2.220	2.230	2.240	2.250	2.260	2.270	2.280	2.290	2.300
3	3.674	3.708	3.743	3.778	3.813	3.848	3.883	3.918	3.954	3.990
4	5.446	5.524	5.604	5.684	5.766	5.848	5.931	6.016	6.101	6.187
5	7.589	7.740	7.893	8.048	8.207	8.368	8.533	8.700	8.870	9.043
6	10.183	10.442	10.708	10.980	11.259	11.544	11.837	12.136	12.442	12.756
7	13.321	13.740	14.171	14.615	15.073	15.546	16.032	16.534	17.051	17.583
8	17.119	17.762	18.430	19.123	19.842	20.588	21.361	22.163	22.995	23.858
9	21.714	22.670	23.669	24.712	25.802	26.940	28.129	29.369	30.664	32.015
10	27.274	28.657	30.113	31.643	33.253	34.945	36.723	38.592	40.556	42.619
11	34.001	35.962	38.039	40.238	42.566	45.030	47.639	50.398	53.318	56.405
12	42.141	44.873	47.787	50.895	54.208	57.738	61.501	65.510	69.780	74.326
13	51.991	55.745	59.778	64.109	68.760	73.750	79.106	84.853	91.016	97.624
14	63.909	69.009	74.528	80.496	86.949	93.925	101.465	109.611	118.411	127.912
15	78.330	85.191	92.669	100.815	109.687	119.346	129.860	141.302	153.750	167.285
16	95.779	104.933	114.983	126.010	138.109	151.375	165.922	181.867	199.337	218.470
17	116.892	129.019	142.428	157.252	173.636	191.733	211.721	233.790	258.145	285.011
18	142.439	158.403	176.187	195.993	218.045	242.583	269.885	300.250	334.006	371.514
19	173.351	194.251	217.710	244.031	273.556	306.654	343.754	385.321	431.868	483.968
20	210.755	237.986	268.783	303.598	342.945	387.384	437.568	494.210	558.110	630.157
21	256.013	291.343	331.603	377.461	429.681	489.104	556.710	633.589	720.962	820.204
22	310.775	356.438	408.871	469.052	538.101	617.270	708.022	811.993	931.040	1067.265
23	377.038	435.854	503.911	582.624	673.626	778.760	900.187	1040.351	1202.042	1388.443
24	457.215	532.741	620.810	723.453	843.032	982.237	1144.237	1332.649	1551.634	1805.975
25	554.230	650.944	764.596	898.082	1054.791	1238.617	1454.180	1706.790	2002.608	2348.765
30	1445.111	1767.044	2160.459	2640.881	3227.172	3941.953	4812.891	5873.172	7162.785	8729.805
40	9749.141	12936.141	17153.691	22728.367	30088.621	39791.957	52570.707	69376.562	91447.375	120389.375

Period	31%	32%	33%	34%	35%	36%	37%	38%	39%	40%
1	1.000	1.000	1.000	1.000	1.000	1.000	1.000	1.000	1.000	1.000
2	2.310	2.320	2.330	2.340	2.350	2.360	2.370	2.380	2.390	2.400
3	4.026	4.062	4.099	4.136	4.172	4.210	4.247	4.284	4.322	4.360
4	6.274	6.362	6.452	6.542	6.633	6.725	6.818	6.912	7.008	7.104
5	9.219	9.398	9.581	9.766	9.954	10.146	10.341	10.539	10.741	10.946
6	13.077	13.406	13.742	14.086	14.438	14.799	15.167	15.544	15.930	16.324
7	18.131	18.696	19.277	19.876	20.492	21.126	21.779	22.451	23.142	23.853
8	24.752	25.678	26.638	27.633	28.664	29.732	30.837	31.982	33.167	34.395
9	33.425	34.895	36.429	38.028	39.696	41.435	43.247	45.135	47.103	49.152
10	44.786	47.062	49.451	51.958	54.590	57.351	60.248	63.287	66.473	69.813
11	59.670	63.121	66.769	70.624	74.696	78.998	83.540	88.335	93.397	98.739
12	79.167	84.320	89.803	95.636	101.840	108.437	115.450	122.903	130.822	139.234
13	104.709	112.302	120.438	129.152	138.484	148.474	159.166	170.606	182.842	195.928
14	138.169	149.239	161.183	174.063	187.953	202.925	219.058	236.435	255.151	275.299
15	182.001	197.996	215.373	234.245	254.737	276.978	301.109	327.281	355.659	386.418
16	239.421	262.354	287.446	314.888	344.895	377.690	413.520	452.647	495.366	541.985
17	314.642	347.307	383.303	422.949	466.608	514.658	567.521	625.652	689.558	759.778
18	413.180	459.445	510.792	567.751	630.920	700.935	778.504	864.399	959.485	1064.689
19	542.266	607.467	680.354	761.786	852.741	954.271	1067.551	1193.870	1334.683	1491.563
20	711.368	802.856	905.870	1021.792	1152.200	1298.809	1463.544	1648.539	1856.208	2089.188
21	932.891	1060.769	1205.807	1370.201	1556.470	1767.380	2006.055	2275.982	2581.128	2925.862
22	1223.087	1401.215	1604.724	1837.068	2102.234	2404.636	2749.294	3141.852	3588.765	4097.203
23	1603.243	1850.603	2135.282	2462.669	2839.014	3271.304	3767.532	4336.750	4989.379	5737.078
24	2101.247	2443.795	2840.924	3300.974	3833.667	4449.969	5162.516	5985.711	6936.230	8032.906
25	2753.631	3226.808	3779.428	4424.301	5176.445	6052.957	7073.645	8261.273	9642.352	11247.062
30	10632.543	12940.672	15737.945	19124.434	23221.258	28172.016	34148.906	41357.227	50043.625	60500.207

Table A-3   Present Value Interest Factor

Period	1%	2%	3%	4%	5%	6%	7%	8%	9%	10%
1	.990	.980	.971	.962	.952	.943	.935	.926	.917	.909
2	.980	.961	.943	.925	.907	.890	.873	.857	.842	.826
3	.971	.942	.915	.889	.864	.840	.816	.794	.772	.751
4	.961	.924	.888	.855	.823	.792	.763	.735	.708	.683
5	.951	.906	.863	.822	.784	.747	.713	.681	.650	.621
6	.942	.888	.837	.790	.746	.705	.666	.630	.596	.564
7	.933	.871	.813	.760	.711	.665	.623	.583	.547	.513
8	.923	.853	.789	.731	.677	.627	.582	.540	.502	.467
9	.914	.837	.766	.703	.645	.592	.544	.500	.460	.424
10	.905	.820	.744	.676	.614	.558	.508	.463	.422	.386
11	.896	.804	.722	.650	.585	.527	.475	.429	.388	.350
12	.887	.789	.701	.625	.557	.497	.444	.397	.356	.319
13	.879	.773	.681	.601	.530	.469	.415	.368	.326	.290
14	.870	.758	.661	.577	.505	.442	.388	.340	.299	.263
15	.861	.743	.642	.555	.481	.417	.362	.315	.275	.239
16	.853	.728	.623	.534	.458	.394	.339	.292	.252	.218
17	.844	.714	.605	.513	.436	.371	.317	.270	.231	.198
18	.836	.700	.587	.494	.416	.350	.296	.250	.212	.180
19	.828	.686	.570	.475	.396	.331	.277	.232	.194	.164
20	.820	.673	.554	.456	.377	.312	.258	.215	.178	.149
21	.811	.660	.538	.439	.359	.294	.242	.199	.164	.135
22	.803	.647	.522	.422	.342	.278	.226	.184	.150	.123
23	.795	.634	.507	.406	.326	.262	.211	.170	.138	.112
24	.788	.622	.492	.390	.310	.247	.197	.158	.126	.102
25	.780	.610	.478	.375	.295	.233	.184	.146	.116	.092
30	.742	.552	.412	.308	.231	.174	.131	.099	.075	.057
40	.672	.453	.307	.208	.142	.097	.067	.046	.032	.022
50	.608	.372	.228	.141	.087	.054	.034	.021	.013	.009

Period	11%	12%	13%	14%	15%	16%	17%	18%	19%	20%
1	.901	.893	.885	.877	.870	.862	.855	.847	.840	.833
2	.812	.797	.783	.769	.756	.743	.731	.718	.706	.694
3	.731	.712	.693	.675	.658	.641	.624	.609	.593	.579
4	.659	.636	.613	.592	.572	.552	.534	.516	.499	.482
5	.593	.567	.543	.519	.497	.476	.456	.437	.419	.402
6	.535	.507	.480	.456	.432	.410	.390	.370	.352	.335
7	.482	.452	.425	.400	.376	.354	.333	.314	.296	.279
8	.434	.404	.376	.351	.327	.305	.285	.266	.249	.233
9	.391	.361	.333	.308	.284	.263	.243	.225	.209	.194
10	.352	.322	.295	.270	.247	.227	.208	.191	.176	.162
11	.317	.287	.261	.237	.215	.195	.178	.162	.148	.135
12	.286	.257	.231	.208	.187	.168	.152	.137	.124	.112
13	.258	.229	.204	.182	.163	.145	.130	.116	.104	.093
14	.232	.205	.181	.160	.141	.125	.111	.099	.088	.078
15	.209	.183	.160	.140	.123	.108	.095	.084	.074	.065
16	.188	.163	.141	.123	.107	.093	.081	.071	.062	.054
17	.170	.146	.125	.108	.093	.080	.069	.060	.052	.045
18	.153	.130	.111	.095	.081	.069	.059	.051	.044	.038
19	.138	.116	.098	.083	.070	.060	.051	.043	.037	.031
20	.124	.104	.087	.073	.061	.051	.043	.037	.031	.026
21	.112	.093	.077	.064	.053	.044	.037	.031	.026	.022
22	.101	.083	.068	.056	.046	.038	.032	.026	.022	.018
23	.091	.074	.060	.049	.040	.033	.027	.022	.018	.015
24	.082	.066	.053	.043	.035	.028	.023	.019	.015	.013
25	.074	.059	.047	.038	.030	.024	.020	.016	.013	.010
30	.044	.033	.026	.020	.015	.012	.009	.007	.005	.004
40	.015	.011	.008	.005	.004	.003	.002	.001	.001	.001
50	.005	.003	.002	.001	.001	.001	.000	.000	.000	.000

Period	21%	22%	23%	24%	25%	26%	27%	28%	29%	30%
1	.826	.820	.813	.806	.800	.794	.787	.781	.775	.769
2	.683	.672	.661	.650	.640	.630	.620	.610	.601	.592
3	.564	.551	.537	.524	.512	.500	.488	.477	.466	.455
4	.467	.451	.437	.423	.410	.397	.384	.373	.361	.350
5	.386	.370	.355	.341	.328	.315	.303	.291	.280	.269
6	.319	.303	.289	.275	.262	.250	.238	.227	.217	.207
7	.263	.249	.235	.222	.210	.198	.188	.178	.168	.159
8	.218	.204	.191	.179	.168	.157	.148	.139	.130	.123
9	.180	.167	.155	.144	.134	.125	.116	.108	.101	.094
10	.149	.137	.126	.116	.107	.099	.092	.085	.078	.073
11	.123	.112	.103	.094	.086	.079	.072	.066	.061	.056
12	.102	.092	.083	.076	.069	.062	.057	.052	.047	.043
13	.084	.075	.068	.061	.055	.050	.045	.040	.037	.033
14	.069	.062	.055	.049	.044	.039	.035	.032	.028	.025
15	.057	.051	.045	.040	.035	.031	.028	.025	.022	.020
16	.047	.042	.036	.032	.028	.025	.022	.019	.017	.015
17	.039	.034	.030	.026	.023	.020	.017	.015	.013	.012
18	.032	.028	.024	.021	.018	.016	.014	.012	.010	.009
19	.027	.023	.020	.017	.014	.012	.011	.009	.008	.007
20	.022	.019	.016	.014	.012	.010	.008	.007	.006	.005
21	.018	.015	.013	.011	.009	.008	.007	.006	.005	.004
22	.015	.013	.011	.009	.007	.006	.005	.004	.004	.003
23	.012	.010	.009	.007	.006	.005	.004	.003	.003	.002
24	.010	.008	.007	.006	.005	.004	.003	.003	.002	.002
25	.009	.007	.006	.005	.004	.003	.003	.002	.002	.001
30	.003	.003	.002	.002	.001	.001	.001	.001	.000	.000
40	.000	.000	.000	.000	.000	.000	.000	.000	.000	.000
50	.000	.000	.000	.000	.000	.000	.000	.000	.000	.000

Period	31%	32%	33%	34%	35%	36%	37%	38%	39%	40%
1	.763	.758	.752	.746	.741	.735	.730	.725	.719	.714
2	.583	.574	.565	.557	.549	.541	.533	.525	.518	.510
3	.445	.435	.425	.416	.406	.398	.389	.381	.372	.364
4	.340	.329	.320	.310	.301	.292	.284	.276	.268	.260
5	.259	.250	.240	.231	.223	.215	.207	.200	.193	.186
6	.198	.189	.181	.173	.165	.158	.151	.145	.139	.133
7	.151	.143	.136	.129	.122	.116	.110	.105	.100	.095
8	.115	.108	.102	.096	.091	.085	.081	.076	.072	.068
9	.088	.082	.077	.072	.067	.063	.059	.055	.052	.048
10	.067	.062	.058	.054	.050	.046	.043	.040	.037	.035
11	.051	.047	.043	.040	.037	.034	.031	.029	.027	.025
12	.039	.036	.033	.030	.027	.025	.023	.021	.019	.018
13	.030	.027	.025	.022	.020	.018	.017	.015	.014	.013
14	.023	.021	.018	.017	.015	.014	.012	.011	.010	.009
15	.017	.016	.014	.012	.011	.010	.009	.008	.007	.006
16	.013	.012	.010	.009	.008	.007	.006	.006	.005	.005
17	.010	.009	.008	.007	.006	.005	.005	.004	.004	.003
18	.008	.007	.006	.005	.005	.004	.003	.003	.003	.002
19	.006	.005	.004	.004	.003	.003	.003	.002	.002	.002
20	.005	.004	.003	.003	.002	.002	.002	.002	.001	.001
21	.003	.003	.003	.002	.002	.002	.001	.001	.001	.001
22	.003	.002	.002	.002	.001	.001	.001	.001	.001	.001
23	.002	.002	.001	.001	.001	.001	.001	.001	.001	.000
24	.002	.001	.001	.001	.001	.001	.001	.000	.000	.000
25	.001	.001	.001	.001	.001	.000	.000	.000	.000	.000
30	.000	.000	.000	.000	.000	.000	.000	.000	.000	.000
40	.000	.000	.000	.000	.000	.000	.000	.000	.000	.000

Table A-4   Present Value Interest Factor Annuity

Period	1%	2%	3%	4%	5%	6%	7%	8%	9%	10%
1	.990	.980	.971	.962	.952	.943	.935	.926	.917	.909
2	1.970	1.942	1.913	1.886	1.859	1.833	1.808	1.783	1.759	1.736
3	2.941	2.884	2.829	2.775	2.723	2.673	2.624	2.577	2.531	2.487
4	3.902	3.808	3.717	3.630	3.546	3.465	3.387	3.312	3.240	3.170
5	4.853	4.713	4.580	4.452	4.329	4.212	4.100	3.993	3.890	3.791
6	5.795	5.601	5.417	5.242	5.076	4.917	4.767	4.623	4.486	4.355
7	6.728	6.472	6.230	6.002	5.786	5.582	5.389	5.206	5.033	4.868
8	7.652	7.326	7.020	6.733	6.463	6.210	5.971	5.747	5.535	5.335
9	8.566	8.162	7.786	7.435	7.108	6.802	6.515	6.247	5.995	5.759
10	9.471	8.983	8.530	8.111	7.722	7.360	7.024	6.710	6.418	6.145
11	10.368	9.787	9.253	8.760	8.306	7.887	7.499	7.139	6.805	6.495
12	11.255	10.575	9.954	9.385	8.863	8.384	7.943	7.536	7.161	6.814
13	12.134	11.348	10.635	9.986	9.394	8.853	8.358	7.904	7.487	7.103
14	13.004	12.106	11.296	10.563	9.899	9.295	8.746	8.244	7.786	7.367
15	13.865	12.849	11.938	11.118	10.380	9.712	9.108	8.560	8.061	7.606
16	14.718	13.578	12.561	11.652	10.838	10.106	9.447	8.851	8.313	7.824
17	15.562	14.292	13.166	12.166	11.274	10.477	9.763	9.122	8.544	8.022
18	16.398	14.992	13.754	12.659	11.690	10.828	10.059	9.372	8.756	8.201
19	17.226	15.679	14.324	13.134	12.085	11.158	10.336	9.604	8.950	8.365
20	18.046	16.352	14.878	13.590	12.462	11.470	10.594	9.818	9.129	8.514
21	18.857	17.011	15.415	14.029	12.821	11.764	10.836	10.017	9.292	8.649
22	19.661	17.658	15.937	14.451	13.163	12.042	11.061	10.201	9.442	8.772
23	20.456	18.292	16.444	14.857	13.489	12.303	11.272	10.371	9.580	8.883
24	21.244	18.914	16.936	15.247	13.799	12.550	11.469	10.529	9.707	8.985
25	22.023	19.524	17.413	15.622	14.094	12.783	11.654	10.675	9.823	9.077
30	25.808	22.397	19.601	17.292	15.373	13.765	12.409	11.258	10.274	9.427
40	32.835	27.356	23.115	19.793	17.159	15.046	13.332	11.925	10.757	9.779
50	39.197	31.424	25.730	21.482	18.256	15.762	13.801	12.234	10.962	9.915

Period	11%	12%	13%	14%	15%	16%	17%	18%	19%	20%
1	.901	.893	.885	.877	.870	.862	.855	.847	.840	.833
2	1.713	1.690	1.668	1.647	1.626	1.605	1.585	1.566	1.547	1.528
3	2.444	2.402	2.361	2.322	2.283	2.246	2.210	2.174	2.140	2.106
4	3.102	3.037	2.974	2.914	2.855	2.798	2.743	2.690	2.639	2.589
5	3.696	3.605	3.517	3.433	3.352	3.274	3.199	3.127	3.058	2.991
6	4.231	4.111	3.998	3.889	3.784	3.685	3.589	3.498	3.410	3.326
7	4.712	4.564	4.423	4.288	4.160	4.039	3.922	3.812	3.706	3.605
8	5.146	4.968	4.799	4.639	4.487	4.344	4.207	4.078	3.954	3.837
9	5.537	5.328	5.132	4.946	4.772	4.607	4.451	4.303	4.163	4.031
10	5.889	5.650	5.426	5.216	5.019	4.833	4.659	4.494	4.339	4.192
11	6.207	5.938	5.687	5.453	5.234	5.029	4.836	4.656	4.487	4.327
12	6.492	6.194	5.918	5.660	5.421	5.197	4.988	4.793	4.611	4.439
13	6.750	6.424	6.122	5.842	5.583	5.342	5.118	4.910	4.715	4.533
14	6.982	6.628	6.303	6.002	5.724	5.468	5.229	5.008	4.802	4.611
15	7.191	6.811	6.462	6.142	5.847	5.575	5.324	5.092	4.876	4.675
16	7.379	6.974	6.604	6.265	5.954	5.669	5.405	5.162	4.938	4.730
17	7.549	7.120	6.729	6.373	6.047	5.749	5.475	5.222	4.990	4.775
18	7.702	7.250	6.840	6.467	6.128	5.818	5.534	5.273	5.033	4.812
19	7.839	7.366	6.938	6.550	6.198	5.877	5.585	5.316	5.070	4.843
20	7.963	7.469	7.025	6.623	6.259	5.929	5.628	5.353	5.101	4.870
21	8.075	7.562	7.102	6.687	6.312	5.973	5.665	5.384	5.127	4.891
22	8.176	7.645	7.170	6.743	6.359	6.011	5.696	5.410	5.149	4.909
23	8.266	7.718	7.230	6.792	6.399	6.044	5.723	5.432	5.167	4.925
24	8.348	7.784	7.283	6.835	6.434	6.073	5.747	5.451	5.182	4.937
25	8.442	7.843	7.330	6.873	6.464	6.097	5.766	5.467	5.195	4.948
30	8.694	8.055	7.496	7.003	6.566	6.177	5.829	5.517	5.235	4.979
40	8.951	8.244	7.634	7.105	6.642	6.233	5.871	5.548	5.258	4.997
50	9.042	8.305	7.675	7.133	6.661	6.246	5.880	5.554	5.262	4.999

Period	21%	22%	23%	24%	25%	26%	27%	28%	29%	30%
1	.826	.820	.813	.806	.800	.794	.787	.781	.775	.769
2	1.509	1.492	1.474	1.457	1.440	1.424	1.407	1.392	1.376	1.361
3	2.074	2.042	2.011	1.981	1.952	1.923	1.896	1.868	1.842	1.816
4	2.540	2.494	2.448	2.404	2.362	2.320	2.280	2.241	2.203	2.166
5	2.926	2.864	2.803	2.745	2.689	2.635	2.583	2.532	2.483	2.436
6	3.245	3.167	3.092	3.020	2.951	2.885	2.821	2.759	2.700	2.643
7	3.508	3.416	3.327	3.242	3.161	3.083	3.009	2.937	2.868	2.802
8	3.726	3.619	3.518	3.421	3.329	3.241	3.156	3.076	2.999	2.925
9	3.905	3.786	3.673	3.566	3.463	3.366	3.273	3.184	3.100	3.019
10	4.054	3.923	3.799	3.682	3.570	3.465	3.364	3.269	3.178	3.092
11	4.177	4.035	3.902	3.776	3.656	3.544	3.437	3.335	3.239	3.147
12	4.278	4.127	3.985	3.851	3.725	3.606	3.493	3.387	3.286	3.190
13	4.362	4.203	4.053	3.912	3.780	3.656	3.538	3.427	3.322	3.223
14	4.432	4.265	4.108	3.962	3.824	3.695	3.573	3.459	3.351	3.249
15	4.489	4.315	4.153	4.001	3.859	3.726	3.601	3.483	3.373	3.268
16	4.536	4.357	4.189	4.033	3.887	3.751	3.623	3.503	3.390	3.283
17	4.576	4.391	4.219	4.059	3.910	3.771	3.640	3.518	3.403	3.295
18	4.608	4.419	4.243	4.080	3.928	3.786	3.654	3.529	3.413	3.304
19	4.635	4.442	4.263	4.097	3.942	3.799	3.664	3.539	3.421	3.311
20	4.657	4.460	4.279	4.110	3.954	3.808	3.673	3.546	3.427	3.316
21	4.675	4.476	4.292	4.121	3.963	3.816	3.679	3.551	3.432	3.320
22	4.690	4.488	4.302	4.130	3.970	3.822	3.684	3.556	3.436	3.323
23	4.703	4.499	4.311	4.137	3.976	3.827	3.689	3.559	3.438	3.325
24	4.713	4.507	4.318	4.143	3.981	3.831	3.692	3.562	3.441	3.327
25	4.721	4.514	4.323	4.147	3.985	3.834	3.694	3.564	3.442	3.329
30	4.746	4.534	4.339	4.160	3.995	3.842	3.701	3.569	3.447	3.332
40	4.760	4.544	4.347	4.166	3.999	3.846	3.703	3.571	3.448	3.333
50	4.762	4.545	4.348	4.167	4.000	3.846	3.704	3.571	3.448	3.333

Period	31%	32%	33%	34%	35%	36%	37%	38%	39%	40%
1	.763	.758	.752	.746	.741	.735	.730	.725	.719	.714
2	1.346	1.331	1.317	1.303	1.289	1.276	1.263	1.250	1.237	1.224
3	1.791	1.766	1.742	1.719	1.696	1.673	1.652	1.630	1.609	1.589
4	2.130	2.096	2.062	2.029	1.997	1.966	1.935	1.906	1.877	1.849
5	2.390	2.345	2.302	2.260	2.220	2.181	2.143	2.106	2.070	2.035
6	2.588	2.534	2.483	2.433	2.385	2.339	2.294	2.251	2.209	2.168
7	2.739	2.677	2.619	2.562	2.508	2.455	2.404	2.355	2.308	2.263
8	2.854	2.786	2.721	2.658	2.598	2.540	2.485	2.432	2.380	2.331
9	2.942	2.868	2.798	2.730	2.665	2.603	2.544	2.487	2.432	2.379
10	3.009	2.930	2.855	2.784	2.715	2.649	2.587	2.527	2.469	2.414
11	3.060	2.978	2.899	2.824	2.752	2.683	2.618	2.555	2.496	2.438
12	3.100	3.013	2.931	2.853	2.779	2.708	2.641	2.576	2.515	2.456
13	3.129	3.040	2.956	2.876	2.799	2.727	2.658	2.592	2.529	2.469
14	3.152	3.061	2.974	2.892	2.814	2.740	2.670	2.603	2.539	2.477
15	3.170	3.076	2.988	2.905	2.825	2.750	2.679	2.611	2.546	2.484
16	3.183	3.088	2.999	2.914	2.834	2.757	2.685	2.616	2.551	2.489
17	3.193	3.097	3.007	2.921	2.840	2.763	2.690	2.621	2.555	2.492
18	3.201	3.104	3.012	2.926	2.844	2.767	2.693	2.624	2.557	2.494
19	3.207	3.109	3.017	2.930	2.848	2.770	2.696	2.626	2.559	2.496
20	3.211	3.113	3.020	2.933	2.850	2.772	2.698	2.627	2.561	2.497
21	3.215	3.116	3.023	2.935	2.852	2.773	2.699	2.629	2.562	2.498
22	3.217	3.118	3.025	2.936	2.853	2.775	2.700	2.629	2.562	2.498
23	3.219	3.120	3.026	2.938	2.854	2.775	2.701	2.630	2.563	2.499
24	3.221	3.121	3.027	2.939	2.855	2.776	2.701	2.630	2.563	2.499
25	3.222	3.122	3.028	2.939	2.856	2.776	2.702	2.631	2.563	2.499
30	3.225	3.124	3.030	2.941	2.857	2.777	2.702	2.631	2.564	2.500
40	3.226	3.125	3.030	2.941	2.857	2.778	2.703	2.632	2.564	2.500
50	3.226	3.125	3.030	2.941	2.857	2.778	2.703	2.632	2.564	2.500

GLOSSARY

accelerated method of depreciation an accounting method whereby part of the cost of a fixed asset is charged off yearly at faster rates than under the straight-line method, where equal amounts are charged off each year over the life of the asset

Acceleration Cost Recovery System the depreciation method that must be used for tax purposes on all assets acquired later than 1980

acid test or quick ratio current assets, less inventories, divided by current liabilities

aggressive approach a method of financing in which fixed assets and only part of the minimum level of current assets are financed by long-term debt and equity

amortization the gradual, planned reduction in value of capital expenditures

arbitrage taking advantage of temporary differences in market prices. This is done by buying in the cheap market and then selling in the higher-priced market.

average collection period the number of days required, on average, to collect accounts receivable (a measure of how effectively the firm is getting customers to pay the credit it gives them when they purchase merchandise)

average payment period the number of days, on average, within which a firm pays off its accounts payables

average rate of return (*ARR*) the ratio of average net earnings to average investment

balance of payments a document showing all payments and receipts of a country vis-à-vis the rest of the world for a year

balance sheet an accounting statement that displays the assets, liabilities, and equity of a firm

beta an indicator of the riskiness of a stock's returns, as compared to the riskiness of general market returns. A beta of 1.0 indicates the same risk as the general market; a beta lower than 1.0 is less risky, and a beta higher than 1.0 is more risky, than the market

bond a long-term debt security issued by a borrower, either a public or private institution

book value (of a firm) assets minus liabilities

book value weights valuation of a firm's financial structure according to the book values of its securities

break-even approach a method used to evaluate the point where sales equal operating costs. It serves as a guideline to determine the profitability of a firm.

call option an option that gives the holder the right to buy

call option buyer an investor who speculates that the price of a stock will increase beyond a strike price

call price the price at which an issuing firm may call in its bonds. Usually the call price is set above the par value and in the case of convertible bonds is a feature used to force conversion into common stock.

capital the net worth of a company's assets

capital account an account in the balance of payments that shows the net capital inflows and outflows resulting from various types of investment

capital appreciation the percentage upward change in the price of an asset, such as a stock, from one period to another

Capital Asset Pricing Model (CAPM) a theoretical concept that measures the required rate of return of an asset by taking into account the sensitivity of other assets' returns to market returns

capital budgeting a method for evaluating, comparing, and selecting projects to achieve the best long-term financial return

capital expenditures long-term expenditures that are amortized over a period of time determined by IRS regulations

capital gains profits from the resale of assets that have been held longer than 6 months

capital impairment rule a requirement in most states that firms limit the payment of cash dividends. This is generally done to protect the claims of creditors in case of insolvency.

capitalization rate the discount rate employed to determine the value of earnings as dividends

capital lease a long-term lease, usually extending over 6 years or more

capital structure the financing mix of a firm. The more debt in relation to equity, the more financial leverage the firm is said to have.

cash cycle the number of days between the purchase of raw materials and the collection of sales proceeds for finished goods

cash flow a measure of a company's liquidity, consisting of net income plus noncash expenditures (such as depreciation charges)

cash turnover the number of times a firm's cash is collected in a year

certainty equivalent factor a factor used to convert projected cash flows into certain cash flows

coefficient of variation a statistical factor that measures the relative variability of risk and return; it is calculated by dividing the standard deviation of outcomes by the mean expected value of returns

common equity the value of common stock issued by the firm. Common stockholders are the owners of the equity in the firm and are the last to receive payment in case of insolvency.

conservative approach a method of financing in which long-term loans and equity are used to finance fixed assets and the minimum level of current assets

contingency payments monetary incentives offered to target company managers as inducements to merge

contractual obligations restrictions on dividend payments that a firm may agree to in a contract with a creditor

contribution margin selling price less variable cost

conversion premium the difference between the current price of a firm's stock and the conversion price of a convertible security

conversion price the stock price at which a convertible security may be exchanged for common stock. It is found by dividing the par value of the security by the conversion ratio.

conversion ratio the number of shares of stock for which a convertible security can be exchanged. It is calculated by dividing the par value by the conversion price.

conversion value the current market price of a firm's stock multiplied by the conversion ratio

convertible bond a security that gives its owner the option to exchange it for a specified number of shares of common stock

corporation a form of organization that is a legal entity and whose owners have limited liability

correlation coefficient a measure of the degree of relationship between one variable and another

cost of capital (CC) the rate a firm must pay to investors in order to induce them to purchase the firm's stock and/or bonds

coupon rate the rate of interest received by a bondholder on an annual, semiannual, or quarterly basis

covariance the degree of correlation between the returns of one asset and those of another asset

current account a combined account in the balance of payments that reflects the sum of the trade account and service account balances

current expenditures short-term expenditures that are completely charged to income the year in which they occur

current ratio current assets divided by current liabilities (a liquidity measure)

cutoff rate the standard discount rate chosen by a firm, against which the profitabilities of potential projects are measured

debt/capitalization (D/C) ratio the ratio of a firm's debt to its capitalization. The higher this ratio, the greater the risk and the financial leverage.

debt equity (D/E) ratio the ratio of a firm's debt to its equity. The higher this ratio, the greater the financial leverage of the firm.

degree of financial leverage the extent to which EPS will change, given a change in EBIT. High financial leverage means high financial exposure and a greater risk that the firm may not be able to meet its debt obligations.

depreciation the allocation of an asset's cost, for tax or management purposes, based on its age

direct investment investment in a foreign asset representing at least 10% ownership

discount rate the required rate of return that a firm must achieve to justify its investments

dividend a return on an investment, usually in the form of cash or stock. Directors decide periodically to declare (or to forgo) dividends, and they set the amount to be paid and the form of the dividend.

dividend income income generated by the receipt of dividends from another company's stock held by the firm

dividend yield the annual dividend payment divided by the market price of a share of the stock

double-declining balance method a method that uses a constant rate (usually double the straight-line ratio) to depreciate the book value of an asset

EBIT earnings before interest and taxes

economic order quantity (EOQ) the quantity of an item that, when ordered regularly, minimizes ordering and storage costs

economies of scale the increasing returns derived from spreading output over a fixed amount of assets, capacity, or investment. These gains are derived from research or from highly efficient machinery.

efficient frontier sophisticated mathematical curve, using quadratic programming, that calculates the optimal maximum expected returns at different levels of risk or standard deviations.

EPS earnings per share

EPS-EBIT approach a method for choosing between equity and debt financing

equivalent purchasing cost the discount rate that makes the present value of lease payments and lost tax benefits equal to the purchase price of an asset

Eurodollars U.S. dollars traded outside U.S. borders

ex dividend without dividend; used with reference to a share of stock purchased after a dividend was declared

exercise price the pre-established price at which warrant holders may purchase common stock. The initial exercise price is usually above the current market price of the stock at the time the warrant or option is issued.

expected return the future receipts that investors anticipate from their investments

expiration date the date when a call or put option comes due. After the expiration date options become worthless.

external sources of funds current debts, long-term borrowing, preferred stock, and common stock

face value the value of a bond at maturity, also called the nominal, or par, value

finance the application of a series of economic principles to maximize the wealth, or overall value, of a firm

financial analysis evaluation of the income and balance sheet statements

financial lease See capital lease.

financial leverage the use of debt to finance investments

financial planning the process of estimating a firm's fund needs and deciding how to finance those funds

flotation costs fees paid to intermediaries who help a firm issue stocks and bonds

foreign currency futures a formal contract to sell or to buy a certain amount of foreign currency at a specified rate for delivery at a future time

foreign currency option a contract that gives the purchaser the right to buy or sell a fixed amount of currency at a fixed rate on or before a specified expiration date

foreign exchange rate the price at which the currency of one country can be bought with the currency of another country

forward transaction a transaction that involves the buying or selling of a foreign currency at a specified price for delivery at a future date

future value the value of an initial investment after a specified period of time at a certain rate of interest

general partnership a partnership in which all partners have unlimited liability for future obligations

geographical arbitrage a type of arbitrage that occurs when the price of a given foreign currency in one market is different from the price in another market

golden parachute large compensation package given to senior management; it provides generous benefits if the firm is taken over and the executive loses his or her job. Payment guaranteed top officers.

goodwill the intangible assets of a firm, calculated as the excess purchase price paid over book value

greenmail payment made by a takeover target company to a holder of a large block of company stock who is regarded as a corporate raider. To induce the raider to go away, the company offers to buy his shares at a price substantially higher than the current market value.

income statement an accounting statement of a firm's sales, operating costs, and financial charges

inflation a general price increase in the economy

insolvency the inability to repay debt

internal rate of return (*IRR*) the discount rate that makes the net present value of a project equal to zero

internally generated funds monies that a firm generates from retained earnings and depreciation

international firm a firm that exports or imports goods and/or services or has overseas activities

intrinsic value the value of an asset or a firm, as perceived by an investor, a manager, or anyone else, based on the person's judgment of all the facts at hand; also, the difference between the exercise price of a put or call option and the market value of the underlying stock

inventory management the process of determining and maintaining the optimal inventory levels

inventory turnover ratio the costs of goods sold divided by the inventory. Usually, the faster the turnover, the better for a firm.

investment value of convertibles the straight bond value of convertibles; the price at which a convertible would sell in the absence of its convertibility

junk bond unsecured debenture with an assigned rating of Baa or lower. It features yields 3% to 5% higher than good quality bonds. Many of these bonds are issued by acquiring companies to finance a merger.

lease a legal contract under which the owner of an asset gives the right to use the asset to another party for a certain period of time in return for a specified payment

lessee the user of an asset that is leased from another party

lessor the owner of an asset that is leased to another party

leverage leasing involves a lessor who does not buy the equipment outright. The lessor puts up roughly 20% to 25% of the purchase price; the rest of the funds are supplied by lenders.

limited partnership a partnership in which one or more partners may have limited liability provided that at least one partner has unlimited liability

liquidity a measure of how easily assets can be converted into cash

liquidity management the process of ensuring adequate cash for the operation of a firm

long-term debt borrowing over a long period of time, usually through bank loans or the sale of bonds. On a balance sheet, any debt due for more than one year is classified as long term.

macro factors factors that pertain to developments in the general economy and government fiscal policy

marginal cost of capital the incremental cost of financing above a previous level

market efficiency a theory that prices of securities or foreign currencies reflect all information, transmitted so quickly that differences between prices are corrected before arbitrage can take place

market value weights valuation of a firm's financial structure according to the market prices of its securities

maturity, maturity date the date on which the issuer of a bond is obligated to pay the principal or face value of the bond

maximize the wealth to achieve the highest level of profits attainable at a given risk level

maximum return the highest possible profit

maximum wealth the highest possible stock price attainable at the least risk

merchandise balance See **trade account.**

merger a combination of tw< firms, with one firm maintaining its identity

merger exchange ratio a ratio derived by dividing the EPS of the acquired company by those of the acquiring company. The result is the number of shares that the acquiring companv will accept to consumn ate a merger.

micro factors factors that pertain to supply, demand, and pricing

multinational corporation a firm with significant operations outside its national borders

negotiating range the minimum and the maximum price an acquiring company is willing to consider when entering in merger negotiations with a target company

net present value (*NPV*) the present value of a project's future cash flow less the initial investment in the project

net profit margins net profits after taxes divided by sales

net residual principle a rule for determining dividend payments, based on investing retained earnings to the point where the *IRR* and *MCC* curves meet, and distributing the remainder as dividends

net working capital current assets minus current liabilities; it may be used as an indication of liquidity from one year to another

NI theory the theory that changes in a firm's capital structure affect its value or its cost of capital

NOI theory the theory that changes in a firm's capital structure do not affect its value or its cost of capital

nominal value See **face value.**

operating lease a lease, usually lasting for 5 years or less, in which the lessor handles maintenance and servicing

operating profit margins the rates of profits earned from operations, excluding taxes and interest from consideration

opportunity cost the rate of return on the best alternative investment that is not selected

optimal capital structure the theoretical structure of debt and equity that results in the lowest cost of capital and the maximum wealth of a firm

option the right to purchase stock at a specified price

option writer an investor who enters into a contract to sell stock (in case of a call) or buy stock (in the case of a put) at a stated price for a specified time in exchange for a premium

ordinary income income from the main activities of a firm and from the sale of assets that have been held for less than 6 months

overall account an account in the balance of payments that reflects the sum of the balances in the current account and various capital accounts

par, par value the face value of a share of stock or a bond. In the case of stocks, par value is merely a bookkeeping entry and serves no other purpose.

partnership an operation owned by two or more persons and conducted for a profit

payback period the amount of time required to recover the initial investment in a project

payout ratio the cash dividend per share divided by the earnings per share

permanent financing the minimum level of current assets plus fixed assets

perpetuity an annuity forever; periodic equal payments or receipts on a continuous basis

poison pill defensive practices by a target company to make an unfriendly merger less attractive to the acquiring company

pooling of interest a merger that involves the combination of the assets, the liabilities, and the equity positions of the two firms. This method differs from the purchase approach, which involves goodwill or any excess payment over book value.

portfolio the sum total of all the assets owned by a firm or an individual investor

portfolio investment an investment in a foreign asset in which there is less than 10% ownership

preference for liquidity the assignment of more value to available cash than to future income

preferred stock a kind of equity whose owners are given certain privileges over common stockholders, such as a prior claim on the assets of the firm. Preferred stockholders usually have no voting rights and are paid a fixed dividend.

present value the cash value, today, of future returns

price/earnings (*P/E*) ratio the price of a firm's stock divided by its EPS. It is usually stated that stock price is a multiple of earnings per share.

probabilities the chances that specific events will occur. Probabilities are used to weight an estimated range of outcomes in order to reduce the range to a single figure.

profitability index (*PI*) the ratio of the present value of future cash flows from a project to the initial investment in the project

proprietorship an operation owned by one person and conducted for a profit

purchase acquisition method payment of cash for another corporation, taking into account goodwill (or cost over book value)

put option an option that gives the holder the right to sell

put option buyer an investor who speculates that the price of a stock will decline

quick ratio See acid test.

rating agencies agencies that study the financial status of a firm and then assign a quality rating to securities issued by that firm. Standard and Poor and Moody are leading rating agencies.

recaptured depreciation the selling price of a used asset minus the book value and capital gain (if any)

required rate of return (*RRR*) the minimum future receipts an investor will accept in choosing an investment

return the gains or losses incurred by the owner of an asset over a period of time; usually measured as the sum of the periodic payments (dividends or interest) and the capital appreciation of the asset (total return)

return on equity (*ROE*) net profits after taxes divided by stockholders' equity

return on investment (*ROI*) net profits after taxes divided by assets. This ratio helps a firm determine how effectively it generates profits from available assets.

risk the degree of uncertainty associated with the outcome of an investment. It is a measure of the volatility of returns obtained from a project, and takes into consideration the probability of loss in any investment venture.

risk instability; uncertainty about the future; more specifically, the degree of uncertainty involved with a project or investment

risk-free rate, riskless rate a discount rate equal to the return on a riskless asset. A U.S. treasury bill is usually considered a riskless asset, and its yield provides a riskless rate.

risk premium an additional required rate of return that must be paid to investors who own risky assets. The riskier the asset, the higher the premium.

risk/return trade-off the relationship between the riskiness of an asset and its expected returns. This can be measured by using the coefficient of variation or the SML model.

sale and leaseback leasing arrangement whereby a firm that owns a piece of equipment sells it to another firm and leases it back, agreeing to pay periodic annual rentals. The contract provides for the original owner of the equipment to buy the equipment back at the termination of the lease.

salvage value the estimated selling price of an asset once it has been fully depreciated

SDRs (Special Drawing Rights) credit extended by the International Money Fund to importing countries. SDRs are exchanged only among central banks and are convertible into other currencies

seasonal financing the amount of current assets minus a minimum (fixed) level of current assets. In other words, seasonal financing can be viewed as that portion of current assets that fluctuates from one month to another.

securities company assets guaranteed to lenders to ensure repayment of loans

security market line (SML) a way to measure the relationship between beta (systematic risk) and expected returns. All points on the SML represent required rates of return for a given beta.

sensitivity analysis a measure of the extent to which one factor varies when another factor changes; a "what-if" technique

service-and-other-intangible account an account in the balance of payments that reflects transactions involving technical know-how, financial services, trade and military aid, and other intangible items

service lease See operating lease.

simulation the use of a hypothetical situation, similar to the real one, as a help in making a decision

simulation software computer programs that randomly generate variables for simulations and calculate the results of these simulations, creating useful distribution curves

Small Business Administration an organization established by Congress in 1958 to assist small companies in solving their financial (e.g., borrowing) problems

sources and uses of funds analysis analysis of how a firm generates and applies funds

spontaneous asset an asset that changes in value as a result of increases or decreases in sales

spot market the market for buying and selling a specific commodity or foreign currency at the current price for immediate delivery

standard deviation the volatility of returns, or the average deviation from an expected value or mean

stock dividend a dividend in the form of additional shares of stock, issued in lieu of a cash dividend. It increases the common stock par value and capital surplus and is taken out of retained earnings.

stock split the issuing of more shares of stock to current stockholders without increasing stockholders' equity. It reduces the par value of common stock but does not alter the equity values in the balance sheet.

straight-line depreciation depreciating an asset by equal dollar amounts each year over the life of the asset

strike price the price at which an option to purchase stock can be exercised

sum-of-the-years'-digits method an accelerated depreciation method whereby a greater portion of an asset is depreciated in the early part of its life

synergism economies and other gains created by the combination of companies in a merger

tax-loss carry-forward a situation that allows a firm to charge off ordinary losses for 3 years against the past and for 15 years forward against income. Capital losses can be carried back 3 years and forward 5 years.

tender offer an offer from an acquiring firm or any other source to purchase a number of shares from stockholders at a stated price per share

theoretical value of a warrant the current price of a share of common stock less the exercise price, multiplied by the terms of exchange

times interest earned ratio EBIT divided by annual interest expense (a measure of how well the firm meets its fixed interest expenses)

trade account an account in the balance of payments, also called the merchandise balance, that shows exports and imports of goods and services in the local currency

transaction risk a type of foreign exchange risk arising when a future foreign currency cash flow is exposed to a possible adverse currency movement before the transaction can be completed

translation risk a type of foreign exchange risk arising from the need to translate the assets and liabilities of a foreign subsidiary into the currency of the home country

variance the standard deviation squared; see **standard deviation**

volatility the degree of fluctuations that occur away from a common denominator such as the mean, or average value, of a series of figures. The greater the volatility in returns, the higher the risk.

warrant a security that gives a bond or preferred stock buyer the right to purchase shares of common stock at a given price

weighted average cost of capital (WACC) a measure of a firm's overall cost of capital, based on the percentage values of the components comprising its financial structure

weighted marginal cost of capital (WMCC) See cost of capital.

white knight in cases of unfriendly takeover bids, the target company seeks out other more compatible firms to merge with, hence preventing the original bidder from acquiring the target company

INDEX